Developing India

'The research that has gone into writing [this book] is impressive, the angles of inquiry variegated and insightful, and the bibliography is rich. No doubt, it is a valuable work for prospective researchers on the subject.'
—*The Indian Historical Review*

'The book deserves to be essential reading for students of Indian nationalism. It is elegantly written, extraordinarily detailed, and analytically polished.'
—*Economic and Political Weekly*

'reflect[s] impressively self-confident judgements about important and intellectually significant questions, and an ability to relate their explorations to wider conversations'
—*The Indian Economic and Social History Review*

'[Zachariah] rightly points out that this mainstream discourse ... permeated the Five Year Plans and the rhetoric of Indian politicians. Therefore Zachariah's book should be required reading for all those who try to understand this rhetoric.'
— *Economic Development and Cultural Change*

Developing India
An Intellectual and Social History, *c. 1930–50*

Benjamin Zachariah

OXFORD
UNIVERSITY PRESS

OXFORD
UNIVERSITY PRESS

Oxford University Press is a department of the University of Oxford.
It furthers the University's objective of excellence in research, scholarship,
and education by publishing worldwide. Oxford is a registered trademark of
Oxford University Press in the UK and in certain other countries

Published in India by
Oxford University Press
22 Workspace, 2nd Floor, 1/22 Asaf Ali Road, New Delhi 110002, India

First Edition published in 2005
Oxford India Paperbacks 2012
Digitally Printed in 2024

ISBN-13: 978-0-19-808607-9
ISBN-10: 0-19-808607-5

Typeset in Times New Roman 10/12
by InosoftSystems, Noida
Printed at Manipal Technologies Limited, Manipal

Contents

Abbreviations   vii
Preface to the Paperback Edition   ix
Preface   xv

1. Introduction   1

2. The Context   25

3. A Reformed Imperium?   80

4. The Debate on Gandhian Ideas   156

5. Development: Possible Nations   211

6. Conclusions   291

Glossary   301
Select Bibliography   306
Index   326

Abbreviations

ADC   Aide-de-Camp
AICC   All-India Congress Committee
AIVIA   All-India Village Industries Association
CPGB   Communist Party of Great Britain
CPI   Communist Party of India
CS   Congress Socialist
CSAS   Centre for South Asian Studies, Cambridge
CSP   Congress Socialist Party
DNB   Dictionary of National Biography
FICCI   Federation of Indian Chambers of Commerce and Industry
HMSO   Her/His Majesty's Stationery Office
ICS   Indian Civil Service
IOR   India Office Library and Records, Oriental and India Office
         Collections, British Library, London.
ISI   Indian Statistical Institute, Calcutta
JCK   J.C. Kumarappa Papers
JNP   Jawaharlal Nehru Papers
JNU   Jawaharlal Nehru University, New Delhi
LSE   London School of Economics
NAI   National Archives of India, New Delhi
NML   Jawaharlal Nehru Memorial Museum and Library, New Delhi
NPC   National Planning Committee
PCJA   P.C. Joshi Archive
PCMA   P.C. Mahalanobis Archive
RSS   Rashtriya Swayamsevak Sangh
TP   N. Mansergh (ed.), *India: The Transfer of Power* (12 volumes,
         London, HMSO, 1970–83)
UP   United Provinces
YMCA   Young Men's Christian Association

Preface to the Paperback Edition

Seven years is not a long time in the history of a book; and the author's re-engagement with his own work is not always the best way to situate that work. But a new edition calls for a new preface, and I have grown rather fond of this book, disregarding sensible voices that advise writers not to get too attached to work that after all relates to fragments of who they once were, and to which they now bear no necessary resemblance. In the spirit of being a part of all I have met, and the experiential arch through which I attempt to fade out backwards into the travelled, this therefore becomes an attempt to regress to a previous phase of existence and retravel the route taken. A reader might wish to ignore this preface for now, and perhaps return to it after having read the book—it is said that connoisseurs of detective stories read their books backwards, skipping to the end and then returning to the beginning to see how the author shapes and takes them to that end; and if this is the case, those who wish to read this book as if they were connoisseurs of detective fiction and this were such a book will find that I have provided an end in the beginning.

Sitting uneasily as it does amidst fields that do not habitually talk to each other—accounts of economic development, histories of science and science policy, intellectual histories of the pre-Cold War era, socialist accounts of 'incomplete' or 'failed transitions', nationalist histories of Indian national 'awakening'—the silences that appear to surround the book are perhaps understandable. An old academic adage is that one should not read reviews of one's own work. I have ignored this one; and reading the reviews, I realized that one of the problems *Developing India* faced in its Being-in-the-World was that of the lenses the reviewers brought to their reading. If readers were to seek answers to the once-classic questions such as 'Why did the Indian developmental project fail?', 'How does it compare with Korea and Brazil?', 'Is land reform a prerequisite for capitalist development?', or 'Are there non-communist routes to socialism?', they would be disappointed. An academic and political nostalgia for the so-called 'Nehruvian project', especially among left-leaning readers, was not best served by the book's account of the disciplinarian tendencies and eugenicist assumptions of much of the developmental imagination. The neo-liberals' flattening of the world's developmental experiences into the freedom of the market versus the tyranny of the planners did not find much support in the book either.[1] A shared distrust for the developmental project among the so-called 'post-developmentalists',[2] self-proclaimed anarchists,[3] and privateers who sought to break off small and/or allegedly 'sustainable' bits of developmentalism and run them as profitable 'non-profit' non-governmental organizations found little support in a book that differently damaged each set of expectations without providing enough appropriable material for any of the causes.

More than being an opportunity to argue with other people, for which other fora are more productive, a new preface provides an opportunity to revisit and re-engage with one's own limitations, and perhaps to attempt a few (self-)clarifications. What would I have liked to do differently? What should I have liked to point out more strongly?

One difficulty in writing about 'development' has tended to be that even as it relates to wider conceptions of progress, it is always on the verge of being instrumentalized; indeed, it is this capacity to be instrumentalized that is its rationale. Or, as it is so often put, 'development' is about tangible and practical matters rather than abstract thought. This of course makes a scrutiny of the abstract lurking behind and permeating the (often literally) concrete structures a less self-evident subject of study; but fortunately this apparently Manichean world of thought and action is now accepted not to exist, and what had been difficult in the 1990s, when some of the book began its life as a PhD thesis, is now considered worthy of academic time and space. It might be worthwhile here to make a distinction between what I have come to think of as *the developmental imagination* in contrast with *developmentalism*, the latter associated with states, state-building, and statist projects, the former a more diffuse set of hegemonic assumptions (in the Gramscian sense) shared among state and non-state actors, and a crucial set of political lenses for the actors themselves, though of course the *term* is analytic and external. The two are connected, but distinct: it is often

---

[1] This is an argument that can claim some antecedents in F.A. Hayek, *The Road to Serfdom* (London, 1944); but not many neo-liberals are so concerned with political liberalism or the political democracy that was central to Hayek's polemic on the loss of freedom resulting from economic planning.

[2] See Preface to the hardback edition, note 3.

[3] James C. Scott, *Seeing Like a State: How Certain Schemes to Improve the Human Condition Have Failed* (New Haven, 1998).

the developmental imagination that enables the process of legitimation of developmentalism. A statist project of developmentalism, by contrast, contains constituent elements that must be hidden, underplayed, or disavowed lest they come into conflict with the developmental imagination.[4] Perhaps the French would say it better, an *imaginaire* rather than an imagination, but everything sounds more intellectual in French.

It is tempting here to invite an outline of the vicissitudes of the developmental imagination, from its beginnings in self-conscious aspirations to industrialization and progress among intellectuals in the parts of the world that sought to 'catch up' along an apparently pre-ordained developmental trajectory, through to the technologist and import-substituting regimes of the Cold War era, from the Colonial Development Act to the Truman Doctrine, from socialism to scientism, from modernization to dependency theory, and through many stages in between. This would, I think, be possible if we distinguish between different sets of actors whose divergent projects are paradoxically facilitated by a shared language that creates the formulae and the appearance of agreement on the basis of which divergences are possible: the 'language of legitimacy' that is a recurrent theme in the book. Which is to suggest that there exists the possibility of mapping, for other parts of the world, similar but possibly distinctive developmental imaginations.

The deliberately centrist focus of the book was also a difficulty for an author whose principles of selection were even to himself somewhat tendentious: in deciding upon a broad as opposed to a narrow understanding of 'development', I nevertheless left out a number of approaches that in my judgement did not make their way to centre stage, that is, were not taken seriously enough by those who sought to build a state.[5] In retrospect, this makes a point that I wanted to make and should have made better. A more consistent engagement with developmentalism *as a form of* statist nationalism, rather than merely as *driven by* nationalism, might have been better worked out for the book. This becomes far more evident in the post-independence era, where representatives of government exhorted the people to make sacrifices for the development of the 'nation' (by which

[4] The clarification of this distinction I owe to Dhruv Raina and Rohan D'Souza, who suggested that what I was using as a casual distinction was potentially more important than I thought it was. I take the opportunity here to thank them both for their intervention.

[5] In this connection, see Ian C. Petrie, 'Village Visions: Science and Technology in the Bengal Countryside, c. 1860–1947', unpublished Phd dissertation, University of Pennsylvania, 2004, which takes up some of the ideas that I left out, over a longer time-frame, and framed in terms of different concerns.

was meant the state); in effect, to avoid definitions of national belonging that were potentially exclusionary, common participation in a national developmental project in which all citizens belonged and from which they benefitted became a form of compulsory nationalism. To refuse to participate on the terms imposed by the state, the corollary ran, was to exclude oneself from belonging to the Indian state.[6] A more disturbing question is whether the state's developmentalism was built upon a hegemonic developmental imagination that accepted a top–down, state-led view of progress, a set of hierarchical assumptions about greater and lesser civilisations, and the right of an 'enlightened' and self-appointed elite to speak for the 'masses'. That a number of these assumptions map easily onto caste-based moral orders, perpetuate class distinctions in a language of equality and empowerment, lead to the marginalization or use as internal colonies of the recalcitrant residual category referred to as 'the north-east', or subordinate workers' rights to the alleged greater good of the 'nation' is now better known than it used to be; but for all the academic critiques of development that we have had over the last three decades or so, the public acceptability of these assumptions are very resilient.

Which brings me to what was certainly a misjudgement on my part, or perhaps a result of my own internalization of a part of the *imaginaire* that I can now describe. A view of 'development' as a set of concerns different from religious, sectarian, and 'communal' ideas was a separation crucial to the rhetoric of what we now call the 'Nehruvian project'; it was a distinction that I accepted far too readily. For one thing, a tendency towards social or religious reform could draw on a similar set of ideas about 'developed' and 'less developed' morals and morality to those on 'the economy', or mute its religious language by mixing it with or subsuming it within a language of development.[7] As I outlined the closeness of assumptions about racial hierarchies and eugenic assumptions about 'healthy' societies, it would have been a sensible step to see this in continuum with other attempts to discipline and order a 'nation-building' project. However, 'development' has so long been positioned as an *alternative* to 'communal' imaginings

---

[6] Benjamin Zachariah, *Playing the Nation Game* (New Delhi, 2011), pp. 205–54, develops this argument.

[7] Although I show this for Gandhi's thinking about hierarchies of moral development and its connections with caste, I do not do this as consistently elsewhere. I thank Soumen Mukherjee for pointing this out to me; see also Soumen Mukherjee, 'Community Consciousness, Development, Leadership: The Experience of Two Muslim Groups in Nineteenth and Twentieth Century South Asia', PhD dissertation, Heidelberg University, 2010, esp. pp. 170–203.

of the national entity that it was easy to miss this. (In my defence I can only say that I was probably the first to take any account of eugenics as a strong theme in Indian nationalism, and of its corollary, the yearning to discipline and control populations.) In fact, an implicit set of eugenicist assumptions, framed in 'secular' terms, could be bent to a number of purposes. A consequent closeness to a number of themes we would now call 'fascist' needs to be examined with some stringency, while at the same time resisting the tendencies towards concept-inflation that have so damaged serious scholarship since the 'f' word began to be used in mere polemics rather than in systematic scholarship.[8] And although there is now some scholarship on the theme of 'Indian eugenics', its restriction to the themes of population and reproduction is likely to miss the larger picture.[9] The entire mobilizational and disciplinary paraphernalia of an Indian 'national movement', or rather of various 'national movements' that sought to imprint their particular visions of the nation on the future state, relied on similar eugenic assumptions.[10]

The temptation of turning this preface into an imagined rewriting of the book must be resisted. However, some potential or actual directions to debates on development in the Indian context might be described here. Recent research seems to further vindicate the idea that the rhetoric of socialism within developmentalism was not incompatible with the furthering of capitalism, which was often the intended goal of development (not least for socialists themselves, for whom it was a necessary stage *en route* to socialism). The 1950s, when the alleged socialist project was at its height, were also the time of the greatest growth of private capital, which never again

[8] This is the basis of a productive set of disagreements between myself and Franziska Roy. See Benjamin Zachariah, 'Rethinking (The Absence of) Fascism in India, c. 1922–1945', in Sugata Bose and Kris Manjapra (eds), *Cosmopolitan Thought Zones: South Asia and the Global Circulation of Ideas* (Basingstoke, 2010), pp. 178–209; Franziska Roy, 'Paramilitary Volunteer Organisations and Mass Mobilisation in India, 1918–1948', forthcoming PhD dissertation, University of Warwick, 2012.
[9] Sarah Hodges, 'Indian Eugenics in an Age of Reform', in Sarah Hodges (ed.), *Reproductive Health in India: History, Politics, Controversies* (Hyderabad, 2006), pp. 115–38; Sarah Hodges, *Contraception, Colonialism and Commerce: Birth Control in South India, 1920–1940* (Aldershot, 2008); Sanjam Ahluwalia, *Reproductive Restraints: Birth Control in India, 1877–1947* (Urbana and Chicago, 2008).
[10] Franziska Roy, 'Paramilitary Volunteer Organisations and Mass Mobilisation in India, 1918–1948'.

had it so good, even during the period of 'liberalization'.[11] The exclusions of the developmental imagination, viewed from a statist—and centrist—perspective are also worth dwelling upon. The creation of new centres and peripheries within the (nation-)state as developmentalism demanded of its population the required sacrifices for the greater good, or punished non-conformity and 'backwardness', can be best illustrated by approaching the narrative from the new peripheries and internal colonies within the now-independent Indian state: the Armed Forces Special Powers Act (AFSPA) as the accompaniment of and corollary to a statist developmentalism that seeks to control and contain within its boundaries those that it seeks to 'develop', if necessary by force.[12] The difficulties of citizens attempting to resist the designs of the state, or of private capital, both of which situate themselves within a hegemonic developmental imagination, from within that developmental imagination, must be addressed through an understanding of the functioning and the limits of that imagination.[13]

These are strands of argument that are now beginning to take shape, and if this book contributes something to their trajectories, its writing will have been well worth the effort. I remain engaged with a number of these strands myself, academically and politically. I take this opportunity to thank, in addition to those already mentioned in the footnotes, Franziska Roy and Hanna Werner for their close and critical engagement with this book, and with the debates of which it is a part.

Benjamin Zachariah

Berlin/Heidelberg, July 2012

[11] See Pulapre Balakrishnan, *Economic Growth in India: History and Prospect* (New Delhi, 2010); on Indian capitalism, see Terence J. Byres, 'State, Class and Development Planning in India', in Terence J. Byres (ed.), *The State and Development Planning in India* (New Delhi, 1994), pp. 5–50; see especially pp. 7, 37.

[12] For the model of internal colonialism, see Michael Hechter, *Internal Colonialism: The Celtic Fringe in British National Development, 1536–1966* (Berkeley, 1975). See also Zachariah, *Playing the Nation Game*, pp. 205–54; William R. Avis, 'Fractured Identities: Constructions of Assamese Identity in Post-independence India', unpublished PhD dissertation, University of Sheffield, 2011. The text of the AFSPA is available online at http://www.satp.org/satporgtp/countries/india/document/actandordinances/armed_forces_special_power_act_1958.htm (last accessed on 9 July 2012).

[13] Hanna Werner, 'Arguing with Dams: Developmental Perspectives and Social Critique in 20th Century India', forthcoming PhD dissertation, Heidelberg University, 2012.

Preface

This is a book about ideas which were crucial for the articulation of a vision of a future independent India. Such ideas were organized around notions of 'development'—a term which encompassed far more than the narrowly economic meaning to which it was later reduced. These wider conceptions of 'development' were crucial to attempts to legitimize models of ordering the society of a future India; and the debates surrounding them were crucial to the formation of the language of legitimacy which was to become the obligatory rhetoric of politics in post-independence India.

A major part of this book started life as my doctoral dissertation. Perhaps, fortunately for prospective readers, a substantial part of the dissertation did *not* find its way into the book. As subsequent work added to what I began in the dissertation, it began to acquire a life of its own and to grow uncontrollably, reminding me uncomfortably of various wise (wo)men's strictures about the autonomy of the text; but I was less than prepared to grant it this autonomy until after I had placed it in the public domain, so it had to be called to order again. This involved disciplining myself *not* to write about a number of themes, at least within the framework of this study. (There is therefore an implicit sequel to this book; but it would be providing a hostage to fortune to claim that I shall be the one to write it.)[1]

What follows, then, is a work that deals with underlying notions of progress, self-government and nation-building contained in developmental goals articulated in India in the late colonial period, the middle of the twentieth century. It concentrates on the period c. 1930–1950, reaching back to earlier debates where relevant, and carrying the narrative into

---

[1] To some extent I have dealt with issues that belong in such a sequel in a piece of work that overtook this one to publication, but in doing so confirmed to me the value of publishing this work: Benjamin Zachariah, *Nehru* (London, 2004).

the 1950s to show the significance of the ideas discussed. It studies three main groups of contributors to the debates in some detail: British Indian administrators, Gandhians, and other Indian nationalists, the last often loosely referred to as 'modernizers' or incorrectly lumped together as 'Nehruvians'. It attempts to show the interactions and interconnections among these ideas, and the processes through which the ideas were articulated and placed before an audience.

Examining the language of the debates and the conventions that took shape through them makes it possible to disaggregate the divergent political projects contained in a conventional language. For instance, it enables us to understand how imperialist, capitalist, and socialist projects could use a similar language of legitimacy without sharing the political or developmental goals that the language seemed to imply. This work provides a study of a formative period in the history of the aspiration to development that was later to be an integral part of the post-Second World War world. However, it argues that 'development', as it was conceptualized by international organizations and governments after 1945, was a different project from that articulated before that period by Indian nationalists, even as both sometimes seemed to share the conventionalized language of development that took shape earlier. In part, the acceptability of a developmental practice post-1945 that worked with and within Western Cold War agendas was built on the use of a language of legitimacy that *appeared* to emanate from an anti-imperialist consensus.

This is, therefore, an intellectual history of 'development' in India before 'development' became the Cold War-related project that we now recognize—if called upon to classify it, I would call it an intellectual history with a corresponding, and sometimes implicit, political narrative. It is also a social history of influential social circles, their political and intellectual alignments, and the intellectual and moral horizons within which they operated.

The nature of my work, despite the necessary illusions of agency and autonomy that accompany authorship, may well have been dictated by the times and spaces in which I found myself. This book was started at a time when interest in 'development', especially of the state-led variety, was led by disillusionment with science, 'modernity', 'post-enlightenment rationality', and connectedly, 'socialism', among many who considered themselves on the 'left'. The disillusionment had led, variously, to the so-called 'impasse' in 'development studies', to an assault on science as a tyrannical system of knowledge/power, to a discomfort with anything that had anything to do with even the word 'socialism' because of its association with the tyranny of states.[2] (This elusive disillusionment was, it may be added, peculiar to those who saw themselves as 'progressive'; the right suffered no such agonies. A determined offensive by what we now politely call 'neo-liberalism', which tends to hide the fact that it is neither new nor liberal, was at the same time manifesting itself.)[3] In this context, a conventional study of practices of development in India in the 1940s, which failed to engage with the anxieties of our times, would have been most dissatisfying.[4]

It is now fashionable to claim that the work one did was unfashionable at the time it was done, and that it has been vindicated by later trends.

[2] Representative works from this period include W. Sachs (ed.), *The Development Dictionary: A Guide to Knowledge as Power* (London, 1992); F.A. Marglin and S. Marglin (eds), *Dominating Knowledge: Development, Culture and Resistance* (Oxford, 1990); Claude Alvares, *Science, Development and Violence: The Revolt Against Modernity* (Delhi, 1992); for an assessment of the 'impasse', see Colin Leys, *The Rise and Fall of Development Theory* (London, 1996).

[3] The move from the concerns of work such as Gunnar Myrdal, *Asian Drama: An Inquiry into the Poverty of Nations* (3 vols, London, 1968), or the Soviet scholars V. Solodovnikov and V. Bogalovsky, *Non-Capitalist Development: An Historical Outline* (Moscow, 1975), to Jagdish Bhagwati, *India in Transition: Freeing the Economy* (Oxford, 1993) was a large one. A flavour of the then current debates can possibly be found in Ian Duncan, 'The Politics of Liberalization in Early Post-Independence India: Food Deregulation in 1947', *Journal of Commonwealth and Comparative Politics* Vol. XXXIII No. 1 (March 1995), which recast Gandhi as an early ally of 'liberalization'; this essay can be read in radical ways.

[4] A study of the Indian war economy and post-war development(s) remains nevertheless a worthwhile project, potentially the sequel to this book hinted at earlier: for possible starting points, see B.N. Banerjee et al., *People's Plan for Economic Development of India* (Delhi, 1944); L.J. Pressnell, *External Economic Policy Since the War, vol. 1: The Post-War financial Settlement* (London, 1986); Alan S. Milward, *War, Economy and Society, 1939–1945* (Harmondsworth, 1987); Dietmar Rothermund, 'Die Anfaenge der indischen Wirtschaftsplanung im Zweiten Weltkrieg', in Peter Habluetzel, Hans Werner Tobler & Albert Wirz (eds): *Dritte Welt: Historische Praegung und politische Herausforderung: Festschrift zum 60. Geburtstag von Rudolf von Albertini* (Wiesbaden, 1983); Kevin Watkins, 'India: Colonialism, Nationalism and Perceptions of Development', unpublished DPhil thesis, University of Oxford, 1986; B.R. Tomlinson, 'Indo-British Relations in the Post-Colonial Era: The Sterling Balances Negotiations, 1947–49', *Journal of Imperial And Commonwealth History* 13 (1985); Anita Inder Singh, *The Limits of British Influence: South Asia and the Anglo-American Relationship 1947–1956* (London, 1993). Such a history of events could have been written before this book; or perhaps by me, instead of this book; but I think it will be far easier to write after this book.

I can make no such claim, having worked from a base in Cambridge University that often valorized the unfashionable in order to make a virtue out of its intellectual insularity. However, contextualizing myself outside the bubble, I should say this: coming from a generation that had grown up with disillusionment, and consequently being disillusioned with disillusionment, I was willing to confront some of the trends that I recognized as reacting to terminology rather than to what the terminology attempted to describe. To the extent that generic attacks on Science, Socialism or Development appear to be less frequent or respectable now than they were in the 1990s, things have moved along in directions that I might have desired. If the final version in which this work now appears eschews much of the polemical debate that it once contained, it is because the polemic is no longer quite so relevant; but its vestiges can still be recognized in the text, as it can in public and academic domains.

Although it is tempting to claim a multi- or inter-disciplinary perspective, I shall refrain from doing so. As I happily trespassed on other people's disciplines, I remained acutely conscious that my disciplinary background was that of history. However, such is the indisciplined nature of that discipline, that, chameleon-like, it is capable of acquiring the characteristics of all or some of the things it seeks to write or talk about—it is, in fact, necessary for the historian to know something about what s/he seeks to write about, lest s/he impose upon the disciplines of others the imperialism of his/her own categories and his/her own categorical imperatives. In other words, I have eschewed the methodology of the historian of a science who refrains from engaging with the internal consistency of that science lest s/he be tainted by the tyrannies of scientific practice. Instead I have tried, to the best of my ability, to acquire an understanding of what people thought they were doing or saying. I hope I have nonetheless remained discursively unviolated, and that I have retained a critical perspective.

It was also necessary to avoid the problem experienced typically (though not exclusively) by the economic historian, of writing his or her histories in conformity with the prevalent standards of the master discipline: current economic theory thus becomes a yardstick for judging a world in which one looks for, and finds, only its economic aspects. It became clear from even a cursory reading of the sources conventionally used to write about 'economic development' that the discussions then going on were about much more than economic development: they had a surplus meaning and an emotive significance—an emotional cathexis, in Freudian language—which could not be explained merely with reference to the state of the discipline of economics at the time, or even to conventional political economy explanations regarding 'interests'. A rule of thumb which I found useful was to separate my own, retrospective understanding of something from that of my contemporaries.

This is a book that concerns itself primarily with debates conducted within the historiography of South Asia. What this means is that it does not engage substantially or in great detail with debates in 'development studies', in 'cultural studies' or 'postcolonial theory' (however one wishes to constitute these fields). This is not to say that these debates are irrelevant, or that I refuse to engage with them, this refusal constituting my desire to wish them out of existence (the contextualizing remarks above constitute just such an engagement). On the other hand, the wordiness of some writing that overwhelms its readers with theoretical and comparative material before getting to the point has always had the effect of intimidating me. I did not, therefore, wish to put a reader through the same experience. Therefore, what this book owes to the thinking of Foucault, Habermas, Gramsci, Said, or the poststructuralist/postcolonial turn, as also to the less doctrinaire aspects of the Marxist tradition, is left implicit in many cases, although the debts should be obvious to the discerning reader. I do touch upon some theoretical or comparative material in historicizing 'development': historical work on the subject of development is relatively rare, and the separate (inter-disciplinary?) discipline of development studies uses history very selectively. While development as a disciplinary formation has now conducted an extensive self-criticism of its assumptions, it has often done so by stereotyping its own intellectual and political histories. There is, I hope, enough in this book to suggest that a creative listening-to-each-other across disciplinary boundaries might sometimes be more productive of new ways of seeing things than an obliteration of the boundaries. I have tried to indicate in the text where I feel this is necessary. Disciplinary boundaries are of course no more than heuristic devices, and if the division of labour implied by them is useful in any way, it is in the particular emphases of particular disciplines. The advantage of history is that it can provide a sense of detail. And yet nothing is more tiresome than detail for its own sake, without reference to current debate. History-writing can also be a trifle old fashioned, in that it still seeks to provide *information* (obviously coloured by the historian's selectiveness and agenda) as well as an argument; and some of that information can survive the end of the debate within which the argument once situated itself.

I have incurred many debts, intellectual, social and personal, in the course of researching and writing this book, and I take this opportunity to acknowledge some of them. Geoffrey Hawthorn supervised the PhD thesis in the process of becoming this book, and provided meticulous comments on successive drafts. Chris Bayly and Sudipta Kaviraj, who examined the thesis, made many suggestions that were immensely useful in preparing a manuscript for publication, as did two anonymous readers for Oxford University Press. This work has also been influenced by conversations with, and in some cases comments from, several persons. None of them is responsible for what I have written; many of them may not even recall the conversations which I now acknowledge; some, indeed, may wish to deny being implicated in this work even by association. 'Influence' is an intangible thing, and its traces are hard to catalogue; nevertheless, I believe it to be worth the effort, in accordance with my conviction that for all its emphasis on originality, academic work is a collective exercise performed alone. I therefore take this opportunity to thank Michael Adas, Ravi Ahuja, Robert Anderson, G. Arunima, Amiya Bagchi, Barnita Bagchi, the late Sudarsana Bagchi, Ganesh Bagchi, G. Balachandran, Crispin Bates, Tarun Bhartiya, Debraj Bhattacharya, Sanjoy Bhattacharya, Sugata Bose, Lionel Carter, Partha Chatterjee, Basudev Chatterji, Bhaskar Chakrabarty, Subhas Chakraborti, Uttara Chakraborti, Peter Clarke, Markus Daechsel, John Darwin, Suranjan Das, Clive Dewey, Margret Frenz, Nandini Gooptu, Jharna Gourlay, Stephen Gourlay, Tapati Guha Thakurta, the late Partha Sarathi Gupta, S. Irfan Habib, Sohail Hashmi, Ištvan Hont, A.G. Hopkins, Aparna Jack, Ayesha Jalal, Roger Jeffery, Umbreen Khalid, Sunil Khilnani, Toufique Kitchlew, Aparajita Koch, Kerstin Lehr, John Lonsdale, John Marriott, Dilip Menon, Rudrangshu Mukherjee, Biswamoy Pati, Dhruv Raina, Rajat Kanta Ray, Peter Robb, Sulagna Roy, Tanika Sarkar, Sumit Sarkar, Amartya Sen, Samita Sen, Suhit Sen, Sujaya Sen, Ajay Skaria, Jayeeta Sharma, Subir Sinha, Ashley Tellis, B.R. Tomlinson, Hari Vasudevan, Ian Zachariah. In particular, Robert Anderson, Subhas Chakraborti, Rajat Kanta Ray, Sulagna Roy, and Hari Vasudevan might recognize in some of my writing traces of discussions I have had with them. I am one of many who owes much to the genius of Jeff Vernon; special thanks are due to him.

Financial and institutional support is of course essential in the production of academic work. I would like to thank Trinity College, Cambridge, for its award of an External Research Studentship, and for a supplementary grant which made my research possible. I would like particularly to thank Chris Morley, erstwhile Tutor for Advanced Students, and then Vice-Master of Trinity College, and Hazel Felton, whose running of the lives of Trinity's Advanced Students made the obligatory bureaucratic details of graduate life far smoother than they might have been. I would also like to thank the Committee of Vice-Chancellors and Principals of the Universities of the United Kingdom for their award of an Overseas Research Studentship; the Smuts Memorial Fund for their award of a travel grant which enabled me to go to India on field work; and the Charles Wallace Trust for providing me with additional funding towards later research. The Department of History, Sheffield University, provided me with the last stages of financial and institutional support that enabled me to finish this book.

I would like to thank the Master and Fellows of Churchill College, Cambridge, for permission to consult the Grigg Papers. I would also like to thank the staff of the following libraries and archives for their assistance: the Centre for South Asian Studies, Cambridge; the Centre for Studies in Social Sciences, Calcutta; the Oriental and India Office Collections, British Library, London; the School of Oriental and African Studies, London; the Churchill College Archives Centre, Cambridge; Presidency College, Calcutta; the Indian Statistical Institute Library, Calcutta; the West Bengal Secretariat Library, Calcutta; the West Bengal State Archives, Calcutta; the P.C. Joshi Archive, Jawaharlal Nehru University, New Delhi; the National Archives of India, New Delhi; the Jawaharlal Nehru Memorial Museum and Library, New Delhi; and the British Library of Political and Economic Sciences, London School of Economics, London. The Department of History at Sheffield University should also be thanked for providing me with a quiet corner that is my own.

As the cliché goes, all errors are of course also my own.

Benjamin Zachariah
March 2005

1

Introduction

The Problem

This book is concerned with ideas of 'development' in India—often claimed as the defining goal of both imperialism and nationalism—in the late colonial period, circa 1930–50. This was a period of uncertainty during which the debates surrounding that word evoked a wide and exciting range of possibilities, not yet limited by the later impositions of 'development economics', and relatively unconstrained by the demands of practical politics. This book seeks to recover some of the variety of meanings encompassed by 'development' in the first half of the twentieth century, particularly in the 1930s and the 1940s; the contexts in which conceptions of 'development' operated in this period; and, consequently, to relocate those contemporary debates on 'economic development' in the wider context of the stated and unstated assumptions upon which they were based. I locate concerns with 'development' within wider notions of progress, self-government, and nation-building which, for contemporaries, were inseparably entwined with 'development'. I examine, through ideas of 'development', larger questions of the nature of intellectual formations under colonial rule, and the problems of transition to a post-colonial polity.

This work is not intended as a history of development policy, the literature dealing with which is vast, mostly pertaining to a period outside the chronological framework of this book.[1] It is not a history of 'economic thought' in India; such histories can be found elsewhere.[2] Nor is it a direct successor to the large body of literature dealing with the effects of colonial rule on Indian economic growth: its distortion of Indian economic life and the stunting of indigenous capitalism; or the beneficial effects of colonial order, commercialization, expansion of transport and markets in pioneering capitalism in India, or subtler variations on these themes—although I shall have occasion to engage with many of the concerns dealt with in that literature.[3] Moreover, the absence in this book of an analysis of the details of political debates, in the more conventional sense of day-to-day manoeuvres and specific problems, should not be read as an indication that such debates did not exist; they were, indeed, going on. This book does not, however, deal centrally with them; instead, it attempts an analysis of the ideas which went into, and the conventions within which such debates occurred. I argue that the more specific arguments cannot be understood without reference to the wider framework within which they were placed. This work seeks to provide an essential re-reading of ideas and influences which have long been subject to decontextualized readings and, therefore, have often been completely misunderstood, their unfamiliar elements dissolved into a spurious familiarity in consonance with the prevailing ideological or methodological concerns of later periods.

Given the discursive framework of the period, most protagonists had to address economic questions, and the social questions that emerged therefrom, to a large extent in a language of economics. However, the main thrust of many of the points the various protagonists sought to make were moral or ethical, which was often where the protagonists differed. Such moral questions were entered through a discursive framework not actually suited to moral arguments: the prevalent language of economics. The moral arguments, transparent in the arguments of Gandhi and the Gandhians, were less directly moral, because they were not foregrounded, in the arguments of the British or of other nationalists.

The concerns which, by the 1930s, were phrased in economic terms, therefore, encompassed issues well beyond the economic. Moreover, these were often long-standing concerns with strong lineages and pre-histories in earlier periods, which took new forms and were catalysed differently in this period. Many of the trends of thought which crystallized around the events, examples, or trends of the 1930s and the 1940s, were reconfigurations of late nineteenth-century debates. Some of the crucial differences among nationalists can, nonetheless, be traced to common starting points. Many of the intellectual resources drawn upon by Indian nationalists, or indeed British imperialists, originated in Orientalist scholarship emphasizing the splendours of the civilization of ancient India or, in British accounts, of the particular features of the stereotypical Indian, dating back in some cases to the late eighteenth or early nineteenth centuries. These early origins were often only dimly remembered or altogether forgotten by the protagonists in the debates of the 1930s and 1940s, who had acquired them at second or third remove—through more recent texts which themselves often cited secondary sources, or through popular and vulgarized usage. More recent debates were better remembered, and their earlier resolutions repeated in the new language. This book attempts to show that an understanding of these earlier lineages is necessary to an understanding of 'development' in the post-1930s period; and that the relative consistency of the concerns that were articulated reflected long-standing anxieties prevalent in a colonial society.

There is a surprising absence of literature that acknowledges this. All too often, in the existing writing on the subject of 'development', 'economics', narrowly defined, acts as the scissors which shear off all ideas not assimilable to 'economics' proper; as a result, many interesting ideas of 'development' have been written out of the story by later editing, with writers projecting into the past the narrower definitions of their own times.[4] It is not inaccurate to say that the term 'development' came to be, from the mid-twentieth century, a term whose meaning has largely been bounded by the discipline of economics; it caught on in liberal usage after the Second World War, and largely in the context of 'cold war' thinking: in which well-meaning desires to raise standards of living and incomes in the 'Third World' merged with the need for containing communism by ensuring that poor countries felt they had a stake in the economy of the 'free world'; and, on the other side, took shape in the 1950s' and 1960s Soviet discussions of possible 'alternative paths' to socialism so as to claim non-communist developing countries as allies.[5] As an idea, however, it had an earlier and richer history than the merely economic: it had long been a crucial part of contending world views. 'Development' was a crucial part of the Marxist tradition, though not always in the sense intended by its non-Marxist users; the Marxist usage was extremely important in the Indian case.[6] The word was widely applied in colonial discourse—where it acquired an extremely interesting semantic and political range, entwining itself with a great many of the crucial political, economic, and intellectual problems of the inter- and post-War world.[7] It appeared, for instance, in the Colonial Development Act of 1927, and the subsequent versions of the Act, culminating in the Colonial Development and Welfare Acts of the 1940s.[8] In the last years of British colonial rule—and in the context of the rising strength of anti-colonial movements and sentiment in the dependent world, the metropole, and outside, notably in the USA, Britain's claim to furthering the 'development' of the colonies provided the basis of her defence of empire before home and world opinion, a claim which had implicit or explicit links with the idea of a colony's need to qualify for self-government.[9] The importance of economics as a framework for the justification of colonial rule was more visible in such matters as colonial development (a Colonial Office idea which never directly applied to India), where it was explicitly argued that a benevolent, improving colonialism was preferable to self-rule—especially in countries not yet 'ripe for self-government': the two strands of the argument were meant to be mutually reinforcing, and even found expression in assertions from the Labour Party that certain colonies should be given 'socialism' before they were given independence.[10] 'Development', in all these usages, retained less well-defined connotations which were connected with ideas of regeneration and progress.[11]

In India, 'development' was an idea around which converged both the British justification of Britain's right to rule and Indian opposition to British ideas of the 'backwardness' of the subject people—racial, social, political, and economic. By the 1920s and the 1930s the idea of 'backwardness' was framed in predominantly economic terms, in British colonial as well as nationalist arguments: earlier British arguments regarding Indian 'backwardness' lost their effectiveness, partly as Indian nationalists developed strong counter-arguments, partly as arguments which defined 'backwardness' in terms of other categories became less respectable in Britain itself. Race and religion, for instance, had long played a role in this—as had a number of 'scientific' theories of evolution, the strands being mutually reinforcing. By the 1920s, however, the 'difference' between British standards of political behaviour and those of the Indians needed to be underplayed if an increasingly difficult-to-govern India had to be convinced of the sincerity of Britain's claim to be progressively granting self-government to Indians. Though the indication of the existence of such differences remained an important element in imperial arguments, this was expressed in a form tempered by the hope that, with time, things would improve. This was not, therefore, any longer an argument regarding the intrinsic qualities of Indians, but an argument regarding where Indians stood in the stages of civilization: backward, but not incapable of catching up. The two elements were not clearly separated, although by the 1930s it was more common to rephrase beliefs of the first kind in terms of the second, at least in public argument. This also justified the British reluctance to set a concrete time for its grant of self-government: the period of apprenticeship was almost, but not quite, over. (Archibald Wavell, the penultimate Viceroy of India, was quite impatient with the British tendency to treat Indians like backward children; this, he felt, was outdated and not appropriate to the times. He did not, however, question the validity of the analogy; India, he wrote in his journal, could no longer be treated like a child because it was now a 'tiresome adolescent'.)[12]

The strategies of argument adopted in these debates are well known. The official British argument in India, as elsewhere, was centred on the beneficial nature of the colonial connection for finance, trade, and commerce, its 'modernizing' role through contact with the scientific and developed West and its crucial role in preserving internal peace, law, and order. The subject people responded by attributing 'backwardness' to the effects of colonial rule itself; in this scheme of things, economic backwardness, which was a consequence of colonial rule, was itself the cause of other forms of backwardness.

Conceptions of 'economics' were crucial to these arguments. The language of economics provided an apparently neutral way of talking about 'backwardness', based on supposedly impartial criteria. This did not create agreement among imperialists and nationalists on terms, propositions, or theories in economics. On the contrary, several economic theories which could be advanced in opposition to the orthodox economics of balanced budgets, 'sound finance', and relative inaction on the part of the government, became part of the nationalist armoury of arguments against the colonial government and against colonialism. On the nationalist side, although to advocate 'development' was to concede the point regarding Indian 'backwardness', to acknowledge this particular form of 'backwardness' was less offensive, it being a contingent 'backwardness', capable of being overcome.

At the same time, the significance of these debates, even when framed in predominantly economic terms or containing strong claims to economically rational argument, extended well beyond the merely economic. The terms of reference for these debates—'development', 'modernization', 'industrialization', 'backwardness'—contained in them connotations not too far removed from other categories of 'backwardness', which remained scarcely veiled under colonialism. British colonialism in India was dependent on justifications based on ideas of British expertise in the arts of government, economics, and administration, and on assumptions of the inadequacy and inferiority of Indians in these fields. Indians on their part sought to combat the imperial claim to a monopoly of expertise in government, economic and otherwise, but also to come up with their own conceptions of 'development'. This was more than a search for a model economic plan (though there were many of those); not just a question of material betterment: it was also one of the 'moral health' of the 'nation', as Sir M. Visvesvaraya, engineer, civil servant, and former dewan of the princely state of Mysore, put it.[13]

'Development', along with the implied or stated terms it conjured up along with itself, therefore, became in many cases a synecdoche for the more general problem of the search for a framework within which to conceptualize a future or possible Indian nation—a nation in the act of becoming. In the context of the need to anticipate a framework for the desired independent Indian state, 'development' set off a chain of thought on various matters seen to be related to it: a not atypical request received by Jawaharlal Nehru as national leader in 1933 asked him to '"educate" public opinion', on 'the economic policy (and interconnected other policies—Educational, Domestic that is, relating to Marriage and the *division* or the *assimilation* of social work and functions between man and woman, Religious and Communal, Recreational, and Political that is, relating to the 'form' of the gov[ernmen]t. It would be useful if you also compared or contrasted, as the case maybe, [sic] your scheme with the main ones on which the world's eyes are now fixed, Bolshevism on the one hand and Fascism–Nazism on the other'.[14] It was felt necessary by some to make explicit certain connections between economic regeneration and development and the wider processes of 'nation-building', 'national discipline', the 'modernization' of the masses, or forms of government.

This was not, however, conceived merely in terms of a political problem of 'constructing the nation', but situated in the context of wider philosophical, social, and moral questions: what 'improvement' consisted in, the conditions of human well-being, the laws of history, the social responsibility of science. This rather large set of concerns was raised by the evocative and potentially limitless connotations of 'development'. A burning question of the time was the relative merits of capitalism and socialism—a thread that runs through most of the arguments. Intermeshed with, and often cutting across, this thread was the debate on the relative merits of a centralized, state-administered, industrialisation-oriented direction to development and a decentralized, village-self-sufficiency-based agriculture-and-cottage-industry-oriented order—the latter position championed by Gandhi.

Such wider questions and their connections with 'development' were explored in the writings and speeches of a significant band of proselytizers, among them academics, economists, technocrats, scientists, and 'scientific socialists': members of an articulate intellectual bourgeoisie. They addressed a variety of issues connected to a general project of regeneration, uplift, and liberation.

The impact of the Great Depression and the emergence of alternatives to the largely non-interventionist liberal economics of the pre-1914 era[15] played a strong catalysing role in incorporating and transforming various existing economic nationalist arguments[16] as well as a number of existing, and previously discrete, non-economic concerns into a recognizable nationalist discourse on 'development'. Yet, while various strands of thought were brought together by these events in the world's political economy and the responses they provoked, the latter often provided not much more than a starting point for a chain of thought which incorporated these events into wider and more intricate arguments.

These events also provided examples which were seen to be emulable in India; but as emulable examples which were also appropriated in selective and eclectic ways. In the 1930s the Soviet Union's planning was extremely influential in this regard, and not merely among socialists. This was not the only example: the economic successes of Japan, of the USA through the New Deal, of Fascist Italy, or Nazi Germany were commonly cited as examples worthy of emulation in some of their aspects, with the emphasis varying according to political orientation. It became necessary at times to separate the economic achievements of some of these countries from their political behaviour: thus, from about 1937, Nazi Germany and Fascist Italy were less quoted examples; praise for Japan's economic success was explicitly stated as not to imply support either for her aggression in China or her behaviour during the Second World War.[17] The Soviet example remained the most cited one, if only by virtue of being apparently the most successful, such success being in large measure responsible for ensuring that its influence extended beyond socialists and cut across the political spectrum. But the goals of most of those citing that example were quite un-Soviet, seeking only to try to emulate its material successes.[18] The term 'socialist' was also used loosely; everyone, from the communists through Nehru to the Gandhians, and even Indian capitalists and some British imperialists, laid claim to that term at various points.

The fora for many of the discussions of 'development'—in its separate themes and on particular issues through official reports and enquiries— were often provided by the government; and also in the discussions promoted by nationalist political groupings around the Congress. These fora were, however, peopled not just by the main protagonists in politics (who undoubtedly gave to the discussions a legitimacy and immediacy which they lacked in their purely academic setting), but also by academics and professionals, participants in the wider concerns connected with 'development', as well as those considered 'experts' in their particular fields, and businessmen, whose demands for space within which to operate more freely were seen as national demands.[19] But the discussions in organized and official fora operated according to the rules of the forum concerned. This automatically ensured that a number of ideas were muted; but, nonetheless, echoes of these ideas could often be heard.

At the same time, the participation of people from various fields, who brought diverse ideas of eclectic origin to shared concerns on the subject of 'development', created new fora and drew more people into the debates. A great deal of writing on and around the theme of 'development' was also published at this time.[20] Many of the important discussions surrounded moral, cultural, and spiritual matters, and took place in the realms of academic discourse as well as in more informal fora, such as in private correspondence. There were, thus, on the one hand, those with a wide variety of concerns about India's future who were drawn into fora and debates in which they came to characterize their concerns as concerns of 'development'; there were others who had already characterized their concerns in this way. Thus, in the 1930s 'development' came to be increasingly a way of connecting and, to a degree, ordering, a wide variety of issues. By the 1930s 'development', and its invariable concomitant, 'planning' (the latter being the means through which the former would be achieved), began to imply a further cluster of closely related ideas, with earlier ideas incorporated into the later formulations.[21]

The Approach

It would be an exaggeration to claim that this book is the first to perceive and address these connections; indeed, originality is a vain and dangerous claim to make in a field that has attracted as much attention as 'development' has in India. However, it might be possible to claim that, so far, there has been no sustained attempt to examine the intellectual history or conceptual framework within which 'development' was discussed in India.[22] The theme of the 'origins' of Indian developmental ideas has too often been subordinated to histories of the 'nationalist movement', been addressed as the 'pre-history' of Indian development planning, or dealt with in passing in biographical writing relating to those concerned with development. A properly contextualized intellectual history, taking debates, conversations, movements on their own terms, has been notably absent.

Looking at a set of debates, the assumptions behind them, and the series of related ideas which were consciously invoked, or at times unconsciously triggered off, is essential to this work. This range of ideas is difficult to illustrate unless followed up in the strange fragmented way in which it emerged. The best solution to this problem seems to me to be to write a history of overlapping personal, social and institutional histories, held together by a narrative of intellectual and socio-political contexts. It is crucial to assess the influences on the main protagonists—what they read, whom they knew, and the social contexts in which their ideas took shape. The history of the protagonists themselves, the fora in which they were communicating what they were, who they imagined their audiences to be, and how far they were able to reach them, is obviously related to this.

The transformations that many ideas which were borrowed from outside India encountered in the Indian context were often dependent on the ways in which they interacted with the specific concerns and anxieties of the Indian intellectual bourgeoisie under colonialism, who then adopted these ideas and projected them on to the public in certain ways. In this process, in many cases the well-worked-out genealogies of these ideas in other contexts have very limited resonances for the Indian context because of the peculiar ways in which they are interpreted. (This is not a case for 'indigenism' of any kind, however; I am merely making a case for the study of the peculiar ways in which certain ideas were adapted to new contexts, often accompanied by the claim that these were new, perhaps 'indigenous', ideas. I do not endorse such claims.) Or, indeed, there might be a simple borrowing of terminology to a greater or lesser degree of consciousness, in which the term acquires a wholly different meaning in the new context, or is borrowed unconsciously and so stands sometimes for less than an idea—perhaps a pre-idea or an unconscious trace.

There has been a relative lack of engagement among historians of India with the history of ideas, certainly in a field as apparently 'material' as that of 'economic' matters—unless in some sense it can directly be related to policy or attempted policy. If such 'hard' matters are acknowledged to have an intellectual history, this is not considered to be important, for ideas are overpowered by 'hard-headed' considerations of power, profit, and politics.[23] The virtue of this rather reductionist view of human behaviour undoubtedly lies in its conceptual simplicity. The connection between ideas and policy is often a tenuous one, after all, the linkages being intangible and difficult to trace, and the relative importance of ideas and practical constraints in the framing and, thereafter, the execution of policy is often impossible to establish.[24] On the other hand, the concentration on self-interest as the moving force of history can highlight the less-than-noble motives behind the articulation of particular ideas and political positions, either in terms of individual self-interest or the class interests at work (although some writing is reluctant to acknowledge the relevance of 'class' as a tool of analysis). The question arises, however, as to whether 'interest' always operates at a conscious and cynical level or whether it may be unconscious, tending towards the promotion of these 'interests' though phrasing its arguments in broader and more universalistic terms. This is usually a problem of historical evidence: in the absence of such evidence, it seems questionable to attribute intentions to historical players; though it is certainly possible to point to the logic a particular position tends towards.

The intellectual antecedents of the 'self-interest' approach to writing history, usually centred on high politics or organized interest-groups, are often ambiguous. Some of this writing, though resolutely anti-Marxist, seems to deal with 'ideology' at times in a mechanistically Marxist sense (as 'false consciousness'?); at times a vulgar Freudian sense (ideology as the justification of one's unconscious desires, but then being dismissed as irrelevant rather than explored in terms of the anxieties they might represent), or drawing on earlier traditions originating in the philosophy of Jeremy Bentham and John Stuart Mill regarding the pursuit of pleasure (in the form, perhaps, of power, profit, and politics?) as the fundamental motive behind human actions. In any case it would seem—and this has been said long ago and often—that this approach, emphasizing the ultimately self-interested nature of political ideas as justification for often cynical desires and acts, is less than rigorous in its attribution of motives.[25] Ideas may, at times, be elaborate disguises for self-interest, but they need not always be so; the question as to whether they are conscious attempts at disguises or unconscious rationalizations of desires needs also to be addressed.

Perhaps more importantly, whether politicians or ideologues believe what they say is often beside the point. Ideas which form the basis of the accepted political rhetoric of public arenas are ideas which define the boundaries of publicly acceptable political behaviour—and, therefore, define public standards to which people are expected to conform: a language of politics which becomes inescapable in that claims to political legitimacy must be made in that language. This creates the basis for public debate and the standards for acceptable action, both crucial for the appearance of democracy (I use the word 'appearance' in both senses here—'coming into being' as well as 'what it looks like'). Deviations from such norms need to be hidden, or justified as only apparent deviations, ultimately assimilable within the bounds of the norms. In the case of 'development', its importance as a catchphrase for legitimizing all manner of action in India is still too familiar to require elaboration.

The 'materialists', Marxist or non-Marxist, have been relatively marginalized by the emergence of alternative lines of approach to the study of 'development' in recent years, which link 'cultural' critiques of 'development' and 'state power' with an examination of the ideas and assumptions which went into them. Some important work has succeeded in emanating from such approaches; but its pitfalls need to be pointed out, at least in the context of dealing with India, without entering too deeply into a long-running and already clearly defined polemic.[26]

It is widely accepted that the process of formation of a new nationalist state was represented in Indian nationalist thought as a struggle, on the one hand, against an economic 'backwardness' enforced by colonialism and, on the other, between the 'modern' trends in national life and obscurantist, 'communal', traditionalist, 'backward' forces. A legitimate national state, as opposed to an economically retarding colonial one, was expected to play a strong role in developing the economy; therefore the legitimacy of the postcolonial state came to be crucially linked to its ability—or rather the ability of the directors of economic planning, identifying themselves with the state—to direct a programme of economic development on behalf of the nation. Arguments critical of this formulation diverge from this point onwards, in directions ranging from a wholesale critique of 'modernity' and its alleged allies, science and reason,[27] to a less ambitious questioning of the relationship between the nation and the state in India.[28] A good deal of the recent writing on the subject has, however, approached it from the former perspectives, through a critique of 'modernity' and its relationship with 'Western', 'post-Enlightenment rationality', which has become increasingly important in academic circles worldwide, in part as a response to the Eurocentrism of some earlier scholarship.[29] Unfortunately, such a critique either tends to conflate a variety of social, intellectual, and political positions within a somewhat flat conception of 'modernity', leaving little room to explore the intricacies of the negotiation of particulars thereof; or seeks to discover a separate, 'indigenous' epistemological framework for an 'Indian modernity'. The corresponding delegitimization of 'modern'/'Western' positions tends towards an empowerment of a variety of positions which justify often reactionary, obscurantist or ethnocentric positions as 'indigenous', equally 'modern' and/or better because they are 'authentic'. This can link up with a growing tendency to see projects which claim 'development' as their goal as *a priori* cultural imperialism or the 'tyranny of the state', perhaps because they emanate from a 'Western' or an 'Enlightenment paradigm'. This has important consequences, not merely confined to India, in providing (perhaps unintended) justification, in academically respectable terms, for right-wing politics. In addition to the dangers of political appropriation, there is the danger of an 'indigenism' of the academic variety closing down possibilities of exploring differences and tensions within 'indigenous' 'modern' society; for instance, in the privileging of 'indigenous' positions (presumably retrievable from a past of pre-colonial 'innocence') in writing of Indian pasts,[30] and an inadequate exploration of the numerous borrowings, conscious or unconscious, and the reinterpretations of such borrowings, which go into concepts of 'Indianness'. ('Nationalism', in the Indian context, because of its connections with anti-colonialism, has seldom been subjected to the degree of searching scrutiny that other normalized categories have been; its legitimacy and desirability has to a large extent been taken for granted.)

The dominant concern of much of this writing is a concentration on the theme of 'modernity'. A subject such as 'development' is often dealt with in terms of this grand theme. It seems to me to be an unnecessary academic project to continue to insist on the importance of 'modernity' as anything other than a claim, the characteristics or hallmarks of which are bound to significantly diverge across contexts and time-periods. The term 'modernity', in the period under consideration, carried with it extremely positive connotations for a people called 'primitive' and 'backward'; the tendency to excavate the past for a similar-sounding term to those in current use should recognize that such terms often did not then carry the overtones they acquired in late twentieth century debates.[31] Similarly, the focus on 'culture', another term for which great claims are made and which appears to have replaced 'economic man' at the centre of a good deal of social sciences discourse, is not particularly useful, especially when used (implicitly or explicitly) in opposition to 'economics'.[32] This is an approach which, moreover, has a tendency to look at ideas in rather anachronistic contexts, interrogating them for traces of contemporary ideologies reflecting the state of late twentieth or early twenty-first century academia rather than nineteenth or early twentieth century colonial contexts. In this study, therefore, terms such as 'modernity', 'culture', or 'Westernization' are treated as important ideas in the debates examined, but are not given extraordinary powers of their own across the specifities of time and place: they were indeed normative terms in their own times, as they are now, but their normative significance as well as their descriptive content was often different.

Why and how, then, might it be relevant—and productive—to approach 'development' in India in terms of the clusters of ideas surrounding it and the contexts within which they operated, which were used to conceptualize and/or justify 'development', rather than in terms of the political machinations and compromises contained therein, force of circumstance, *Realpolitik*; or in terms of development-as-Western-enlightenment-tyranny? The dilemma of how to situate the role of ideas, as I have already mentioned, stems from the attempt to make too direct a link between ideas and policy. My work, however, as I have also mentioned, does not deal directly with the connection of ideas to policy or the execution of policy; it seeks to establish the place of ideas in terms of the public standards and the contours of public rhetoric which they generate.

This approach to dealing with the importance of ideas in history has analogies in the approach used by Quentin Skinner, which succeeds in avoiding the contrasting purities of strongly idealist or crudely materialist positions. Skinner's placing of influential ideas within their ideological and practical contexts, and his focus on the question of legitimation of social action (or potential social action) through ideas, is a methodology which might be profitably employed in other work. In particular, Skinner's contention that 'political life itself sets the main problems for the political theorist, causing a certain range of issues to appear problematic, and a corresponding range of questions to become the leading subjects of debate', and that, consequently, ideas are a part of politics, needs to be kept in mind here.[33] Also relevant is his contention that the possibilities for ideological manoeuvre are constrained by an existing political vocabulary which is 'intersubjectively normative'[34]—containing 'evaluative-descriptive' terms (that is, terms which are both descriptive and evaluative at the same time).[35] It is through the 'manipulation' of these terms 'that any society succeeds in establishing and altering its moral identity'.[36] An agent who wishes to legitimize what he is doing cannot simply instrumentally tailor his normative language to fit his projects; in part he must tailor his projects 'in order to make them answer to the pre-existing language of moral principles'.[37]

There are obvious disanalogies, methodological as well as empirical, with Skinner's material which come to mind when discussing the Indian situation. There are no 'classic' texts; there was no relatively stable political consensus in the 1930s in most parts of the world, not just in India, giving rise to writing within contending paradigms.[38] Skinner's ideologues seem to be extremely conscious of the terms which they seek to manipulate; in the Indian situation, the terms along which debates are structured often operated implicitly, constraining and moving ideas along. As a result, I prefer the term 'ideas' to 'ideology'; the latter often seems to imply a more coherent, consciously employed set of ideas than is indicated by my material, though, of course, some relatively coherent ideologies were articulated. The contexts which need to be kept in mind in the Indian situation are more complex, spanning several cultural and discursive contexts, metropolitan, colonial, and international.

What can be established, however, is that in India, from the 1930s onwards, a certain normative language was coming into being. In part it was emerging from the dialectical relationship between two mutually opposed normative languages, one explicitly imperialist, another broadly nationalist. This was the formative period for a normative framework which, arguably, lasted till the 1990s liberalization wave, and in certain aspects still survives.

Such a history as this cannot be comprehensive; it certainly is not intended to be. On the other hand, it may well be representative. This is made easier by the nature of the problem I deal with. The main protagonists in the debates and the main protagonists who later found themselves in bodies formulating developmental policy in the 1950s were often of the same set. They came from an easily identifiable social milieu, and were all from the colonial intellectual bourgeoisie. They debated the ethics, principles, and philosophies of contending paths to 'development'. They claimed the right to speak for all classes and all sections of Indian society, as an enlightened leadership. Yet most often the ways in which they conceptualized problems of 'development' were intimately bound with the anxieties and limitations of their class ('anxieties and limitations' rather than 'interests': the former formulation does not imply deliberate cynicism)—even when many of them claimed to speak for 'socialism' and the 'masses'.

Constraints of space and time played a role in the selection of examples; for instance, the milieu of each presidency town and of the capital provided different specifics in terms of the ways in which social circles among the intellectual bourgeoisie took shape, institutions worked, and individual intellects were moulded. Yet I think it is possible to establish that these were variations on an identifiable theme; not only were the milieus not significantly different, but they also overlapped and communicated with each other. If there was in colonial India an all-India class, it was the intellectual bourgeoisie. This does not imply that there were no internal differences: ideological differences existed, and in some cases tensions on 'community' lines could come into operation which divided intellectual from intellectual.[39]

Certain other aspects of the selective addressing of the problem need also to be dealt with here. One is the exclusion of ideas and contexts which did not emerge at the national centrestage, but operated according to regional or local imperatives; another is the relative lack of importance given to writing on 'development', written both in economic terms and in broader terms, which did not find a place in the main currents of thought on the subject. This is explained by the focus of this book on ideas which were accommodated in the nationalist mainstream—I believe that this accommodation was itself a sign of the importance given to those ideas. This does not altogether overlook specifically local contexts, especially when an originally local context in conjuncture with a more all-India concern can be seen in operation. On the other hand, for instance, the importance of 'development' in the relations among the princely states of Mysore and Travancore and the British paramount power may be less significant to the larger picture. Similarly, many interesting formulations of the problem of 'development' were not significantly engaged with by a wider audience and, as a result, they did not significantly find their way into the mainstream debates. On the other hand, some ideas which were marginalized were adopted in dilute or modified forms in the mainstream; the dilution or modification was crucial in that it usually changed the content while maintaining aspects of the initial formulation which assisted the search for legitimate arguments. The question to be asked in such cases is how the context for various ideas served to highlight and amplify some ideas while rejecting others.

In this connection, a brief comment in anticipation of arguments made in the rest of the book might be made here on the relationship between metropolitan and Indian ideas—a relationship which is explored in this book in connection with 'development', but which would repay further exploration in other contexts. One of the major problems of understanding politics in colonial India is that the terminology is misleadingly familiar to readers from a metropolitan context, while the meaning of the terminology is often subtly but significantly different. This is often a factor of a borrowed terminology whose meaning is shifted as it is related to Indian concerns—a tendency shared among British colonial officials as well as Indian nationalists.

Political arguments in colonial India were interventions into arenas structured by the British colonial power. An effective intervention had to appeal to principles which the colonial power recognized as valid. These were often principles which had already secured political and/or academic respectability in Britain—both British colonial government officials and Indian opponents of the government linked their arguments to these principles, whose legitimacy was reinforced by their *prior* status as valid principles in the metropolis. Metropolitan ideas were, therefore a potential source of legitimacy for Indian arguments. This explains the familiarity in terminology.

The shifts in meaning of that terminology in Indian usage related to the specific arguments which protagonists in India sought to make. Long-standing concerns could often be reframed or rephrased in terms of newer ideas or principles which had acquired legitimacy in the metropolis. The importance of metropolitan ideas of dissent from the mainstream (such as 'socialism'), to which ideas of dissent from imperialism were attached, and in terms of which the latter ideas were rephrased, should be noted in this connection. This process often required a translation of Indian concerns into new idioms. This is where the shift occurred. As metropolitan ideas were used to provide a language for particularly Indian concerns or anxieties, the meaning of the ideas shifted (as in Gandhi's incorporations of turn-of-the-century anti-industrial romanticism). The terminology often remained the same despite the shift in meaning. At the same time, in its rephrasing in the language of the metropolis, to an extent the idea in Indian usage came closer to its metropolitan host idea. The 'original' idea may have been lost in translation.

Yet another problem remained: standards of legitimacy in India could not be seen to lean too strongly on metropolitan standards alone. Hence, the importance of denying charges of adopting 'foreign' elements. This was an implicit problem of the existence of two potential standards of legitimacy in the colonial situation: Indian (nationalist) and British (colonial). In practice, the distinctions were not quite so rigid, with certain arguments capable of being represented within either convention, and both conventions coexisting ambivalently. This also meant that 'indigenous' intellectual resources were sought to be drawn upon as standards of legitimacy, which were said either to reinforce or to undermine the sanctity of outside principles. Ironically, these 'indigenous' resources had themselves been crucially shaped by British interventions in earlier periods. Thus, in reading arguments, the historian is faced, in addition to the problem of the sameness of terminology masking differences in meaning, the problem of differences in terminology masking similarities in meaning.

None of this is to suggest that 'discourses'—by which I mean the less-than-explicit assumptions within which debates or arguments functioned—fundamentally determined the outcome of arguments, or indeed determined the practical politics resting on the principles articulated in such arguments. There was considerable autonomy within the conventions, as long as the boundaries of the conventions were observed; this autonomy, as I shall argue in this book, was crucially dependent on the ability of protagonists to place their arguments within the conventions.

Endnotes

1. For a convenient route through this literature, see Sukhamoy Chakravarty, *Development Planning: The Indian Experience* (Oxford, 1987); T.J. Byres (ed.), *The State and Development Planning in India* (Delhi, 1994); T.J. Byres (ed.), *The Indian Economy: Major Debates Since Independence* (Delhi, 1997); for earlier work dealing with planning see A.H. Hanson, *The Process of Planning: A Study of India's Five-Year Plans, 1950–64* (Oxford, 1966); Francine R. Frankel, *India's Political Economy 1947–1977: The Gradual Revolution* (Princeton, 1978).

2. For instance, in Bhabatosh Datta, *Indian Economic Thought: Twentieth Century Perspectives* (New Delhi, 1978), Ajit K. Dasgupta, *Gandhi's Economic Thought* (London, 1996), Ajit K. Dasgupta, *A History of Indian Economic Thought* (London, 1993), and for earlier periods in B.N. Ganguli, *Indian Economic Thought: Nineteenth Century Perspectives* (New Delhi, 1977); to an extent, Bipan Chandra, *The Rise and Growth of Economic Nationalism in India: Economic Policies of Indian National Leadership, 1880–1905* (New Delhi, 1966) as well as in sections of Sumit Sarkar, *The Swadeshi Movement in Bengal 1903–1908* (New Delhi, 1973).

3. On the negative economic impact of colonial rule, see, for instance, William Digby, *'Prosperous' British India* (London, 1901); Dadabhai Naoroji, *Poverty and Un-British Rule in India* (London, 1901); Romesh Chunder Dutt, *The Economic History of India* (two volumes, London, 1906); for a restatement of the 'benefits' case, see Vera Anstey, *The Economic Development of India* (London, 1929). For later continuations of the debate, see, for instance, Amiya Kumar Bagchi, *Private Investment in India 1900–1939* (Cambridge, 1972); Basudev Chatterji, *Trade, Tariffs and Empire: Lancashire and British Politics in India 1919–1939* (Delhi, 1992); Dietmar Rothermund, *India in the Great Depression 1929–1939* (Delhi, 1992); Dietmar Rothermund, 'The Great Depression and British Financial Policy in India, 1929–1934', *Indian Economic and Social History Review*, Vol. 17, No. 4 (1981), reprinted in his *The Indian Economy under British Rule* (Delhi, 1983); Clive Dewey, 'The End of the Imperialism of Free Trade: The Eclipse of the Lancashire

Lobby and the Concession of Fiscal Autonomy to India' in Clive Dewey and A.G. Hopkins (eds), *The Imperial Impact: Studies in the Economic History of Africa and India* (London, 1978); B.R. Tomlinson, *The Political Economy of the Raj 1914–1947* (London, 1979). On the relationship of business to politics, see Bipan Chandra, 'Jawaharlal Nehru and the Capitalist Class, 1936', *Economic and Political Weekly*, Vol. X, No. 33–35 (August 1975); *The Rise and Growth of Economic Nationalism in India* (New Delhi, 1966); Sumit Sarkar, 'The Logic of Gandhian Nationalism: Civil Disobedience and the Gandhi–Irwin Pact (1930–31)', *Indian Historical Review*, Vol. III, No. 1 (1976); Aditya Mukherjee, 'The Indian Capitalist Class: Development 1927-1947', in S Bhattacharya and Romila Thapar (eds), *Situating Indian History: for Sarvepalli Gopal* (Delhi, 1981); Aditya Mukherjee, 'Indian Capitalist Class and Congress on National Planning and Public sector, 1930–47', in K.N. Panikkar (ed.) *National and Left Movements in India* (New Delhi, 1980); Aditya Mukherjee, *Imperialism, Nationalism and the Making of the Indian Capitalist Class 1920–1947* (Delhi, 2002); Basudev Chatterji, 'Business and Politics in the 1930s: Lanceshire and the making of the Indo-British Trade Agreement, 1939', *Modern Asian Studies* 15, 3 (1985); Alan Ross, *The Emissary: G.D. Birla, Gandhi and Independence* (London, 1986) (a commissioned biography); Medha Malik Kudaisya, *The Life and Times of G.D. Birla* (Delhi, 2003); A.D.D. Gordon, *Businessmen and Politics: Rising Nationalism and a Modernising Economy in Bombay, 1918–33* (Delhi, 1978); Claude Markovits, *Indian Business and Nationalist Politics* (Cambridge 1985); R.S. Chandavarkar, *The Origins of Industrial Capitalism in India* (Cambridge, 1994)—the last linking the concerns regarding industrial capitalism in India with concerns regarding industrial labour in India. For an attempt at an overall assessment of the business–politics linkages and the industrial development question, see Rajat Kanta Ray, *Industrialisation in India: Growth and Conflict in the Private Corporate Sector 1914–47* (Delhi, 1979). For a recent restatement of the 'benefits' argument, see Tirthankar Roy, *The Economic History of India 1857–1947* (Delhi, 2000). This is a representative, but by no means an exhaustive list.

4. See Bhabatosh Datta, *Indian Economic Thought: Twentieth Century Perspectives*, informative on the strictly economic aspects of these twentieth century debates. Datta often raises interesting questions only to close them again, speaking of 'romantic' strains in economic thought which he marginalizes in his narrative, highlighting its economic dimensions without asking where the 'romantic' strain came from, assuming it to be dispensable. Only a partial exception to this trend is Ajit Dasgupta, *Gandhi's Economic Thought*, which deals with a subject that has become a strong ally of anti-developmentalists, environmentalists and advocates of 'sustainable development'. Dasgupta is sympathetic to Gandhi's ideas and takes into account the moral and ethical bases of Gandhi's conceptions of economics—an approach essential in understanding Gandhi. Nevertheless, it attempts to

systematize Gandhi's writings on economic matters into a consistent body of thought which can be expressed intelligibly in the language of economics.

5. See, for instance, H.W. Arndt, *Economic Development: The History of an Idea* (Chicago, 1987); Raymond Williams, *Keywords: A Vocabulary of Culture and Society* (revised edition, third impression, Glasgow 1989), pp. 102–4; and less self-consciously, W.W. Rostow, *How it All Began: Origins of the Modern Economy* (London, 1975); *Politics and the Stages of Growth* (Cambridge, 1971). On the Soviet Union's views, see S. Clarkson, *The Soviet Theory of Development: India and the Third World in Marxist-Leninist Scholarship* (Toronto, 1978).

6. For a summary of the Marxist assumptions behind 'development' as related to India, from a contemporary viewpoint, see R. Palme Dutt, *India Today* (London, 1940; second revised Indian edition, Bombay, 1949).

7. Britain was not alone among the colonial powers in claiming 'development' to be one of the goals of colonialism, although some of them (such as Belgium or Portugal) were rather less energetic about 'development' —in practice and theory.

8. On 'colonial development', see, for example, Partha Sarathi Gupta, *Imperialism and the British Labour Movement 1914–1964* (London, 1975), *passim*; J.M. Lee, *Colonial Development and Good Government: a Study of the Ideas Expressed by the British Official Classes in Planning Decolonisation 1939– 1964* (Oxford, 1967); S. Constantine, *The Making of British Colonial Development Policy 1914–1940* (London, 1984); Herward Sieberg, *Colonial Development: die Grundlegung moderner Entwicklungspolitik durch Grossbritannien, 1919–1949* (Stuttgart, 1985).

9. Most importantly, American public opinion and its opposition to the British Empire and Commonwealth as a bloc which gave the USA too little access to its markets—see William Roger Louis, *Imperialism at Bay, 1941–1945: The United States and the Decolonization of the British Empire* (Oxford, 1977).

10. See Partha Sarathi Gupta, *Imperialism and the British Labour Movement 1914–1964* (London, 1975), pp. 10–13 and *passim*.

11. In connection with the intellectual pre-history of the presumptions of 'development' and its relationship with ideas of progress, see J.W. Burrow, *Evolution and Society* (Cambridge, 1966). Burrow concentrates on the wider social and political meanings rather than the economic, though the latter are implicit in the first. The importance of India in providing examples and intellectual ammunition in these debates is notable.

12. Penderel Moon (ed.), *Wavell: The Viceroy's Journal* (London, 1973), p. 61, entry for 19 March 1944, and p. 108, entry for 31 December 1944.

13. Sir M. Visvesvaraya, *Planned Economy for India* (Bangalore City, 1934), preface.

14. Babu Bhagavandas to Jawaharlal Nehru, 24/9/33, Jawaharlal Nehru Papers (JNP), Nehru Memorial Library (NML), Vol. 7, f. 273.

15. It would not be entirely accurate to call it laissez-faire—this never was

completely so, except in economic doctrine. See Sabyasachi Bhattacharya, 'Laissez-faire in India', *Indian Economic and Social History Review*, Vol. II, No. 1 (January 1965).

16. See Bipan Chandra, *The Rise and Growth of Economic Nationalism in India* (New Delhi, 1966); also B.N. Ganguli, *Indian Economic Thought: Nineteenth Century Perspectives* (Delhi, 1977).

17. See the early writings of Sir M. Visvesvaraya, for instance, *Reconstructing India* (London, 1920), or the speeches and essays reprinted in G.D. Birla, *The Path to Prosperity: A Plea for Planning* (Allahabad, 1950).

18. The Bombay Plan, Sir M. Visvesvaraya, and the Government of India all cited the Soviet experience as an example of the great possibilities of planning—all operating within a capitalist framework. See P. Thakurdas, J.R.D. Tata, G.D. Birla, Sir Shri Ram, Kasturbhai Lalbhai, A.D. Shroff, and John Matthai, *A Plan of Economic Development for India* (Parts I & II, Bombay, 1944); M. Visvesvaraya, *Planned Economy for India*; Government of India, *Second Report on Reconstruction Planning* (New Delhi, 1944).

19. On the ambivalence of nationalist intellectuals and professional elites to business, see Chapter 5 in this book: for British government circles' hostility to Indian 'capitalists' despite the urgent need to find a formula for occasional cooperation with them, especially with regard to the mutual need to put down labour unrest or 'communism', see Claude Markovits, *Indian Business and Nationalist Politics* (Cambridge 1985); Basudev Chatterji, *Trade, Tariffs and Empire*, (Delhi, 1992).

20. Kitabistan, Allahabad, Vora and Co., Bombay, and Oxford University Press, Delhi, the last named, with its 'Oxford Pamphlets on India' series, were major publishers on 'development' as a theme.

21. See the section, 'Terminology', in Chapter 2 of this book.

22. Terence Byres, in *State, Class and Development Planning in India*, called for an historical understanding of development planning in terms of 'a political economy framework, broadly construed and not attenuated by disciplinary specialisation' (p. 6)—a history which, he believes, begins in the 1930s but 'remains to be written'. This book may be seen as a step towards the writing of such a history, but is not intended to be the 'full history' which will 'transcend the specialisation which has fractured social science' that Byres calls for (p. 9). Earlier calls for such an historical understanding largely went unheard—see, for instance, Colin Simmons, 'Economic Development and Economic History', in Barbara Ingham and Colin Simmons (eds), *Development Studies and Colonial Policy* (London, 1987), especially pp. 28–31. This does not, however, escape from the narrow focus on economic arguments. For a more recent attempt, see Sudipta Kaviraj, 'Democracy and Development in India', in Amiya Kumar Bagchi (ed.), *Democracy and Development* (London, 1995), in which *inter alia* he speaks of the 'vernacularisation' of political languages as they enter India, and points to the 'movement of the entire ideological language to the left, to the detriment of leftist politics and clarity

of political language itself' (p. 103)—though he dates this second trend to the 1960s rather than earlier. See also David Washbrook, (still in the economic mode as far as development is concerned, as well as being unreferenced and speculatory); Sugata Bose and Ayesha Jalal, 'Nationalism, Democracy and Development', in Sugata Bose and Ayesha Jalal (eds), *Nationalism, Democracy and Development: State and Politics in India* (Delhi, 1997); David Ludden, 'India's Development Regime' in Nicholas Dirks (ed.), *Colonialism and Culture* (Ann Arbor, 1992); Sugata Bose, 'Instruments and Idioms of Colonial National Development: India's Historical Experience in Comparitive Perspective', in Frederick Cooper and Randall Packard (eds) *International Development and the Social Sciences* (Berkeley, 1997).

23. See Christopher Baker, Gordon Johnson, and Anil Seal (eds), *Power, Profit and Politics*, special issue, *Modern Asian Studies* Vol. 15, No. 3 (1981).

24. A notable attempt at looking at the importance of ideas in the framing of policy ran into this dilemma and its author frankly admitted his inability to resolve it. See S. Ambirajan, *Classical Political Economy and British Administration in India* (Cambridge, 1978), pp. 17–22, 268. Other works dealing with ideas and their influence on administration in India have been more circumspect, dealing essentially with influences and the formation of official attitudes: Eric Stokes, *The English Utilitarians and India* (Oxford, 1959); Ranajit Guha, *A Rule of Property for Bengal* (Paris, 1963). Recently Clive Dewey has attempted to make a case for 'vested ideas rather than vested interests' being responsible for the governing of the Empire in India; but his examples point to the failure of these 'vested ideas' in practice, so the question must be said to remain unresolved; see Clive Dewey, *Anglo-Indian Attitudes: The Mind of the Indian Civil Service* (London, 1993).

25. See, for instance, specifically in the case of Indian history, Howard Spodek, 'Pluralist Politics in British India: The Cambridge Cluster of Historians', *American Historical Review*, Vol. 84, 1979; and, in connection with the 'Namierite' approach to history-writing, E.J. Hobsbawm, 'Where are British Historians Going?', *The Marxist Quarterly*, Vol. II, No. 1, (January 1955), especially, pp. 19–23. Hobsbawm points out that consequent to post-Namier bourgeois historians adopting an approach of 'vulgar materialism', 'Marxists have had to remind them that history is the struggle of men for ideas, as well as a reflection of their material environment' (p. 22); he also acknowledges that a number of Marxist-inspired histories have been rather mechanistically materialist.

26. For a sense of the polemic in relation to India, see D.A. Washbrook, 'Progress and Problems: South Asian Economic and Social History, c. 1720–1860', *Modern Asian Studies*, Vol. 22, No. 1 (1988); Partha Chatterjee, *The Nation and its Fragments* (Princeton, 1993), pp. 29–32; Bose and Jalal, 'Nationalism, Democracy and Development', pp 2–3; Sumit Sarkar, 'The Decline of the Subaltern in Subaltern Studies', *Writing Social History* (Delhi, 1997), p. 108. The important points made here are in danger of getting lost in the polemic;

two, however, should be taken seriously —the first, by Partha Chatterjee, opposes revisionist histories which appear to reduce the importance of the colonial experience in India to insignificance (*The Nation and its Fragments*, pp. 27–32); the second, made more generally, opposes strong conceptions of 'culture' upon which a good deal of recent academic writing seems to rely in arguing for the distinctiveness of South Asian society and ways of relating to the world.

27. See Ashis Nandy, *Tradition, Tyranny and Utopias: Essays in the Politics of Awareness* (Delhi, 1987); Ashis Nandy (ed.), *Science, Hegemony and Violence: A Requiem for Modernity* (Delhi, 1988); Ashis Nandy, 'The Political Culture of the Indian State', *Daedalus*, Vol. 118, No. 4, (Fall 1989); Claude Alvares, *Science, Development and Violence: The Revolt Against Modernity* (Delhi, 1992). Some of this writing contains valid points of criticism of science, reason, or development as it has been practised; but where such criticism is valid, it is conducted on the basis of tools of analysis provided by reason, science or development themselves, for instance in Alvares' analysis of the Green Revolution in chapter two of his *Science, Development and Violence* or in Nandy's pointing to the educated middle-class nature of Indian political culture until quite recently or, more generally, in the environmentalist position, emerging through this sort of academic work, on the limitations and dangers of unfettered technology, much of which criticism is based on science itself. These intellectual debts to the enemy are seldom acknowledged.

28. For examples of this approach see Sugata Bose and Ayesha Jalal (eds), *Nationalism, Democracy, Development: State and Politics in India*, of which two essays are particularly interesting: Bose and Jalal, 'Nationalism, Democracy, Development', and Amartya Sen, 'On Interpreting India's Past'.

29. See, for instance, Partha Chatterjee, *Nationalist Thought and the Colonial World: A Derivate Discourse?* (London, 1986); Partha Chatterjee, *The Nation and its Fragments*; Dipesh Chakrabarty, *Provincialising Europe* (Princeton, 2000); Dipesh Chakrabarty, *Habitations of Modernity: Essays in the Wake of Subaltern Studies* (Chicago, 2002); Ranajit Guha, *History at the Limits of World History* (New York, 2002). The theme is, now at least, a little stale.

30. See Ashis Nandy, *The Intimate Enemy: Loss and Recovery of Self Under Colonialism* (Delhi, 1983), p. ix; Ashis Nandy, 'The Political Culture of the Indian State'.

31. Marshall Berman has argued in this connection that the terms 'modernism' and 'modernization' grew apart after the 1920s. The first was seen as a cultural, aesthetic, and philosophical standpoint; the second was related to economics and the organization of industry; although these two aspects of modernity were dialectically related, those interested in the one were not necessarily interested in the other. Marshall Berman, *All that is Solid Melts Into Air: The Experience of Modernity* (London, 1983). In India, however,

invariably the modernists were the modernizers; they viewed the two as inseparable, and the same people dominated economic and cultural life; the linking of the two positions was embodied in public phenomena such as the successful running and circulation of such journals as *Science and Culture* and the *Modern Review* (for which, see Chapter 5 of this book).

32. See Partha Chatterjee, *The Nation and its Fragments,* pp. 74–5. This is in line with his distinction between two domains in which nationalism operated: the 'inner' and the 'outer' spheres: in the 'inner' sphere, Indians attempted to maintain a cultural domain, in which they sought to develop a culture which was modern, but not 'Western' (pp. 6–7). His distinction between an 'inner' sphere of 'culture' and an 'outer' sphere of statecraft, politics, etc, in which the 'West' might be imitated, is not reflected in the debates on 'development'. The postulation of a distinction between 'culture' and 'economics' in Indian nationalist discourse is not peculiar to Chatterjee: for instance, see Sudipta Kaviraj, 'On the Structure of Nationalist Discourse' in T.V. Sathyamurthi (ed.), *Social Change and Political Discourse in India, volume 1: State and Nation in the Context of Social Change* (Delhi, 1994), p. 316. The distinction may be viable for earlier periods—Kaviraj contrasts the 'cultural' approach of Bankim Chandra Chattopadhyay and the 'political economy' approaches of Dadabhai Naoroji or Romesh Chunder Dutt, and Chatterjee formulates the distinction between the 'inner' and 'outer' spheres from the case of early nineteenth century Bengali responses to British social engineering projects— but the separation of these two spheres or of 'culture' and 'economics' is not present in debates on 'development': the spheres mingle, and the themes are embedded in one another.

33. Quentin Skinner, *The Foundations of Modern Political Thought* (Cambridge, 1978), Vol. 1, p. xi, quoted in James Tully, 'The Pen is a Mighty Sword: Quentin Skinner's Analysis of Politics', in James Tully (ed)., *Meaning and Context: Quentin Skinner and his Critics* (Cambridge, 1988), pp. 10–11.

34. The phrase is not Skinner's own, but an useful abbreviation used by James Tully, 'The Pen is a Mighty Sword', in Tully (ed.), *Meaning and Context*, p. 13.

35. Quentin Skinner, 'Some Problems in the Analysis of Political Thought and Action', in Tully (ed.), *Meaning and Context*, p. 111.

36. Skinner, 'Some Problems in the Analysis of Political Thought and Action', p. 112.

37. Quentin Skinner, 'Language and Social Change', in Tully (ed.), *Meaning and Context*, p. 132.

38. It is not just texts which work as sources in my work; minor texts may well form part of the ideological context, but so do live political and social debate. The problem of reading authorial intention is both methodological and empirical—in his methodological writing Skinner makes it clear that the intention(s) of the author in writing a text and the reception of it by his targeted audience are important: see Skinner, 'Meaning and Understanding in

the History of Ideas', in Tully (ed.), *Meaning and Context*—and is a complex question when unconscious influences are taken into account, as in my work; but when I do this I read these influences from the context in which the writing or 'statement' appears, and cross-check the anxieties with other 'statements' related to other subjects—that is, which have the broad context in common but a different content.

39. The latter case was especially evident in the Muslim intellectual's need to work out problems specific to Muslim society, whether within the framework of an all-India identity or outside it. For examples of this tension, though not in the context of 'development', see Sulagna Roy, 'Communal Conflict in Bengal, 1930–1947', unpublished PhD dissertation, University of Cambridge, 1999. It has often been said that the tensions could be related to the separate development of the Hindu and Muslim bourgeoisies—this was the official Congress explanation and also the official communist one. But this could also be read against Gramsci's comments on the position of the intellectual. Antonio Gramsci, *Selections from the Prison Notebooks,* edited and translated by Quintin Hoare and Geoffrey Nowell Smith (London, 1971), pp. 5–18. See also below, Chapter 5 of this book.

2

The Context

This chapter attempts an understanding of the setting in which 'development' was discussed in India in the 1930s and 1940s: the discursive and socio-political context, and the implicit ground rules, in which the debates operated. I examine why the protagonists asked the questions they did—what, practically, prompted their questions; what, discursively, shaped them; and why they gave the answers they did. I also point to the ways in which these might have been circulated and disseminated. This will illustrate the contention that there is no simple connection between material context and response, between 'reality' and perceptions of that 'reality'. Consequently, the emergence of a nationalist discourse of 'development' needs to be seen not merely, or primarily, in relation to material 'facts', 'events', etc., but also in relation to other discourses, that is, to the ways 'facts', 'events', etc. were ordered and made sense of, publicized, and disseminated.

I do not, of course, want to suggest a rigid distinction between (a) a 'practical' and (b) a 'discursive' context or to put it differently, between (a) a context with a basis in 'facts', 'events' or 'projects', that is, 'what things are', (from my external vantage point, or where I broadly agree with the readings of contemporaries), as well as, in terms of the projects set out for themselves by contemporaries, 'what is to be done' (from their perspective)—the two taken either separately or together as the 'practical context': 'what is being talked about'—and (b) a context set out by the conventions of political debate, that is, 'how things are talked about' (my reading of 'discourse') and which might have been taken for granted by contemporary participants in debates who, consequently, would have been less conscious of them as governing conventions (but which could have talked about things which I consider to have been 'true' with the benefit of hindsight, as well as things which I do not consider to have been 'true'). In some cases, from an external point of view, a 'practical context' is also a part of the 'discursive context': 'what is being talked about' is not altogether separable from 'how things are talked about'. (To contemporaries, of course, the distinction was not always apparent, and would certainly not have been phrased in those terms.) The distinction is, therefore, a heuristic one.

The chapter outlines the background debates regarding political economy in colonial India, and points to the dependence of these debates on the attribution of essentialized and stereotypical economic and social roles to particular groups of people by British imperial discourse. It raises the question of how far counter-arguments were able to break down these essentialisms, or how far they required the creation of counter-essentialisms. It examines the interplay between allegedly universal principles—'economics' or 'political economy'—and particular exceptions, based, for instance, on the 'nature' of Indians. It was, I argue, extremely difficult to break out of this cycle and make a valid argument if the adjudicators—British imperial officials—were always in the last analysis able to particularize opponents' positions, refusing to accept their universality. However, in the 1930s, the porous and changing conceptions of the central universal—'economics'—made an appeal to the universal easier, because the adjudicators lost their stranglehold on it.

At the same time, Indians did not abandon their own right to appeal to particular arguments. I examine the interconnectedness of the terminology used in the cluster of debates surrounding 'development', and point to the strong extra-economic connotations of some of them. The chapter points out that many of the debates on development emerged from categories and concepts intrinsic to everyday situations of imperial administration, but threw up the need to formulate alternative arguments.

Political Economy: Precedents and Ideas, Metropolitan and Colonial

Since the debates on 'development' were, to a large extent, framed in terms of political economy or economics—although political economy was often used merely as a starting point—an understanding of what 'political economy' or 'economics' meant to the protagonists in the debates is necessary in order to make sense of many of the details, examples, and contexts which the debates drew upon. This focus requires that I shall not draw substantially upon the retrospective and external judgements of present day economic historians, though I shall draw on their judgements of the perceptions internal to the periods they describe.

The earlier history of Indo-British economic relations was the background to later debates on 'development' from the 1930s onwards. This was largely a record of the British government's claim to having been an agent of economic progress and Indian counter-claims that the British had been an agent of economic destruction. It is important here to provide an outline of that early history, concentrating on information which was also widely known by the protagonists in the debates on 'development'; it was not only a history which made up the practical context of the need to escape from economic backwardness, it was also a discursive context which nationalists drew upon. I also provide a survey of the ideas in metropolitan thinking on economic matters; and of how conventions of argument used 'political economy'.

At the height of the British Empire in India, from roughly the last third of the nineteenth century to the First World War, laissez-faire was the proclaimed doctrine of government, although the ideology of laissez-faire admitted of exceptions in practice, especially in India, where government intervention had been, selectively, far greater than that acceptable in Britain.[1] Exceptions to the doctrine were often necessitated by a genuine concern for levels of agricultural production.[2] With a certain amount of tenancy legislation the government was able to provide some security to peasants of a certain level and above, as the basis of production for a growing export market; other legislative measures included protecting peasants from having their land pass into the hands of their creditors, who were from so-called 'non-agricultural castes'.[3] At other times, laissez-faire appeared to be rather absurdly applied: for instance, the government did not, apparently on principle, interfere in the internal grain market even in times of famine.[4] Deviation from laissez-faire was particularly evident in certain areas like the Punjab, which seems to have provided a prototype for an 'improving' colonialism—whose logic, in the Punjab case, fitted in well with the contours of the imperial economy and the need for expanding agricultural production. Its irrigation system, sturdy peasant farmers, canal colonies, its cooperative movement, and its actively benevolent civilians, contributed to creating a positive image of a 'Punjab School' of administration which was greatly influential for the more public-spirited, or often merely the more romantic, Indian Civil Service (ICS) men coming to India; the Punjab was regarded as the most desirable posting for a civilian.[5] 'At the heart of the Punjab political tradition lay the desire to create and preserve a stable rural base'; the Punjab tradition 'discounted the political importance of the town, the trader and the educated Indian', and believed in 'the races that can fight'.[6] The idea of martial races, along with the idea of sturdy and honest peasants, it might be noted, were two examples of the colonial tendency to ascribe essentialized economic and social roles to particular groups—which stereotypes were influential, in many cases, in providing the rationale for actual policies.

The colony as a market and a source of raw materials had its justification, when one was required, in the classical economists' ideas of international division of labour and comparative advantage.[7] With the drying up of European markets under the impact of the depression of the 1880s and the consequent protectionism in Europe, India also proved its worth as a sphere of capital investment, with the active assistance of a government willing to protect returns.[8] India, in this period and until after the First World War was, in terms of international trade, the most open market in the world.[9]

The government was not unaware of the problems of the Indian economy, despite few signs of action to tackle them. The 1880 Famine Commission had pointed out, for instance, that the root of much of the poverty of the people of India and the risks to which they were exposed in times of scarcity was the fact that agriculture formed almost the sole occupation of most of the population. A remedy for this situation had to include the introduction of a diversity of occupations, through which the surplus population could be drawn from agricultural pursuits to employment in manufactures or elsewhere.[10] The Indian Industrial Commission of 1916–18 addressed the problem of the lack of manufacturing industries in India, largely as an outgrowth of the concern with India's lack of military potential during the First World War, and linking up with Lord Curzon's desire, expressed earlier, to turn India into a second military centre of the British Empire;[11] concrete results following its report were insignificant.[12] Specific problems with British handling of agrarian policy were also being articulated; but these did not make their way to the top of the priorities list.

The First World War ended the old imperial equilibrium, though the adherence to a proclaimed doctrine of laissez-faire continued through the 1920s.[13] Tariff protection, when finally introduced by the Government of India in the 1920s, apparently as a concession to nationalist demands, was described by the government as 'discriminating protection', which was still 'free trade with legitimate exceptions'.[14] Tariffs also allowed the government the better to balance the budget and pay the home charges,[15] the latter having been justified in 1911 by Sir Theodore Morison as a fair price for good government, infrastructure, and the privilege of borrowing in the world's cheapest capital market.[16] The concomitants of that privilege—balanced budgets and a rupee strictly linked to sterling at a statutory ratio—were the prerequisites of British Indian finance, the official argument being that unbalanced budgets or a floating rupee might damage India's creditworthiness in the eyes of the City of London and might even lead to a default on her debts.[17] The effects of tariff protection were largely cancelled out by the continued British control over the rupee–sterling exchange rate.[18] The call for tariff protection was also often linked to the problem of labour militancy, in which regard Indian businessmen and the colonial government found that their interests coincided: the former often claimed that a particular tariff concession or reduction in excise duty would strengthen their hand in dealing with strikes or labour's demands for a wage increase, and that without these concessions from the government they could not afford to pay the wage increases which alone could curb the Red threat.[19]

The 1920s saw the evolution of many of the mechanisms of economic administration that were carried into the 1930s, after the First World War had disrupted the old imperial equilibrium. The arguments and issues raised in the former period—fiscal autonomy, discriminating protection, imperial preference—all acquired greater importance in the 1930s when the balancing of imperial and Indian interests in an overall imperial system became more difficult.[20] The Depression undermined the economic assumptions which mediated India's imperial connection—in particular, the drastic decline in the money value of agricultural products (and, consequently, the ability of the state to collect land revenue) and the collapse of the external market for agricultural goods posed serious problems for balanced budgets[21]—and created a new context for arguments which challenged the accepted economic orthodoxies.

At the same time, the old debates were well remembered by the protagonists in the new ones (they were often the same people), and details from the older debates—which to nationalists were grievances— remained part of the standard armoury of nationalist argument: they became part of the historical memory which was to be drawn upon as a political resource-base by nationalists.[22]

The general assumptions on which British economic thinking rested need to be understood in this connection; with the caveat that although British intellectual currents had always been important in influencing trends in British India, such currents did not work in India in any simple sense. In the most direct sense, the imperatives of imperialism ruled out certain options in terms of the adoption of policies and dictated the cementing of certain economic and political structures of control in India.

Indirect influences also operated in a variety of ways; for instance, in the possibility of India being a sort of laboratory for conceptions of property[23] or for testing utilitarian social theories[24] which were not as yet influential or acceptable in Britain. On the imperial side, some arguments hinged on the universal applicability of certain principles—'economics', 'laissez-faire'; others on the exceptional nature of India, in which principles universal in Britain or Europe were inapplicable to India—parliamentary democracy, equality, or even in more 'economics'-based arguments, the irrational tendencies of the Indian peasantry to hoard, the lack of the entrepreneurial temperament, and so on.[25]

Changing perceptions within Britain itself of the economic role of the state ought to have made it possible to hold slightly broader economic ideas with which to deal with the crisis years of the 1930s. Free trade had remained the dominant doctrine of British official economic thinking through the 1920s, made possible by a hope that economic conditions would return to 'normal' until the Depression forced a realization that the multilateral trading world of the pre-First World War era could not be taken for granted, and was not likely to be restored in a hurry.[26] The 1930s was a period of great uncertainty, in which multiple possibilities for the future seemed to open out before the world, not just in matters of economic policy. As it happens, in terms of doctrine, many tried to defend free trade and to treat the Depression as an aberration; new ideas met with great resistance, governments operated on the basis of trial and error, and very few people seemed to be able to grasp what was going on.[27] John Maynard Keynes' ideas appeared to epitomize 'unsound' finance and caused great nervousness in the City which, as the leading sector of the British economy and staffed by Britain's most powerful elites, commanded a great deal of influence on official policy.[28] Keynes' forays into government began at the India Office, his first posting as a young civil servant, and continued over the years, notably as a member of the Economic Advisory Council,[29] and later as adviser to the Treasury during the Second World War; it was not until this last stage that he was able to make his most crucial impact on official economic thinking in Britain.[30] But perceptions changed all too slowly and selectively, with even the New Deal being watched nervously and suspiciously in British financial circles.[31] The 'Keynesian Revolution', as it is now known, was a long time in the making, facing the opposition of the pillars of the British financial establishment, the Treasury, and the Bank of England.[32] In the formative period of 'Keynesianism', some of the ideas which were being tentatively tried out were arrived at independently of Keynes in a number of countries—such as the unbalanced budget in the New Deal. The ideas that went into the writing of Keynes' *General Theory* were probably gleaned by Keynes through his experiences of the early 1930s. The examples of the New Deal in the USA, Soviet planning, and Fascist and, later, Nazi experiments in economic management became available through the 1930s. These were intimately connected with the ideological positions they represented, and if measures which had precedents in any one system were advocated as emulable examples, it was necessary to delineate adherence to or divergence from the ideological positions they represented. The easiest way of avoiding the issue of ideology was to declare a position on the basis of economic principles alone, thereby apparently defusing the debates of their political content and appealing to a supposedly neutral arbiter in the rational science of economics.

Such questions of changed perceptions as did arise emerged from immediate practical problems: of protecting Britain as far as possible from the worst effects of the Depression, of keeping a colonial state financially 'sound', and of the need for a containment policy against socialists and communists, whose increasing appeal was being felt all over the Empire, and whose prediction of the impending collapse of capitalism seemed to be materializing. In the Indian context, as far as policy was concerned, as a colony it was not to be granted the same measure of right to reassess the principles of its political economy. The need for a balanced budget in the colonies was considered especially important in the Depression when incomes in primary goods producing countries collapsed spectacularly along with agricultural prices and, therefore, also export-earnings and colonial governments' incomes.[33] A number of ideas which were discussed in official and semi-official circles in this period never found their way into policy, partly because of official discomfort with some of the ideas, but largely because they did not fit in well with the priorities of the imperial economy. Nevertheless, the ferment of economic ideas was noted in official as well as unofficial circles in India, with interest and concern, and found its way into current and subsequent debate.

The changes in economic orthodoxy which were adopted under the national government in Britain owed a good deal to the Conservative element within it, although for various reasons most groups in British politics went with the changes to a greater or lesser extent. The call for tariff reform was revived, and protective tariffs adopted in 1931; this was coupled with a demand for conscious efforts towards the integration of the Empire in a trading bloc through imperial preference, agreements towards which were drawn up at the Imperial Economic Conference in

Ottawa in 1932.[34] These two initiatives were intellectual contributions of the Conservative Party, but became acceptable across political boundaries. The Labour Party had been an opponent of both tariffs and imperial preference until the 1930s—in the 1920s largely due to the fear of the rise in the cost of food.[35] The retreat from this position was largely forced on Britain by the Depression; imperial preference, as a defence against its effects, was seen as a possible way out.[36] Keynes, a liberal, and G.D.H. Cole, a Fabian, as members of the Economic Advisory Council, were in favour of introducing tariffs, stimulating domestic investment, import controls, and subsidies for exports.[37] Philip Snowden, Chancellor of the Exchequer in the Labour government of 1929 and of the national government that followed, was a dedicated free trader representing the liberal side of the Labour Party and, consequently, inclined to deal with the situation by deflationist policies; he resigned on the issue of tariffs in 1932.[38] A section of the Conservatives welcomed the recommendation on tariffs, a demand which its supporters dated back to Joseph Chamberlain in 1903; among its supporters was Leopold Amery, future Secretary of State for India, who combined the recommendation of tariffs with a renewal of the call for imperial preference within an 'Empire–Commonwealth', a new and more palatable term for the British Empire which envisaged eventual equality of the nations within it.[39]

The Government of India's finance members in the 1930s, Sir George Schuster and Sir James Grigg, had opposing views on economic matters that reflected these conflicts in metropolitan circles: Schuster was suspected of Keynesianism (though this is to attribute too much consistency to his views), and Grigg was very much a 'sound finance' man. They have been seen as exemplars of contrasting attitudes within imperialist ranks.[40] Neither of them, however, abandoned a fundamental faith in the right of British imperialism to hold India.[41] The study of British economic thought in India at the highest official levels in the 1930s, therefore, provides no great surprises by way of innovative political economy. Whether this is seen as cynical exploitation or an adherence to a principled 'discriminating intervention',[42] the old values of sound economics and firm administration remained in evidence, Schuster's private views notwithstanding, manipulated as far as possible from London.[43] Schuster's private advocacy of economic planning for India on a quasi-Soviet model remained confined to the filing cabinets.[44] (Somewhat incongruous with this, at least at an apparent level, was Schuster's claim that India should not industrialize excessively, in line with Gandhi's strictures with which he claimed to be sympathetic:

apparently, British rights to plan India's future development involved the power of Soviet planners used for rather un-Soviet goals.)[45]

This was also the period of the search for a new constitutional framework for India, which had to find a balance between apparently conceding the principles of self-government, claiming to defend the rights of 'minorities' and protecting the interests of British business and finance. Related to and concurrent with this was the conflict between the Tory 'die-hards', led by Winston Churchill, who opposed any concessions to India—playing on the insecurities of Lancashire mill-owners trying to defend their Indian market and Lancashire workers' fears for their jobs—and the more apparently progressive section of the Tories, who saw the old forms of imperialism as unviable and sought to find new ones.[46] The solution envisaged by the latter section was within an imperial framework which was to be redefined as a partnership of equals—actual (those who had attained Dominion status) and potential (the latter category comprising those who had not yet qualified, in British eyes, for self-government)—and of many shades in between. Amery had already emerged as a champion of this position, in which domestic tariffs, imperial preference, and colonial development were integrally connected. In such a framework, the 'British Empire and Commonwealth', as he called it, would provide a large and more or less self-sufficient protected market within which the interests of its constituent members would be adjusted by negotiation.[47] Imperial preference—'a form of protection by which the Empire and the Dominions would become a single economic unit'[48]—was to be merged with 'a wider patriotism, blended with and yet transcending our several national patriotisms', in Amery's conception of the Commonwealth.[49] Member countries would all be entitled to have tariffs, but such tariffs would differentiate between Empire and other goods, allowing the former preferential access to their markets. The connection between this gradualist and evolutionary egalitarianism and Amery's white supremacist views, or his pioneering contribution to the development of aerial bombardment of civilian populations from the air is difficult to ascertain.[50]

Within this framework, colonial development could, by increasing the purchasing power of the colonies, enable them to buy more British goods.[51] Amery's views on the Empire were therefore, not too different from aspects of what came to be called Keynesian economics, adopted in domestic policy after the War. Amery himself was not particularly impressed by Keynes' work: he was later to write of Keynes' *General Theory* that it was 'enveloped in a vast cobweb of abstract definition, eked out by algebraical formulas ... [and] contains [only] a few commonplaces'.[52] The aspect of Amery's 'forward view' which came to be taken most seriously in Britain, and encouraged cross-party collaboration, was that of the importance of the imperial market, which was, in the propaganda of the 'Empire Marketing Board', to be embodied in the 'Empire Christmas Pudding'.[53] The economic fate of the British Empire was thus sought to be kept integrated. In such integration, however, India was an exception to the 'colonial development' aspect; while 'colonial development' had limited beginnings elsewhere before the Second World War, as an idea emerging from Colonial Office thinking, it did not find echoes in the India Office.[54]

This integration was maintained and remained crucial during and after the Second World War. During the War, given the material demands made by wartime production, the sheer impossibility of maintaining norms of 'sound finance' brought Keynesianism to the Treasury—in the person, in fact, of Keynes himself—and an anticipation of the welfare state in the Keynes-supported Beveridge Plan, two liberal statesmen's contribution to the identity of a future Labour government.[55] In India, the insistence on balanced budgets collapsed with India turning from a debtor to a creditor of Britain's, the rhetoric of maintaining India's creditworthiness with the City vanishing with it.[56] New equations now came into play.

In the 1930s and the 1940s, most participants in debates on 'development' in India would have known and understood these debates; and indeed followed them with interest. This shared public awareness had roots in a long debate which, by the 1930s, had become the basis for two kinds of conventional wisdom. The first, minus its internal differences for the purpose of its outward, anti-imperialist orientation, can be described in broad terms as a strong and articulate economic nationalism, and was a long-standing tradition in India; it had grown up from the second half of the nineteenth century, one of the earliest spheres of the articulation of a recognizably nationalist position, critical of the economic effects of British rule in India, rejecting laissez-faire in favour of the continental protectionist model of developing new industries as advocated by Friedrich List.[57] The demand for positive government intervention in order to create industries in India was integral to this, in which the argument of economic necessity—the need for alternative avenues of employment to agriculture— merged with that of national interest and right—objection to lack of industrialization other than that by foreign capital protected and subsidized by the British Government of India.[58] A well-informed and detailed critique of colonial economics on the Indian side, carried on continuously through the press and through academic and other publications, provided annotations and commentary on all things considered significant from a political economy point of view, and ensured that an awareness of these issues was part of the everyday awareness of an educated readership. Most of the newspaper-reading public would have been aware, in a general way, of the wider issues related to imperial domination of the Indian economy and of Indian politics and society, but also of issues such as the relative merits of a rupee–sterling exchange rate of 1s 4d, as opposed to 1s 6d, the Indian arguments in favour of tariffs but against imperial preference, the Central Banking Enquiry Committee, fears related to the sterling balances, and so on. These occupied a great deal of space in the daily papers, and were not simply matters of specialist concern, although many among the general readership might have been able to relate to them mainly in terms of further evidence of British imperial domination of India, fitting into a pre-existing conventional framework of understanding; which tended to ensure that even if the details of the arguments were not fully intelligible, the points sought to be put across were absorbed. In addition to this, political publications emanating from parties or pressure groups provided a continuous stream of information on political economy issues in simplified popular form, which were translated into several languages.[59]

On the other hand, there was the long-standing British argument of India being basically an agricultural country, temperamentally unsuited to industrialization, with industrial goods being capable of cheaper production in Britain; an appeal to this idea of the international division of labour was combined with a denial of the incompatibility of British and Indian positions on economic issues, and claims that the painful transition to an industrial society which Britain had undergone was unnecessary for India.[60]

By the 1920s and the 1930s these positions were so well established, the debates so well worn, as to trigger almost automatic appropriate responses on both sides of the nationalist–imperialist divide. The positions were carried forward into conceptions of 'development', linked up with a wider range of issues, and sought to be systematized. Nationalist writing on economic themes functioned largely in order to educate its public, generally on the basis that things could not be any different under a colonial government. British official responses in India were most often aimed at the same audience, claiming that the charge of inaction on the part of the government was untrue, that nationalist prescriptions for the economy were impractical, and that the British government was willing to assist India in realizing her 'legitimate national aspirations'.[61] The government also began directly to address charges that colonial rule was responsible for economic and, in particular, industrial backwardness.[62] Official arguments, however, began to sound less convincing with the emergence of various forms of strongly interventionist state elsewhere in the 1930s, which provided more fuel to nationalist arguments.

Shared Spaces of Domination and Resistance

There was always the imperative of keeping up appearances; and British imperialism in India took procedure extremely seriously. The highest official recognition that could be given to a problem in British India was through the appointment of a Royal Commission—in 1927 the Royal Commission on Agriculture, chaired by the future Viceroy of India, Lord Linlithgow, and in 1931 the Royal Commission on Labour conducted their enquiries. The appointment of these commissions represented the pressing need to take official cognisance of long-standing problems and to be seen to be doing something; it is possible to take them too seriously.[63] Public criticism of the narrowness of the Royal Commissions' reports or terms of reference was always widespread; and though this criticism was attributed by the government to nationalist hostility, the narrowness of the framework of solutions recommended was indeed striking, even by the standards of the time. The Linlithgow Commission, for instance, recommended the establishment of the Imperial Council of Agricultural Research, which dealt with such technical matters as soil quality and strains of seeds, but the commission could be justifiably accused of avoiding larger questions of land tenure except by the relatively safe measure of recommending the promotion of the cooperative movement.[64] The royal commissions played far less of a part in political economy than they did a performative part in the theatrical display of benevolent rule, while attempting to disguise the fact that no significant change, and certainly no radical change, could be expected from a Royal Commission report; and that India would continue to be managed for British benefits; this was recognized and highlighted by nationalists. That there was an element of humour in the pomp and circumstance of the visit of a Royal Commission, slowly making its way across the country, and winding up its enquiries before the end of the cool season, was not lost on one of the correspondents of the *Congress Socialist*, who was moved to verse:

Three Cheers for the Royal Commission!
By the end of fifteen months

We shall have all the facts.
A year later
And the Government will have a plan.
But by that time, of course,
The situation will have entirely changed
And it would be clearly unwise to interfere.[65]

A working framework was sought in allowing non-official Indians in various capacities to participate in and contribute to certain levels of political and economic debates. Indian voices were increasingly audible in these debates, and from within an officially recognized institutional framework. The fiscal commission, the tariff boards, royal commissions and various other committees of enquiry accommodated Indians, whose contributions to their proceedings were considerable. This was relatively safe: actual implementation of various decisions was outside their control. It is easy to make too much of the representation of Indians on these committees. Representation in British India was not meant to be representative; nor was it intended to extend actual powers. Hand-picked Indian notables were either loyalists of dependable lineage, or often businessmen whose interests the committees were meant to be dealing with, selected, at least, as much for their moderation as their 'expert' opinions, their dependence on the continuance of order and, consequently, on the state's law and order apparatus ensuring their moderation. They could, it was generally assumed, be trusted with playing the 'constitutional' game.[66] These notables were a select group. The same few names appear in various combinations on committees on economic matters from the First World War to 1947—and, indeed, after. It was only towards the last years of the Empire that they could no longer be relied upon to act as moderating influences on nationalist, especially Congress politics, to which the government knew they gave their financial, if not always political, support. (This is not to say that the government treated them as allies: their potential and actual opposition to government policies was preferred by the government to more radical forms of opposition; they, on their part, were content to hedge their bets and carve out as much space for their activities as possible.) The smaller and less consequential committees might consist of a larger proportion of Indians, or entirely of Indians, and even include a certain proportion of fairly militant nationalists; the last named might find their way onto an important Royal Commission or a committee on fiscal and monetary matters if they were safely outnumbered.

These men were allowed to smell political power, but not to exert it. The elaborate procedures of committees and commissions of enquiry carried with them something of the characteristics of the theatre of the absurd. Many months of long and complex enquiries would end with a report which invariably reaffirmed the main principles of government policy, recommended a few minor changes or conceded a principle which could not be put into practice due to claimed technical or administrative difficulties.[67] A great many Notes of Dissent and Minority Reports were written; but the point of view of Indian 'interest groups' seemed so often to get lost despite these, the 'majority' generally only needing to carry one or two well selected Indians with them, if that. The pattern of economic discourse in British India and the slow bureaucratic process with which it went was strongly geared towards the existence of precedents to justify an idea or policy initiative: the best justification found for an idea in such official discussions was the claim that the principle had already been conceded by its predecessor committee or commission. Committees followed up previous committees on similar subjects, drew strongly on the majority findings of the previous committee, ignored dissenting voices in its own and its predecessor committee and reaffirmed the latter's conclusions; dissenting voices drew on Minority Reports, Minutes of Dissent, principles conceded by, and evidence recorded before predecessor committees to argue their case. (Committees regularly recirculated and recycled evidence, opinions, and findings, both in their majority and minority capacities: for instance, the chain of arguments on monetary and fiscal policy can be traced through various committees quoting each other, and the Minutes of Dissent similarly quoting previous reports.)[68] Some committees did not much more than recommend the setting up of new committees.[69] As far as the rules of this game were concerned, the 'economic truths' that they recognized inhabited a parallel universe which vanished from the time and space which marked the distance between successive committees; when the Congress and other Indian political parties formed provincial governments, they, of course, appointed their own committees.[70]

It is also worth noting that the ostensible principles along which such enquiries operated, were those of interest and of expertise. These two principles might seem to be mutually exclusive; but the unresolved contradiction between them was the basis of certain manoeuvres which might explain why it was possible for the conclusions in the report to often be greatly at variance with the main currents contained in the Minutes of Evidence. The committee itself was composed of members selected for their 'expertise': government servants of various kinds; if the committee was important enough, a few 'experts' or professionals from 'home' (Britain); and a few Indians. The Indians were the ambiguous participants; they were implicitly to play the part both of 'expert' and of 'representatives of interests'.[71] They were members of the committee as 'experts'; if they disagreed with the findings the government wished to endorse, they were mere 'representatives of interests'. This logic was repeated in the examination of witnesses, in which an explicit separation of categories was maintained between the principles of 'interest' and 'expertise', those called upon to give an opinion before an official committee belonging to one or the other category. This categorization of witnesses might make an interesting field of study; but it was the 'expert' whose opinion held more water, as it was construed as being 'disinterested'.

The (often merely implied) criticism of an opinion as not that of a disinterested 'expert' could, of course, justifiably be levelled against other members: that they represented the government's 'interests', and were not mere 'experts'; but the government, by virtue of the fact of governance, by repeated assertion as well as by holding the ultimate power to appoint committees, could paint itself as neutral. This claim to neutrality was also the crucial link in late colonial justifications of the British right to rule: as an impartial arbitrator among Indian 'interests'. To acknowledge that these committees were merely conglomerations of (often mutually exclusive) 'interests', 'expertise' being subordinate to this former logic, would be to destroy the rationale for the committees: in an attack on the government's claim to neutrality, the committees themselves, which were the only official spaces in which Indian opinion had to be officially noted, would be discredited. (This was an attack which was implicitly or explicitly made on the committees system by the left wing of the nationalist movement, combined with an argument that the sort of 'notables' who were appointed to such committees—usually big business 'interests'—were not unambiguously anti-imperialist, as a result of which they could not altogether antagonize the government and would, to a greater or lesser extent, remain collaborators: in making this argument, the left was, of course, attacking the very basis of the game.)[72]

I have already referred to the scepticism with which these committees were treated. However, it is important to realize that this took place within a shared framework of imperialist discourse, in which Indians participated: whether they agreed or disagreed with the official position, the assumptions and questions that were raised were dictated by imperialism. This should not be confused with a version of the 'collaborator' argument:

'collaboration' was permitted to Indians on vastly inferior terms; the discursive framework was dictated by imperialism, and though the participation of Indians themselves worked towards changing that framework, it only succeeded in changing rhetorical forms and creating further layers of discourse in which legitimacy could be construed in terms of the participation or non-participation of Indians. In participating in these committees, therefore, the desire to oppose official arguments and to subvert the terms of imperialist discourse was not incompatible with a strengthening of the terms of that discourse, in which Indians participated without necessarily intending to—another sphere in which the argument made by Nehru and the Congress left against forming provincial governments in 1937 demonstrated its validity:[73] by participating in the imperial system, nationalists became complicit with, and part of, that system. But to be complicit with imperialism was not the same as 'collaborating'.

An example might be useful here. The forum provided by an official enquiry was often used by Indian nationalists as a means of articulating nationalist grievances, and putting them on record. Enough of these had come and gone for them to be aware that little or nothing practical would come of them on the basis of Indians' evidence before them. Even this articulation had the limited effect of placing grievances on record in a forum recognized *as* legitimate by the British imperial administration; much of the more effective articulation of grievances came from the reporting of its proceedings or conclusions in the press. In a committee, the possibilities of protest were limited and formulaic. The assertion of Indian arguments similarly drew on by now formulaic assertions; the need for protest, not immediately recognizable as protest, often found its way into relatively non-controversial committees and commissions in strange ways:

From the earliest times there is record of roads and wheeled vehicles in India ... good roads, easy communications, necessarily go with civilisation and civilised administration; and Indian civilisation goes back not less than five thousand years according to the latest discoveries of the Archaeological Department.....[74]

This passage, in a report of 1928 which agreed that the Indian road system had to be 'developed' for the 'general welfare of the country' and, in particular, for better marketing of agricultural produce, 'for the social and political progress of the rural population', and as a complement to 'railway development'[75]—reaffirming the usefulness of transport facilities to an export-oriented primary-producer colony—also manages to cite the latest discoveries at Harappa and Mohenjo-Daro (a civilization then dated back to circa 3300 BC by Sir John Marshall, whom the report cites), the *Rigveda*, the *Arthashastra*, the *Jatakas*, the reigns of Chandragupta Maurya and Ashoka; the accounts of Fa-Hien, Hiuen-Tsang, Ibn Batuta, Tavernier, and more. All this was squeezed into the confines of an official report. It was customary for such reports to contain a section on the historical background, on previous legislation, or the evolution of a problem. A notable paradox here in this evident need to draw on a glorious past before colonialism, and the implicit accusation of colonialism it contains, is that this past is only accessible through colonial sources— in this case, explicitly the Archaeological Department, and implicitly the achievements of Orientalist (in the pre-Saidian sense) scholarship.[76] This is a recurring, and surviving, paradox of the need for various 'indigenist' arguments.

An example from a better known committee might also be provided as illustration of the strong divergence between minutes of evidence and conclusions to which these enquiries were prone: that of the Indian Central Banking Enquiry Committee of 1931. The enquiry, beginning in 1929, was split into three stages. First, provincial committees dealt with agricultural credit and cooperative credit, credit facilities for small industries, mortgage banks, financing of internal trade, and the stimulation of habits of investment and attraction of banking deposits. The All-India Committee then dealt with regulation of banking, banking education, and credit facilities for India's main industries such as cotton, jute, and coal. A small body of 'foreign experts' (that is, neither British nor Indian), selected by the government and having experience of rural credit and industrial banking, was appointed to assist the Central Committee in coming to its conclusions.[77] The Committee's terms of reference were to investigate banking and the organization of credit in India under the following main headings:

(a) the Development of Banking with a view to the expansion of indigenous cooperative and joint-stock banking with special reference to the needs of agriculture, commerce, and industry;
(b) the Regulation of Banking with a view to protecting the interests of the Public; and
(c) Banking Education with a view to the provision of Indian personnel in adequate numbers and with the necessary qualifications to meet the increasing needs of the country for a sound and well managed national system of banking.[78]

One of the official arguments underlying the Banking Enquiry Committee, reiterated in its report, was that there was a great need for capital in the form of British banking in India. The assumption behind the 'banking education' part of the enquiry was that Indians had to be taught the art of banking. Many Indians who provided evidence before the Committee strongly objected to this; they also pointed to the racially discriminatory practices of the Imperial Bank of India;[79] and some defended the long existence of 'traditional' banking in India as against 'Western' banking.[80] As regards banks' alleged reluctance to finance Indian industry, the government as well as British bankers in India claimed that credit was always forthcoming when the venture was 'sound'.

Manu Subedar wrote the Minority Report on his own—all 484 pages of it.[81] Subedar claimed to have 'looked upon the problem as an Economist. The two great beacons lighting my path were an impoverished mass of people in the country on the one hand, and powerful vested interests on the other hand, both Indian and foreign'.[82] On the other hand, in chapter two—a well-written summary of nationalist economic grievances—he rejected the idea of 'the grounds of pure banking' as relevant criteria for a national policy.[83] Subedar, here at least, and in common with the main currents of nationalist criticism of the government, sought to explode the device of apparently neutral terms.[84] For himself, however, he claimed the neutrality of economics: his opinion was that of an 'expert', not an 'interested party'.

This kind of argument was made on both sides. A direct predecessor committee, the External Capital Committee of 1925,[85] had rejected the idea of controls on external capital on the grounds, inter alia, of the rights of the consumer.[86] The Committee cited its own predecessor commission in opposing certain interests: '"no one", in the words of the Fiscal Commission, "would advocate a policy of protection merely to enrich capitalists".'[87] Moreover, '[n]othing could be more disastrous to the industrial development of India than measures which would scare away the external capital invested in it or prevent the local investment of its profits'.[88] The Note of Dissent argued, however: 'The very foundation of protectionism, as has been said by eminent economists, is the idea of nationality';[89] or, economics is subordinate to the interests of nations, not the other way round. Yet there seems to have been the need to claim the authority of economics itself in making this statement.[90]

Imperialists and nationalists inhabited this familiar framework of conventionalized and repeated arguments. The outlines along which 'development' was to be discussed were already visible in these conventions, as was the penumbra of related concerns, of 'legitimate national aspirations' and British 'expertise', reaching out to older arguments of the restoration of a glorious past or the necessity of British rule. The constraints of these conventions are clear: there were major divisions of political position, but one economic discourse within which each position was articulated; and the economic discourse was framed by the British (because they possessed the authority to set the frames within which the exchanges took place). Nationalists had to shift the boundaries of the 'economic' to a certain extent to accommodate their concerns: to claim 'economics' as their ally.

To these existing conventions were added the further examples and precedents thrown up by world events: Soviet planning, the New Deal, Nazi and Fascist economics, and Japan (which had been an earlier influential example, from the Meiji Restoration onwards).[91] Yet the interactions between the various strands, from the older conventions and the new examples, were unpredictable and non-linear; the integrity of an argument borrowed from a different context was not necessarily maintained, as elements were eclectically borrowed from it and put into the service of arguments concerned with shifting the boundaries of the discourse of 'economics'. Such a shifting of boundaries also involved an enlargement and partial submersion of 'economics', in which 'development' transcended the merely economic, incorporating originally separate concerns, in an attempt to arrive at new conventions on better terms for nationalists.

Terminology

The interconnectedness of terminology, and the series of concerns reflected therein, in the debates on 'development' from the 1930s, becomes evident from a close reading of a variety of sources outside the constraining spaces of official committees or reports. The connections might at first glance elude a later reader; yet the protagonists seem in no way to regard these apparent long digressions as tangential, participating in the discussions in terms of a shared discursive framework. It is the opacity of this discursive framework to later readers which seems to have been a contributing factor in the privileging of the economic—as familiar and accessible—in their writing, and to the dismissal of the rest as romantic or irrelevant. This is a good example of the imposition of later paradigms on the writing of earlier periods, and the consequent tendency to either praise the writers for having reached a conclusion desirable to the later paradigm or to castigate them for having failed to reach it.[92]

'Development' in India was related to a wide variety of problems and questions, which pointed the way to a comprehensive 'reconstruction'—

another popular term—of Indian life. Related terms within this discursive framework had the propensity to start a free association which linked up with the wider social and moral questions implied by 'development' and carried these along into what were ostensibly 'economic' debates: 'progress', the need to overcome 'backwardness', the moral nature of nationhood. 'Development' in the 1930s incorporated themes which had earlier been autonomous—'social reform', 'village uplift', 'rural reconstruction', 'constructive work'; 'cooperative farming', and 'cooperative credit'; 'self-reliance', 'technical education', 'science'; 'socialism'; improvement of the human material constituting the 'nation'; 'nation-building'—many of which had strong extra-economic connotations. The term 'development' itself—in the sense of evolution and in India in the sense of developing institutions—had been in use at least since the end of the nineteenth century. From the 1930s, with hopes of a soon-to-be-won independence emerging, 'development' as 'improvement' or 'progress' was wholeheartedly embraced within the comprehensive framework implied by 'planning'—the means by which 'development' could be consciously aimed at. The all-encompassing framework which 'planning' implied was extremely important; it could thus serve as an umbrella category in which the various ideas surrounding 'development' could be described and discussed. 'Development' and 'planning' in the 1930s, when used without the qualifying adjective 'economic', tended to mean far more than 'economic development' or 'economic planning'.

The apparent exception here is the Gandhian opposition to planning as embodying the tyranny of a centralized system of state control; but it is only an apparent exception: 'constructive work' similarly envisaged wide-ranging changes in the conditions of life and psyche of its participants, and (at least in terms of its proclaimed aims) in the economic and political framework in existence. (Gandhian writing, though generally anti-centralization and anti-state, tended to be remarkably silent on questions of private property, and how the socio-economic order then in existence, dependent, in Gandhi's interpretation, on the 'trusteeship' of capitalists who ran the machine-based industries that he so strongly opposed, would give way to the social and economic order he proposed.) By the 1940s, 'Gandhian planning' had entered the terminology.[93] Similarly, Gandhians' opposition to 'socialism' as something outside the framework of the Indian psyche did not prevent versions of his ideas from being put forth, by his followers as well as himself, as a Gandhian version of 'socialism', sufficiently in harmony with the Indian temperament so as to be acceptable.[94] The specific problems to which the constituent terms referred were seen as interlocking with the wider issues. For instance, wider moral concerns were equally linked up with the village uplift initiatives of Tagore, Gandhi, the Punjab civilians, or the Young Men's Christian Association (YMCA), though in different ways; and with matters of 'national discipline', work efficiency and control over leisure in the writing of J.C. Kumarappa and M. Visvesvaraya, despite their markedly different approaches to 'development'.

A clue to this sharing may once again be sought in long-standing conventions of imperial discourse. From the 1858 Government of India Act, 'for the better Government of India',[95] until the 1935 Act, the Government of India was required annually to present to Parliament a 'Statement ... exhibiting the Moral and Material Progress of India'.[96] There was no clear separation of its moral and material aspects. Successive reports remained basically statements of accounts and administrative reports of the Government of India. The merging of the two categories did not, however, mean that the moral aspect was ignored. Though it was clear that the material aspect was more immediate a concern, the general tone implied that moral progress would accompany the material, thereby allowing the imperium to claim the moral high ground. By the 1920s and 1930s, though the format of the reports had substantially changed—they were written by a single author (the Director of Public Information, Government of India), and contained more continuous narrative and far less of the facts and figures kind of reporting characteristic of its nineteenth century predecessors[97]—their moral tone remained intact, and they continued to claim an authoritative voice in representing the political, economic, and administrative year that had just passed. The moral tone was often based on specific characterizations of Indian society as peculiar, and implicit or explicit references to the need for British rule to maintain the moral order. Thus, speaking of the need to police the countryside against dacoits, the report for the year 1925–6 observed,

Indian society contains many potentially criminal elements which need only opportunity to come to the fore. Most villages of any size have their Badmashes, i.e., bad characters, who are known to turn their hand to theft, burglary, or even more serious crimes when circumstances permit. There are many criminal and wandering tribes in India, who, *from time immemorial,* have lived by the same sort of nefarious arts as were practised by Gipsies in Europe until a generation or two ago.[98]

This assumption that moral and material progress were crucially related permeated both imperialist and nationalist thinking. Nationalist rhetoric had to incorporate this in claiming for Indian pasts a suitably respectable history: in 1920, Radhakumud Mookerji, at the time Professor of History at Mysore University, wrote, '... no student of early Indian history could deny the marked triumphs and achievements of the Hindu genius in the domain of mental, moral, and spiritual progress'.[99] Such borrowings could be less than conscious, and the contexts in which they were used could be quite different. One of Gandhi's stronger arguments was that, unlike other socio-economic systems, the society he envisaged would not delink the moral and material aspects of human progress, and that the moral would lead the material.[100] His strongest opponents in the nationalist movement were equally convinced of the interrelatedness of the two; but for them, most often, the material would have to lead the way to the moral.[101]

Within this framework, the specific importance of 'development', and of 'planning' to that end, lay in its importance for 'nation-building'. The term 'nation-building' itself had an interesting genealogy of usage in imperialist rhetoric. 'Nationhood' being set forth in imperial discourse as a goal to strive towards, it was convenient to refer to 'nation-building' as a process by which to arrive at that—which, needless to say, had not been achieved yet. Under the Government of India Act of 1919, popularly known as the Montagu–Chelmsford Reforms, a system of provincial government had been set up, along the road to 'responsible government' á là the white Dominions, which provided provincial legislatures in which Indians could discuss certain things. This system was to be in operation for ten years, after which a Statutory Commission would review the 'progress' made by India in constitutional terms, and recommend further constitutional changes. In the provinces, under the 1919 Act, areas of legislation were divided into 'reserved' and 'transferred' subjects; the former were to be legislated on only by the governor, as imperial proconsul; the latter were 'transferred' to Indian ministers—selected from among members of legislative groups or parties elected to the legislature on an extremely limited property franchise.[102]

The 'transferred' departments came to be referred to in British official parlance as the 'nation-building', departments. These 'nation-building' departments included subjects such as industry and agriculture which, as a result of the shift of charge to Indians, were in theory no longer to be handled by British administrators, and became the responsibility of Indians. This could be, and was often, used as an excuse to avoid parliamentary questions in Britain and legislature questions at the centre regarding the lack of industrialization in India or the lack of government initiatives when the rest of the world was resorting to a more interventionist economics: any action by the British government in this regard would, it was argued, be considered an invasion of the sphere of authority of Indian ministers.[103]

Despite the obvious limitations of the 'nation-building' departments, the project itself was recognizable and acceptable to Indians. This apparent paradox of 'nation-building' for Indians being supported as a desirable project by India's British rulers fits into a general trend which has been noted before. 'It is the colonialists who become the defenders of the native style,' Frantz Fanon wrote.[104] This phenomenon, visible in the arena of artistic endeavour, with Sir George Birdwood's enthusiasm for Indian arts and crafts[105] and in Government Art College Principal, E.B. Havell's, support for the 'Bengal School' of art,[106] had its parallels in politics and governance as well. In Fanon's reading, this phenomenon is not necessarily related to conscious manipulation of terms, or to direct participation in some colonial project; it has more to do with the comforting feeling engendered in the colonizer that the 'native' will remain the 'native'. Comforting stereotypes of Indianness on the part of British officials and of British opinion can often be attributed to this as much as to the occasional strategic use of such arguments to cloak British imperialist interests.

The curious thing about this defence of 'the native style' is that it could be put to use in differing and opposed arguments; the 'natives' and the colonialists both, for different reasons, resorted to arguments based on fundamentals of the 'native' character. In 1911, the historian, Sir Jadunath Sarkar, lamented the lack of entrepreneurial spirit in the Indian.[107] Whereas for him this was a matter of some frustration and anguish, for his reviewer, Theodore Morison, this merely established what the British already knew—and what is more, as the review put it, this was being acknowledged by an indigenous, therefore more authentic, voice.[108] This authenticity could cut both ways; a voice was authentic when it confirmed British preconceptions, or, otherwise, was of an Anglicized, inauthentic elite. Sarkar's argument was attractive in that it accepted the dominant imperialist paradigm to a large extent, in which the 'native style' was defined by its lack of something desirable; Morison's appropriation was, therefore, that much simpler.

More complex appropriations were necessary for British arguments which insisted on the superiority of 'indigenous' practices, traditions, or ideas to 'Western' ones; but at times this was also possible. In this context it might be mentioned that selective appropriations of Gandhi's 'economic' ideas (as opposed to his 'political' ideas) were found to be appealing to certain British official circles; Gandhi's concern for the villages was lauded as correct, as the 'real' India lived in its villages; therefore, industrialization was undesirable, as it would damage this 'real' India.[109]

The Circulation of Ideas and Information

The circulation of ideas and information in connection with the debates on 'development', it should be clear by now, was dependent on a number of connections and currents. It might be useful to indicate the general features of this circulation. It will be necessary here also to distinguish analytically between disseminator and audience, if only to indicate that the distinction is blurred; where much writing and many conversations were the collective soliloquy of the intellectual bourgeoisie.

This is not to suggest that attempts were not made to circulate ideas; merely that their effective circulation was limited. As I have said, there was a significant band of proselytizers for 'development' among the intellectual bourgeoisie. Large parts of the debates were conducted in public arenas; but this 'public' was a limited one. Proselytization operated by drawing on ideas whose primary appeal, as a vision of the future, was in providing an escape from imperialist domination—a goal which all concerned agreed upon. Although this audience grew with time, it still remained comparatively small.

Arguments on 'development' attempted to address an audience which in part had to be created. On the other hand, this created audience had to be drawn from an audience of the politically and economically literate; merely accepting the conventions of anti-imperialism was inadequate for understanding the details of the new positions. The size of the audience shrank in proportion to the subtlety and quality of the arguments. Consequently, the effective audience for the 'development' debates was not much larger than the number of participants themselves. And the participants were not that many. Inasmuch as 'development' came to mean anything to a wider audience than this, it was in the equally conventionalized forms in which it was presented. (This, of course, is in the nature of languages of legitimation: it is in their conventionalized forms that they achieve most effectiveness.)

This argument requires a certain amount of elaboration. To begin, then, with the question of audiences, and attempts to reach them: access to information on matters which went into the debates on 'development' was relatively easy for a literate public, as has been mentioned before. The nationalist press fed this need; opportunities to print and discuss various grievances against British rule were provided by various immediate instances: world events, reporting on the proceedings of official committees of enquiry, or the implications of particular policies. 'Information' of this kind can be seen as the unformed raw materials of more well-formulated ideas. The nationalist daily papers, however, reproduced this information for its readership in relatively structured form, in terms of a general anti-imperialist position. As a result of this, the outlines of nationalist arguments against British rule in India were conventional knowledge: the details of the arguments may not have been fully intelligible, but the points sought to be put across were absorbed.

A general readership was thus provided with information which could fit into the conventional arguments against colonial rule, the primary target. The conventional nature of this information needs to be noted; its awareness-raising value was limited, as it operated largely by reiterating well-known arguments against British rule. (Let it be repeated here that, as far as the anti-British-rule content of 'development' was concerned, the matter was fiercely political; it was not 'technical' and neutral.) But the presentation of these arguments usually maintained the consistency of the nationalist voice, and did not talk about internal divergences.[110] Arguments about 'development' were thus, by the time they were presented to such an audience, already pared down to this conventional level, and presented shorn of the debates and uncertainties which characterized the internal debates among various strands of the nationalist movement, as well as the conceptual complications they contained. By the time they reached this general readership through the daily papers, therefore, a process of dilution and simplification had been underway.[111] Feedback from this general readership was also not expected to be substantial.

There were, however, other publications: specialist periodicals read by far fewer people, dealing with finance, agriculture, or economics.[112] Some other journals, which sought to popularize their specialist field, were also read by a lay public.[113] There were also more general journals which had a literary-miscellany slant but which inter alia dealt with specific issues related to 'development'.[114] The first category might have constrained the expression of wider ideas by the rules of the disciplines concerned, but in many cases did not. The second and third gave more free rein to related concerns, which might have been assumed to have a wider appeal to its readership. The readership of all these categories was a sub-set of the 'general readership' of the daily papers, but smaller; assumed a greater amount of active political interest, a wide set of interests and some versatility and ability to understand and take an interest in various philosophical as well as technical subjects. This involved people not merely literate but possessing a certain amount of cultural capital. What all this assumed was an interest in such matters as 'development' in wider philosophical senses. This wider interest may, in fact, have been generated by the conventions visible in the daily papers: the problem of the economy as defined in terms of the problems of British rule; 'development' as a framework for a solution; but it went beyond the limited formulations thereof. This readership was also capable of participating in a more informed manner in the debates.

In addition to this, political publications emanating from parties or pressure groups provided a continuous stream of material on political economy issues in simplified popular form, which were translated into several languages. Many of the pamphlets and books published under the banner of the All-India Congress Committee (AICC) also linked up with questions of 'development'.[115] Inasmuch as these at all went beyond the generally accepted nationalist line, they had a Gandhian slant, which apparently was not seen as disturbing to the nationalist consensus. These were priced at between two annas and a rupee each, most costing four annas or less.[116] These were widely circulated, both in English and in translation,[117] with requests for copies flooding in from Provincial Congress Committees, colleges, newspapers, magazines, as well as professionals and private persons. Apart from the regular Congress bulletins, reports of sessions, resolutions and so on, pamphlets on political and economic issues were in particular demand.[118] In the period of the Congress ministries, these materials were further publicized.[119] The Gandhians had their own publishing networks in Ahmedabad and Wardha. Books were printed on handmade paper, and quickly went through several editions in English, as well as in several Indian languages.[120]

In the 1930s, a National Publications Society was set up, the board of editors comprising Jawaharlal Nehru, Narendra Dev, and K.T. Shah, the Managing Committee comprising, among others, Nehru, Narendra Dev, K.T. Shah, Govind Ballabh Pant, Syed Mahmud, Jayaprakash Narayan, and S.A. Brelvi.[121] The board of editors was 'entitled to write or have written by competent writers on behalf of the Society, books, monographs and other works in order to carry out the Objects of the Society'[122]— which were to publish literature 'describing, analysing, explaining or criticizing the institutions and organizations of Public Administration in India, as also those affecting the collective life and consciousness of the community'; to publish other literature 'for the enlightenment of the masses, and dealing with day-to-day problems that affect them'. The material was to be '... selected and written up .... to promote most effectively the freedom and collaborative well-being of the Indian people and their development in every respect, in order to realise to the fullest, their inherent possibilities ... (It) will provide material for the drawing up of (a) National Plan of Social Reconstruction ... The publications will provide for a reconstruction of the social system on the basis of the socialisation of the means of production, distribution and exchange of material commodities and services needed for the maintenance and advancement of the community'.[123]

The Congress Socialist Party (CSP) also did a good deal of serious pamphleteering on the subject of 'development', specifically connected to questions of socialism. There was clearly an attempt here to extend the reach of the information contained, to raise political awareness, and to go beyond the formulae of articulating conventional anti-British statements—though without denying the truths behind the conventions. These pamphlets, again, were translated into several Indian languages. It is unclear as to how successful they were in widening the reach for these ideas. The CSP pamphlets were often confiscated, banned, or destroyed by the government—there are several accounts of such action reported in the *Congress Socialist*, the official weekly of the CSP—and these were events which happened relatively randomly, for the government did not appear to have a clear policy regarding what was to be considered subversive or communist literature.[124] The arguments they contained were often complex, though clearly argued; the *Congress Socialist* was perpetually in financial crisis because of a lack of subscribers,[125] and the publications advertised in the *Congress Socialist* were probably bought by party workers, but could hardly have sold many copies if the CSP had not been able to persuade its workers to support the *Congress Socialist*. (It folded in 1939.)

The AICC's pamphlets did relatively better in terms of circulation and sales, judging from the AICC's own records.[126] This may in part have been a result of the AICC's own reputation as an anti-imperialist organization, which consequently generated sales.[127] There was, however, a recognition that the chances of a wide circulation and understanding of the ideas would be proportional to their simplicity. A circular letter to potential translators from the AICC's Economics and Political Department emphasized that the pamphlets, some as yet unwritten, were 'to be written in popular and non-technical style by persons who are qualified for the task'.[128] The Socialist Book Club, an initative of Nehru's, proposed to provide 'socialist classics' suitably 'abridged' for Indian readers.[129]

Effectively, then, the public arguments remained simplified and formulaic, perhaps because of, rather than despite, intentions to widen 'mass awareness'. It was generally recognized, implicitly at least, that the primary audience would be an educated, middle-class, mainly urban readership; nonetheless, it was hoped that they would play a vanguard role of sorts in raising awareness among the 'masses'. The public arguments were also full of certainties which were not reflected in the less public aspects of the debates.

Of the widening of debates that did occur, it was the urban intellectual bourgeoisie as an audience which was drawn into the smaller circles of the disseminators and was able to participate in the debates. This smaller 'public' was still large enough to become a target audience of some significance, and not merely in mobilizational terms. Of the great deal of writing on and around the theme of 'development' published at this time, much of it was taken up by private publishers,[130] of whom not all could be seen as 'nationalist': there was a good market for ideas of this kind, and publishers were keen to feed it.[131] These were often written by academic men at the fringes of politics. At this point, clearly, *the distinction between audience and disseminator begins to blur*. Quite apart from an attempt to reach an audience 'out there' connected to an often vague desire to mobilize, the debates in these inner circles addressed each other more firmly, reflecting the desires and aspirations of the participants.

The possibilities of circulation of ideas in these small circles took more informal forms as well, through personal connections, in private correspondence, and casual social intercourse. It is here that certain tensions between public versions of the arguments, both for the consumption of the general public and the smaller circles of the intellectual bourgeoisie, and the complexities and anxieties behind such resolutions as found their way into these public arenas, can be traced. Given that it was from within these smaller circles that the initatives to proselytization emerged, these tensions are significant; they run through various levels of debate, which enables a reader to reconstruct the concerns which cut across the hitherto highlighted differences. In this connection, another significant aspect of these tensions needs to be pointed out here. I have said that the presentation of certain ideas to a wider audience was marked by a process of dilution and simplification. But this dilution and simplification also involved a process of self-clarification on the part of the disseminators; a variety of positions can be read as different resolutions of similar tensions.

The closeness of the inner circle of the disseminator/audience category is made clearer if one moves away from media to look at the role of various institutions, and the persons involved with them, in the propagation of these ideas: institutions such as Bombay University's School of Economics, with C.N. Vakil and K.T. Shah; Presidency College, Calcutta, and the University of Calcutta, from which emerged a long and respectable lineage of intellectuals concerned with 'development';[132] Mysore University, under the initiative of Sir M. Visvesvaraya, in whose mind it was to be an alternative place of learning to Madras University; Patna University, at which Gyan Chand taught; the Gokhale Institute in Poona; Allahabad University; all these became academic establishments with a lively interest in problems of 'development' and 'nation-building'. The involvement of these institutions and men with teaching assisted to a certain extent the circulation of their ideas regarding 'development', at least among those with access to higher education. The circulation of personnel among these establishments also parallels that of ideas to a certain extent: Mysore University drew on the talents of the Mookerjee brothers, Radhakamal and Radhakumud, and of Brajendranath Seal, all formerly from Calcutta; Radhakamal Mukherjee and Meghnad Saha both taught at Allahabad (the term 'Allahabad–Calcutta axis' was, in fact, used in connection with physics research).[133] Calcutta connections tended to predominate, with a significant *bhadralok* presence in the intellectual professions both within and outside Bengal.[134]

The Gandhians, with their apparent aloofness from the intricate world of formal academics, their professed reliance on the inherent instincts of the peasant, and aversion to 'Western' forms of social organization, might have been expected to address a different audience. On closer inspection, however, on the issue of 'development' they can be seen to address essentially the same audience: with 'development' being closely bound up with issues of leadership and direction, it was a matter of importance to enter into a dialogue with the intellectuals, who were increasingly pulling away from Gandhian arguments. Gandhi's success with mobilizing the peasantry and his insistence on the primacy of the village as a moral and economic unit can obscure the fact that the Gandhian position, despite its anti-centralisation emphasis, is far from anti-leadership; on the contrary, it demands leadership and control.[135]

No corresponding uncertainty to that which was suffered in nationalist circles was entertained in imperial circles when defining its audiences. The government at least was sure that there were two main audiences; and they had to be told different things. This was not necessarily only because there were consciously recognized double standards (though there often were), but because it was understood that things had to be handled with a certain amount of tact. As a result, the British public at home was to read and hear arguments about the importance of British rule for the Indians' well-being, and later on the guidance of the colonies towards self-government in terms of the achievements of British imperialism; in India, the corresponding emphasis had to be on the government's ultimate benevolence, its recognition of legitimate national demands and its willingness to help achieve the goals envisaged therein. These were not radically different messages, but the difference in tone and emphasis was crucial: it was not possible to claim too strongly in India that Indian economic progress or representative government were British achievements; for one thing, they were not seen by nationalists as achievements, but as inadequate travesties of what they ought to be, and for another, inasmuch as they were better than nothing, they were seen as concessions which had been wrung out of a reluctant government by force of nationalist agitation. Even in the latter case, however, there was a recognition of the scepticism with which such claims on the part of the British government would be received; the policy was, therefore, more in terms of producing arguments which avoided the main lines of disagreement. It was also clear to the British government that they were competing with the nationalists for an audience. During the Second World War, this competition was made explicit: the time for convincing the peasant of the government's benevolence was over; it was educated middle-class opinion which counted; the latter were the target group, therefore, of much wartime propaganda.[136] This group, which can be taken as roughly corresponding with the general newspaper readership outlined above, was taken by the British as a pre-defined unit: particularly susceptible to, and carriers of, nationalist ideas (metaphors related to disease were common in the official rhetoric relating to nationalism or communism), they had, in turn, to be targeted by the British and to be convinced that the British were wholeheartedly conceding nationalist demands. In this attempt, the urge for 'development' was identified as a key concern which had emotive significance for this class; promises of 'development', economic progress, and industrialization were crucial to wartime propaganda efforts. And it was the conventional rhetoric of the nationalist public arguments on 'development' which were projected: state-controlled heavy industry, protective tariffs, guarantees for private capital of post-War protection for new industries set up during the War.[137]

Imperialism, however, had a secondary audience for these ideas, and perhaps at times an inadvertent one: its own personnel. These new versions of a 'nationalized' imperial mythology fit in well with British civilians' self-image of benevolent and dedicated service, while erasing the unpleasantness of the implications of exploitation. The wine of nationalist rhetoric in imperial bottles was for them well worth buying; only it could now be confused with imperial rhetoric, or imperial truth.[138]

The international and metropolitan linkages of ideas of 'development' in India which have been referred to earlier were further aided by the circulation of personnel along certain well-defined lines facilitated by the colonial connection. The obvious aspect to this circulation was in the recruitment of imperial personnel from the public schools and Oxbridge or, as towards the latter part of the Empire, perhaps from the less exalted backgrounds of Manchester Grammar School and Oxbridge.[139] The connections with home trends have been explored, for instance, in the case of Darling and his peripheral connection with the Bloomsbury group.[140] But these home connections were liable to erosion and overwriting in the light of experiences in and exposure to India.

There were also certain crossover linkages. A university education in Britain was reasonably common among the Indian aristocracy and upper middle class, usually upper-caste and affluent though, with some exceptions made possible through academic achievement or financial patronage. Below the level of university education or specialization, access to education was a possible means of social mobility in colonial India, though to a limited extent. Two examples may be provided in this latter connection: Meghnad Saha, the son of a lower-caste grocery shopowner from East Bengal, whose academic performance at school gave him access to Presidency College in Calcutta, which was his stepping stone to fame in physics and his point of access to the intellectual bourgeoisie among whom 'development' was being discussed;[141] and B.R. Ambedkar, later to be spokesman and leader of the Depressed Classes, whose patron was the ruler of a princely state.[142] The trajectory of academic success, the acquisition of cultural capital or its further consolidation, could be immensely assisted by a degree from a foreign university, usually in Britain—in which case it was usually Oxford, Cambridge, or London—or somewhere in the USA; in the latter category were Jayaprakash Narayan, who came in contact with the Communist Party of the USA while a student at Madison, Wisconsin,[143] and Kumarappa, who became relatively popular as a lay preacher while a student at Columbia University in New York.[144]

The British connection was, however, of further importance because of its political significance in imperial politics; and London was a 'junction-box' for anti-imperialist politics of various shades.[145] Students from India acquired a taste for and some sort of contact with some of these shades, in the form, perhaps, of the Communist Party of Great Britain (CPGB) in Cambridge, or the Fabianism of the London School of Economics (LSE); political involvement in anti-imperialist politics often created links with the same circles. A commitment to the left, broadly defined, characterized these connections; communist linkages were often the most coherent, but were also not always maintained; and communist ideas were never permitted to become mainstream in India; on the other hand, a (sometimes less than conscious) Fabian slant can be discerned. This might have been more compatible with the experiences of a class of students who had relative access to figures of authority and power in India, but whose identification with oppressed peoples was made evident for them in Britain as representatives of an unfree nation; the Fabian idea of gradualism and intellectual influence on higher circles of authority might, therefore, have seemed appealing.

There were also certain key figures who provided both international and domestic linkages for the circulation of ideas. Nehru was one such figure, and in some respects the most important one. In the context of what might be called a second wave of socialism in India in the 1930s, Nehru, through his pivotal position in the Congress and, consequently, in the nationalist movement, combined with his own socialist sympathies, acted as a sort of sounding board and junction box for many of the ideas and programmes of the left, and for ideas of 'development' with which the left was associated; he was also involved in influencing the political ideas of a number of people. He had various important ideas routed through him, for his comments, acceptance, or rejection, even when these ideas originated elsewhere, and did not particularly seem to need his stamp of approval; and as one regarded as the spokesman for the left within the Congress, was often instrumental in the acceptance or rejection of these ideas.[146] His own political importance was also greatly enhanced by his being regarded by influential sections in British politics as the acceptable face of Indian nationalism, and the most desirable man to deal with when India eventually had to be granted independence.[147]

It has been possible so far to delineate certain modes of circulation of information and ideas, in terms of social and political milieu, universities and schools attended, intellectual environments, influences of the print media, personal connections, and so on. The importance of patronage and access to finance should also be mentioned. The apparent academic or political purity of various positions was somewhat sullied by the demands for finance and patronage as operative in a colonial environment. Scientists operated either through government grants or in institutions financed by industrialists. Most Gandhian ventures would not have survived without regular provision of finance from G.D. Birla or some other industrialist. In an example which epitomizes the non-congruence of political ideas and material constraints, Saha, a consistent opponent of private capital in national life, appealed to Nehru, a self-proclaimed socialist, to request funds from the Tatas for the setting up of a cyclotron in Calcutta.[148] Eventually he received funds from both the Tatas and the Birlas. (The most crucial parts of the cyclotron—its high-vacuum pumps—were lost when the ship carrying them was sunk by a Japanese torpedo in 1942.)[149]

The expected corollary of government or business patronage might be expected to be a degree of control over activities and of ideas circulated. Certain loopholes nevertheless remained, resulting in a relative autonomy from control in the circulation of ideas, given the peculiarities of the demands of colonial politics: the coalitional nature of 'nationalist' positions and the need of the colonial government to appear to tread softly when treading upon nationalist dreams. 'Technical' or academic work funded by the government was not considered dangerous; and work considered dangerous would not secure funding. Among 'nationalists', the constraints of coalitional politics created a somewhat artificial, though necessary consensus in which divergences of opinion were not to be too strongly emphasized and the funding of a project with which the fund-giver may not have been in agreement was an act of expressing commitment to the coalition. For businessmen, these were investments in patronage; association with nationalism was desirable as political and economic insurance against the uncertainties of colonial politics. Moreover, a battle could be fought on an ostensibly academic ground with relatively greater freedom; Birla's investment in hiring an academic editor, P.S. Lokanathan, for his *Eastern Economist*, to provide a capitalist view with an Indian flavour as opposed to the capitalist view from the metropole provided by the *Economist*, attempted such a battle.[150] Quite logically, however, the difficulties with circulating ideas with a strong socialist or anti-capitalist content were greater in terms of access to funds, media, or fora; business was not liable to fund such ventures, and the government prevented or constrained their circulation.[151] On the other hand, the umbrella claim of 'nationalism' permitted variations within that professed framework to circulate; ideas constrained within that framework were relatively safe, but could not be permitted to break out of it.

Conclusions

Thus we may conclude that imperialism, viewed not merely in terms of political economy, but also as a social and intellectual environment, was crucial in shaping the debates on 'development' in India. It was the taken-for-granted setting (the status quo); it provided the discursive framework which writers and audiences shared even as they resisted it; and was the reference point for attempts at alternative discursive frameworks. The imperial context shaped and channelled the debates on 'development', providing the questions to which answers had to be sought.

Arguments framed in terms of 'economics', and ordered by the constraints of official discourse could not become enough of a basis for a nationalist view of 'development', which aspired to be more than merely economic. However, in order to legitimately secure a hearing in the imperial environment, arguments on 'development' had, to a large extent, to conform to 'the rules of political economy', which had a long-standing respectability. The fact that these rules, as applied to India, were based on a number of stereotypical assumptions on the part of the British about what Indians were and how they ought to progress, was not acknowledged, and was not an adequate resource for the discrediting or readjustment of the rules. Thus, not only were the existing terms of debate set by the British, but the spaces in which arguments might proceed were British as well, and its discursive rules worked to the benefit of the British.

The solution was to seek to move the boundaries of 'economics'; to widen the scope of existing fora as far as possible to express the wider views; and to create new fora, drawing more people into sharing the wider concerns. Intellectual resources in this regard were provided to a certain extent by new conceptions of political economy emerging in the 1930s which helped to make the boundaries of 'economics' more permeable. In the context of the wider concerns, existing fora proved not to be particulary widenable; but new fora were created, in which 'development' was expressed as far more than merely 'economics', and successfully drew in people with separate concerns, who were now able to express these diverse concerns in terms of planning India's future.

However, this period also saw a reassessment of imperialism on the part of many of its functionaries, from the highest level downwards; and perhaps for the first time an explicit acknowledgement in some circles of the underlying principles behind British rule in India. This reassessment was in part generated by a disrupted imperial system and the need to find new governing principles or to modify old ones.

Endnotes

1. Sabyasachi Bhattacharya coined the term 'discriminating intervention' to describe this scenario: see Sabyasachi Bhattacharya, 'Laissez-faire in India', *Indian Economic and Social History Review*, Vol. II, No. 1, January (1965). See also E.J. Hobsbawm, *Industry and Empire* (Harmondsworth, 1969): India was 'the only part of the British Empire to which laissez-faire never applied' (p. 123). By way of contrast, see S. Ambirajan, *Classical Political Economy and British Policy in India* (Cambridge, 1978), which treats British policy in India as attempting to be more or less consistent with its proclaimed laissez-faire ideology, though acknowledging that exceptions had to be made for the peculiarities of the Indian situation. This latter case, of which Ambirajan provides almost as many examples as the former, tends to strengthen the argument that laissez-faire never properly applied to India. What Ambirajan's arguments do tend to point towards, however, is that the normative standard on the basis of which much policy was debated was laissez-faire, which as it 'percolated down to the interested layman and civil servants' was shorn of any subtleties it might have had, and was reduced to 'a set of clear-cut principles that seemed to have universal application'. S. Ambirajan, *Classical Political Economy*, pp. 23–6. As far as practice was concerned, Sabyasachi Bhattacharya's formulation is more helpful.
2. From the government's point of view, remittances to the metropolis were financed by India's quite substantial favourable balance of trade, composed mainly of agrarian exports; this, in turn, helped cover Britain's trade deficit with the rest of the world. See S.B. Saul, *Studies in British Overseas Trade, 1870–1914* (Liverpool, 1960).
3. B.R. Tomlinson, *The Economy of Modern India* (Cambridge, 1993), pp. 63–6; Dietmar Rothermund, *An Economic History of India* (London, 1988), pp. 44–9; N.G. Barrier, *The Punjab Alienation of Land Bill of 1900* (Durham, NC, 1966); P.M.H. van den Dungen, *The Punjab Tradition* (London, 1972); Neil Charlesworth, *Peasants and Imperial Rule: Agriculture and Agrarian Society in the Bombay Presidency, 1850–1935* (Cambridge, 1985).
4. Ambirajan, *Classical Political Economy*, pp. 76, 90.
5. van den Dungen, *The Punjab Tradition* (London, 1972); Clive Dewey, *Anglo-Indian Attitudes: The Mind of the Indian Civil Service* (London, 1993); on the attraction of Punjab as a posting, as opposed to Bengal, which was seen as a hardship posting, see Michael Carritt, *A Mole in the Crown* (Calcutta, 1986), pp. 13–15.

6. van den Dungen, *The Punjab Tradition*, pp. 299, 31.
7. This was an argument which John Maynard Keynes was still using in 1911 to refute Theodore Morison's contention that India would inevitably industrialize: Keynes' review of Theodore Morison, *The Economic Transition in India* (London, 1911), in *The Economic Journal* XXI, (September 1911), pp. 426–7.
8. To take a notable example: a strong boost was provided to British iron and steel by Indian government spending on railways, or to private railway companies who were guaranteed at least 5 per cent returns on investment by the government—again in stark contrast to proclaimed orthodox laissez-faire principles of government. John M Hurd, 'Railways', pp. 741, 743, in Dharma Kumar (ed.), *Cambridge Economic History of India*, volume II, (Cambridge, 1983).
9. Amiya Kumar Bagchi, *Private Investment in India 1900–1939* (Cambridge, 1972), chapter one.
10. Cited in Tomlinson, *The Economy of Modern India*, p. 104.
11. *Report of the Indian Industrial Commission* (Calcutta, 1918); see, especially, pp. 1–2 for the Commission's account of its own antecedents. See also Indian Munitions Board, *Industrial Handbook 1919* (Calcutta, 1919), intended as a comprehensive survey of the then existing industries in India, their advantages or problems, and their potential for growth and profitability, in the particular context of industrial potential for war. The Industrial Commission itself was an outgrowth of the Board, and had the same chairman or president, T.H. Holland.
12. B.R. Tomlinson, *The Political Economy of the Raj, 1914–1947: the Economics of Decolonization in India* (London, 1979), pp. 58–60.
13. See Tomlinson, *The Political Economy of the Raj*, pp. 1–30.
14. Note by C. Kisch, 20 January 1923, quoted in Basudev Chatterji, *Trade, Tariffs and Empire: Lancashire and British Policy in India, 1919–1939* (Delhi, 1992), p. 220.
15. Chatterji, *Trade, Tariffs and Empire*, pp. 91–2.
16. Sir Theodore Morison, *Economic Transition in India* (London, 1911).
17. See Dietmar Rothermund, *India in the Great Depression 1929–1939* (Delhi, 1992); G. Balachandran, 'Towards a "Hindoo Marriage": Anglo-Indian Monetary Relations in Interwar India, 1917–35', *Modern Asian Studies,* Vol. 28, No. 3 (1994).
18. Amiya Kumar Bagchi, 'Private Investment and Partial Planning in India', unpublished PhD dissertation, University of Cambridge, 1963, pp. 44–6; John Darwin, *Britain and Decolonisation: The Retreat from Empire in the Post-War World* (Basingstoke, 1988), p. 9; P.J. Cain and A.G. Hopkins, *British Imperialism: Crisis and Deconstruction, 1914–1990* (London, 1993), p. 199.
19. For instances, see Basudev Chatterji, *Trade, Tariffs and Empire: Lancashire and British Policy in India 1919–1939* (Delhi, 1992), pp. 247–60, 301–5.

20. Chatterji, *Trade, Tariffs and Empire*, passim.
21. See Dietmar Rothermund, 'The Great Depression and British Financial Policy in India, 1929–1934', in Dietmar Rothermund, *The Indian Economy under British Rule* (Delhi, 1983).
22. For the purpose of the above argument, I have used 'imperialists' and 'nationalists' to refer to two cohesive sets of positions. However, although broadly speaking, it is perfectly accurate to speak of the imperialist–nationalist divide as the dominant one, and although both imperialists and nationalists usually did not break ranks in arguments against each other, there were, of course, tensions underlying the apparent unity of positions. The imperialist position, as I will argue in the next chapter, was more conducive to unity and coherence despite internal differences. On the nationalist side there were more complex internal equations.
23. Ranajit Guha, *A Rule of Property for Bengal* (Paris, 1963).
24. Eric Stokes, *The English Utilitarians and India* (Oxford, 1959); Javed Majeed, *Ungoverned Imaginings. James Mill's The History of British India and Orientalism* (Oxford, 1992).
25. This tension between the universal and exceptional in British thinking on India has been noted implicitly in S. Ambirajan, *Classical Political Economy*, and explicitly by Thomas Metcalf, *Ideologies of the Raj* (Cambridge, 1994), both of which deal with earlier periods than this study. Equally, 'nationalists' also vacillated between claims to equality on the basis of universal principles, and exceptionality—on the basis of the inapplicability of 'Western' systems of thought to India.
26. During the First World War there had been necessary departures from the ordinary norms of balanced budgets and a non-interventionist government; food rationing and price controls had come into operation from 1915. But this was considered an exceptional situation, and controls were dismantled after the War. This was considered both necessary and desirable even by the economic heretics of later years: see, for instance, Peter Clarke, *The Keynesian Revolution in the Making, 1924–1936* (New York, 1988), pp. 14–17.
27. See Charles Kindleberger, *The World in Depression 1929–1939* (Munich, 1973; new edition, Harmondsworth, 1987).
28. In this regard P.J. Cain and A.G. Hopkins' 'gentlemanly capitalism' argument is relevant: the interests of the City predominated over the interests of industrial producers; and it was the interests of the former which were represented in imperial policy. 'Sound finance', embodied in balanced budgets and a stable currency, was thus the cardinal principle for the colonies. For a reiteration of this argument, see P.J. Cain and A.G. Hopkins, *British Imperialism: Innovation and Expansion 1688–1914* (London, 1993); Cain and Hopkins, *British Imperialism: Crisis and Deconstruction 1914–1990*. The Cain and Hopkins thesis places finance capitalism at the core of British imperial interests for the duration of the Empire; it is usually

acknowledged as the dominant interest in the final stages of British imperial rule, that is from the late nineteenth century onwards, as surplus capital sought fields of investment overseas. See, for instance, R. Palme Dutt, *India Today* (second revised Indian edition, Bombay, 1949).

29. See Robert Skidelsky, *Politicians and the Slump: The Labour Government of 1929–1931* (London, 1967), pp. 203–15. For details of Keynes' involvement with India, see Anand Chandavarkar, *Keynes and India: A Study in Economics and Biography* (Basingstoke, 1989). Despite its adulatory tone, it provides some useful details on Keynes' own views on India, which were unsurprisingly conventional. It is possible to conclude, as Amiya Kumar Bagchi does, that Keynes' views on India, with which after his first book, *Indian Currency and Finance* (London, 1913), he was only peripherally concerned, did not go beyond the bounds of the India Office. Amiya Kumar Bagchi, *The Presidency Banks and the Indian Economy, 1876–1914* (Calcutta, 1989), pp. 102–8. This is the view accepted by Keynes' biographer: D.E. Moggridge, *Maynard Keynes: An Economist's Biography* (London, 1992), p. 203 and p. 211n.

30. Keynes was one of the main architects of the post-War financial settlement, especially with regard to post-War international and inter-allied indebtedness, and was a key figure at the Bretton Woods conference in July 1944—see Charles P. Kindleberger, *A Financial History of Western Europe* (Oxford, 1984; revised edition, 1993), pp. 416–17, 431—although his own scheme of an international clearing bank to deal with such debts was rejected in favour of the scheme for an International Monetary Fund. He was also, along with Sir William Beveridge, one of the architects of the welfare state.

31. See the notes on the New Deal that the director of the Bank of England, Montagu Norman, sent to the finance member of the Government of India, James Grigg. Grigg Papers, Churchill College Archives Centre, Cambridge, PJGG 2/16/1(c).

32. See Clarke, *The Keynesian Revolution in the Making, 1924–1936.*

33. For an example of the Indian case, see Dietmar Rothermund, *India in the Great Depression, 1929–1939* (Delhi, 1992); 'The Great Depression and British Financial Policy in India, 1929–1934', *Indian Economic and Social History Review*, Vol. 17, No. 4 (1981) and *Indian Economic and Social History Review*, Vol. 18, No. 1 (1981), reprinted in Dietmar Rothermund, *The Indian Economy under British Rule*. For an account of the Bank of England's attempt to ensure control of Indian financial policy through the soon-to-be-formed Reserve Bank of India, see G Balachandran, 'Towards a "Hindoo Marriage": Anglo-Indian Monetary Relations in Interwar India, 1917–35', *Modern Asian Studies*, Vol. 28, No. 3 (1994). The absence in India of a right to reassess its political economy principles became evident in the confrontation between Finance Member, Sir George Schuster, and Secretary of State for India, Sir Samuel Hoare, regarding Schuster's attempt to delink the rupee from sterling and to let it float after sterling had abandoned the gold standard in 1931. See George Schuster, *Private Work and Public Causes* (Cowbridge, 1979), p. 114; Rothermund, *India in the Great Depression*, pp. 42–4.

34. See Ian Drummond, *British Economic Policy and the Empire, 1919–1939* (London, 1972), pp. 89–120, and on India pp. 98–9; Drummond's claim, elsewhere, that British politicians did not have 'exploitation in mind' because they were primarily preoccupied with the Dominions, where they lacked the political power to impose policies, and 'to a much lesser extent with India, where in economic policy-making they systematically abstained from using what little political power they still posssessed'—Ian Drummond, *Imperial Economic Policy 1917–39: Studies in Expansion and Protection* (London, 1974), p. 422—has been systematically destroyed by subsequent work, notably Basudev Chatterji, *Trade, Tariffs and Empire*, which demonstrates that the rhetoric of British powerlessness vis-à-vis India was useful in conceding the appearance of fiscal autonomy and an independent tariff policy, while in practice policies were still dictated by overall imperial interests as understood by London—as he puts it, disagreements between Delhi and London were 'disagreements regarding how best British interests were to be preserved' rather than disagreements based on protecting Indian interests (p. 23).

35. Partha Sarathi Gupta, *Imperialism and the British Labour Movement 1914–1964* (London, 1975), p. 60; Kindleberger, *The World in Depression*, p. 126.

36. Initially, the Trade Union Congress was prepared, even after the fall of the Labour government, to continue consultations with the Federation of British Industries for a joint approach to the Ottawa Conference. Hopes were expressed for planning investment in a sterling area commonwealth in which there would be 'the development of complementary production': TUC Annual Report 1932, pp. 220–2, quoted in Gupta, *Imperialism and the British Labour Movement*, pp. 234–5.

37. Kindleberger, *The World in Depression*, p. 126.

38. See Drummond, *Imperial Economic Policy 1917–1939*, pp. 112, 145, 151–77; Gupta, *Imperialism and the British Labour Movement*, pp. 156–7; Peter Clarke, *Hope and Glory: Britain, 1900–1990* (Harmondsworth, 1996), pp. 175–7.

39. See L.S. Amery, *The Empire in a New Era* (London, 1928); Amery, *The Forward View* (London, 1935); Amery, *India and Freedom* (Oxford, 1942), Amery, *The Framework of the Future* (Oxford, 1944). See also Amery's memoirs: Amery, *My Political Life, volume three: The Unforgiving Years 1929–1940* (London, 1955).

40. See, for instance, B.R. Tomlinson, *The Political Economy of the Raj 1914–1947* (London, 1979); Dietmar Rothermund, *India in the Great Depression* pp. 38–78; Raghabendra Chattopadhyay, 'An Early British Initiative in the Genesis of Indian Planning', *Economic and Political Weekly*, Vol. XXII, No. 5 (1987).

41. See Chapter 3 of this book.

42. The term is Sabyasachi Bhattacharya's 'Laissez-Faire in India', *Indian Economic and Social History Review*, Vol. II, No. 1 (1965).

43. The continued need for economic control over India was stressed even as the need for political concessions was realized. Note, for instance, the conservative policies of Sir James Grigg, Schuster's successor, and the role envisaged for the governor of the new Reserve Bank of India by Montagu Norman, Governor of the Bank of England: 'no agreement, no document, nothing that could be quoted or enquired into but complete freedom in form ... to do as he likes with his money and simply a voluntary arrangement by which he tells us of his actions and intentions and we tell him whether or not they would suit our book'. Quoted in Balachandran, 'Towards a "Hindoo Marriage", p. 635. For this to work, the Reserve Bank had to be kept 'white'.

44. See Raghabendra Chattopadhyay, 'An Early British Initiative in the Genesis of Indian Planning', *Economic and Political Weekly*, Vol. XXII, No. 5, *Review of Political Economy* (31 January 1987).

45. Sir George Schuster, 'Empire Trade Before and After Ottawa: A Preliminary Reconnaissance', *The Economist:* Special Supplement, 3 November 1934; Sir George Schuster, 'Indian Economic Life: Past Trends and Future Prospects', *Journal of the Royal Society of Arts*, LXXXIII, 31 May 1935, address delivered 8 March 1935; Sir George Schuster, *Private Work and Public Causes: A Personal Record, 1881–1978*, (Cowbridge, 1979), pp 39–89.

46. The long-drawn-out negotiations and discussions eventually led to the passing of the Government of India Act of 1935, which crucially contained certain commercial and financial safeguards for the protection of British commercial and financial interests, as well as additional and disproportionately large representation of the 'European' business community in the provincial legislatures, especially of Bengal—defined as an Indian 'minority'. See R.J. Moore, 'The Making of India's Paper Federation', in R.J. Moore, *Endgames of Empire*, (Delhi, 1988); Carl Bridge, *Holding India to Empire*, (Delhi, 1986).

47. Implicit in this, of course, was the fact that the less equal members would end up having their position represented by Britain, and could justifiably feel uneasy about this. For an example from the Indian case, see Basudev Chatterji, 'Business and Politics in the 1930s: Lancashire and the Making of the Indo-British Trade Agreement, 1939', *Modern Asian Studies*, Vol. 15, No. 3 (1985).

48. William Roger Louis, *In the Name of God, Go! Leo Amery and the British Empire in the Age of Churchill*, (New York, 1992), p. 32.

49. L.S. Amery, *The Forward View*, p. 112, quoted in Louis, *In the Name of God, Go!* p. 32.

50. Amery wrote to Valentine Chirol, Foreign Editor, *The Times*, on 7 July 1900, while working as a reporter on the Boer War, that 'South Africa must develop as a white man's country under the guidance of white men, and not a bastard country like most of South America. In five hundred years' time I expect the South African white man will contain a strong dark blend, and the end of all things may be a brown South African race, comparable to the Abyssinians or

Somalis. That doesn't matter, what does matter is that there should not be too quick a mixture now or for the next few centuries'. He further stated, 'We have done one good thing towards conciliating the Dutch: that is, we have shown our resolve not to let the natives get out of bounds'. Quoted in Louis, *In the Name of God, Go!*, p. 46. Perhaps only his practical sense caused him to compromise this principle for the greater good of the Empire. See his parallel remarks on the possibility that the British Empire might have been saved if Indian maharajas had been allowed to marry British women to ensure cementing of ties between Britain and India, which he believed might have led to Britain continuing to hold India: Penderel Moon (ed.), *Wavell: The Viceroy's Journal* (London, 1973), Wavell's account of a conversation with Amery, entry for 1 August 1943, p. 14. On 'the control of tribal areas by aerial bombardment', see William Roger Louis, *In the Name of God, Go!*, pp. 26–7.

51. Louis, *In the Name of God, Go!*, pp. 23–8, 37; see also S. Constantine, *The Making of British Colonial Development Policy 1914–1940* (London, 1984). Amery's approach to the integration of the Empire was economic, as opposed to those of Lionel Curtis and the Round Table group with whom he was associated in the first decade of the century: Louis, *In the Name of God, Go!*; p 37. On Oxford, the Round Table group, and the Commonwealth, see also Frederick Madden and D.K. Fieldhouse (eds), *Oxford and the Idea of the Commonwealth* (London, 1982), of which see especially Frederick Madden, 'The Commonwealth, Commonwealth History, and Oxford, 1905–1971', pp. 9–24, and Deborah Lavin, 'Lionel Curtis and the Idea of the Commonwealth', pp. 97–119; and on another prominent member of the group, Philip Kerr, see the official biography: J.R.M. Butler, *Lord Lothian (Philip Kerr) 1882–1940* (London, 1960), pp. 35–60; for a list of Lothian's articles for *Round Table*, see pp 323–5. On Lothian's desire for a 'Liberal Socialism', as he put it in a letter to Lloyd George on 25 November 1935, see pp. 172–3.

52. Amery, *My Political Life*, Vol. I, p. 252, quoted in William Roger Louis, *In the Name of God, Go!*, p. 77.

53. S. Constantine, '"Bringing the Empire Alive": The Empire Marketing Board and Imperial Propaganda, 1926–33', in J.M. MacKenzie (ed.), *Imperialism and Popular Culture* (Manchester, 1986). In Amery's view, imperialism as propounded by the Empire Marketing Board (EMB) and imperial preference could be not just a solution to economic problems, but an antidote to socialism. Tariff reform would, he had written in 1906, be part of an imperial policy that 'will be capable of detaching the working people in this country from the anti-imperialist leaders of socialism'. When the Scottish trade unionist, Thomas Johnstone, was suggested by the Labour Member of Parliament (MP), J.H. Thomas, to Leo Amery, whose brainchild the EMB was, as a member of the Publicity Committee. Amery wrote, 'I think this is a good move'. Amery believed, as he put it in 1923, that the 'real healthy and

natural division of parties' in Britain should be between 'constructive Conservatism on the one side, with a policy of Empire Development and national economic organisation, and on the other hand Labour Socialism with its ideas of levelling up by taxation, nationalisation, etc.'. The EMB itself, however, seen as a means of influencing consumer choice, did not reflect this 'natural division'. In 1929 the Labour government took over the EMB, its new chairman was Sidney Webb, Lord Passfield; and Amery received and accepted an invitation to remain on the EMB. Constantine, 'Bringing the Empire Alive', pp. 196–8. The art critic of the *Times* commented that the EMB campaigns had made the words 'Empire' and 'imperial' respectable again. Cited in Constantine, 'Bringing the Empire Alive', p. 217.

54. On 'colonial development', see S. Constantine, *The Making of British Colonial Development Policy*; and specifically on the Labour Party's perspective, Gupta, *Imperialism and the British Labour Movement*, pp. 135–42, 243–59, 309–25.

55. William Beveridge, *The Pillars of Society* (London, 1943); *Full Employment in a Free Society* (London, 1944). The welfare state, although implemented by a Labour government, was, it may be noted, largely conceptualized by these two liberals, with earlier measures by Lloyd George's governments as predecessors in policy terms.

56. Rothermund, *An Economic History of India*, pp. 118–19.

57. Bipan Chandra, *The Rise and Growth of Economic Nationalism in India: Economic Policies of Indian Nationalist leadership, 1880–1905* (New Delhi, 1966).

58. Bipan Chandra, *The Rise and Growth of Economic Nationalism in India*, pp. 90–141. What should be done to bring about industrialization was something on which no clear consensus had emerged at the end of the nineteenth century.

59. See section, 'The Circulation of Ideas and Information' in chapter 2 of this book.

60. Variations of this series of arguments were ubiquitous in British thinking; but for a statement, updated for the 1930s, see George Schuster, 'Empire Trade Before and After Ottawa: A Preliminary Reconnaissance', *The Economist*: Special Supplement, 3 November 1934.

61. For the question of the audiences being addressed, see section, 'The Circulation of Ideas and Information' in chapter 2 of this book.

62. See, for instance, A.G. Clow, *The State and Industry: A Narrative of Indian Government Policy and Action in Relation to Industry under the Reformed Constitution* (Calcutta: Government of India Central Publication Branch, 1928). This reiterated the government's arguments that it had always been concerned with economic improvement in India, had promoted industrial education and commercial intelligence; and assserted that the previously-held but now outdated doctrine of laissez-faire had prevented more active intervention on the part of the government, but that the acceptance of tariffs for India was an indication that this attitude had changed. It is worthwhile to contrast this statement with that of 1923 quoted above ('free trade with

legitimate exceptions'), which might be useful in contrasting publicity statements with policy statements; both cases involved 'official' statements, though Clow's book contained the conventional disclaimer that the opinions expressed therein were not necessarily those of the Government of India.

63. As an enormous amount of the historiography of colonial India relies on such official reports as source material, the rules underlying these sources need to be pointed out. In particular, the use of such sources for understanding the 'official mind' creates certain dangers. (A good example of the problems which can arise from this approach, pioneered by the Gallagher–Robinson team, is B.R. Tomlinson, *The Political Economy of the Raj*, in which Tomlinson reads the 'official mind' as desiring the progressive decolonization of India from after the First World War). The dangers of regarding the 'official mind' as the source of imperial ideas, impulses, or policy have often been pointed out. Among the notable difficulties with studies of 'ministerial head-scratchings', as Victor Kiernan put it, is that the 'official mind' selectively creates its records through a process of reducing debate and dissent to certain bureaucratic formulae; and it is certainly not as disinterested as its files make it out to be: Victor Kiernan, 'Farewells to Empire: Some Recent Studies of Imperialism', in *Marxism and Imperialism* (London, 1974), p. 78. To abandon the storms of nationalist and left critiques of colonialism for the calmer waters of official discourse is often to fall victim to imperialism's own mythologies. (There may also, as Stephen Howe points out, be several 'official minds' at a given political juncture. Stephen Howe, *Anticolonialism in British Politics: The Left and the End of Empire 1918–1964* (Oxford, 1993), pp. 13–14, 21.) I would argue that the rhetoric and arguments—the concentrations and silences—of the commissions needs to be read against those of conservative imperialism at home and of imperialists and nationalists in India. The assumption of many of these studies seems to be that the arguments put forward in 'official sources' can be arranged in terms commonly understood by everyone (even if these terms were not available to the protagonists at the time), and then analysed on the basis of these terms. An understanding of the contexts in which these conventionalized arguments operated, I would argue, is essential for a proper understanding of the arguments themselves.

64. See *Report of the Royal Commission on Agriculture in India* (London, 1928). By contrast, the Bengal Land Revenue Committee of 1938, chaired by Sir Francis Floud, recommended the abolition of the Permanent Settlement of Bengal, which it claimed had led to parasitic landlords living off their tenants and contributing nothing to the improvement of agriculture, while the government share in land revenues remained static. See Government of Bengal, *Report of the Land Revenue Commission, Bengal, Vol. I (with Minutes of Dissent)* (Calcutta, 1940). The latter was, of course, a land revenue committee, not an agrarian reforms committee; but it saw such reform as the only way to increase revenue receipts.

65. F.R. Scott, in the *Congress Socialist*, 16 May 1936, p. 6.

66. This point is made quite often in the historiography on the subject. See Chatterji, *Trade, Tariffs and Empire*; Claude Markovits, *Indian Business and Nationalist Politics 1931–1939: The Indigenous Capitalist Class and the Rise of the Congress Party* (Cambridge, 1985); J.A. Gallagher and Anil Seal, 'Britain and India between the Wars', *Modern Asian Studies*, Vol. 15, No. 3 (1981).

67. See, for instance, the *Report of the Central Banking Enquiry Committee, 1931* (Calcutta, 1931); the *Report of the Royal Commission on Indian Currency and Finance, 1926* (London, 1926) (the Hilton Young Commission): Sir Purshotamdas Thakurdas' Note of Dissent; the *Report of the Indian Fiscal Commission, 1921–22* (Simla, 1922), Minute of Dissent signed by Ibrahim Rahimtoola (president), T.V. Seshagiri Ayyar, G.D. Birla, Jamnadas Dwarkadas, Narottam Morarjee. This last is worth quoting briefly, as it was drawn upon in a number of subsequent debates. It declared that the goal to be aimed at was that India 'should attain a position of one of the foremost industrial nations of the world'. *Report of the Indian Fiscal Commission*, p. 176. The 1918 Industrial Commission had been debarred from considering Indian fiscal policy; but they would have come to the same conclusion regarding protection as these people are now. 'We believe that the industrial backwardness of India is in no way due to any inherent defects amongst the people of India, but that it was artificially created by a continuous process of stifling, by means of a forced tariff policy, the inborn industrial genius of the people'. *Report of the Indian Fiscal Commission*, p. 180.

68. The Majority Report of the Central Banking Enquiry Commission drew heavily on the Royal Commission on Agriculture in India's 1927 report for its section on agricultural and rural credit; it also drew on the Hilton Young Committee's 1925 report. See the *Report of the Indian Fiscal Commission*; the *Report of the External Capital Committee, 1925* (Calcutta, 1925) (IOR: V/26/330/1); the *Indian Central Banking Enquiry Committee, 1931*.

69. For instance, the *Report of the Committee on the Subject of Imperial Preference* (Calcutta, 1920) (Wacha Committee) recommended the establishment of a fiscal commission to answer the question of imperial preference as part of a general concern with fiscal questions (p. 2).

70. See Claude Markovits, *Indian Business and Nationalist Politics 1931–1939: The Indigenous Capitalist Class and the Rise of the Congress Party* (Cambridge, 1985), chapter six, on some of these committees between 1937 and 1939.

71. In this connection, it might be worth mentioning Sir J.C. Coyajee, Principal of Presidency College, Calcutta, in the 1920s. Known as a man of great integrity, he had learnt his economics from Alfred Marshall at Cambridge, and regarded the principles of his science to be sacrosanct; his 'sound' neo-classical views found him in great demand by the government as an 'expert' on various committees, notably the Royal Commission on Indian Currency and Finance (the Hilton Young Commission) of 1926.

72. See J.P. Narayan, *Why Socialism?* (Benares, 1936), pp. 135–43. The CSP, it

need hardly be added, was not called upon to send representatives to these committees.

73. Nehru had argued in 1936 that office-acceptance 'would inevitably mean our co-operation in some measure with the repressive apparatus of imperialism, and we would become partners in this repression and in the exploitation of our people'. Quoted in Bipan Chandra, 'Jawaharlal Nehru and the Capitalist Class, 1936', *Economic and Political Weekly*, Special Number, (August 1975). The debate can be followed in some detail in the pages of the *Congress Socialist*. (The Congress, in its period of office from 1937 to 1939, considerably toned down its pro-*kisan* and pro-labour rhetoric to accommodate capitalist and zamindar demands. See Markovits, *Indian Business and Nationalist Politics*, chapter six; Dietmar Rothermund, *India in the Great Depression*, p. 274.)

74. *Report of the Indian Road Development Committee, 1927–28* (Calcutta, 1928), chapter two, 'Indian Roads in the Past', p. 3. The Committee was chaired by M.R. Jayakar, the Liberal (the Liberals broke away from the Congress in the 1920s); among its members was Lala Lajpat Rai, who probably wrote that chapter.

75. *Report of the Indian Road Development Committee, 1927–28*, p. 53.

76. The term 'Orientalism' has become rather ambiguous since Edward Said's *Orientalism* extended its usage far beyond its original specific usage. For an outline of the problems of such usage see Aijaz Ahmad, '*Orientalism* and After: Ambivalence and Metropolitan Location in the Work of Edward Said', in *In Theory: Classes, Nations, Literatures* (London, 1992); see also J.M. MacKenzie, *Orientalism: History, Theory and the Arts* (Manchester, 1995).

77. *Indian Central Banking Enquiry Committee, 1931 Volume I, Part I; Majority Report* (Calcutta, 1931), pp. 2–3.

78. *Indian Central Banking Enquiry Committee, 1931 Volume I, Part I; Majority Report*, p. 5. As the Report explained, the Enquiry's terms of reference did not include the formation of the Reserve Bank which had been discussed for some years and had been recommended by the 1926 Hilton Young Commission. The 1928 Reserve Bank Bill had been defeated in the Assembly, as a result of pressures on the government from the Assembly, and the two most important Chambers of Commerce—the European-dominated Associated Chambers of Commerce (ASSOCHAM) and Indian business' Federation of Indian Chambers of Commerce and Industry (FICCI), for different reasons.

79. *Indian Central Banking Enquiry Committee, 1931 Volume II: Evidence (Written)* (Calcutta, 1931), pp. 5–6, 25–6, 36.

80. *Indian Central Banking Enquiry Committee, 1931 Volume II: Evidence (Written)*, pp. 335–8.

81. *Indian Central Banking Enquiry Committee, 1931, Volume I Part II: Minority Report* (Calcutta, 1931).

82. *Indian Central Banking Enquiry Committee, 1931, Volume I Part II: Minority Report*, p. 7.

83. *Indian Central Banking Enquiry Committee, 1931, Volume I Part II: Minority Report*, pp. 8–15.
84. For instance, he pointed out that the proposed Reserve Bank was meant as a means to 'divert blame from Government in respect of charges of manipulation'. He accepted the idea of 'automatic conditions' only if a country was on 'a full and proper gold standard'; India was not, therefore 'manipulation' was necessary; and the government's manipulation was against Indian national interests. *Indian Central Banking Enquiry Committee, 1931, Volume I Part II: Minority Report*, p. 286. Subedar recommended that Indian deposits be taken away from foreign banks under new licensing arrangements that reserved the field of internal banking for Indian banks – the standard argument for protection advanced by nationalists in India. This arrangement might, he argued, induce foreign banks 'to bring cheaper money from their country, which will enrich the Indian money market. It would be the test of England's boast regarding financial internationalism and the free use of the savings of English depositors abroad in institutions which finance her own foreign trade as well as the foreign trade of India'. *Indian Central Banking Enquiry Committee, 1931, Volume I Part II: Minority Report*, p. 425.
85. Chaired by the then finance member of the Government of India, Sir Basil Blackett; its terms of reference 'to consider the question of the flow of capital into India from external sources'; how such capital enters India, in what forms it was necessary and unobjectionable, how far it was possible to replace external by internal capital, and so on. *External Capital Committee: Report (1925)*, (Calcutta, 1925), IOR: V/26/330/1, pp. 1–2.
86. 'As a general principle', the Report stated, external capital was not only 'unobjectionable', but 'a valuable factor in assisting the economic development of a country and in increasing its wealth and employment'. At the same time it was desirable that new requirements of capital be supplied from internal sources, as far as it was forthcoming. *External Capital Committee: Report (1925)*, p. 4. This was the standard formulaic statement with which a compromise formula was arrived at, reducing an argument to a slogan. Unfortunately, the Report went on to say, India's 'large store of potential capital' was 'unproductively locked up in bullion and jewellery' (another standard argument); hence, the continued need for external sources while internal capital resources, credit, and investment facilities, were 'developed'. Measures for controlling external capital were rejected on the grounds of impracticability, the consumers' right to low prices, and because it would 'require a very elaborate system of trade licensing and the most inquisitorial government control'. *External Capital Committee: Report (1925)*, p. 10.
87. *External Capital Committee: Report (1925)*, p. 11.
88. *External Capital Committee: Report (1925)*, p. 13.
89. Madan Mohan Malaviya's Note of Dissent, dated 15 Septemeber 1925, *External Capital Committee: Report (1925)*, p .18.
90. 'When we Indians asked for protection we did so in order to promote Indian enterprises with Indian capital and under Indian control', *External Capital*

Committee: Report (1925), p. 19. 'If a foreigner invests behind Indian tariff walls with foreign capital and repatriates profits, the Indian consumer suffers and inadequate benefit accrues to the national economy'. *External Capital Committee: Report (1925)*, pp. 19–20.

91. See M. Visvesvaraya, *Reconstructing India* (London, 1920).

92. Quentin Skinner discusses this problem in Skinner, 'Meaning and Understanding in the History of Ideas', in James Tully (ed.), *Meaning and Context: Quentin Skinner and his Critics* (Oxford, 1988). Existing writing is replete with examples of this: Radhakamal Mukherjee having reached certain economic truths despite his 'romantic' views on the Indian village; Gandhi or J.C. Kumarappa having been environmentalists or advocates of 'sustainable development' ahead of their times. Bhabatosh Datta, *Indian Economic Thought: Twentieth Century Perspectives*, pp. 28–9; Devendra Kumar, 'Kumarappa and the Contemporary Development Perspective', *Gandhi Marg* 14, 2 (July–September 1992), Madhav Gadgil, 'On the Gandhian Economic Trail', *Gandhians in Action*, April–June 1994.

93. See later editions of J.C. Kumarappa, *Why the Village Movement?* (first published Wardha, 1936; fifth edition, Wardha, 1949); S.N. Agarwal, *The Gandhian Plan of Economic Development for India* (Bombay, 1944).

94. This tendency increased in the so-called 'Nehruvian' period; though Gandhi at times put forward the view, especially when accused of being anti-socialist, that his ideas were also socialist, albeit better suited to India than the socialism of his opponents, he did not do this more than polemically.

95. The Act of the 21st and 22nd Vict. Cap., passed in 1858 'for the better Government of India', quoted in IOR: L/PARL/2/150: Moral and Material Progress Reports: Parliamentary Sessions 1860–61 (Report for 1859–60), p. 1.

96. Clause 53 of the above Act. The requirement was maintained in the 1909 and then the 1919 Acts—see, for instance, the 26th Section of the Government of India Act 1919 (5 & 6 Geo. V, chap. 61).

97. Compare, for instance, the *Statement* for 1861 (IOR: L/PARL/2/150) with, say, the *Statement* for 1925–6 or 1934–5; the former is basically an account book full of tables of money spent and taxes collected; the latter are good-natured, well-written narratives of the administrative year gone by from a government point of view. The origins of the latter reports in the Directorate of Public Information, simultaneously published in India under the more innocuous title of *India in [year]*, is significant in that they were meant to be adjuncts to the providing of the Government of India with a more acceptable face. For the rationale behind and the working of the Central Bureau of Information, under which the Directorate fell, in the period from its inception after the First World War to before the Second World War, see Milton Israel, *Communications and Power: Propaganda and the Press in the Indian Nationalist Struggle, 1920–1947* (Cambridge, 1994), chapter one: 'The Government of India: images and messages in the defence of authority'. L.F.

Rushbrook Williams, who had been, from 1914, a historian at the University of Allahabad, where he had combined teaching and research with literary and publicity work for the government, was appointed director, in 1919, of the newly-formed Central Bureau of Information, attached to the Home Department, Government of India; among his tasks was the preparation of the annual 'Moral and Material Progress Report'. Israel, *Communications and Power*, pp. 30, 33.

98. *Statement Exhibiting the Moral and Material Progress and Condition of India during the year 1925–26* (London: His Majesty's Stationery Office [HMSO], 1927), p. 189. (Emphasis added). The linking of stereotypes about India to European racism and animosity towards the gipsies is worth noting. In a similar vein, a report in the India Office Information Department records by H.B. Holme, 'circulated to the Executive Committee of the Indo-Burman Association by the Secretary' regarding a Fabian Society conference on India, held at Oxford in September 1942, claimed that the audience had included 'a number of Jews and many foreigners', in addition to six or seven Labour MPs, who, the report implied, were guilty by association of being of the same mettle; and that the Fabians, 'affiliated to the Labour Party', as Holme felt it necessary to remind his readers, were busy spreading 'their poisonous doctrines of British 'shame' in India and anti-Imperialist cant'. Report, n.d., IOR: L/I/1/95. This account was endorsed by Sir John Woodhead, former Governor of Bengal, and later to be chairman of the 1945 Famine Commission in Bengal, who had been present and had spoken at the conference: Sir John Woodhead's letter to India Office Information Department, dated 1/10/1942, IOR: L/I/1/95; though perhaps he might himself have put things a little more politely.

99. Radhakumud Mookerji, *Nationalism in Hindu Culture* (London, 1921), p. 1. (Here, of course, he identified the 'national' with the 'Hindu genius'.)

100. See Chapter 4 of this book.

101. See below, Chapter 5 of this book.

102. *Report on Indian Constitutional Reforms* (Calcutta, 1918), pp. 124, 153–4, 167–8, 230–1; 234–7. See also J.A. Gallagher and Anil Seal, 'Britain and India between the Wars', *Modern Asian Studies*, Vol. 15, No. 3, (1981).

103. This was a system of responsibility without financial control: finance was not a 'transferred' subject; and the Meston Award resulting from the 1919 Act gave the inelastic sources of revenue—from land, irrigation, excise, and stamps—to the provinces, leaving the more flexible sources—income tax, opium, salt, and customs—to the centre. See Gallagher and Seal, 'Britain and India between the Wars', p. 400. The lack of financial control or of evident sources of finance did not stop Indians from thinking along ambitious lines. Although the lack of financial control was noted strongly by Indians, there was an optimism that, with the departure of the British, sources of finance would be forthcoming.

104. 'It is the colonialists who become the defenders of the native style. We remember perfectly, and the example took on a certain measure of importance

since the real nature of colonialism was not involved, the reactions of the white jazz specialists when, after the Second World War, new styles such as the be-bop took definite shape. The fact is that in their eyes jazz should only be the despairing, broken-down nostalgia of an old Negro who is trapped between five glasses of whisky, the curse of his race, and the racial hatred of the white men'. Frantz Fanon, *The Wretched of the Earth* (Harmondsworth, 1967), pp. 195–6.

105. See George Birdwood, *The Industrial Arts of India* (London, 1880). Birdwood (1832–1917) was connected with the arts and crafts movement in Britain, and was regarded as an expert on Indian art. Dictionary of National Biography (*DNB*) *1912–1921* (Oxford, 1927), pp. 46–7.

106. See Tapati Guha Thakurta, *The Making of a New 'Indian' Art: Artists, Aesthetics and Nationalism in Bengal, c. 1850–1920* (Cambridge, 1992). Guha Thakurta does not state her case as strongly as Fanon did, although she points out the importance of the British contribution to what constituted 'genuine' Indianness as part of 'a wider imperial commitment' (p. 147), as well as the importance of this category of 'Indianness' to Indian nationalists, around which the whole debate on 'national art and 'Indian-style' painting revolved. She points out the importance to these debates of the Arts and Crafts Movement's idea that design and handicrafts were where artistic 'traditions' were kept alive: see, especially, chapter five. This was despite strong disagreements, such as that between George Birdwood, who completely denied the existence of 'fine arts' in India, and E.B. Havell, the discoverer of Abanindranath Tagore as the first 'genuine' modern Indian artist. Havell 'argued for the abolition of all 'artificial' distinctions between "fine" and "applied" arts and for a rethinking of art and industry, highlighting design as the basis of all art and any sound art instruction' (p. 151), but, nonetheless, shared Birdwood's concern with 'industrial arts'. It might also be noted that the implications of a view of industry as arts and crafts, in aesthetic terms rather than as an economic proposition concerned with employment and income generation, was not disruptive of a view of India as essentially an agricultural civilization with a long, unchanged 'tradition'.

107. Jadunath Sarkar, *The Economics of British India* (Calcutta, 1911). This is referred to by Bhabatosh Datta as '[o]ne of the earliest books on Indian economic problems' (Datta is, of course, excluding nineteenth century perspectives from his consideration): Bhabatosh Datta, *Indian Economic Thought: Twentieth Century Perspectives*, p. 5.

108. Morison began by stressing the importance of an authentically Indian voice: 'In India religion and social usage must powerfully affect the operation of economic laws, but in what way they accelerate or retard the wheels of industry few Europeans are in a position to say. Upon this aspect of the economics of his own country an Indian speaks with unrivalled authority, and his point of view is so essential to a thorough mastery of the problem that it may confidently be asserted that an authoritative work on Indian

economics can only be written by an Indian.' Morison praised Sarkar's 'courage and independence' in differing from the opinions 'which are popular with his countrymen', but was generous enough to take a more charitable view of the Indian character than Sarkar himself did: 'He [Sarkar] frequently emphasises the unpalatable truth that the backwardness of Indian industry is due to faults of Indian character; in so far as he assumes these faults to be permanent and ineradicable, I am inclined to think he is over-pessimistic'. Theodore Morison's review of Jadunath Sarkar, *The Economics of British India*, in the *Economic Journal*, Vol. XXI (September 1911), pp. 424–5. Morison apparently did not see the contradiction in selecting as worthy of praise an authentically Indian voice which he himself described as a minority opinion: was it authentic because it was a minority voice, despite being a minority voice, or simply because it was an Indian voice? Which raises the question of whether Morison's own endorsement of that voice was simply due to the fact that it endorsed a commonly held British prejudice about the uneconomic character of Indians. Yet Morison's own views were not conventionally British: for instance, though he opposed protection for Indian industries—and was pleased to note that Sarkar did as well (p. 424)—he was not too displeased at the prospect of gradual but inevitable Indian industrialization: Theodore Morison, *The Economic Transition in India* (London, 1911). For this view he was rather patronizingly criticized by the young Keynes; on the grounds that it paid no attention to the 'specialisation of nations'. Keynes continued: 'if regard be had to climatic conditions and to the aptitudes and habits of her people, it seems hard to believe that India will not obtain more wealth by obtaining from the West, in exchange for her raw products, most of those commodities which she now obtains in this manner, than by diverting her capital and her peasants from the fields of the country to Bombay, in order to make them herself'. John Maynard Keynes, review of Theodore Morison, *The Economic Transition in India*, in *Economic Journal*, Vol. XXI (September 1911), p. 427. It might be noted that Keynes held classically imperialist views, far more rigidly stereotypical in their postulation of climatically determined occupations and unchanging native character than Morison's. Yet it was Keynes, ironically, who accused Morison of arguing 'too lightly from the past to the future and from the West to the East' (p. 428).

109. See Chapter 3 of this book.

110. The question of ownership and control obviously comes into the equations here. Much of the press was controlled by 'nationalist' capital, whose support of the Congress and attempts to control it went side by side. GD Birla, for instance, owned a great deal of the press. For details of Birla's involvement with various papers and journals, both as financier and as controlling influence, see Medha Malik Kudaisya, 'The Public Career of GD Birla, 1911–1947', unpublished PhD dissertation, University of Cambridge, 1992, pp. 56–8. The *Hindustan Times*, the main pro-Congress daily paper, was owned by him and edited by Gandhi's son. The *National Herald* was

possibly an exception as a mainstream daily with a left slant, run by Jawaharlal Nehru. But Nehru was usually careful about maintaining the outward unity of nationalism, as the primary goal of the Left was also independence, to which end anti-imperialist unity was a priority. Conventional arguments were the best that could be hoped for in a daily paper.

111. It is difficult to get reliable circulation figures for the major national dailies. Approximate figures were collected by the Government of India's Bureau of Public Information for intelligence purposes. In 1944 they stood as follows: *Hindustan Times*, 15,000; *Hindu* (Madras), 38,824; *Bombay Chronicle* 21,000; *Hindusthan Standard* (Calcutta), 26,500; The *National Herald* (Lucknow), Nehru's paper, ceased publication in August 1942, at which point its estimated circulation was 8000 (it resumed publication on 30 November 1945). Source: Government of India, Bureau of Public Information, *Guide to Prominent Newspapers and Periodicals in English and Indian Languages Published in British India and Indian States* (New Delhi, May 1944) (IOR: V/27/960/10). These figures do not show any significant change from the figures published for the period upto December 1937, and it may be suspected that many of the figures were just carried forward into the later Bureau of Public Information guides, except in the case where a significant change was expected from other sources of evidence or when a new publication entered the records. See Government of India, Bureau of Public Information, *Guide to Prominent English and Vernacular Newspapers and Periodicals Published in British India and the Indian States, Corrected up to December 1937* (New Delhi, 1938) (IOR: V/27/960/9).

112. For instance, the *Mysore Journal of Economics*, the *Indian Journal of Economics*, or the *Indian Agricultural Journal*. Circulation figures for these, or other specialist journals such as *Science and Culture* or the *Eastern Economist,* were not provided in the Bureau of Public Information's publications—they were probably not considered important for intelligence-gathering purposes.

113. *Science and Culture* is a good example of a journal with a bearing on 'development' from a science angle.

114. *Modern Review* (approximate circulation 5500); *Prabashi* (approximate circulation 6500): *Guide to Prominent Newspapers and Periodicals* (1944).

115. They included titles such as *Agrarian Problem in India*, the first publication of the recently-formed Political and Economic Information Department; *Village Industries and Reconstruction*; *Non-Violent Revolution*; *The Gandhian Way*; *Revolution and Counter-Revolution*; as well as much material on public debt, constitutional issues, reports of various Congress conferences and resolutions. 'All-India Congress Committee, Swaraj Bhavan, Allahabad: List of English publications', n.d. (but c. 1938—after the Haripura Congress), File on Congress Publications, AICC papers, C-I/1938, ff 29–30.

116. The exceptions were Pattabhi Sitaramayya's *History of the Congress*, which cost two rupees eight annas, *The Gandhian Way*, which cost two rupees, the *All Parties' Convention Report*, which also cost two rupees, K.T. Shah's

Federal Structure, which cost two rupees eight annas, and the [Motilal] *Nehru Committee Report*, which cost one rupee eight annas. All-India Congress Committee, Swaraj Bhavan, Allahabad: List of English publications', n.d. (but c.1938–after the Haripura Congress), File on Congress Publications, AICC papers, C-I/1938, ff. 29–30.

117. Appeals for translation were made by the AICC; the politics of translation and of language occasionally made brief appearances: a circular letter dated 14 July 1936 appealed for translators into Urdu, Hindi, Gujarati, and Bengali for Z.A. Ahmed's *The Agrarian Problem in India—A General Survey* and for the shortly-to-be-published *Indian Struggle in World Perspective*. AICC Papers, G-47/1936, ff. 1–3. A reply from one Sibtay Hasan of the daily *Payan* in Hyderabad (Deccan), offered to translate them into *Hindustani*. The Hindustani translation does not seem to have materialized; a letter dated 5 July 1937 to one P.N. Dikshit, Pleader, Patkapur, Cawnpore, mentions a Hindi edition of *The Agrarian Problem* shortly to come out, and an Urdu edition, out already, publishers Sasta Sahitya Mandal and Jamia Milia, respectively.

118. These were all sales, not free distribution. AICC papers, C-I/1938; C-I (KW 1-7)/1938.

119. The Public Information Department, Civil Secretariat of the UP, for instance, requested five copies each of the Wardha Educational Scheme, a scheme of education on Gandhian lines, in English and Urdu. AICC papers, C-I (KW-6)/1938, f. 383. Occasionally, requests came in from outside nationalist circles. The advertising agency, D.J. Keymer, wrote to J.B. Kripalani to request, on behalf of an unnamed client, 500 copies of a brochure entitled 'Indian Transport', by S.R. Soni, published by the Congress on the occasion of its golden jubilee. The book was out of stock. C-I (KW-6)/1938, f. 399.

120. Publication details of Gandhian publications are usually very clear—they provide dates of each reprint or edition, the number of copies printed; and lists of publications and the languages in which editions existed.

121. JNP, NML, Vol. 110, Subject Files No. 19 (Part I), f. 8. Others were R.S. Pandit, V.L. Mehya, M. Iftikhar Ud-Din and Raghunandan Saran.

122. JNP, NML, Vol. 110, Subject Files No. 19 (Part I), f. 5.

123. JNP, Nehru Memorial Library (NML), Vol. 110, Subject Files No. 19 (Part I), ff 2–3.

124. This confusion is corroborated in the files of the Indian Political Intelligence organization (IPI)—for instance, what books were to be excluded from India and so on: see IOR: L/P&J/12/26, L/P&J/12/493, L/P&J/12/677–8, L/P&J/12/680. The consistent underling concern was to prevent the circulation of communist ideas, 'communist' being a category which was extremely broadly defined in a rather paranoid manner. But this was probably not decisive in stopping information and debates about development matters per se, because even though one might be able to include some agitational material in such pamphlets, it was difficult for the government to treat apparently technical arguments regarding planned economies as agitational.

125. *Congress Socialist* circulation figures were about 2000. *Guide to Prominent English and Vernacular Newspapers and Periodicals* (1938).
126. AICC Papers, G-47/1936; C-1/1938; C-1 (KW-1-7)/1938.
127. It is possible to attempt to gain an idea of the circulation of pamphlets from sales records. The records contain such items as a request for a copy of the new Congress Constitution of 1938 from a jeweller from Jaipur: Letter from one Padam Chandra, dated 5 September 1938, AICC papers, C-1/1938, f. 89. The 1938 Constitutional amendment concerned mainly procedural matters, but it stemmed from a concern to deal with the problem of genuine and opportunist members, 'bogus membership', and voting malpractices. See AICC Papers, C-1 (KW-6)/1938, ff 95–105, 181–99. This problem can be said to have become more pressing as the Congress was seen to be closer to power in the period after it formed ministries in several provinces. The petite-bourgeois class position of the Jaipur jeweller is consistent with his support for the Congress and, consequently, for his concern with organizational matters—as has been indicated before in studies which deal with the support bases of Congress. There is no indication, however, that this support translated into the interest in economic and political matters which was desired. This is reflected in sales records—see AICC Papers, G-47/1936; C-1/1938; C-1 (KW-1-7)/1938—pamphlets dealing with economic and political matters, education, and other matters related to 'development' were bought mainly by institutions, academic or political, and, consequently, presumed to have been read mainly by members of the intellectual bourgeoisie. Institutional sales, however, often do not provide a good indication of readership, merely of potential readership. On the other hand, since the pamphlets were often published by private publishers, and priced rather low, enough sales seem to have been generated.
128. Circular letter dated 14 July 1936, AICC papers, G-47/1936 f. 3.
129. Prospectus of the Socialist Book Club, copy in AICC Papers 21 (Part 1)/1936, ff. 661–3(b).
130. Kitabistan, Allahabad, and Vora and Co., Bombay, were major publishers on 'development' as a theme.
131. Oxford University Press, Delhi, with its *Oxford Pamphlets on India* series, is a case in point. I have benefitted from conversations with Rimi Chatterjee in this connection; her forthcoming book, to be published by Oxford University Press, Delhi, deals with the production of textbooks for the colonial market up to 1940. See, in this connection, Rimi B Chatterjee, 'A History of the Trade to South Asia by Macmillan & Co. and Oxford University Press, 1875–1900', unpublished DPhil thesis, University of Oxford, 1997; unfortunately, it does not deal with the period under consideration in this dissertation.
132. In 1909, Calcutta University instituted an honours degree in economics, the first Indian university to do so. Before that specialization, economics was the domain of the historian, of which Calcutta circles produced more than their fair share; for instance, Jadunath Sarkar, better known as a historian of the

last great Mughal emperor, Aurangzeb, or Benoy Kumar Sarkar (1887–1949), 'an ardent nationalist, interested in economic development, technical training and educational experiments', who 'like others in his generation' had his basic training in history, philosophy, and literature. Bhabatosh Datta, *Indian Economic Thought: Twentieth Century perspectives*, pp. 4–5. Datta omits to mention Benoy Sarkar's more than passing interest in fascism, as is evident from his articles in the *Modern Review*.

133. See Robert S. Anderson, *Building Scientific Institutions in India: Saha and Bhabha* (Montreal, 1975), p. 40.

134. The best approach to describing the bhadralok is that of John McGuire: 'the *bhadralok* cannot be seen as a fixed social group, but rather as the embodiment of changing sets of organic social relationships'. John McGuire, *The Making of a Colonial Mind: a Quantitative Study of the Bhadralok in Calcutta, 1857–1885* (Canberra, 1983), p. 2. Put differently, the bhadralok or 'respectable people', was a social group which admitted new entrants as and when it was thought that these prospective entrants met the required social standards. Although caste did play a role in this, it was, as McGuire argues, never a major factor in securing admittance to the category 'bhadralok'—and education was a powerful way of securing such access. It is thus easier, at any given point of time, to discern who was not a 'bhadralok'. An ambiguity remains as to whether Muslims could be bhadralok. Existing literature seems for the most part to take it for granted that they could not; but there are instances of the term being used to refer to, for instance, Muslim teachers at Presidency College, Calcutta—this should, at least, be noted as an ambiguity which needs to be explained.

135. See Chapter 4 of this book.

136. During the Second World War, the middle class was specifically targeted as an audience for British propaganda and publicity programmes: see Sanjoy Bhattacharya, *Propaganda and Information in Eastern India, 1939–45.* (Richmond, 2000)

137. See Sanjoy Bhattacharya and Benjamin Zachariah, "A Great Destiny': The British Colonial State and the Advertisement of Post-War Reconstruction in India, 1942–45', *South Asia Research*, Vol. 19, No. 1 (1999). For a description of the government's wartime plans, see Raghabendra Chattopadhyay, 'The Idea of Planning in India 1930–1951', unpublished PhD dissertation, Australian National University, Canberra, 1985'.

138. See Chapter 3 of this volume.

139. See Carritt, *A Mole in the Crown*. I am also grateful to Sidney Bolt for allowing me to see a draft of his memoirs, *Pseudo-Sahib*.

140. See Clive Dewey, *Anglo-Indian Attitudes*, (London, 1993).

141. Robert Anderson, *Building Scientific Institutions in India*, pp. 6–12; Benjamin Zachariah, Subhas Ranjan Chakraborti, and Rajat Kanta Ray, 'Presidency College, Calcutta; An Unfinished History', in Mushirul Hasan (ed.), *Knowledge, Power and Politics: Educational Institutions in India* (New

Delhi, 1998), pp. 332–3, 385–6. Saha's bhadralok status was hard won through his educational and scientific achievements.

142. The Maharaja Sayajirao of Baroda. Ambedkar's acknowledgements in the published version of his doctoral dissertation, which he completed at Columbia University under the supervision of E.R.A. Seligman, outline his debts in this regard. See B.R. Ambedkar, *The Evolution of Public Finance in British India: A Study in the Provincial Decentralisation of Public Finance* (London, 1925). For Ambedkar's early life and education, see Dhananjay Keer, *Dr Ambedkar: Life and Mission* (Bombay, 1954; this edition, Bombay, 1987), pp. 26–34; W.N. Kuber, *B.R. Ambedkar* (New Delhi, 1978), pp. 9–15.

143. Narayan 'had been a Communist during his student days in America, and though he had since renounced Bolshevism he was willing to regard the Indian Communists as good Marxists'. Gene D. Overstreet and Marshall Windmiller, *Communism in India* (Berkeley, 1959), p. 156, referring to the formation of the CSP in 1934.

144. On Kumarappa, see Chapter 4 of this book.

145. Ian Duffield, 'History and the Historians', *History Today* (September 1981), pp. 34–6, quoted in Stephen Howe, *Anticolonialism in British Politics*, p. 25.

146. This is rather convenient from a researcher's point of view, because the play of ideas can be viewed in rather rich representative sample in the JNP; unfortunately, these are closed to researchers without the requisite connections for the period after 1946. An important transitional period, therefore, remains relatively opaque.

147. See H.N. Brailsford to Nehru, 8/3/36, JNP, NML, Vol. 10, f. 15; Brockway's letters to Nehru, JNP Vol. 10, ff. 105–131, 8/9/33, 25/5/36, 20/6/38, 30/6/38. Fenner Brockway to Nehru, 30/6/38, JNP, NML, Vol. 10, f. 125, Cripps to Nehru, 14/1/40, JNP, NML, Vol. 14, ff. 221–2. For an elaboration of this argument, see Benjamin Zachariah, *Jawaharlal Nehru* (London, 2004). Sir James Grigg, who was not exactly known as an enemy of the British Empire in India, acknowledged retrospectively in his memoirs that Nehru was the most sensible of the Indian nationalists—he attributed this to the latter's having been to Harrow and Cambridge. P.J. Grigg, *Prejudice and Judgement* (London, 1948), p. 288.

148. Jawaharlal Nehru to Ardeshir Dalal, 26 June 1940, JNP, NML, Vol. 16, ff. 133–4; Meghnad Saha to Jawaharlal Nehru, 27 October 1941, JNP, NML, Vol. 90, ff. 24–5.

149. Anderson, *Building Scientific Institutions in India*, pp. 43, 45.

150. Lokanathan was the author of two books on industrialization and industrial relations, the former financed by the Methodists, and making an impassioned appeal for the preservation of industrial peace for the betterment of the nation—which, he argued, was better for workers as well: P.S. Lokanathan, *Industrial Welfare in India* (Madras, 1929); P.S. Lokanathan, *Industrial Organisation in India* (London, 1935).

151. See IOR: L/P&J/12/26, L/P&J/12/493, L/P&J/12/677-8, L/P&J/12/680.

3

A Reformed Imperium?

This chapter examines a few selected moments at which 'development' came to the forefront in British imperialist debates on India. In so doing, it attempts to explore the tensions in approach to imperialism contained within these approaches to 'development'. These were for the most part separate debates from those conducted contemporaneously by Indian nationalists; the trajectory of practices the former debates sought to justify were often different from the latter, although there were, of course, points at which the debates overlapped, and there were certain crossovers of ideas.

Although claims to developing the colonies and, therefore, to holding them as trustees for their peoples, were always implicit in the justification of the Empire, there were times at which these claims were brought to the foreground in a more explicit manner. ('Trusteeship' was the formula used after the Great War in recognizing the right to self-determination of all nations but, nonetheless, redistributing the colonies of the central powers among the victorious allies. The idea of trusteeship carried with it the assumption that this was a temporary relationship, to be terminated when the territories held in trust were ready for nationhood. This was perfectly in accord with the British claim that colonies needed a period of tutelage in self-government.)[1]

In reading these debates, attention needs to be drawn to the narrow framework within which official thinking operated; to the occasional moves outside this framework; and to the wider implications of the term 'development' in the confrontation between colonial discourse and nationalism: the 'backwardness' of the subject people, by the 1930s framed in predominantly economic terms, was used as justification for the continuance of colonial rule: the beneficial nature of the colonial connection for finance, trade, and commerce, its 'modernizing' role through contact with the scientific and developed West, and its crucial role in preserving internal peace and law and order, was stressed in imperial arguments, these assumptions being challenged in nationalist arguments.[2] Here I shall explore internal debates within official and government circles on ostensibly economic matters, related to the nature of the role to be fulfilled by British rule in India. These were debates which sought to sustain the justification of imperial rule in India, but which were capable of leading to doubts about the justice of the position. This justification, though viewed as an economic one by those who resorted to it, also drew strongly on a number of assumptions regarding India or Indianness which, although normally presented in their economic versions, had respectable lineages in well-established mythologized views of the Empire and imperialism; it was colonial rule's favourite self-congratulatory principle that it had brought the natives a higher level of moral and material civilization—the one went with the other.[3]

The period under consideration was one of the erosion of certainties. The relative internal consistency of earlier ideologies of the Empire was not achieved in this period. Attempts by imperialists to justify and reorder imperialism in India, while trying to connect an older imperialist discourse with the immediate needs of government, or while attempting to read the impending independence of India in terms of the achievements of imperialism itself, tended, paradoxically, to lean on older conventions of imperial thinking: speaking, as it were, from the past rather than the future in trying to reconcile their belief in imperialism as a positive force with the realities before them.

Levels of Governance and the Narrow Range

Discussions on development, as far as the governments in the colonies or His Majesty's government and its personnel were concerned, were constrained by considerations which subjugated the interests of the colonies to those of Britain, although the specifics of the conflict of interests might vary from instance to instance. This is not a surprising or new statement; a huge proportion of the historiography of imperialism—outside the imperialist framework of thought itself—has explored the structures of colonial exploitation. Yet almost in the same breath, contained within the framework of balancing imperial accounts, it was possible to trace the voice of a benevolent imperialism, defining its benevolence through economic uplift of 'backward' colonial peoples. It remained ambiguous—deliberately so in public pronouncements—whether the colonies were to be developed instrumentally, merely as a subsidized market for Britain, especially British heavy industry and/or an avenue for profitable investment, or whether, taking a slightly broader (and possibly more paternalistic) view of things, British governments in the colonies should also concern themselves with problems such as nutrition, social welfare, disease, and famine control.

It was, nonetheless, clear that the claimed benevolence of 'development' through imperialism could at best be a constrained benevolence.[4] The fact that a concern with 'developing' India would not translate into the sacrificing of British interests was, of course, clear to a number of people who, nonetheless, involved themselves in claiming the 'development' of India through imperialism—both as an essential element of the public rhetoric of imperialism, and in ideas and practices which worked on a narrow scale that was not seen as disturbing the wider priorities of the Empire. There was also an emergent school of thought which believed that particular paths of 'development' for India would be mutually beneficial to Britain and India and, in fact, link up with a coordinated programme of economic benefits and prosperity for the 'Empire–Commonwealth' as a whole.[5] For those who ignored this aspect, it was partly an exercise in self-delusion, achieved by people who ignored or suppressed the facts of exploitation upon which the Empire was based—or, alternatively, regarded them as unavoidable results of the pressures of Realpolitik which should not be allowed to stand as evidence of the destructive nature of imperialism in general. Such dissociations, as in the first case, or creations of exceptions, as in the second, were not uncommon—and, indeed, were necessary in order that a well-intentioned individual did not find himself being swallowed up by his own negative definition of imperialism, a self-disempowering act which left no space for the legitimacy of his own activities—though they might have been somewhat harder to sustain if those who made them had had the entire range of evidence from the confidential official record before them. Yet it would be too easy simply to dismiss this strand of thought as self-delusion, unimportant in the perspective of the real working of imperialism; for its existence did a great deal to sustain the will to maintain the Empire among its personnel.

By the 1930s, the single-minded consistency and confident dogmatism which had characterized official thought in the late nineteenth and early twentieth centuries was evaporating. It became difficult to hold on to simplistic views regarding the Empire as India became increasingly difficult to govern.[6] Assumptions which had worked for a younger and more stable Empire during its time of confidence and strength were gradually eroded, and some serious rethinking had to be done, through the

Depression, the War, and tremendous political unrest. At the same time, this rethinking process had to reckon with the institutional rigidities of a system of governance whose default settings, as it were, had been put in place in the course of the nineteenth century, and whose priorities were overwhelmingly imperial. As a result, new ideas, which were increasingly being articulated in this period, seldom made their way into policy;[7] by the 1930s, British imperialism had acquired fairly rigid default settings, and the elaborate and ceremonial procedures of British rule made change an extremely difficult process.[8] (The idea of a 'ceremonial', as applied to the more mundane processes of bureaucratic work, also has echoes in psychoanalytic usage, which sees the construction of a ceremonial as a psychological mechanism of avoiding addressing uncomfortable realities by the repetitive and ritualized performance of certain practices.) If these new ideas managed to get to the stage of stated policy, their implementation was doubtful. Nevertheless, in being discussed, they brought to the forefront the difficulties in sustaining a justification of imperialism based on 'good government', both to imperial administrators and their nationalist opponents.

By the 1940s, when the first extensive discussions on development plans for India were held under the auspices of the government, realistic thinkers in Britain accepted that India might well be lost to the Empire— or, from another point of view, was 'ripe for self-government'.[9] These discussions were entwined with the practical situation of wartime needs, ensuring that the government emerged from the War running a severely controlled economy, with rationing of food and cloth, requisitioning of shipping and other transport, controlling factories and making decisions regarding production towards the War effort forming part of its necessary duties; with the urgent need for post-War reconstruction as a policy to prevent large-scale unrest due to unemployment or excessive inflation; and as part of the general campaign during the War to advertise the British government's good intentions for India;[10] these also linking up after the War with schemes to bolster Britain's weakened economic position.[11]

The rhetoric of benevolence notwithstanding, the framework of the Empire imposed a straitjacket on creative thinking on political economy issues, as on other issues not directly affecting its administration; and in part the rhetoric itself can be seen as detrimental to such thinking, for it was also the basis for the claim that the government had always acted for the best in economic matters, had always had a constructive policy and, therefore, did not need to do much more. This is not to say that the government had nothing to say on the problems which clearly stared everyone in the face in India; but there was a particularly narrow range available for the play of ideas, and those outside this range would be met with hostility or suppressed.

Two things follow from this. The first is that the government often appeared to those outside it as a largely consistent body of ideas and policies operating in the service of Britain—a view held by Indian nationalists—because dissenting voices within it would either be suppressed or confined within the civilized bounds of committee rooms and filing cabinets, not reaching the outside world. (At any rate, among anti-imperialists or nationalists it was not considered particularly useful to make distinctions among kinds of imperialism.) The other is that creative thinking by officials of the government, even views perfectly compatible with imperialism, would have to be sustained only on the fringes of a rather dogmatic imperial administration, among those not directly concerned with the higher imperatives of imperial balancing of accounts.

Nevertheless, the uncertainty and increasing lack of confidence felt by the colonial government in India from the 1920s, both in 'political' matters and in economic matters, provided more space, even within the homogenized territory of official discourse, for dissenting voices to be heard. Although certain methods and practices based on existing principles continued to be followed (partly due to administrative inertia, but largely due to imperial constraints such as the need for 'sound finance'), the reassessment of the role of colonialism, past, present, and future, and the questioning of principles which went with it, also saw the emergence of a strand of thought which could be quite critical of the previous record of British colonial rule, and determined to make amends in some way before the inevitable end of the Empire.[12] Yet even in the throes of self-doubt, British officials and private citizens in India would acknowledge mistakes, occasional brutality, and even malicious intent on the part of certain officials but assert that, on the whole, British rule had brought benefits to India. Some were able to appropriate Karl Marx's assertion that imperialism had had an inadvertently progressive effect in dragging India into the modern world—the only question now was to complete the job successfully.[13] Like nasty medicine, colonial rule had done some good, although nasty medicine need not be taken for its own sake after it had done its job. Hence, the increasing liberal-left belief in the 1940s that Britain had finished her work in India and should go home—this was, of course, assisted by the extreme difficulties of staying on.

It will be useful at this point to provide certain caveats which might seem self-evident to many, but which need to be placed in the foreground, since they will, in many instances, be refered to later in the text. The dangers of focusing on the 'official mind', especially given that it is often difficult to identify among contending voices within official circles which one of them may be considered the best representative of the 'official mind', have already been pointed out. And although, viewed from the outside, various strands of imperial thought may have tended towards justifying similar approaches or breeding the same sort of practical consequences (there is a practical logic of imperialism which is above the good intentions of the occasional imperial official), for the purpose of an analysis of the ways in which claims to legitimate action were made, the differences are indeed significant. Thus, it is not particularly useful to see the Empire as one consistent and systematically worked out conspiracy. However, nor was it a system which was not a system, a system with a rationale which was inadvertently worked out, or not worked out at all, merely having evolved accidentally in a certain way. There were a number of clearly articulated and supposedly systematic principles on which the Indian, under the British Empire, was governed. These always admitted of exceptions when Realpolitik was at stake but, nonetheless, remained the ostensible basis of policy. When called upon to justify its actions, it was these principles which were resorted to as explanations by the government.

Which brings us to the next point: there were several layers of imperial governance. Lower levels were often not 'in the know' regarding the wider perspectives involved in governing India, though with experience some might guess at a number of them. At the top of the ladder, the India Office had different immediate priorities and pressures—responsibility to Parliament and fitting into the overall governance and electoral perspectives of the British political scene—from those of the Government of India, who had to be somewhat responsive to political pressures in India—certainly from the 1920s with provincial governments and transferred subjects, and the too regular resort to the state's coercive apparatus beginning to be considered politically unwise. This was even more so with the coming of provincial autonomy with the 1935 Act and Indian ministerial government in the provinces from 1937. Provincial governors had their own pressures to balance; and this involved a level of bargaining with the viceroy who might take his council into confidence, and/or, in more important cases, make out a case to the secretary of state for India at the India Office. He, in turn, might be involved in a lengthy bargaining process with the cabinet regarding Party or 'national' interests, those of various manufacturing lobbies such as Lancashire, or the interests of the City, championed by the Bank of England, whose Governor, Montagu Norman, was an influential figure at the India Office.[14]

These were the higher levels at which hard bargaining and often blatantly cynical measures could be sanctioned and approved, as long as some justification could be found to present them to the various audiences or interests to whom they had to be justified—because the government in Britain and, to a lesser extent, in the colonies, was supposed to be amenable to public opinion and, consequently, had to manage its publicity as best it could.[15] In the colonial context, 'public opinion' was effectively more narrowly defined: the electorate was narrower, based on a property franchise, and various legal and semi-legal measures of overriding public dissent—viceregal certification of laws not passed by the central legislature and various useful coercive laws for policing—existed.[16]

It is at the lower levels that the justification for imperialism was so important. The 'man on the spot', the local civilian or district officer, saw himself as tremendously important in knowing the true picture, and often derided the central bureaucracy (who were taken into confidence regarding wider imperial perspectives), the government at Delhi (or Simla), and the India Office at home for their inadequate reading of the situation at hand. (This did not imply that the picture provided by the 'man on the spot' took into account a wider 'public opinion' unless he feared unrest or disruption of law and order—after all, he was the 'expert' who knew what was good for 'his' peasant or district.) The central bureaucracy in their turn valorized their closeness to India and their knowledge of the country, as against the India Office or members of the government appointed after experience at home or in other colonies or Dominions. There was also a divergence in perspectives between the ICS man at the Secretariat and the 'man on the spot' who thought the former was too rigid in insisting on existing principles and precedents being followed. This was especially true of the occasional ICS man who devoted a career, and often a lifetime, to being an 'expert' on a particular aspect of India; these men were prone to be particularly difficult by challenging the well-worn attitudes of government to the work they did.[17] ('Knowing India', in these terms, nonetheless, remained a matter for discussion among British officials; there was a marked distance between these discussions and those of Indians, and it was seldom that a British discussion on India did more than appropriate an Indian voice. Indians were not meant to be active agents in discussing their future: they remained 'native informants', whose opinions were to be recast in terms of British concerns.)

In such a political scenario, the ostensible adherence to principles was not merely important in terms of the outside observer (the Empire had to be seen to be operating on the basis of some transparent principles, its violence and brutality could not be paraded before everyone and had to be held in reserve); it was also necessary that the Civilian, an integral part of the intimate details of local administration, believed in his job; and if he saw the violence and brutality, he could regard them as exceptions. The system of self-justification which the Civilians brought to bear upon their work leaned hard on the mythologies of the Empire. Nonetheless, it was sometimes possible to make an argument against the rigid insistence on precedents which characterized imperial government, through an appeal to higher principles derived from the same mythologies of the Empire.

There were, of course, Indians in the imperial administration itself; but they were peripheral to these debates about the restructuring of imperialism. Debates between an Indian imperial administrator and a European imperial administrator on the terms of legitimacy or the goals of imperialism do not appear to exist in the written record. This does not, of course, mean that there were never any such debates, though it does seem that they were not regarded as important enough, and would certainly not have been conducted on terms of equality. The race factor to the internal equations among imperial officials has not been directly dealt with in the existing literature. In the official apparatus of government, Indians were seen as disruptive to the system, Indian ministers or ICS men were considered corrupt and inefficient, and not considered true participants in the internal debate on the best way to govern India. There are numerous instances of claims that Indians were unfit to govern themselves; this took the form, within the ICS, of European complaints that there had been a degeneration in the quality of administration proportional to the rise in numbers of Indians in it. It was also characteristic of (possibly self-interested) arguments made by some European members of the Service that complaints against inefficiency, nepotism, or corruption on the part of particular Indians were generalized to support the contention that all Indians could not be trusted, especially not in the ICS.[18] On the other hand, there are instances of Indian ICS men (the self-justification for whose participation in the imperial experience has also not yet been properly studied) as participants in the system often being compelled to go by the book even more than their European counterparts, being in a somewhat ambiguous position in an essentially racially difficult environment. There was a need for them to establish to their British colleagues and superiors, if not loyalty, at least efficiency within the given system. If the ICS were 'guardians' of India, the white men in the ICS were the guardians of the brown men in the ICS, in a hierarchical system of guardianship.[19] This feeling had apparently been internalized by a number of Indian civilians.[20] From the Indians' point of view, being in the ICS epitomized the difficulties of operating in a discriminatory environment, in what might usefully be called a participation/dissent paradox. Success in entering the ICS was seen by Indians as a triumph in the face of major obstacles, and a positive blow struck for the cause of nationalism. At the same time, by becoming a member of the ICS, an Indian became a party to, and an agent of, imperialism, complicit in the system, and in danger of being seen—by others and, to an extent, by himself—as a 'collaborator'.

The 1930s: Aberrations and Default Settings

The few attempted innovations of approach within government circles which have caught the attention of historians were justified internally within imperial circles in terms of certain principles, and externally in terms of these principles modified for wider consumption. This was part of a dual search for legitimacy at home in Britain as well as in India for the running of the Empire. However, on closer reading they are not as innovative as they might have seemed.

Sir George Schuster came to India with some colonial experience in the Sudan and East Africa, and as a self-confessed Liberal among Conservative and Labour men with friends among Labour's political and economic advisers.[21] He called for more active intervention in the Indian economy on the part of the government, to which end he initiated discussions within the Government of India on the possibility of economic planning for India.[22] On the main contentious issues of Indian economic administration, he often tended towards—in private—views seen as 'nationalist'.[23] Being overruled in these efforts, Schuster, like a good soldier, brought the Government of India through the worst of the Depression period with orthodox balanced budgets.[24] Schuster's India years are an excellent example of the structural constraints of imperial sound finance reclaiming a dissenter and forcing him back upon the right path.

Despite the problems he faced, however, Schuster's approach to Indian economic problems did not imply a lack of commitment to the Empire. Schuster made this explicit for a British audience in the pages of the *Economist* in 1934, and before the Royal Society of Arts in 1935.[25] Planning India's economy was also part of a wider process of reconciliation of British and Indian business interests, and 'rationalisation of economic effort throughout a group like the British Commonwealth'.[26] Especially aware of the debates surrounding imperial preference,[27] he pleaded for a recognition of 'the value to the Empire countries of the United Kingdom market', which was, despite the Depression, relatively stable.[28] In advancing these opinions Schuster the Liberal and suspected Keynesian was not particularly far away from Leo Amery the Conservative, who was advocating work towards similar ends,[29] though Schuster's methods may have been slightly different. The complementarity of colonial development and imperial preference had already been outlined to the British public; and the old industrial capitalism of textiles and steel was being sacrificed for newer industries organized within the Federation of British Industry and the finance capitalist interests of the City.[30] As far as India was concerned, Schuster believed, there would continue to be 'a mass of manufactures which India cannot possibly manufacture herself and for which, with increasing prosperity, the demand will grow'. He hoped for a 'complementary plan' which would involve cooperation of Indian and British interests. Schuster believed that the rise of some Indian industries, which had resulted in the reduction of her cotton and iron and steel imports from Britain, was acceptable; but he saw great 'possibilities of future development in India and of the trade which more highly industrialized countries may have with her'.[31]

Within Schuster's rationalizing scheme, therefore, India's place was to be defined in terms of widely held British views of what India ought to be: these shibboleths, which a British public both within and outside government circles had come to recognize easily and to relate to strongly, were extremely useful as bases upon which to build a new argument. To Schuster, a 'balanced' Indian economy was, and should remain, basically agricultural—a contention which he knew would be completely unobjectionable to his audience. Agriculture was, however, he argued, to be 'supplemented by moderate-sized industrial establishments on a sufficient scale to provide a sound commercial basis, but set down away from large towns so that the workers could still keep in touch with the land'. He was sceptical about the wisdom of large urban concentrations and industrialization, especially as the consumer would still pay more for his goods than if they had been imported:

Can it be said that the 180,000 additional workers in the cotton mills are happier or are even performing a higher human function than they would have been if working in the fields? On the economic plane, has it paid? The consumers of cotton goods are certainly not getting these cheaper....[32]

This claim to his argument working 'on the economic plane' seems to be separate from what in the previous sentence sounds like a philosophical and ethical question: 'happiness' and 'higher human functions'. He went on to remark that he had 'great sympathy with some of Mr Ghandi's [sic] economic ideas': India, differing as it does from the advanced industrial powers, and less materialistic in temperament,[33] should not aspire to advanced levels of industrialization. though he did not wish to go as far as Gandhi in denouncing all urbanization and modern industry.[34]

The economic parameters claimed by Schuster's argument were well within the framework of a liberal world view of maintaining the 'international division of labour'. This was, however, not cited by Schuster, since he framed his appeal on the basis of the need to abandon laissez-faire—the latter principle traditionally having gone with the former—and the need for the adoption of a more interventionist government where economic matters were concerned. He attempted to persuade his audience of this on the basis of consistency with the general principles claimed for British imperialism, which he claimed overrode the commitment to laissez-faire. One of these was that of the British responsibility to provide the conditions of progress in the colonies; he began from the general premise that '[t]he general standard of living in India falls so far below the minimum that there can be no question that it is the duty of any Government in India to strive to raise it'.[35] This duty was made more urgent by the fact that in part the current situation was a British creation; he admitted that 'the more a country has been dependent on foreign markets, the more acutely has it felt the depression and the slower is its recovery proving'—and that India, of all the empire countries, had relied most on foreign markets.[36] As 'part of a world organism', she was 'vulnerable to changes in the rest of the world over which she has no control'; but she could not detach herself 'without a serious economic disaster to masses of her people'.[37] Consequently, however, moves towards economic self-sufficiency (as advocated by nationalists) were not the solution to her problems; the solution had to be sought at a wider level, through an attempt at a more rational worldwide consumption pattern, in which poor people and poor countries could increase their levels of consumption.[38] This could only be achieved by careful planning; which, he argued, was not incompatible with the principles of private enterprise which laissez-faire had stood for.[39]

Effectively, Schuster was arguing before an audience accustomed to regarding the older conventional imperialist arguments as axiomatic, at two levels: that of mutual self-interest, in which he argued that Indian economic 'development', if contained within certain parameters, was not damaging to British interests and was, in fact, mutually beneficial; and that of *principles*, both moral and material: the moral responsibility of British imperialism to look after the material progress of India; the protection of India from the vicissitudes of the world market to which Britain had attached her; the overriding of laissez-faire as a guiding principle in consideration of the former two imperatives; but at the same time the need to protect India from the evils of excessive industrialization. Despite the selective appropriation of Gandhi's arguments—Schuster was anti-'excessive' industrialization but not, as a consequence, pro-self-sufficiency—the basic premise of Britain's right (or duty) to decide the course of India's moral and material future remained unchallenged in these arguments, in consonance with the unchallenged existence of that assumption for his audience. It also needs to be remembered that Schuster's arguments were linking up with debates and strands of ideas related to tariffs, imperial preference, and market-sharing which were beginning to be earnestly discussed in Britain in the 1930s and, therefore, with an already-created audience awareness.[40]

The significance of Schuster's years in the Government of India—and in his subsequent interventions in debates on matters related to India in his capacity as a senior India hand—lay in his ability to think beyond the confines of official policy, in his recognition of the need to rethink imperial economics, and in his forcing government officials, albeit momentarily, to do the same. However, although it was apparent by the 1930s that the economic assumptions of a more stable capitalist economic order needed to be reassessed, such reassessment was only reluctantly undertaken, and certainly did not include the right of a colony to reassess long-standing assumptions, even with a British administrator speaking on its behalf. In 1930 Schuster phrased his appeal for government intervention in the economy to his fellow members of the Government of India in a polite proposal which suggested, among other things, the setting up of an economic advisory council for India along the lines of the British Economic Advisory Council established by the Labour Government in January of that year.[41] Schuster's own account of the proposals is contained in his 'Note on Economic Policy'.[42] As far as policy matters are concerned it is insignificant;[43] it is insignificant even as a precedent, for it seems to have been quietly buried: not a whisper of Schuster's 1930s' ideas on planning were extricated in the 1940s' discussions on post-War development when large numbers of old paper schemes and reports were being unearthed and pasted together by both the centre and the provinces to constitute 'post-war reconstruction and development'.[44]

In his Note, Schuster argued that there was a need for the better coordination of the various government departments involved in economic matters, and also a need for contact between official and non-official opinion. The third and most important requirement was:

the creation of an intelligent public opinion on economic questions. it is of course too much to hope that the whole 'public' will become instructed but at present it is hardly too much to say that all economic discussion in India is conducted, not with scientific accuracy on the basis of reliable statistics and impartial evidence but in an atmosphere of political bias, pre-conceived ideas, and loose statements.

Schuster related this to nationalist propaganda on economic matters, which he felt was wrong and could, therefore, be disarmed by educating 'public opinion'—or, at least, a crucial part of it—in true economics.[45]

What was required was a constructive economic policy on the part of the government and a greater unofficial say in its framing—he acknowledged the legitimacy of this especially in the light of the Great War having 'upset the ordinary processes of economic life and created forces and oscillations of an unprecedented kind which have forced Governments to intervene and give a lead to the concerted national effort which is required to cope with these conditions'. Consequently, governments in all countries were seeking advice on policy from 'expert economists and fact-finding commissions'—Australia, Hoover's USA, and Weimar Germany. There was also 'much to be learnt from Japan to whose example India always looks'. The 'most energetic national plans' were, however, being undertaken by the two 'forms of despotism' represented by Italy and Russia.

The case of Russia perhaps merits special consideration because there is said now to be a tendency for the 'advanced' youth of India to look more and more to Russia as an example and a guide. Just for this reason alone it may be worth while to consider what is happening in that country....[46]

Along with his Note, therefore, Schuster appended a review by Maurice Dobb from the *Spectator*, from which he quoted at length.[47] Though Schuster distanced himself from the advocacy of 'the methods of Mussolini or the Soviet Government' and remained sceptical about the possibility of the success of 'the Russian programme', he felt it was interesting because (and here he agreed with Dobb), 'in the words of the review, "They represent an attempt to carry out the industrialisation of an *agrarian semi-Asiatic* country at an unprecedented speed, and for the first time in history to do so ... on the basis of centralised control and

planning and of approximate economic equality ...'".[48] This represented
the beginnings, on the part of British Indian officials, of a curious
engagement with the Soviet Union regarding matters of economic uplift
and social reform—an engagement which was able to coexist with a deep
mistrust and intense paranoia regarding communism and urban or rural
labour unrest.[49]

Behind the failure of Schuster's conception of an accommodating
imperialism to get a significant hearing in government circles lay a strong
conception of what was acceptable in terms of political economy. It was
these default settings which dominated the government for the most part.
Sir James Grigg, Liberal sympathizer and Schuster's successor, brought an
explicitly Treasury and Bank of England approach to India, having
previously served as Principal Private Secretary to successive Chancellors
of the exchequer from 1921 to 1930. Grigg's rigid views made him almost
a caricature of the sound financier; when Philip Snowden wrote to him
about having joined Lloyd George's unemployment campaign,[50] he
expressed his misgivings and asked to know the reasons for Snowden's
'conversion'; he conceded that 'in England where they have a reputation
for common sense and stability, large expenditure on public works would
not do much harm', but

I am still a firm believer in individualism and my experience in India has
confirmed my view that there is no real hope for the world until it gets back much
more nearly to Free Trade, but now it looks as if even you have deserted....[51]

Snowden denied this charge in his reply: 'I am still an unrepentant Free
Trader, only more so'; his support to Lloyd George was only provisional,
though he did feel that money being cheap but the confidence to invest
being lacking, '[t]his is the opportunity for the State to be enterprising
and to do things which need to be done'.[52] In subsequent correspondence
between Grigg and Snowden, both complained that the trade situation had
not improved and that tariffs did not work. Grigg's correspondence with
Montagu Norman in 1934 was marked by the shared assumption, as they
commented on the New Deal, Nazi Germany, and Australia's handling of
the world crisis, that none of this would work; this was accompanied by
the occasional dig at Keynes and the Keynesians.[53]

Grigg's personal crusade was against the 'particularly virulent form of
economic nationalism' that existed in India; on the hopeful side, he
reported 'faint glimmerings of a recognition that economic nationalism is
only a device for big employers to exploit their workmen, the consumers
and the taxpayer generally'.[54] He detested businessmen more than he

detested the Congress. Nehru was 'an academic but fanatical revolutionary'; others in the Congress were 'merely the jackals of big business and most people think that Gandhi is really a prisoner of these'. Businessmen in India had a 'habit of posing as the people of India and getting higher protection as a result'. Nehru's current ascendancy, he noted, had frightened the 'jackals' to say to Zetland and Linlithgow that 'they want to be reconciled to the British and that Gandhi is the only possible instrument for effecting this reconciliation'. This was not only 'from the point of view of checking communism'. These 'buccaneers of business' knew that the 'reappearance of Gandhi again in any active form would mean that the markets would be hopping about like mad and so they would be able to make enormous speculative profits'.[55]

This sometimes rather perceptive reading of the internal workings of Congress politics coexisted quite happily with his imperialism. While apparently accepting a left critique of the Congress and of Indian politics, Grigg was able to leave the British government out of it. He also discovered a stronger imperialist self in India.

Do you remember once saying to me at the Hague that whenever you saw the Union Jack in a foreign country, you invariably became extremely Imperialistic[?] Well, I am undergoing something of the same process; I am not becoming Imperialistic in the rather vulgar sense of the word but I am firmly convinced that India's destiny is inextricably mixed up with ours and that it is essential that we should make it clear that there is no question of our being kicked out.[56]

His views on 'development' were expressed in a letter to the Chancellor of the Exchequer, Neville Chamberlain, soon after his arrival in India, in the nature of a full report to enlighten Chamberlain about the real situation in India. This letter was a reinforcement of the standard perspectives of British Indian administration; but, forcefully put in Grigg's inimitable style, made explicit the older imperial attitudes which the Indian administration was trying its best to underplay in order to create an atmosphere conducive to political peace.

... India is the most desperately poor and inefficient and backward country you can imagine. The representative Indian is not to be found among the few tens of thousands of noisy politicians, journalists, stock exchange gamblers and clerks; he is an almost naked creature clad in a loin cloth and an umbrella who squats about among his crops by day and breeds like a rabbit by night. And in my view we have for years neglected the second class for the first. It is quite true that we have removed from the peasant the fear of famine and murder but what with his entire neglect of Malthusian teaching and the slump in agricultural prices his economic position is if anything worsened. As an antidote to the misfortunes of the cultivator we have played up to the idea of a rapid industrialisation of India by means of stupendously high duties but the effects haven't been too happy. The prices to the consumer have been grotesquely high (and the consumer is the peasant plus the European), import trade has been cut down enormously and (though you won't agree with this) the ability of the agriculurist [sic] to export still further reduced while except in the case of steel the enterprise and uprightness of the industrialist have been insufficient to enable the new industries to become established securely. Thus we have pleased nobody not even the industrialist or the politician to whom we have been playing up. The last named is a queer creature mainly because his own mind reflects the incurable divisions (racial as well as religious) of India. At the moment he hates England or, if he doesn't he finds it necessary to say that he does. At the same time he is afraid of her and is afraid that he can't do without her. His pride demands power or at any rate office while his conscience or rather his historical sense tells him he is unfit for it.[57]

Grigg did not see any easy solutions to this last problem. He felt that it could ideally have been solved by giving Indians, as a placebo, the trappings but not the substance of power; hopefully, after a few years of 'office and prestige and emoluments' they would recognize that they were not governing very well and would 'lean more and more on Englishmen', who would however 'have to stay in the background'.

Of course if we go back to the Company days there would be a very obvious solution to all this viz. give the Indian all the pride and pomp of power and retain the reality ourselves. But after nearly a hundred years of domination by the heaven-born it is not too easy to go back to being merely the power behind the throne.[58]

This brought Grigg to another of his favourite complaints, that against the 'heaven-born' ICS, who he felt should stay out of the process of governing at the centre although 'good in his district'. As far as the ICS was concerned, Grigg was pleased to use Indian ammunition against them: 'a bureaucracy not amenable to popular control has become arrogant'; it was not efficient either, so 'the Indian has his grievances on the score of competence as well as arrogance'.[59] Grigg was willing to leave the civilian his sphere of influence in the districts, where he could continue to do his good work, while Grigg and his colleagues looked after the wider priorities of empire.

This was, however, more an argument about jurisdiction than a disagreement on principles: most Civilians in India, especially those at the local level, shared with Grigg—and the socialists—a dislike of capitalists, especially greasy, comprador, sycophantic Indian capitalists, but often from a different perspective to that of the socialists. The Civilian, if not by birth a gentleman, became one through his normally-public-school-and-Oxbridge training and the company and social graces he had to keep and acquire respectively when in European society in India. Such training had not yet a very easy acceptance of people who had risen from trade (which Indian capitalists certainly had, in the quite recent and measurable past); by contrast, British businessmen whom the Civilian met were, by the 1920s and 1930s, educated at the same institutions as the Civilians, polished, rich, and with a knighthood, baronetcy, or even an earldom to their name—a far cry from the crude freebooters of the early days of the Company, whom the Civilian could, at a pinch, easily bring himself to despise as ignoble characters who looted poor innocent natives, until a wiser and better English imperialism rescued them. Grigg shared this background himself; he had plebeian origins and had had to acquire his gentleman's status; as a Liberal he had a self-image of himself as a left-winger, though a 'moderate' one.[60]

Grigg was also a racist. Racism was not uncommon among the British in India in the 1930s, either as explicit hatred or as more gentle prejudices against Indians, justified in terms of national character, incompetence, corruption, and so on. It was, however, a characteristic both of the administration and of the individuals in the administration, which could not be admitted in public. Grigg did not apparently believe in these rules of silence; he quite unselfconsciously (though privately) attributed his colleague Sir Joseph Bhore's support for a 'madly protectionist fiscal policy' to his 'mixed marriage and the parti-coloured results of it'. Grigg saw Bhore as a 'nationalist' and a co-conspirator of '[Sir Homy] Mody & Co'.[61]

The unabashed imperialism of Grigg could at times be embarrassing to other imperial administrators who were not quite so comfortable with imperialism. Lord Lothian, who had headed the Indian Franchise Commission, and with whom Grigg had shared some of his thoughts on Congress,[62] agreed that the Congress–big business nexus was corrupt; but

....in the long run the battle with financial privilege can only be fought by Indians themselves. The Marxist criticism that the British power in fact is the principal support of landlordism, the Princes, predatory finance etc., has a considerable measure of truth in it. While we can protect Indians against certain obvious forms of administrative corruption so long as we have real power, but Indians themselves, like Nehru, can alone tackle the fundamental vested interests.[63]

This was, of course, 'in the long run'; the timetable for that run was to be set by the British. It was not before the Second World War that the time frame began to look more concrete.

Conceptions of economics thus appeared in such arguments as inseparably entangled with views regarding the necessity of imperialism even as they selectively engaged with aspects of socialist, nationalist, or Gandhian arguments appropriable within the framework of imperialism. Yet it was important to maintain the language of economics in presenting the government's position. This was provided from 1938 by the new office of Economic Adviser to the Government of India, in the person of Theodore Gregory. Gregory, as a former academic, put the Government of India's arguments into respectable academic language; an alumnus of the London School of Economics, he taught there from 1913 as assistant lecturer, and was Cassel Professor of Economics at the University of London from 1927 to 1937. The creation of his post was an indirect result of Schuster's initiatives in the early 1930s.[64] The appointment of Gregory, a conservative neo-classical economist, to the post, suited Grigg, the then Finance Member, who placed Gregory at the forefront of his campaign to convince his colleagues of the wisdom of ignoring Indian nationalist demands on economic matters. Logically, among Gregory's first efforts at writing official memoranda were papers on the demand for industries and the tariff question. These attempted to articulate and justify government policy in the economist's terms—rather than making a case for new policy, they aimed either at justifying existing practice, or at calling a halt to concessions made already—until the War changed the equations.

Industries were demanded in India, Gregory wrote, 'whether it be for purposes of self-protection, of "economic balance", of coping with a growing population or of mere self-esteem'.[65] But were such industries really necessary? He phrased the question as:

Given that diversification of occupation is desirable, is there any reason to suppose that in the absence of state-aid, such diversification is impossible in any country where the theory of comparative costs indicates that in the international division of labour, the production of agricultural products yields the greater gain?[66]

This was a resort to Ricardo within a standard imperialist argument, phrased in the language of laissez-faire which, it may be recalled, government spokesmen had explicitly repudiated.[67] Gregory went on to argue that agriculture did, in fact, breed some secondary occupations— agricultural implements 'must be made and kept in repair', motor transport and railway transport is required, and this breeds the need for repairs:

railway workers, road builders, dock workers, drivers of vehicles, canal builders, 'commercial and technological organisation'.[68] Regarding competition for Indian industries, he wrote:

Some marginal competition no doubt exists: "foreign" coastal lines may divert traffic which might otherwise have been carried on interior railways or roads, for instance. But it is obvious that transport and communications facilities of all kinds have to be constructed, worked and maintained in full repair *on the spot* ... The same applies to the "commercial" activities involved in agricultural production. Thus by far the larger part of the indirect activity generated by agriculture is incapable of being replaced by foreign products. It follows that it is simply not true to suppose that secondary industries cannot exist without state-aid being afforded by tariff or subsidy or both.[69]

This somewhat peculiar argument amounted to the fact that India did not really need further industries not directly stimulated by and serving agriculture, so India did not need tariffs or state aid. Gregory, however, admitted that this argument did not 'dispose of the whole problem of how to provide adequate employment for a growing population' or 'deal with the assumed necessity of providing state-aid for the purpose of establishing *particular* industries in India'. Nor, he argued, was it intended to do so. His intention was 'to dispose of a particular intellectual complex—the fear that without state-aid there would be no ancillary employment at all, or only ancillary employment of a negligible amount in a predominantly agricultural country'.[70]

It was strange that Gregory should find it worthwhile to challenge the principles of state-aid and tariffs which, by 1938, had long been accepted. This can only be seen as part of Grigg's counter-nationalist economic propaganda. Grigg wrote that he had read the note 'with much interest'.[71] The attack was carried further in the first of a new series of publications issued by the Office of the Economic Adviser in 1939, concentrating on the impact of tariffs on revenues and the import trade.[72] The study, generally free from polemics, corroborated Grigg's contention that the burden of the tariff had risen to a level at which, in revenue terms, diminishing returns had come into play. It argued, therefore, that the duties imposed on goods such as cotton piecegoods, sugar, iron and steel, and matches, were protective duties, not revenue duties: imports had fallen enormously in value as a result of the tariffs imposed, as had, consequently, the duties collected. In general, imports of consumer goods had fallen substantially both in relation to imports and in terms of contribution to import duties, imports of raw materials and capital goods had become more important, and luxuries had remained stable.[73] The absolute figures, and the figures for Indo-British trade, were not highlighted. The sub-text to this argument was that British–Indian tariff policy had been, if anything, too successful. The tone of Gregory's notes and writings changed substantially in the 1940s; he was far more uncertain as to how to position government policy as the changes in the British–Indian economic relationship brought about by the Second World War began to manifest themselves.

Post-War Reconstruction and Development

My concern with the conceptualization of post-War reconstruction and development does not deal with the intrinsic qualities and viability of the various projects themselves, nor on their actual implementation, or rather lack of it, for most of the schemes arising in this period remained elaborate paperwork. A bureaucrat acting according to a specific brief produces work according to that brief; accordingly, in the best traditions of the ICS, a good deal of detailed and dedicated work went into the plans.[74] Many of these schemes were produced by Indian bureaucrats who shared at least some of the enthusiasm of the 'nationalists' for the project of planning; and the mythology of 'good government' had its share of sincere adherents among British officials and bureaucrats. What I am mainly concerned with is the changing assumptions regarding India, her character and her future which were reflected in the elaborate discussions surrounding post-war reconstruction planning in India.

Post-War reconstruction and development, as it was called, was an exercise in forward thinking which was expected of governments during the War. Such forward thinking was initiated in Britain from 1939, taking concrete form with the publication of the Beveridge Report in November 1942.[75] The Government of India began its own efforts in this direction by 1941.[76] This was 'an abortive start, brought to an end by Japanese aggression', and it was not until August 1943 that the Reconstruction Committee was reconstituted, thereafter becoming the Planning and Development Department in August 1944.[77] Meanwhile, the process of thinking about post-war economic matters for India had become inextricably entangled with politics in London and general anxieties about the possible weakness of Britain's own post-war situation, especially in relation to the accumulation of the sterling balances.

Anxiety regarding the growing British indebtedness to India, a reversal of the pre-war situation, gradually built up as the war went on. In March

1942, Chancellor of the Exchequer, Kingsley Wood, pointed out that the original estimates of the relative expense for Indian defence to be borne by the British government had shown striking increases since the war began; at the present rate of sterling balances' accumulation, Britain would be unable to convert them into gold, dollars, or other currency except very gradually. Consequently, they would have to be blocked, and 'we shall be told that the City of London is obtaining a forced loan from the impoverished Indians or we shall be accused of defaulting on our debt to India. This would be most dangerous politically'.[78] The War Cabinet, led by Winston Churchill, set about trying to secure a readjustment of the War Financial Settlement in Britain's favour. Secretary of State, Leo Amery, recognizing the political dangers of such a step, pointed out that India's own defence expenditure had also risen substantially with the entry of Japan into the war, and emphasized the fact that a large proportion of the sterling balances were accumulated due to expenses on munitions and other supplies unconnected with the defence of India as such.[79] Viceroy-designate Lord Wavell, added that, in fact, during the first years of the war, it was India who had defended British interests in the Middle East.[80] Nonetheless, options in this regard were kept open, though it was agreed that the question should be temporarily buried.

As these discussions went on, the framework of a possible solution began to emerge gradually. It was suggested that the sterling balances could be considered a source of export earnings after the war.[81] Amery wholeheartedly backed these proposals, even suggesting that the sterling balances could turn out to be 'more ... a blessing than a danger'[82]—a suggestion which prompted Keynes at the Treasury to describe him as a 'dangerous lunatic'.[83] This line of argument gradually began to link up with another, apparently contradictory, scheme—the idea of initiating a social and economic reforms policy in India to divert political criticism from the government and to wean the masses away from Indian political parties.

In May 1942, Amery, in a speculative mood, wrote to Linlithgow:

The current Congress charge, voiced by Nehru, that our administration is incompetent, is no doubt untrue judged by the test of what a Congress Government would do setting itself to the same task. But what if a Congress Government, like the Soviet Government, set itself to much bigger and bolder tasks regardless of conventional financial restraints as to what is possible and not possible? And what if we ourselves during the interval, which may well be one of years, between the war and Indian Self-Government, set ourselves in the same spirit to a complete overhaul of India's national life? ... Might it not be our duty after the war to put ourselves in the position of a bold, far-sighted and benevolent despot, determined in a few years, in a series of five-year plans, to raise India's millions to a new level of physical well-being and efficiency?[84]

Such ideas had been considered at other levels as well. In the general concern connected with getting India to contribute wholeheartedly to the war effort, many former India hands believed that in addition to a clear promise of Dominion status, accompanied by a concrete date, some sort of economic placebo might help rally Indian opinion. In late 1941, Schuster, speaking in London at a meeting of the East India Association in connection with the publication of his new book, *India and Democracy*, advised the British government to '.... go on trying to get representative Indians to come in and join the task of government, men who could go about the country and make speeches, pointing out to the Indian people that this war, although it is a terrible disaster, is also a vast opportunity— an opportunity for India to accomplish something like an industrial revolution, to develop her industries and thus to fulfil dreams which many people in India have long cherished'.[85]

Earlier, in January 1940, Sir Malcolm Darling, then a senior civilian on the threshhold of retirement, had written of 'the almost incurable suspicion which the intelligentsia have of our intentions', and proposed that an indication of British good intentions would have to include the appointment of Indians to high positions in the administration of war activities, or as aides-de-camp (ADCs) to governors, and possibly to provide an Indian a governorship of 'one of the smaller provinces'. In addition, while the Congress remained 'in the wilderness' (the Congress provincial ministries had resigned in 1939 in protest against the Viceroy's declaration of war on behalf of India without consulting Indian opinion), it was necessary to '....take full advantage of the reins of government being in our hands again to go all out for the betterment of the underdog, especially the villager. If, as is possible, this situation continues for a year or two, it is an opportunity to prove to all concerned that we are as much for his interests as any Congress Government. Our motives on this point have been questioned, not without reason. Let there be no doubt about them now, and Congress in their passionate though uninstructed desire to do what they could for the underdog has given us a lead which, with our greater experience of administration, we should be able not merely to follow but to better'.[86]

On his return to England, Darling made similar suggestions to Amery, Secretary of State for India, which he repeated periodically.[87] These suggestions, initially not taken very seriously, seem eventually to have been taken seriously in the crisis situation of 1942.[88] At a cabinet meeting on 24 August 1942, it was decided that in the light of the general disorder in India, attributed to the Congress (the Quit India Movement) and the Japanese, '….urgent attention should be given to the development of a more progressive social and industrial policy in India. Under present conditions discontent with social and industrial conditions was being exploited for political purposes; and this type of exploitation could best be countered by a positive policy for improving those conditions'.[89]

The idea was, however, met with great scepticism. W.D. Croft, Deputy Under Secretary at the India Office, felt that 'India having been self-governing in these respects for some 20 years now, H.M.G. are hardly called upon to obtrude their advice and assistance'.[90] This was not a new argument—from the 1919 Government of India Act onwards, industry and the so-called 'nation-building' departments had been under the provinces, which justified the central government's lack of initiative in matters related to them.[91] 'This is not a time for long-term measures,' he added.[92] Perhaps this was more to the point, as the Cripps Mission had already promised Dominion status after the War, with the right to secession from the Empire thrown in. Sir Atul Chatterjee, Adviser to the Secretary of State for India, also felt that such a move would be seen as encroachment on a field regarded as one of Indian self-government,[93] and Sir Ramaswami Mudaliar, one of the Indian representatives to the War Cabinet, observed that 'it would be resented as a bribe and as a sign of death-bed repentance'— though some steps in such a direction might be taken by the ex-Congress provinces, now ruled under Section 93.[94] Writing home to Linlithgow, Mudaliar reiterated that it would be suggested in India that money so granted was inadequate and 'more ought to be given to make up for all the past "organised loots" of the British Government'.[95] As he had told Bevin, efforts from Britain regarding labour legislation would be construed by Indian businessmen as 'a naive attempt to recapture the lost export markets by pushing up the working costs of [Indian] industry'—this again was an argument that Indian businessmen had been known to use quite strenuously when the colonial government raised the issue of labour conditions or proposed labour legislation. He concluded, 'This is one of the hastily conceived "brilliant" ideas of an intellectual but I am certain it will come to nothing'.[96] The question of finance created further obstacles: proposals to spend more rupees in India, involving further growth of India's sterling balances holdings, would hardly go down well with the Chancellor of the Exchequer. Amery felt that spending money on social reforms could not be a viable policy 'simultaneously with the policy of asking India to refund to us some of her sterling balances'.[97] It would be better to think of some other public relations scheme which involved spending sterling—donations to build mosques for Indian lascars in Britain, or a grant to the School of Oriental and African Studies.[98] On the other hand, economic reforms were quite compatible with the sterling balances problem: they would 'afford to India a very valuable means of raising her whole level of industrial and irrigation plant'[99] and would be 'available for every kind of long-range re-equipment of India, whether for industry, irrigation, railways or other public works. These things would probably do more to raise the standard of living after the war than anything else, and would incidentally dispose of the sterling balances in the shape of orders for capital goods from here, and to that extent help the employment situation during the years of transition from war to peace'.[100] Ernest Bevin, Minister of Labour and National Service in the War Cabinet, agreed that it would be short-sighted of Britain to think of sales of consumer goods to India after the War; it would have to be capital goods, and Britain had to get her act together quickly lest the Americans beat her to it.[101]

Amery's account of the origins of the proposal credits Churchill's 'suggestion that it would really pay us to take up the cause of the poor peasant and confiscate the rich Congressman's lands and divide them up' with starting off discussions on the scheme, after which others, particularly Bevin,[102] chipped in with demands for social reform. But the main initiative seems to have come from Bevin and his Labour colleague Stafford Cripps; its origins notwithstanding, once the idea had been sold to Churchill, it was Cripps, and to a lesser extent Bevin, who were its most enthusiastic supporters.[103]

Expressed as a political move, this began to take the shape of a sort of commitment to social justice. Owing to the opposition it faced and ostensibly anticipating Indian opposition on the grounds that such measures impinged upon provincial autonomy, it was advised that the recommendation should be interpreted in the extremely limited sense of a labour policy. Bevin's main idea was reported to have been that the standard of living and wages of the Indian industrial worker ought to be forced up before she became independent—an idea quite current in Labour circles, which held that the colonies should be given 'socialism' before they could be given independence.[104] The problem was, however, that in India, industrial labour was only a 'microscopic portion' of the population, and standards of living were determined largely by agricultural conditions: the two, therefore, had to be dealt with together.[105]

Amery had, meanwhile, broached the subject somewhat apologetically in a telegram to Linlithgow: 'at a time like this your Government is too fully engaged in repression to think of construction'. Nevertheless, he felt that Linlithgow would 'see positive propaganda advantages and after all it might be a refreshing change from our present activities'.[106] Amery hoped the Whitley Commission recommendations[107] would provide a suitable basis for dealing with the subject.[108] The countryside's needs could be summed up by 'the three words land, nutrition and education'. For industrial workers, 'I imagine that the main consideration is a higher level of wage, and it may well be that the present dearness allowance may be on too low a scale'.[109] But by this time, even officials in the India Office were unconvinced of the value of the Whitley Commission's report, referred to as 'moribund'.[110]

Cripps' Note on the subject had a more radical approach. He raised the proposal that instead of the British government relying for its political viability on negotiations on the basis of community with elite leaders, it should attempt to mobilize popular support, not on the basis of community, but of class. He was not blind to the essentially political purpose of such an initiative; he saw it as 'a good opportunity to rally the mass of Indian Opinion to our side. '...It is most important that the Indian workers and peasants should realise that it is a British initiative which is working for them against their Indian oppressors; this will entail a proper publicity service in India'.[111]

It is not necessary to refuse to credit Cripps with any good intentions for such a move. In order to sell the idea to a cabinet led by so unapologetic an imperialist as Churchill, he could not afford to overemphasize its socially radical content, if that were indeed his intention. He further emphasized that such action would have to be combined with efforts to make the Viceroy's Council 'more representative of the wider class interests of India'. If personnel could not be found to represent 'those communal sections which are prepared to co-operate and also the different class interests', then 'the class constitution should prevail'.[112] Cripps viewed this only as a short-term solution. He emphasized that post-War full Dominion status and 'the inherent right of self-determination' had already been conceded to India; 'the sole question is therefore how can we make India most useful or least embarrassing to the United Nations for the rest of the war'. For the present, such a policy could 'demonstrate to opinion here, in America and in India itself, the determination of the Government to serve the interests of the peoples of India'.[113]

This perspective became increasingly obscured, however, as discussions proceeded. Cripps' approach to the problem was interpreted in different ways as it traversed bureaucratic corridors in a sort of filing-cabinet version of 'Chinese Whispers'. One version described Cripps' purpose thus: 'despairing of creating "agreement" on political issues between the communities, he proposes to substitute for this disagreement a *class war* ' and added that this was 'a rather dangerous policy for the British Gov[ernmen]t to adopt as a means of solving the problems of India's aspirations to nationhood'.[114] A perhaps more 'realist' interpretation was that 'the principal object of the move is to impress Governmental and public opinion in the USA'; in a pessimistic vein it was argued that 'the idea that communal differences will disappear from the political arena if the stage is set for class warfare is both erroneous and mischievous. The latter would be merely superimposed on the former', and it would fail to convince the bulk of Americans.[115]

But the proposals still had to be addressed, not least because the prime minister, an unlikely ally, nudged the discussions forward at crucial stages.[116] Discussions still lingered for some time on the question as to whether community or class was the more relevant category as far as Indian society was concerned. Croft's view was that it was very difficult to say whether various sections of the Indian public were 'defined upon a communal or upon a class basis'. He added that both provincial and central governments had indeed paid some attention to social and economic problems over the years, among other things, through the work of the Royal Commissions on Labour and Agriculture, and claimed that results therefrom would have been even more beneficial but for factors such as the backwardness of education and the rate of population growth.[117]

In late November 1942, a meeting was held at the India Office to discuss issues arising from the proposal. Sir Theodore Gregory, already in charge of post-war reconstruction discussions in India, pointed out that a beginning had already been made with the setting up of various committees on post-war reconstruction problems within the Viceroy's Executive Council. W.D. Croft said that it was recognized that India 'is and must remain primarily agricultural'; industrial development must, therefore, follow agricultural development and the consequent raising of agricultural consumers' purchasing power. Gregory agreed, but said that a large volume of agricultural output automatically created a good deal of secondary employment in terms of transport, distribution, clerical labour.[118] He 'did not feel that Russian methods could be applied to India without a violent reaction', but Sir Frederick Leggett believed this had to be faced if the standard of living of India as a whole was to be raised. Priority was in principle to be accorded to the standard of living of village industry workers and peasants; Sir Malcolm Darling believed that the fundamental point to begin from was education, to which end a small commission of experts should be sent to Russia, '(not now, but at some appropriate time)', since Russia had been successful with its literacy programme. No solution to problems of finance were attempted to be dealt with.[119] Cripps, thereafter, produced a much more detailed note on 'A Social and Economic Policy for India', stressing education, population control, the raising of agricultural productivity, factory legislation and the promotion and control of industrialization through the utilization of the sterling balances. It also recommended the use of 'modern techniques of economic planning and the modern device of the Public Corporation' and the coordination of provincial programmes into an 'All-Indian Programme of Industrial Development'.[120] Amery's response was a reiteration of his earlier objections to the social clauses. The problem of education, he wrote, due to the lack of a wide recognition of its importance among the people, could not be 'greatly affected by the waving of the Viceregal wand'. He added that regarding agriculture, no one knew better than the present viceroy, who had been chairman of the Royal Commission on Agriculture which had set up the Imperial Council for Agricultural Research.[121]

Amery was at the same time following up his own angle to the proposals; he spoke to Lord McGowan of the Imperial Chemical Industries regarding future industrial development in India. McGowan was 'all for British firms throwing themselves frankly into that development, rather than creating the impression that they grudge Indian development in the interests of British exports, and also bringing Indians into partnership in local Indian companies as much as possible'. He suggested the setting up of an Indian Development Commission with branches both in India and Britain, 'to consider what British industry could do to help the most rapid development in India, not only of major industries, but also of simple manufactures which could add to local employment and to the general standard of living'.[122] This was quite in line with what Schuster had proposed in the early 1930s, in the form of Britain permitting or even assisting the development of less complex levels of industrialization in India, while Britain would continue to provide sophisticated products and capital goods, and to which end he had suggested coordinating economic planning for India with imperial preference to create an integrated imperial economic order.

As part of his contribution to the ongoing debate in London, Linlithgow sent home notes from Jenkins and Hutton, Secretaries of the Supply Department and the War Resources and Reconstruction Committee, respectively, whose responses were from interestingly divergent perspectives, but highlighted the problems of approach which existed in the proposals.[123] 'The difficulty lies not in deciding what ought to be done, but in doing it on an adequate scale,' Jenkins observed. Regarding agricultural productivity, except for the consolidation of holdings, the other proposals were administratively easy, but '[t]he point is that all interference with land tenures is highly controversial, and that while success may be impossible without compulsion, compulsion itself may not be practical politics'. Regarding industrial development, he felt that 'Indian opinion favours the establishment of aircraft and automobile industries, whereas the economic facts may indicate agricultural implements, bicycles, typewriters, hurricane lanterns and so on. The pace and nature of industrialisation will depend mainly on what the villager wants and what he can afford to buy; and the villager's purchasing power will depend largely on the extent to which the State can raise him above the bare subsistence level'.[124]

Hutton, with his military training, dealt with the point he felt was the most urgent, politically. He accepted that 'we cannot be wrong in starting a programme of social reform in India, even if it entails taxation remaining at a high level after the war. This may be a case where strict financial canons should give way, as it has elsewhere, to political and social considerations'. But he recognized that actual social reforms were to be subordinated to their public relations value:

Education is important for what it achieves rather [than] for what it is and there is great scope for improvement of the system. What is more important is propaganda ... We have yet to realise that a country can be very largely governed, as well as educated and reformed, by propaganda alone ... The success of government, as of individuals, depends more on what people think of their achievements than on what they have actually done.[125]

Responses to the Cripps–Bevin social reform proposals continued to be hostile. It was, in fact, claims of action taken or contemplated on the domestic front which finally killed the Cripps–Bevin initiative. Linlithgow had been mobilizing governors' reports from the Section 93 provinces which pointed to work already done in the field of social legislation,[126] stressing the constitutional position, the financial and manpower requirements, referring to the existence of a post-war reconstruction committee of the Viceroy's Executive Council and, in general, raising objections, until the proposals were dropped. At the end of his term, he advised that if a new viceroy had to implement such a programme 'he would merely be beating the air'. But Wavell had already got the idea. Unimpressed by his informal discussions with Home Secretary, Herbert Morrison, and Stafford Cripps (by then Minister for Aircraft Production) in London, he attributed it to the Labour Party's ignorance about India:

Morrison spoke of India, about which he really knew little. His idea seemed to be to encourage the masses against the classes by factory legislation, spread of education and mechanisation of farming on the Soviet model, but he had little idea of the problem, and thought that 'depressed classes' and 'untouchables' were merely another name for the poor, and seemed hardly to have heard of the caste system.

Cripps, speaking on the same subject, made a more favourable impression; Wavell acknowledged that he did know a little about India; but not enough, it was implied.[127] At any rate, the inherent difficulties of the Indian situation, a society governed by considerations of community rather than class, where impractical nationalists demanded industrialization of an inappropriate kind and the peasants were steeped in tradition and superstition, was not amenable to the kind of social manipulation that Labour Party idealists (hostility towards whom, coalition or no coalition, was not hidden) were prone to suggest.[128]

While these discussions were going on, Government of India officials were keen to point out that the Government of India already had a number of reconstruction committees, which, with the aid of data from the departments, were considering not only the 'inevitable problems of the post-War period but also a long-term development policy'—including industries, communications, agriculture, and social services. Provinces and states to a lesser extent were doing the same. Linlithgow was quick to point out the obstacles to rapid progress—shortage of staff arising out of the claims of food supplies, war industries, transportation and other matters requiring constant attention and imposing strain on administration, especially in the provinces. The planning of the war economy was naturally governed by military priorities.

As long as a war remains close to India and our economic problems are as serious as they are today, any initiation of a large-scale development policy would, we are convinced, be administratively and financially impossible. We are, however, already carrying out a considerable development of industries and agriculture to satisfy war requirements which have also a long-term value.

Linlithgow had by this time a good idea of the multiple objectives which had to be incorporated into post-War planning for India. He was also more than aware of the problems of public relations which were posed by such an issue, and far less sanguine than Hutton on its potential dividends as propaganda. 'As experience in other countries has shown, no Government can hope to meet the full aspirations of the public hoping for a brave new world after the war. In India, many of the ideas held by the public, for example, as to the expansion of industry, are very impracticable.' Moreover, there was much suspicion of British intentions: 'any well-advertised development policy might well be acclaimed by the people as only a belated attempt to remedy past omissions'.

It is not by such rather blatant methods that we shall alter the political situation and for that reason we have deliberately not courted publicity for our planning activities. Our desire is to assure the people that all preparations are being made for a development policy, in respect of which non-officials will be consulted, and that whatever Government may be in power after the war will find them ready to hand. To attempt to make political capital out of our proposals would perhaps have the effect of damning them in advance, to the future detriment of the people of India. If, however, we are obviously fulfilling a public demand, confidence and reliance on Government will assuredly be enhanced.[129]

Linlithgow's statement is a good indication of the multiple objectives sought to be incorporated into the idea of post-War planning for India. But Linlithgow was not being entirely honest when he claimed that publicity had not been sought for the government's 'planning activities'; in fact, they were an important part of the Government of India's war propaganda programme, their public relations dimension overcoming their practical dimensions.[130] At the same time, the various departments in India had to come up with detailed and viable (or, at least, apparently so) projects in connection with long- and shorter-term economic objectives, many of which were in conflict with each other, and some of which could scarcely have been admitted publicly. It was, moreover, quite impossible for individual projects to reconcile objectives at both the widest level of British metropolitan interests and the more immediate local level to which the projects directly pertained.[131] These wider perspectives were to be kept in mind by the higher ranks of the official hierarchy, but there were clear political reasons why they were not to be widely known. The unprecedented deaths of the Bengal Famine—the example that comes most readily to mind—were, for instance, perfectly compatible with the primary purpose of winning the war, and the negative effect it had on the public morale—already suspicious of the government's intentions—would not have been assuaged if the details of the bargaining and engineering of quid pro quos which were taking place behind closed doors had been generally known.[132]

The Fringes of Government

It is most often to the fringes of official discussions that one needs to look to find the genuine carriers of the imperial mythology of good government and of the 'development' that was an integral part of good government. The ICS man, for so long an absolute ruler in his little territory, and treated with the deference that went with that power, saw himself as one capable of improving the lives of the men and women under him. He prided himself on 'knowing India'; at the most, he knew the area under his command; and he rode his horse across this territory at regular intervals, providing justice of sorts, sorting out small problems and generally dispensing benevolence. This was a useful illusion; a civilian with a sense of mission could set about trying to improve things and achieve a modicum of success in his area. Moreover, his confidence in himself and in the imperial government he represented was based on the fortuitously limited perspective he had: the working of the mechanisms of imperialism were often opaque to him.

Interest in the details of administration among particular civilians or government functionaries produced many of the first systematic academic–administrative studies of India, which continue to be the first references for work in similar fields today. Pioneers included B.H. Baden-Powell on the land systems of British India;[133] successors included Major J.C. Jack on the economic life of a Bengal district; Malcolm Darling on Punjab rural life: the Punjab peasant, military recruitment, debt relief, and cooperatives; Frank Brayne on rural uplift.[134] Yet the central difference between writing in the nineteenth century and in the second decade of the twentieth century was the systematization of British rule in India in the interim period: earlier writing was sometimes taken on board as the basis on which to order politics and society, the advantage due to firstcomers in unexplored territories which had previously been opaque to British perceptions. Once, however, the default settings of imperial policy for India had been in place for some years, and a sense of equilibrium arrived at, the government was reluctant to disturb well-worn assumptions—a matter of frustration for some local administrators, who felt that their knowledge and expertise was not being properly utilized.

   If the higher ranks of the Government of India were generally too locked up in constraints imposed by imperial Realpolitik to afford the luxury of thinking creatively of the problems of developing India and, moreover, were bound to hold their peace in public regarding disagreements with official policy, this was precisely the luxury enjoyed by men below those ranks. Considering the numbers involved, comparatively few of them utilized these possibilities, and even fewer combined such disagreement with a more fundamental critique of the Empire: the point, to their minds, was to make an apparently already benevolent and progressive imperial governance even more so. The civilian usually did not see himself as an agent of a vile system of exploitation, although he was not above criticising the government; for he believed himself to be the one who understood India. Most often the peasant was his ideal of what an Indian ought to be like: certain improvements were, of course, possible—he spent too much on weddings, was prone to get into debt, and, in general, to act in an irrational manner—but on the whole he represented unspoiled innocence.[135] The enemy was, of course, the Indian nationalist politician, or the communist, for he stirred the natives to strange feelings which the Civilian did not feel they had under ordinary circumstances.

   Clive Dewey's *Anglo-Indian Attitudes* focuses on two civilians of the Punjab cadre, Darling and Brayne, their intellectual and social backgrounds, their circle of friends and acquaintances in India, and their attitudes and approaches to the problems of village uplift, economic development, or the administration of social justice. Dewey has argued, among other things, that '[e]ach generation of Civilians took the intellectual fashions of their youth out to the East, and spent the rest of their lives putting them into practice. Sometimes their Indian experience confirmed their preconceptions; sometimes it destroyed their illusions; it rarely suggested new methods of analysing society'. Dewey's work chronicles these influences in the careers of his two ICS men.[136] However, it is necessary to use this generalization with caution: the careers and projects of the two men Dewey selected are exceptional in several ways—a point which Dewey himself acknowledges—for which reason the title of the book is too ambitious for the matter it contains. Moreover, a civilian might have wanted to hold on to his ideas of Empire during his years in the ICS, but circumstances could conspire to modify, and in some cases more significantly, change his attitude—a more complex dynamic than merely confirmation or destruction of preconceptions. This is evident in the writings of a number of civilians, who record how their initial attitudes and those of a number of their colleagues, about imperialism and its role, their own role in India, and their relationship to the natives changed over time.[137] There were also significant variations in the circumstances in which the ICS worked, from province to province and from region to region; to the love of the Punjab Civilians for their peasants could be juxtaposed the suspicion and terror felt for the East Bengali countryside by the Bengal Civilians, many of whom lost their lives to terrorists.[138] It is correct to say that only in very rare instances did a British Civilian lose his commitment to the idea of Empire; but how that idea of Empire was interpreted was subject to significant variations.

One of the projects with which the ICS was engaged was village reconstruction, into which parameters fell the promotion of the cooperative movement. The limited and local meanings of these initiatives allowed for a situation in which it was not impossible that they coexist with the wider priorities of imperialism. At the same time, they grew from beginnings as small local issues to fit into larger debates; they were also sometimes invoked as evidence of an active and constructive economic policy on the part of imperialism.[139] The idea of looking after the welfare of Indian villages was compatible with the general assumption that the 'real' India lived in the villages, that the villager was grateful to his district officer for looking after him so well, and so must continue to be looked after. In addition to this, cooperation and village reconstruction were compatible with the civilian's self-image as one who 'knew the country'. (When the Royal Commission on Agriculture was in India, its Chairman, Linlithgow, was reported by the Viceroy, Lord Irwin, to have been 'having a little trouble with the Punjab Co-operative expert, Calvert, who I understand has told the Commission that the Punjab is the only Province in India which knows anything, and that he is the only man in the Punjab who knows anything too'.[140]) These measures were also well suited to a self-perception of benevolent service on the part of the Civilian.

The rise in importance of village reconstruction was reflected in its terminology. 'There was something which in 1928 was called Village Uplift, later renamed Rural Development. Its beginnings must always be associated with F.L. Brayne in the Punjab, who preached a doctrine of better agriculture and cleaner villages with the fervour of the prophet of a new religion. Grant [District Magistrate of Saharanpur] regarded this new faith with sceptical amusement, but others of his generation were slightly outraged ... George [Fisher, a young Civil Servant at Saharanpur], however, believed that rural development was an essential part of the new approach without which constitutional reforms would be meaningless'.[141] Not everyone, therefore, took the project as seriously; a Brayne or a Darling might go to elaborate lengths, but others had a less ambitious idea of what was necessary or possible. As every imperial administrator had been taught about the Indian, 'the main obstacle to his advance and progress lies in the psychology of the rural worker himself, owing to the custom and habit of caste and tradition that has governed his life and action for generations'.[142] It was the imperial administrator's job, as it was of the good Christian, to encourage 'self-help with intimate expert counsel', hopefully leading to 'spiritual, mental, physical, social and economic' uplift.[143] This could, of course, be a thankless task given the proverbial recalcitrance of the peasant; results were often disappointing,[144] but '[t]he theme of all great romances is the quest ... for its own sake. There is always the quest'.[145]

The project of village uplift, rural reconstruction, rural welfare, or rural development, whatever the preferred term might be, had a mixed genealogy, of government initiatives, '[i]ndividual Indians and voluntary associations of Indians', and 'Missionary bodies'.[146] The Indian Village Welfare Association, founded in 1931, sought to support both official and non-official 'experiments and schemes of rural welfare in India, about which reliable information has been obtained', by means of publicity and finance.[147] The term 'rural reconstruction' was claimed as its own by the YMCA.[148] The practice of 'rural reform' (to use yet another formulation, used by the Indian Village Welfare Association's Review of Rural Welfare Activites for 1932), was also carried out through different agencies: in northern India the main impulse came from officials, and in south India from private agencies. Eastern India, similarly, was felt in 1932 to be 'without an official or semi-official agency for coordinating the labours of the various progressive departments', while private bodies either restricted themselves to a small field or specialized in matters such as women's leagues and anti-malarial societies.[149] The Review noted, in particular, Rabindranath Tagore's Sriniketan experiment, but warned that 'Dr Tagore's conception of a rural university, in which individuality and an artistic spirit will be developed, education conducted through the pupil's natural activities, and a love of country life instilled, is one which may be realised under his personal leadership, and may or may not breed successors ... the spirit of the institution, possibly even the institution itself, may not outlive Dr Tagore, and ... the work done, with lofty intention and unselfish labour, may be unscientific and superficial'.[150]

It needs to be noted here that 'rural reconstruction' worked either within a general imperialist consensus (C.F. Strickland, who authored the

Indian Village Welfare Association's Review, was a former Registrar of Cooperative Societies), or, at least, did not disturb it, seeking to work in the spaces for manoeuvre left by British rule. There was also a strong Christian strain in many official or semi-official initiatives, such as those of the YMCA or of missionary activities.[151] In many cases, this could not be highlighted; Brayne complained that government servants were denied the appeal to religion which was so useful in England. He had, therefore, to interpret Christian teachings indirectly, in what has aptly been described as a 'language of physical cleanliness, rational productivity and disinterested social service'.[152] This combination of elements usually provided a framework within which, by agreeing to disagree, or at least by not talking about disagreements, officials and non-officials, imperialists and anti-imperialists, could find a limited area of cooperation: rural uplift was 'not political'. Similarly, Gandhi's All-India Village Industries Association (AIVIA), set up in 1934 in order to undertake 'constructive work', claimed a space not explicitly political. Some imperial administrators were not unsympathetic to this initiative of Gandhi's, as long as it kept him away from politics and concentrated on '*bona fide* village welfare work'.[153] Surendra Kumar Datta of the YMCA[154] maintained a close correspondence with Gandhi and Mahadev Desai regarding rural uplift and education, and was one of the AIVIA's 'expert advisers'.[155]

'Rural reconstruction' also worked within different local or sectional contexts; and within these contexts there could be strong variations in the aims it was expected to achieve. As observed by Strickland, official involvement with village-level activities was most pronounced in north India and, within north India, it was the Punjab which had the greatest share of reconstructionists. Punjab has usually been seen as a good example of the functioning of an improving imperialism and of committed, if sometimes paternalistic, Civilians, striving for the uplift of their peasants.[156] A contrasting case was provided by Bengal. In 1937, when the Congress Working Committee created a Political and Economic Information Department 'to collect a variety of economic, social and political data and to keep as accurate and comprehensive a record' as possible, the new department appealed to various organizations and individuals to help them out with information and publications.[157] A disarmingly frank letter was received from H.P.V. Townend, the Bengal Rural Development Commissioner, in response to this request. He wrote:

I am afraid that you are under a misunderstanding as to the nature of my work which does not deal with rural development in general. I am concerned only with the problem of debt settlement, propaganda for the restriction of the acreage under jute, legislation regarding water hyacinth and legislation regarding the development of decadent areas which are situated particularly in western, central and northern Bengal. My work thus has related chiefly to the preparation of bills and of rules under the Acts which emerged from them, viz. the Bengal Development Act, the Bengal Agricultural Debtors Act and the Bengal Water Hyacinth Act. I have prepared no reports reviewing the work done and no record of my activities for publication. I regret therefore that I am unable to meet your request.[158]

Rural development was not, however, an unimportant theme in Bengal; and if the Rural Development Commisioner's letter had given that impression and Strickland's survey had claimed a lack of official concern with it, this was because it was handled in an unexpected department: the Publicity Branch of the Bengal government. Rural reconstruction had been part of Bengal governor Sir John Anderson's scheme to wean the rural population away from terrorism—most 'reconstruction' schemes were statements of propaganda which were not meant to be actual schemes in any but the most limited sense and were, consequently, not reflected in practices or organizational networks, being linked instead with anti-terrorist propaganda, in a carrot-and-stick policy of repression combined with promises to provide villagers with economic benefits if they abstained from supporting terrorism. Such propaganda reached its high point between 1932 and 1935. Care was taken to hide the connection between rural reconstruction and anti-terrorist propaganda from the public: records were kept in the Home Political (Confidential) Department, and reports were forwarded to Directors of Public Information in other provinces with the warning that they contained 'matters which if not treated as strictly confidential may prove embarrassing to the Government and involve them in difficulties'.[159] The Rural Development Commissioner might, therefore, not have known much about this secret work; even if he had, he would not have been at liberty to disclose it.

In the United Provinces (UP), similarly, anti-revolutionary propaganda was linked to or dressed up as village uplift for the benefit of the rural public, though the UP government seemed not to be concerned about making the connection obvious, at least to its own servants and to those who had access to government information: several pamphlets explicitly outlining this approach were published, clearly bearing on their covers the Government of India's coat of arms and its motto: *Dieu et mon droit*.[160] The UP government had, by 1921, formed anti-revolutionary leagues, called *Aman Sabhas*, in all its districts for the purposes of counter-propaganda against a combination of local peasant unrest and non-cooperation agitation, the latter organized in *Kisan Sabhas*. Aman Sabhas were organized by district officers and local landlords. This idea was then exported to other provinces.[161] The UP also had, however, active official and semi-official bodies engaged in rural reconstruction, including village-level rural reconstruction societies organized on the initiative of the cooperative department. These bodies dealt mainly with agricultural improvements, education, hygiene, and civic matters such as the encouragement of 'cooperative societies for arbitration and better living, village councils for self-government'.[162] Presumably, the existence of these bodies might have made some of the rhetoric of the government as provider seem a little more realistic. As it happens, the Aman Sabhas were not particularly successful.[163] Nevertheless, they provide one strong context within which village uplift was placed, and illustrate the ways in which the rhetoric of benevolence was articulated—in the particular case of the Aman Sabhas, in an avowedly instrumentalist fashion, but reflecting a projection of the imperialist self-image and a vision of the ideal India the British administrator would have liked to see in existence.

Aman Sabhas were meant to put a simple case of government benevolence before a mainly rural public, for which purpose their message had to be simple and direct. The constitution, aims, and objects of the Agra District Aman Sabha, under the organizational control of the Agra District League, for instance, was laid out in the form of a catechism. Its motto was in two parts: 'Be true to your King and Country', and 'Peace and order are necessary for all human progress'. The question 'Who form Aman Sabhas?' was answered by a list of five characteristics: 'People who believe in peaceful evolution of India with "Dominion status" as the final goal.' 'People who have grown gray in the service of the country and who know too well that the other course is bound to end in chaos and disorder.' 'People who believe that India has everything to gain but nothing to loose [sic] by their living within the British Empire.' 'People who know full well that the present national idea is an outcome of English education, and that in case the centripetal force is weakened or removed, the country is bound to go back and get disinterred [sic] into fragments.' 'Its members are not idealists but practical man [sic] who have weighted the advantages of British connections and can not be ungrateful to a nation that have [sic] restored peace and order in the country.'[164]

A list was also drawn up of what Aman Sabhas were capable of doing. They were to organize entertainments, games, and tournaments in the villages, and city *mohallas* (localities) so as to 'produce a team spirit'—a prescription reminiscent of a housemaster reiterating the public school ethos for the benefit of his wards.[165] They were to bring the villagers' grievances 'to the notice of the proper authorities'; arrange social functions for officials and non-officials to meet and 'get benefitted by each others view point [sic]'; and to enrol volunteers 'for Anti-picketing purposes'. Fifth and last on this list was 'village uplift':

Aman Sabhas have undertaken to do 'Village Uplift' in villages, that is,

1. Village games.
2. Village Sanitation.
3. Village roads, streets and other public ways.
4. Village medical relief.
5. Village education.
6. Co-operative Societies.
7. Agriculturist [sic] improvement.
8. Aman Sabha Propaganda.[166]

This view of 'village uplift', with its rather eclectic list of constituent elements, was embedded in a concern for order and stability: a project 'to try and bring about reapproachment [sic] between the people and the Government so that all classes may join together in working for the uplift, the greatness, the freedom and the prosperity of Mother-Land'.[167] 'Village uplift' was offered as a *quid pro quo* for villagers, as members of the Sabha, to act as informers and propagandists for the government, whose duties included 'to read and explain pamphlets, books, notices and other literature issued by the League to the public', and to report fellow villagers or anti-government agitators to the government. The relationship between village uplift as economic and social progress and village uplift as a publicity measure was ambiguous, but the context made it clear that the latter was considered far more important. A report of the Publicity Office, Agra, noted that the organizations through which publicity work was carried out were the District League, the Soldiers' Board, and 'Village Uplift Leagues which are more or less a product of the District League'.[168] The District League was itself mainly a publicity organization; and village uplift schemes working through them were measured mainly in terms of the publicity they provided.[169] Village *panchayats* (five-member village councils) which were considered the basis of ancient Indian 'village republics' both in nationalist and imperialist histories of India,[170] were entrusted with the task of attending to village uplift; but were not provided any autonomy in this regard; the path to uplift was laid out in a most patronizing tone. The *sarpanch*, head of the panchayat, was instructed in a scheme of village uplift, drawn from Brayne's Gurgaon experiment.[171] He was told that, 'Our object in forming these Panchayats is to train you in self-government and to make you happy. Through these panchayats we hope to remove poverty, as poverty brings disease, misery, sufferings, and unhappiness'.[172]

As propaganda this approach was rather clumsy, but it put forward an idea of the ignorant peasant who had to be told what to do—self-help with intimate counsel once again—and which was widely held in imperial circles. Outlines of the line of approach to be taken tended to insult the villagers in every possible way. They were informed: 'Your methods of farming are bad. Your village is filthy ... You waste all your wealth. You keep your women-folk in degradation and slavery ... You resist all change, you are illiterate and ignorant and you do not make a proper use of your leisure'.[173]

The villager was expected to listen while he was told of the seven-step remedial programme to overcome this gloomy situation, relating to cooperative banking and consolidation of holdings, sanitation, the ending of unnecessary and wasteful expenditure on jewellery and weddings, agricultural improvements, good cattle stock, emancipation of women. These suggestions made no reference to any significant reforms in agrarian property relations, an omission which was logical in a project related to the maintenance of peace, order, and taxes, and instead included recommendations on what 'good zamindars' should do.[174]

Occasionally, the rhetoric of intended speeches (there is no indication in these records as to their impact when delivered or if, indeed, such speeches were actually delivered) attempted to approach the poetic, but succeeded only in indicating the lack of poetic instincts of the bureaucracy:

Why are there no flowers in your villages and your homes? Flowers bloom all the year round in India but there are none in our villages. God gave flowers to mankind to make them bright and happy. You will never have flowers till you humanise the women.
What are the two prettiest things in the world? Clean, healthy, happy children and flowers. Both these grow in the home. Woman is the partner responsible for the home, so train the woman that she may learn how to produce flowers and keep your children clean, healthy and happy.[175]

The confusion of the possessive pronouns 'your' and 'our' in this passage, and the role prescribed for 'humanised' women is worth noting in this connection.

'Rural development' could, of course, be more creatively approached. The Punjab Civilian, Malcolm Darling, for instance, sought to transcend its limited conceptions through recommending more positive government policies and greater funding for constructive projects.[176] He was also open to new ideas. A peripheral member of the Bloomsbury group himself,[177] he had gleaned the basics of Keynesianism from his own conversations—of which he kept notes—with his fellow kingsman, Keynes, before the publication of the *General Theory*.[178] He advocated Keynesian ideas of deficit spending to the Government of India with regard to cooperative societies and attacked the 'Secretarial codes and orthodox finance' which had brought all reconstruction processes to a standstill after the Depression set in by cutting off funds. He pointed to development initiatives being attempted in countries such as Italy, Turkey, and Russia. 'The example of Russia is of particular moment, for in many ways its conditions resemble India's, and whatever one's political views, one must admit that an immense effort is being made, greater than any in history, to improve the conditions of life for over 100 million peasants...'[179]. At the same time Darling was uncertain as to the good of dispossessing the landlord, who admittedly was 'too often a parasite'; he could, nonetheless, be encouraged to 'imitate the German Junker', and ought to realize the advantages of this lest he be 'swept away into the limbo of unregretted anachronisms'.[180]

There was a streak of the romantic in Darling; his was no blanket condemnation of so-called 'backward' institutions. He was ambivalent about the allegedly negative role of moneylenders; he believed that a certain moral economy had operated on them before the advent of the British, which had limited the rate of interest they could charge; they had provided credit facilities where none existed, and nothing the British had done as yet had been able to replace them with better sources of credit— though the cooperative movement was making an attempt in that direction. He blamed the changes wrought by the British-imposed legal system for turning a beneficial institution into an oppressive one.[181] Writing during the Depression, he stated: 'In the village at least, there is more to be said than is commonly supposed for medieval methods of business, and for a system of exchange directly based upon commodities and service instead of upon money, over which the world has lost control.'[182] Of the supposedly unproductive habit of storing wealth in hoarded gold or other jewellery, Darling pointed to the wisdom of this in the Depression—they could be sold to pay debts. He also hoped that the Depression would prove 'a blessing in disguise', teaching thrift to an unthrifty people.[183]

Darling formulated his ideas of the 'medieval' nature of the Indian peasantry in the 1920s, in terms of contemporary academic writing. On 'the relation of economics to ethics' (the former being 'mainly concerned with facts' and the latter with 'values'), he wrote in 1928 that the rule of ethics over economics was a 'medieval' characteristic—this premise he drew from R.H. Tawney's *Religion and the Rise of Capitalism*.[184] In India the village was 'still medieval in outlook'. Rules of 'morality', which Darling saw as 'binding upon economic conduct' in the Indian village, were 'almost synonymous with custom'. Consequently, Darling postulated a static village society and a static village economy. This situation had been changing in the last thirty years due to the impact of better transport and irrigation facilities, making the villagers responsive to the 'more dynamic basis of man-made economics'. This was true of 'Hindu, Muhammedan and Sikh'; the boundaries between economics and ethics were beginning to shift.[185]

Darling believed, however, that this could be carried too far; he advocated a principle of 'sufficiency' rather than of 'the gospel of unlimited gain' and the consequent 'danger of arousing the acquisitive instincts of 320 millions', especially as there was 'not enough to go round'. He feared 'deep unrest' and 'explosive results' if the latter principle were adopted. Quoting Keynes, he emphasized the undesirability of modern capitalism: it was 'absolutely irreligious, without internal union, without much public spirit, often, though not always, a mere congeries of possessors and pursuers'.[186] He rejected the nineteenth century view of leaving economic matters to the 'play of natural forces', and called for the interlinking of ethics and economics. 'For agriculture is more than the mere gaining of a livelihood: it is a way of life which touches mind and spirit far more deeply than the pursuits whose sole object is gain.'[187] It is unclear as to whether he realized that this might be read as, or whether he intended this to be read as, a defence of aspects of a 'medieval outlook'.[188]

Darling's interpretation of the problems of the peasantry came from well within the imperial vision: he was concerned with 'schemes "for the better government of India"', as he put it himself, quoting the introductory phrase in the 1858 Act of Parliament which established the Crown's control over India.[189] The, often merely implicit, framework of his views were made explicit in his writing for outsiders to the Indian situation. In 1941, for an American audience, he summarized his views on the problems of the Indian peasantry for a lay readership. All peasants were fundamentally the same everywhere, he wrote, and the peasant 'is not only the link between East and West; he is also the strongest link in the chain which joins our age to the remote past'.[190] Having emphasized the universality of the category 'peasant' and, thereby, the fundamental equality of man, he proceeded to make exceptions.

Man, said Aristotle, is a political animal. This may be true of urban man, perhaps even of western man, but it certainly is not true of the Indian peasant. On the contrary, he is essentially a nonpolitical animal.

... Three years ago ... he was given the vote. This ... is certainly a hazardous experiment to give the vote to over twenty million peasants, most of whom are illiterate, and who, moreover, represent more than two thirds of the total electorate. Never yet has parliamentary democracy been built on such foundations... If, however, the Indian peasant is illiterate, he is certainly not deaf, and not always dumb....[191]

This non-political animal was, however, endangered by the Depression. The effects of the fall in prices, aggravated by the 'rupee famine' caused by deflationary policies of government,[192] 'profoundly disturbed the peasantry's triple relationship with landlord, money-lender and government'.[193] Darling viewed this situation with concern, because it disrupted the harmony of the village environment: 'The basis of this ancient Indian village culture is interdependence, the interdependence of those who live together with common walls, common needs and common ties, who depend for the means of life as much upon one another as upon themselves, and who feel a common dependence upon the mysterious and overpowering forces of nature'.[194] Such unity and interdependence was now under threat from 'materialism'—'the acquisitive spirit which modern life has greatly developed'.

Certain disturbing tendencies were making themselves felt. Darling attributed the tension between landlord and tenant not to property relations in the countryside (which he did not mention, though contemporaries of his often did) but to the rapid increase in population among the tenants.[195] Debtor–creditor relations had been disturbed the most, with moneylenders being unwilling to lend money.[196] Most provinces had passed legislation to protect debtors, whose debts had rapidly doubled with the fall in prices. Now that the prices were on the rise again due to the War, the moneylender might start lending again. The cooperative movement could not offer a solution, he admitted, because it touched only 15 per cent of the population. The government might be 'forced by political pressure' to step in and take the moneylender's place and, consequently, find itself involved 'in all the difficulties that money-lending in India brings'.[197]

Darling interpreted the problem at hand as 'not so much a case of achieving material progress as of arresting a manifest spiritual decline'.[198] This was a somewhat surprising priority given that, by his own account, the material situation of the peasant was not exactly comfortable. He laid out the symptoms of the decline as the potential results of policies initiated during the Depression. The government, like the landlord and the moneylender, had had to forgo a substantial part of its dues. Now that the peasant had the vote, however, he could attack the general system of revenue itself. This was, he wrote, what had happened in Bulgaria. 'The land revenue system is so well-suited to India that I hope that the example of Bulgaria will not be followed. But ... we may be certain that government dues are not likely to be paid by the peasant in the future with as little question as in the past.'[199]

In this connection Darling also attacked the rationale of the pro-peasant legislation of the autonomous provincial governments, the immediate effect of which had been 'to deprive the peasant of credit, to make it difficult for the enterprising to obtain capital to develop their land but easy for the inefficient to remain on it, however badly they cultivate it, and to undermine *the moral sense of obligation* which makes a man pay his dues and repay his loans'.[200]

Such spiritual decline, he believed, could be arrested through two possible means: a revival of the village panchayat, and the development of the cooperative movement. Both were 'consistent with a democratic constitution'. Of the cooperative movement, he wrote that, '... though entirely unpolitical—and long may it remain so—it performs the great political service of binding all classes together irrespective of caste, community or creed'. It had its limitations, he admitted, largely due to an illiterate and ignorant peasantry 'which uses the great blessing of peace for the blind multiplication of the species ...'.[201]

This article might be read in the light of the need for effective British wartime publicity on the Empire and on India in the USA, which might explain the stress on the dangers of peasant democracy to private property and stability, and his emphasis on democratic solutions and entrepreneurship. Yet there is ample evidence elsewhere that in this case he was not merely tailoring his writing to his audience; fears for the sanctity of existing social relations and the rhetoric of capitalist entrepreneurship merged with anxieties about the moral fabric of society in other writings by him and his contemporaries. Darling had already used most of this article in his presidential address to the Indian Society of Agricultural Economics in February 1940.[202] The concerns articulated in it were also recurrent themes in his writings.

The Malthusian danger loomed large in the writings of Darling. His papers contain long notes from Malthus' writings on the dangers of overpopulation, including Malthus' own citations on the subject from Arthur Young, the Englishman who rode across France on the eve of the

Revolution, and whom Darling was to invoke himself in his own ride across north India on the eve of transfer of power.[203] 'The central idea of Malthus' book [is] that marriage sh[oul]d be deferred till a family can be maintained,' Darling wrote, paraphrasing Malthus in terms of his concern at the unwise and extravagant marriages of his peasants. And '[t]he more active the forces pushing to an increase in pop[ulation] the greater the misery when there is a check upon subsistence. In India a serious check e.g. a famine at once produces misery. *What if we left the country[?]*'[204] Viceroy-designate Linlithgow, was also extremely keen on this approach. Having read a report written by Darling on the cooperative movement in the Punjab, he asked Darling for more concrete evidence that population growth was the prime cause of the decline in the standards of living in Lyallpur. He added: 'I am wondering how far I shall feel able to tell India that the over-growth of population is the factor limiting the standard of living. Someone has warned me that I may come to be known as the "Contraceptive Viceroy". I think I should be rather proud of that epithet if it carried the sense that I had persuaded India to go in for fewer but better babies!'[205]

Like many of his contemporaries, Darling was extremely impressed by the achievements of the Soviet Union, and saw it as a model worthy of emulation by India. He saw this as a method of getting things done: 'Russian methods' applied to the running of imperialism, in terms of the education of the peasant,[206] or collectivization as a form of cooperation for a 'semi-Asiatic country' with a need of economic rather than political democracy.[207] The advocacy of Soviet methods may have been made slightly easier by the fact that the Soviet Union was now an ally in the War; the fact remains that diverse ideas were capable of being adapted and incorporated into the imperial vision.

What might be called a limited or local view of the role of the imperial administrator in 'developing' the countryside was thus not disconnected from wider issues of the role imperialism was to fulfil in India. Rural reconstruction was embedded in assumptions of the power and authority of the ICS to impose solutions to problems and to oversee the moral and material progress of their people; whether particular civilians were energetic or negligent about it, the power to do good over the rural population embodied the ICS' self-justification and their faith in Empire. The 1920s and 1930s saw a decline in the importance and absolute powers of the ICS with the introduction of provincial autonomy and the coming of ministerial government; the Second World War and the political developments which accompanied it further eroded the Service's already threatened sense of importance. Darling noted the decline in power of the civilian: no one came to see the Deputy Commissioner any more, because no one felt he had any power—and they said so to him.[208] The War also brought home to all concerned that the British departure from India, for long a part of the official rhetoric of the Empire (though temporally placed in a near future that receded just out of reach as one approached it), was a matter of a few years.

As this became evident, constructing a retrospective view of the achievements and significance of the Empire became more necessary; for many this was a way of coming to terms with the Empire and its impending end. By the end of the war, to quote Philip Mason, '[a]lmost everyone in the Service ... pictured an independent India and since few believed that it could rightly hold a place for themselves, their old whole-hearted confidence could hardly be maintained', and 'everyone ... was thinking of what was to come next'.[209] The sense of uncertainty which from the 1920s, had bred both a reassessment and a hardening of attitudes—while some continued to cling to fragile certainties which they were too insecure to discard, others were more inclined to look the changes in the eye—now intensified to a point where to cling to certainties could only be seen as wilful blindness. After the war, 'ripeness for self-government' was almost universally acknowledged, with only the 'communal question' and the attempt to transfer power to a united India delaying the British departure.

Such a retrospective survey was provided by Penderel Moon, also a Civilian of the Punjab cadre, and one of the few British Civilians to stay on in India after the transfer of power,[210] who sought to place the legacy of British rule in India, and of the contribution of the imperial connection to India's 'development' within a wider context than that of 'rural reconstruction'. Written just after he had resigned from the Service as a consequence of severe disagreements with the Government of India over the treatment of political prisoners during the Quit India Movement,[211] Moon's evocatively titled *Strangers in India* has as its central theme an exploration of 'the alien character of our rule'.[212] It is possible to discern in this book a certain bitterness generated by a sense of betrayal: of the failure of the imperialism whose noble ideals he had been taught to respect and live up to and, consequently, the genesis in Moon himself of a sense of loss, as well as the guilt of complicity in a vicious system, a guilt he now sought to expiate.

Moon drew on experiences and incidents which he regarded as typical: dilemmas to be faced by every ICS man in the course of his service. In the ICS, as Michael Carritt wrote, 'there were some dedicated men who sincerely struggled against all the odds imposed by the system of Imperial Government to administer justice and to cope with the all-pervading rural poverty and ignorance. Not very many of these, I fear, as the twentieth century proceeded and even the best men in the service were frustrated by the contradiction between dedicated paternalism and their professional faith in the blessings of imperial rule'.[213]

The central question of *Strangers in India*—a question dictated by the political scenario in which Moon operated from the 1930s—was 'why it had been necessary to wait right up till their lifetime to take any substantial step towards Indian self-government, said to have been the goal of English policy for nearly 100 years'. The answer he provided was unequivocal: British national interests required the existence of India as part of the British Empire. What followed was largely a representation of Indian nationalist arguments, whose substance Moon acknowledged. He accepted the 'Plassey plunder', 'deindustrialisation' and 'drain of wealth' arguments; and agreed that the system of exploitation through which India provided unprotected markets for British goods enabled Britain 'from about 1860 onwards to use the proceeds to set up as a vast moneylender'. Gradually, '[w]ith the profits from ... ever-increasing investments steadily rising, England could afford to see her share in Indian trade declining and to grant Indians greater freedom in the management of their tariffs'.[214] India as debtor simply had to pay. 'After all, if you are so poor that you cannot develop your own resources without borrowing money, you must expect to pay for it. It matters not whether your borrowings are wise or unwise, voluntary or involuntary. A bond is a bond. The creditor must take his pound of flesh.'[215]

Here Moon used an interesting reversal of arguments: the moneylender was a stock figure in the rhetoric of British India, representing unproductive parasitism: a creature who took advantage of poverty and weakness to extract his profits.[216] Although it was sometimes acknowledged that he provided an essential service in the absence of organized credit facilities, it was generally agreed that his usurious demands aggravated the problem of rural debt. Representing the British Indian state—which represented itself as the protector of the peasant from the moneylender—as a 'vast moneylender' itself, was calculated to provoke.[217] The analogy also drew on the negative connotations of the original use of the image against the cowardly *bania*: moneylending was un-Christian, immoral, and foreign; in being a 'vast moneylender' and by implication un-Christian, immoral and foreign, British rule was not only foreign to India, but was being foreign to itself.[218]

At the same time, Moon acknowledged the 'remarkable' British achievement in India—conquered by 'a tiny handful of Englishmen'—of planting 'in its somewhat uncongenial soil the great liberal ideals and institutions of England'[219]. The number of English officials in India was exceedingly small; at the time he referred to, some districts had only one, many none at all[220].

Neither the merits nor the defects of the British Raj are attributable solely to the British. Without Indian talent the great fabric of ordered government could never have been built; nor could it have been sustained with such impressive stability without certain qualities—which are also defects—of the Indian character—a respect for authority, a strong sense of personal loyalty, and a quick responsiveness to great ideas. The Indian Empire is the product of joint endeavours. Future generations will perhaps admire it.[221]

The consistency and rigour of Moon's arguments regarding imperial exploitation were not matched by a correspondingly exacting intellectual position with regard to claimed extenuating circumstances for imperialism, as he hesitantly searched for a way to rescue himself and his colleagues from being indicted in the logic of empire. What then, if any, were the good things about the Empire in India? Moon, writing in June 1947, seemed to revert, possibly for a different audience, to the general contention that British rule, at least, maintained order—he never quite resolved this question for himself.[222] The younger generation of Indians were prepared to suffer chaos, he wrote, while the older generation hoped that 'British influence and British administrative and technical personnel will ... still linger on and by their mere presence contrive to preserve order and prevent a complete collapse of standards'.[223] This was an adoption of the widely held line that British withdrawal would lead to the deterioration of standards of administration in India. As for 'the vast, voiceless, illiterate, inconscient masses, who inhabit the villages of India', Moon could comfort himself that '[t]o them, such terms as the "British Raj", "Independence", "Pakistan", if not entirely unknown, are at most meaningless abstractions'. Their lives could not be disrupted by colonialism, or by any other forces, continuing 'as they did before the Moguls came and before the British came and as they will continue to do for generations to come, preserving that age-old village life indestructible alike by calamity or progress'.[224]

This was a good resolution of the problem of imperialism and exploitation, with which Moon began: colonialism is exploitative, yet it provides order in a society which would otherwise revert to chaos. All this, however, receded into the background if it could be argued that the vast majority of Indians, who lived in villages, were not significantly affected by colonial disruption. Yet this was not consistently argued; there was an ambivalence written into it. It was both positive and negative—in the latter sense because the best efforts made by British rule to transform the countryside by benevolence was, it was believed, destined to failure. These inconsistencies provide a clue to the dilemma of the colonial official who was uncertain of the moral propriety of colonialism and, consequently, the moral propriety of his own position in its administration.

Perhaps a perfect resolution of the dilemma was possible only in the realms of propaganda, not viewed as deliberate lies but rather as a gentle smoothing out of lines of conflictual interpretation, providing a softened picture which looked away from ugliness, and was as self-deluding as it was deluding. In January 1941 Moon gave a talk on All-India Radio entitled 'Totalitarian Facts and Fiction-2: Does Great Britain Exploit Her Colonies?', in which he argued that although it was impossible to answer this question truthfully with an unqualified negative, exploitation was 'not the avowed purpose for which Great Britain retains her colonies'. The purpose was the 'dual mandate' of 'adequate development of the resources of her colonies' and, as 'trustees for the native races', the promotion of their 'well-being and progress so that they may ultimately take their places as free and independent peoples'.[225] Moon claimed a divergence of interest between the British colonial government and 'powerful financial interests seeking the development of mineral and other resources', the latter preventing British governments in the colonies from maintaining 'the paramountcy of native interests'.

With the above distinction in place, he proceeded to be extremely critical of colonial 'exploitation'.[226] Thereafter appeared, however, a strange argument: since 'primitive African tribes' were not in a position to develop and use their mineral or other resources themselves, what moral claim might they have to resources 'of whose existence and significance they were wholly ignorant until the intrusion of Europeans'? There was, Moon felt, no moral ground to prevent British companies from developing these resources; but the appropriation of all the profits offended his sense of justice. And yet what would a fair division be? He could not resolve this problem; but he did not feel it could be solved 'by the British people becoming overnight a nation of philanthropists'.[227] Here it is unclear whether he was making a case for a more benevolent imperialism or merely leaving his audience with an apparent dilemma; he ended by quoting an unnamed British communist quoting an unnamed West African doctor on the 'highly progressive role' of British rule in Africa.[228]

In *Strangers in India*, written by December 1943, almost three years down the road, and without the constraints of an official 'war effort' speech, Moon made a surprisingly similar point. British rule itself was not responsible for the poverty of the Indian masses. It was 'largely due to factors beyond our control, and even beyond our ken'; any damage done to the already bad situation were the results of 'mistakes', 'shortcomings', 'unfortunate, though often not consciously intended, consequences of our association with India'.[229] Ultimately, Britain could be looked upon, 'in Marx's phrase, as just "the unconscious tool of history". I am proud that our country should have been chosen by fate, nature, God or whatever you like to call it, to clear up the debris of the Mogul empire and to unlock for India the treasures of Western thought. I think on the whole we were worthy of it'.[230] A worthy epitaph for the Empire had been found, worthy of the principle for which Moon always claimed to have taken up his calling as a civilian in India: finally to hand over India to its own, now politically mature, people.

Most people read *Strangers in India* at the time of its publication as a critique of British imperialism in India; it was not immediately apparent that it was equally a defence of the idea of empire. Reading this alongside his other writings, and alongside the writings, public and private, of other civilians at the time,[231] it becomes clear that the belief that Britain should leave India at the earliest possible date was not incompatible with the belief in the imperial ideal, which was sometimes opposed in such writings to imperial practice and which was more difficult to defend. Darling, while praising *Strangers in India* as a 'remarkable first book'[232] and, in private, writing to Moon to say that it was 'worth resigning to write that',[233] found plenty of room to differ with it. Darling was critical of Moon's mixing up of past and present, but particularly of what he regarded as 'biased' views: he felt that the book was 'tinged by a certain animus against British rule in India'. Darling agreed with the contention that the communal question was a struggle among the middle classes for posts, but disagreed strongly with the view that the British 'were "inhibited" from promoting agreement "by our subconscious adherence to the divide and rule principle and by our dislike of Congress"'. His own experience did not endorse the latter view, nor the view that although the British had promised India self-government they did not really want to relax their hold. Darling indicated as counter-evidence the Cripps offer, and if the relevant passage in *Strangers in India* had intended to indicate the period before the offer, he pointed to the grant of provincial autonomy as 'clearly a step in the direction of full self-government'.[234] He also disagreed with the view that the people of India preferred capitalists to 'the whips of foreigners';[235] and found it difficult to reconcile this view with Moon's observation that 'ruthless exploitation of the weak by the strong is still the rule in India'.[236] He attributed these views to the 'frankness and freshness of comparative youth' (Moon was under forty at the time). Moon's approach, Darling observed,

'... is that of the district officer who knows and loves the village and who is jealous of all that may undermine its welfare. It is this that gives the book not only its special interest but also its importance, for it is the village that must condition India's future'.[237]

It is the stereotypical image of the Kiplingesque district officer that provided the extenuating circumstances for Moon's ignorance; he was blinded by love. But Darling was sympathetic to Moon's idea that democracy might be unsuited to the Indian village, and found the latter's most interesting statement to be that the future of India may lie '"in the backward, obsolete States"'.[238] Moon's contention was, however, that the British system of justice had been imposed from above,[239] from which it followed that democracy might be unsuitable—but Darling did not engage with this first point; nor with Moon's unequivocal advocacy of economic planning and industrialization for India.[240]

Darling saw in British rule much good for the peasant; British improvements—the canal colonies, the opportunity to serve in the army and become enlightened through the experience—had made of the peasant a better peasant. If the British were to leave, who was to speak for the peasant? What did he understand, if anything, about the processes of politics in which he was ensnared? He was likely to be deluded and exploited by politicians. The peasant had no conception of who ruled him; the concept of *sirkar* existed, definitely; but the viceroy, the members of his Council, were alien concepts, and the King's name was not known—as Darling had ascertained in his conversations with the peasant.[241] And if this was the case, how could it be said that parliamentary democracy was at all suitable for him? This question continued to worry Darling. On the eve of Independence, he went on his last ride through India á là Arthur Young, and no longer as a Civilian, to talk to his peasants for the last time.[242]

'In what way are you not free?', Darling asked a Pathan, who was a *Khudai Khidmatgar*[243] and a Congress supporter. The Pathan replied, 'Before this there was no education and great harshness. In England there are factories and men make what they please. Here there are none. We cannot make pistols, guns, aeroplanes, motors or clothes: there is no permission, and this will be so until the English go. It is the same for both Hindu and Muslim. We are still slaves, we have only got to freedom's door.' This was conveyed to Darling through an interpreter—Darling did not speak Pushtu. The interpreter presumably translated this into Urdu and Darling translated it into English.[244] He asked a landlord what he, the landlord, would do with freedom; the landlord replied: consolidation of holdings, *panchayats* with powers to run hospitals and schools, textile mills and a small-arms factory. 'Those who read the newspapers think we should develop India like Russia.'[245] These, Darling was disturbed to discover, were rather vague ideas about opportunities for development in a free India, and were combined with a rather uncomprehending support for the Muslim League or for Pakistan; the landlord, a Muslim, had told him that he desired the British to stay on, but if they left he preferred Pakistan to Hindu domination, but this had been the most coherent answer he had received.[246] Darling felt that rather than democracy of a parliamentary variety, an indirect election system through rural constituencies having an electoral college, and 'efficient village panchayats', was preferable. In support of the latter end he quoted Sidney Webb's approving remarks from Webb's preface to John Matthai's *Village Government in British India*.[247] He earnestly advised the new government to place the peasant at the centre of its vision.[248]

Conclusions

There was a certain circularity in the arguments about 'development' as propounded by the British in India. Armed with a finite set of concepts about India, stereotypes built up over the long years of imperial rule, imperial administrators and officials had limited room within which to conceptualize 'development' for India. These concepts—the eternal peasant, the manipulative politician, the exploitative capitalist—were maintained as barriers against nationalism, serving the attempt to combat the latter's claims of the illegitimacy of colonialism with a counter-claim of nationalism's own illegitimacy and a corresponding legitimacy for colonialism on the grounds of its support for the interests of the poor peasant. It was, therefore, almost impossible to concede this ground.

On the other hand, as Darling pointed out, there were limits to what the colonial government could do within the norms of 'sound finance' even for its beloved peasant, and especially during the Depression. This resulted in a situation in which its claim to acting on behalf of the peasant began to lose the credibility it had once had, albeit in a limited sort of way. This left official thinking with two options: first, to abandon the claims to economic good government and concede the point regarding imperialism's exploitative intent—which many imperial officials were willing to do in private—but which would erode the Civilian's sense of well-being as well as make India politically more difficult to govern; or second, to maintain the claim and to argue that the old principles (obsolete and perhaps misguided but not deliberately exploitative) had to give way to new ones, and to hope that these could reconcile British and Indian interests at least so far as to minimize discontent. It was the latter option which was more viable.

Neither of these options was a priori incompatible with imperialism, even the Soviet example which, it was evident from the ways in which it was being discussed in imperial circles, was to be used in the service of not particularly Soviet goals. Indeed, by the time of the War, with the Soviet Union as an ally, it became much easier to discuss development through planning in pro-Soviet or proto-Soviet forms. It is also possible to suggest that many members of the administration and the bureaucracy were not hostile to a system which represented a level of power for the bureaucracy which the ICS had enjoyed in its heyday and which was quite psychologically appealing; this did not imply that communism or communist-led agrarian radicalism was any more appreciated than it had been before.

In the last analysis this is a chapter about attempts to sustain a framework of legitimacy for imperialism in India whose success was confined to audiences who were already wholly or in part convinced of the legitimacy of imperialism; and then only to some parts of these audiences for some of the time. Nationalists remained unconvinced by the arguments put forward. However, the space given to these ideas can be justified from a wider perspective than that of the internal debates of British imperialism in India. Many of the ideas which went into the arguments used in these debates influenced and reappeared in varying forms in nationalist discussions on 'development'. Many of the premises upon which arguments in support of imperialism were based were shared by arguments which opposed imperialism; the premises were combined in different constellations to produce different arguments. This was often the result of shared conceptual frameworks and discursive practices— partly due to frameworks and practices set in place by colonialism and, therefore, having to be engaged with within those spaces, partly because both sides drew on the academic and political ideas current in Western European and North American thought, and partly because the original sources of ideas, though perhaps now ill-remembered, were often the same. I shall elaborate this argument in the following chapters.

Endnotes

1. R. Hyam, 'Bureaucracy and "Trusteeship" in the Colonial Empire', in W.R. Louis (ed.), *Oxford History of the British Empire*, Vol. IV (Oxford, 1999).
2. See Chapter 1 of this book.
3. See section, 'Terminology', in Chapter 2 of this book.
4. Indicative of this are the writings of Sir George Schuster: see, for instance, 'Empire Trade Before and After Ottawa: A Preliminary Reconnaissance', in *The Economist:* Special Supplement, 3 November 1934; 'Indian Economic Life: Past Trends and Future Prospects', *Journal of the Royal Society of Arts LXXXIII*, 31 May 1935, address delivered 8 March 1935; *Private Work and Public Causes: A Personal Record, 1881–1978* (Cowbridge, 1979), pp. 39–90.
5. See section, 'Political Economy: Precedents and Ideas, Metropolitan and Colonial', in Chapter 2 of this book, especially on the contribution of Leo Amery to these debates, and the idea of imperial preference.
6. The mythologies and organizing ideologies of the British Empire have been studied in some detail now, and there is a rich literature on British attitudes to the Empire, their origins, sustenance, or propagation. Most of this relates, however, to a period of confidence and strength within the British Empire, dealing with the higher ranks of Government officials in India and Britain or the training and manipulation of British public opinion regarding the Empire. See, for a summary in the Indian context, Thomas Metcalf, *Ideologies of the Raj* (Cambridge, 1994). The work of Bernard Cohn is influential in this regard: see, in particular, the collections of essays, *An Anthropologist Among the Historians and other essays* (Delhi, 1986), and *Colonialism and its Forms of Knowledge: The British in India* (Delhi, 1997). See, also, Thomas Metcalf, *The Aftermath of the Revolt* (Princeton, 1965); Francis Hutchins, *The Illusion of Permanence: British Imperialism in India* (Princeton, 1967). On the manipulation of British public opinion and the moulding of British mentalities with regard to the Empire, see, for instance, J.M. MacKenzie, *Propaganda and Empire: the Manipulation of British Public Opinion, 1880–1960* (Manchester, 1984); J.M. MacKenzie (ed.), *Imperialism and Popular Culture* (Manchester, 1986); J.A. Mangan, *Making Imperial Mentalities: Socialisation and British Imperialism* (Manchester, 1990), and other titles in the Manchester University Press 'Studies in Imperialism' series.

7. This was in contrast to the early period of British rule, in which India was a sort of laboratory in which to test new ideas. See, for instance, Eric Stokes, *The English Utilitarians and India* (Oxford, 1959).

8. On the ceremonial aspects of British rule in India, see Bernard Cohn, 'Representing Authority in Victorian India', in Eric Hobsbawm and Terence Ranger (eds), *The Invention of Tradition* (Cambridge, 1983).

9. In 1942 the Cripps Mission explicitly offered India Dominion status after the War, with the right eventually to secede from the Empire—the offer also implicitly recognized Pakistan for the first time: see R.J. Moore, 'The Mystery of the Cripps Mission', in R.J. Moore, *Endgames of Empire: Studies of Britain's India Problem* (Delhi, 1988).

10. Sanjoy Bhattacharya and Benjamin Zachariah, '"A Great Destiny": The British Colonial State and the Advertisement of Post-War Reconstruction in India, 1942-45', *South Asia Research*, Vol. 19, No. 1 (1999).

11. See, for example, Philip Joseph Charrier, 'Britain, India and the Genesis of the Colombo Plan, 1945–1951', unpublished PhD dissertation, University of Cambridge, 1995; Anita Inder Singh, *The Limits of British Influence: South Asia and the Anglo-American Relationship 1947–1956* (London, 1993).

12. See, for example, Penderel Moon, *Strangers in India* (London, 1944); for a less critical—and retrospective—reading of the British record, but for a similar acceptance that by the 1930s it was time to leave honourably, see Philip Mason, *A Shaft of Sunlight* (London, 1978). A more critical reading is provided by Michael Carritt, *A Mole in the Crown* (Calcutta, 1986). All three had been British civil servants in late colonial India.

13. Moon, *Strangers in India*, p. 43.

14. See G. Balachandran, 'Towards a "Hindoo Marriage": Anglo-Indian Monetary Relations in Interwar India, 1917-35', *Modern Asian Studies*, Vol. 28, No. 3 (1994); also Dietmar Rothermund, *India in the Great Depression 1929–1939* (Delhi, 1992); G. Balachandran, *John Bullion's Empire: Britain's Gold Problem and India between the Wars* (Richmond, 1996).

15. For the importance the government gave to the management of its own publicity with regard to India, see Milton Israel, *Communications and Power* (Cambridge, 1994).

16. The Government of India Act of 1935, while widening the franchise, kept it on a property basis which denied voting rights to most of the population. Viceregal certification was a measure written into the Act as a safeguard against the difficulties of running a government which had to get budgets and other unpopular government legislative measures passed even after the Central Legislature had rejected them. All Finance Member, P. J. Grigg's Budgets were passed by Viceregal certification—see Dietmar Rothermund, *India in the Great Depression 1929–1939*, pp. 70–8.

17. On the 'man on the spot', see Clive Dewey, *Anglo-Indian Attitudes: The Mind of the Indian Civil Service* (London, 1993); Clive Dewey, 'Editor's Introduction' to Malcolm Darling, *The Punjab Peasant in Prosperity and*

Debt (fifth edition, Delhi, 1977). Dewey does not comment on the relationship between the 'man on the spot' and 'public opinion'.

18. In 1924, the Lee Commission set targets for admitting Indians to the ICS: see *Report of the Royal Commission on the Superior Civil Services in India* (London, 1924); on the Lee Commission's Indianization targets, see D.C. Potter, *India's Political Administrators 1919–1983* (Oxford, 1986), pp. 90–91, and, on the rate of their achievement, pp. 89–101. The Lee Commission targets were in fact a slowing down of the pace of Indianization, as Indians were increasingly successful in entering the Service; and the Governor of UP reportedly thanked its chairman for 'having changed the entire situation, political and administrative ... whereas two years ago we of the Services felt almost down and out, we have now got the "Wogs" by the short hair and can do what we like with them'. Quoted in Carl Bridge, *Holding India to the Empire* (Delhi, 1986), p. 14.

19. For the use of the term 'guardians' with regard to the ICS, see Philip Woodruff (Philip Mason), *The Men Who Ruled India, Part II: The Guardians* (London, 1965). This is a retrospective justification of the ICS' role in India; 'Indianization' is at best looked upon with anxiety as Mason claims for the civilian an intellectual tradition of Platonic expertise in disinterested governance.

20. See, for instance, S.K. Chettur, *The Steel Frame and I: Life in the ICS* (Bombay, 1962), notably his anecdotes on pp. 70–1 and 89.

21. Sir George Schuster, *Private Work and Public Causes: A Personal Record, 1881–1978* (Cowbridge, 1979), pp. 39–89.

22. See Raghabendra Chattopadhyay, 'An Early British Initiative in the Genesis of Indian Planning', *Economic and Political Weekly*, Vol. XXII, No. 5 31 January 1987.

23. On the rupee ratio question, for instance, Schuster was inclined to support 1s 4d. See Dietmar Rothermund, *India in the Great Depression*, p. 38; Tomlinson, *The Political Economy of the Raj 1914–1947* (London, 1979), p. 85. He did not get a sympathetic hearing. To maintain the high ratio of 1s 6d at a time of falling prices a severe contraction of currency was required. As the Government of India was still the currency authority Schuster had to do this job, and in public he defended it as best he could. In private, he appealed to Montagu Norman, Governor of the Bank of England, in August 1930 arguing that the political unrest in India would spread to the agricultural classes as currency contraction aggravated the problem of falling prices. Norman appreciated the economic logic of Schuster's analysis of the situation, but advised 'Do nothing, stand fast': quoted in Rothermund, *India in the Great Depression*, p. 41. The Treasury was opposed to 'transferring the burden, even contingently, on to the British taxpayer': quoted in Tomlinson, *The Political Economy of the Raj*, p. 87. When Britain went off the gold standard in September 1931 without informing the Government of India in advance, Schuster advised the Viceroy, Lord Willingdon, to issue an

ordinance suspending payments to prevent a run on the reserves, and then to let the rupee float, in order that a lower ratio assist the recovery of trade. In this they were overruled by Samuel Hoare, the new Conservative Secretary of State for India, who ordered that the 1s 6d rate be maintained, sending his telegram directly to the Controllers of Currency in India over the viceroy's head: see Rothermund, *India in the Great Depression*, p. 45. The anticipated political and financial disasters failed to materialize, as the outflow of gold on private account restored the export surplus which enabled the home charges to be remitted easily once more. The departure of sterling from the gold standard led to a fall in the gold value of the rupee, which was tied to sterling. The price of gold rose by the same value as the downswing of the pound, and the discrepancy between the depreciation of the rupee and the pound combined with the government's freezing of gold prices in rupees at the old rate made it profitable to buy gold in India and sell it in London. It is also reasonably clear that much of this gold was dehoarded as a result of distress sales from the countryside, as moneylenders claimed their dues in gold rather than agrarian produce or land, not worth much with the collapse of primary produce prices. See Rothermund, *India in the Great Depression*, pp. 47–50, but B.R. Tomlinson seems not to see that 'enforced disinvestment' and the desire for profits were actually quite compatible since different groups of people were operating under these two motivations. Tomlinson, *The Political Economy of the Raj*, pp. 37–8. See also Benthall Papers, Centre for South Asian Studies, Cambridge, Box II, File '1931–32': letter from Benthall (who was representing the European Association and the Associated Chambers of Commerce at the Conference) to P.H. Browne, President of the Bengal Chamber of Commerce, 5 October 1931: 'As the situation is now, the gold ratio is considerably under 1/4d, and silver has risen so that the only stick which Birla has to beat the Government at the moment is the export of gold, over which he has acted so discreditably [by exporting gold himself] and his only argument is that while he must admit that the alteration of the rupee in relation to gold has benefited India, it would have benefited India more if the rupee had been allowed to find its own level entirely out of relation to sterling.'

24. This was done by a policy of deflation, retrenchment and borrowing mainly on the Indian money market. See Dietmar Rothermund, 'The Great Depression and British Financial Policy in India, 1929-1934', in Dietmar Rothermund, *The Indian Economy under British Rule* (Delhi, 1983). Despite net additions, Schuster was actually able to reduce the total public debt. And despite his advocacy of public spending he presided over cutbacks in public works and irrigation expenditure.

25. Sir George Schuster, 'Empire Trade Before and After Ottawa: A Preliminary Reconnaissance', in *The Economist:* Special Supplement, 3 November 1934; and Sir George Schuster, 'Indian Economic Life: Past Trends and Future Prospects', *Journal of the Royal Society of Arts LXXXIII*, 31 May 1935, address delivered 8 March 1935.

26. Schuster, 'Empire Trade'.
27. See section, 'Political Economy: Precedents and Ideas, Metropolitan and Colonial', in Chapter 2 of this book, for a genealogy of 'imperial preference' as an idea in reasonably common circulation from the late 1920s, largely in Conservative Party thinking. In India, though the debate acquired great significance in and around 1932 consequent to its being discussed at the Ottawa Imperial Economic Conference, in practice, something very similar had already begun. Even in 'traditional' export products like cotton piece-goods and steel, Britain now preferred to share the Indian market with Indians rather than lose it to outsiders due to their own lack of competitiveness. Indian steel was the first beneficiary of this policy, because cheaper Belgian or German steel could be excluded by 'differential tariffs' which did not apply to British steel. After 1932 these were called by their proper name—'Imperial Preference'—and applied increasingly to cotton textiles against Japanese competition. See Rothermund, *India in the Great Depression*, pp. 168–74; see also Basudev Chatterji, 'Business and Politics in the 1930s: Lancashire and the Making of the Indo-British Trade Agreement, 1939', *Modern Asian Studies*, Vol. 15, No. 3 (1985).
28. Schuster, 'Empire Trade' (1934); also 'Indian Economic Life', pp. 662, 655–6.
29. See L.S. Amery, *Empire and Prosperity* (second edition, London, October 1931).
30. Basudev Chatterji, *Trade, Tariffs and Empire: Lancashire and British Policy in India, 1919–1939* (Delhi, 1992), pp. 10–27; P.J. Cain and A.G. Hopkins, *British Imperialism: Crisis and Deconstruction,* pp. 11–30, 198–9.
31. He pointed out that other important heads of manufactured imports had shown a remarkable increase—chemicals, cutlery, dyes, electrical goods, machinery, paper, and motor vehicles—despite the Depression. 'Most of these, especially motor vehicles, are classes of imports which are capable of vast expansion without interfering with India's own natural industrial development'. Schuster, 'Indian Economic Life', pp. 646–7.
32. Schuster, 'Indian Economic Life', p. 654.
33. Schuster, 'Indian Economic Life', p. 642: 'I do not wish ... to suggest that the masses in India, even though they are so poor, are necessarily more unhappy than in the rest of the world. I believe in fact that even as things are, more absolute and intense human misery prevails among parts of the world in highly industrialised countries which have suddenly lost all chances of employment owing to the economic crisis which has cut away the foundations on which their life depended. The very simplicity of Indian life and its less materialistic background have saved the people some of the misery which has fallen on other countries.'
34. Schuster, 'Indian Economic Life', p. 664. Schuster recommended three objectives for Indian policy: (1) maintenance and development of export markets for 'those commodities in the production of which India has special

natural advantages'; (2) raising of standards of living so as to provide new internal demand for the products of her rural population; (3) 'the development of industrial activities as an important means towards achieving the second objective...'. This involved economic planning, which he urged, was the logical conclusion to the Government of India's existing policies: 'Indian Economic Life', p. 662.

35. Schuster, 'Indian Economic Life', p. 642.
36. Schuster, 'Empire Trade...'.
37. Schuster, 'Indian Economic Life', p. 647.
38. '... in a world where an enormous part of the population of all countries are not even adequately fed, and much less adequately supplied with all the other equipment of life, it is ridiculous to talk of overproduction, and that the efforts of all statesmen ought to be concentrated on opening the channels for an increase of consumption.' Schuster, 'Indian Economic Life', p. 649.
39. Schuster, 'Indian Economic Life', pp. 656–7.
40. See Chapter 2 of this book.
41. For an account of the failure of this initiative to make a practical impact on government thinking, see Raghabendra Chattopadhyay, 'An Early British Initiative in the Genesis of Indian Planning'.
42. George Schuster, 'Note on Economic Policy', National Archives of India (NAI): Finance Department, Finance Branch, File No: 15-I-F of 1930, pp. 1–2. The proposals originated in discussions with the Commerce Member, George Rainy, and the then Members for Education, Health and Lands, and Industries and Labour, in anticipation of the Constitutional changes being discussed in the light of the Simon Commission Report, and following from the public demand for a constructive, active economic policy on the part of the government. There appears to have been more to the initial discussions than a demand for an economic advisory council—but there was no paper record of these discussions. A more explicit appeal for intervention was made by Schuster on 8 June 1932, in a Note prepared at the new Viceroy Willingdon's request. Schuster wrote, 'No Government in present economic conditions can afford to carry on with the old laissez-faire policy. The need for some kind of national planning is being forced on all governments...I should like to see the Government of India attempting to design something in the nature of a five-year economic plan.' Quoted in Raghabendra Chattopadhyay, 'The Idea of Planning in India, 1930–1951', unpublished Ph.D Dissertation, Australian National University, Canberra (1985) p. 48.
43. Schuster's colleagues were not enthusiastic; Schuster, nonetheless, asked them to put their objections on paper for him, after which he summarized the objections and put forward his own case. This was also in the light of the opinions of representatives of unofficial opinion who had been invited to discuss the possible benefits which might accrue from such a council, and the views of the governors of various provinces who had been asked to write in their opinions on the matter. The initiative also led to a brief tour and a report

by Sir Arthur Salter, then Director of the Economic and Financial Section of the Secretariat of the League of Nations. See Sir Arthur Salter, *A Scheme for an Economic Advisory Organisation in India* (Delhi, 1931). Salter complained in his Report of the lack of time and the small number of places he visited and made his suggestions 'with considerable diffidence' (pp. 1–2); but came up with extremely detailed proposals, recommending a committee which would be 'predominantly unofficial in character' rather than based on the British model of being expert rather than representative (p. 13). Nothing much came of these proposals, the consensus being that it was politically undesirable to associate representative opinion with government decisions, the former apparently seen as almost automatically hostile. See Sir John Woodhead's note, NAI: File No. 2002-C (in 15-I-F, 1930), ff. 11–12. See also Raghabendra Chattopadhyay, 'An Early British Initiative ...'. (Salter's own account of his 'Oriental interlude' as he described it, is less concerned with the work he did in India than the travels he undertook thereafter, particularly in China, where he was most impressed by the delicate Chinese ladies in Western dress: Arthur Salter, *Memoirs of a Public Servant* (London, 1961), chapter ten, especially pp. 208–11.)

44. The proceedings of the Reconstruction Committee of the Viceroy's Executive Council, and the planning and development department which followed it, can be read in the files of the Government of India, Finance Department, Planning, Planning-I, Planning-II, and Planning-III Branches, NAI, dated 1944–6 (but often incorporating earlier materials). It is unclear as to whether anyone knew of or remembered Schuster's 1930s efforts; though Schuster himself continued to recommend economic planning for Indian development— for the mutual benefit of India and the world: see Guy Wint and George Schuster, *India and Democracy* (London, 1941).

45. George Schuster, 'Note on Economic Policy' NAI: File No: 15-I-F, 1930, p. 1. Interestingly, the first two proposals were not taken particularly seriously; the third was taken to mean the need for pro-government propaganda on economic matters—not the only time this interpretation was given to government economic schemes. See the notes of Sir Geoffrey de Montmorency, NAI: File 15-I-F, 1930, p. 7 (he also claimed that the government 'have always had' an active economic policy—p. 4); and of Sir John Woodhead , 2002-C (in 15-I-F, 1930), f. 12.

46. George Schuster, 'Note on Economic Policy' NAI: File No.: 15-I-F, 1930, p. 1.

47. Maurice Dobb's review of *The Soviet Union Looks Ahead: The Five-year Plan for Economic Reconstruction*, from the *Spectator*, Appendix I, NAI: File No. 2002-C (in 15-I-F, 1930); quoted in NAI: 15-I-F, 1930, p. 1.

48. NAI: 15-I-F, 1930, p. 1.

49. This paranoia is well reflected in the reports written by the Government of India on the communist situation; see Sir David Petrie, *Communism in India, 1924–1927* (Calcutta, 1927); *India and Communism: Confidential: Compiled in the Intelligence Bureau, Home Department, Government of India*

(Calcutta, 1933); *India and Communism: Confidential: (Revised up to the 1 January 1935: Compiled in the Intelligence Bureau, Home Department, Government of India* (Simla, 1935). The general British premise was that all political disturbances in India were potentially appropriable by the communists, whether local, parochial, religious, or secular; all unrest, therefore, should be treated as actual or potential communism. See *India and Communism*, 1933 edition, pp. 20–1—which also quotes Petrie's agreement with this premise. The same text outlines the ways in which the full weight of the colonial state's repressive apparatus could be thrown against 'communist' political unrest: 'India's Legal Armoury Against Communism', chapter twenty-three, pp. 179–204, *India and Communism*, 1933 edition.

50. Philip Snowden to P.J. Grigg, 18 March 1935, Grigg Papers, PJGG 2/19/1(c). Churchill College Archive Centre, Cambridge.
51. Grigg to Snowden, 13 May 1935, Grigg Papers, PJGG 2/19/2(a)-(b).
52. Snowden to Grigg, Grigg Papers, PJGG 2/19/3(b).
53. See Grigg Papers, PJGG 2/16. Norman, rather interestingly, wrote to Grigg after Hitler's party purge in 1934, expressing his approval for that measure, late and therefore 'more bloody', 'but maybe not too late to save and maintain a moderate situation. My friends declare that the lateness of Hitler has been due to his affection for the buccaneers and burglars who stood with him throughout the hard years, of whom he was loth to believe extreme intentions and still less disloyalty'. Norman to Grigg, 4 July 1934, Grigg Papers, PJGG 2/16/1(a)-(b). There is no indication in the letter that either Norman or Grigg was uncomfortable with Hitler being in power; he was a 'moderate'.
54. Grigg to Snowden, 11 November 1935 PJGG 2/19/4(c)-(d).
55. Grigg to Snowden, 27 February 1936, PJGG 2/19/6(b)-(c). See also Grigg to Chamberlain, 30 March 1936, Grigg Papers, PJGG 2/2/3(a)-(c), which is phrased in almost identical terms.
56. Grigg to Snowden, 13 May 1935, Grigg Papers, PJGG 2/19/2(d).
57. Grigg to Chamberlain, 17 August 1934, Grigg Papers, PJGG 2/2/1.
58. Grigg to Chamberlain, 17 August 1934, Grigg Papers, PJGG 2/2/1.
59. Grigg to Chamberlain, 17 August 1934, Grigg Papers, PJGG 2/2/1. In 1936, Grigg announced to Chamberlain, 'We have just beaten the Assembly at Ottawa', and directed him 'you must never again enter into an agreement with India which does not provide specifically for Lancashire'. Grigg to Chamberlain, 30 March 1936, Grigg Papers, PJGG 2/2/3. This was by now a difficult position to hold; and by the 1940s it was freely admitted that Lancashire had been sacrificed—though not, of course, the City.
60. See his memoirs: P.J. Grigg, *Prejudice and Judgement* (London, 1948).
61. Grigg to Sir Findlater Stewart at the India Office, 23 July 1934, Grigg Papers, PJGG 2/20/6(b). Stewart politely agreed that Bhore was a nationalist, but defended him as 'a very moderate and reasonable nationalist', while gently alluding to the possible racist connotations of Grigg's remarks. Stewart to Grigg, 10 August 1934, Grigg Papers, PJGG 2/20/8(a).

62. Grigg to Lothian, 16 April 1938, Grigg Papers, PJGG 2/14/1.

63. Lothian to Grigg, 1 June 1938, Grigg Papers, PJGG 2/14/2(b).

64. Though not Gregory's selection for the post—Schuster would not have backed so conservative an economist. Sir Arthur Salter's trip to India in response to Schuster's requests had led to the recommendation of better collection of economic information for India. See Sir Arthur Salter, *A Scheme for an Economic Advisory Organisation in India* (Geneva, 1931). This had led on to the Bowley–Robertson Report of 1934: A.L. Bowley and H.D. Robertson, *A Scheme for an Economic Census for India, with special reference to a Census of Production and Reorganisation of Statistics* (Delhi: Government of Indian Press, 1934)—which had made further recommendations in this regard, and had inter alia recommended the appointment of an economic adviser to the Government of India. See also Raghabendra Chattopadhyay, 'An Early British Initiative...'.

65. Memorandum on 'Protection and "Secondary Industries"', dated 6/5/1938, Gregory Papers, IOR: MSS.EUR.D.1163/1, f. 4. There was a demand for state aid for the growth of industries; he pointed out that 'State aid is not identical with tariff protection ... a subsidy might equally well meet the case'. Gregory Papers, MSS.EUR.D.1163/1, f. 4.

66. Gregory Papers, MSS.EUR.D.1163/1, f 6.

67. See, for instance, A.G. Clow, *The State and Industry in India* (Calcutta: Government of India Press, 1928); Schuster's arguments, cited above.

68. Gregory Papers, MSS.EUR.D.1163/1, ff. 6–8.

69. Gregory Papers, MSS.EUR.D.1163/1, f. 8.

70. Gregory Papers, MSS.EUR.D.1163/1, f. 12.

71. Note by Grigg on first page, Gregory Papers, MSS.EUR.D.1163/1, f. 1.

72. *Studies in Indian Economics issued by the Office of the Economic Adviser, First Series: Aspects of the Indian Tariff, No. 1: The Burden of the Indian Tariff* by T. E. Gregory, DSc (Econ.) and W. R. Natu, BSc (Econ.) (Delhi: Government of India Press, 1939), copy in Gregory Papers, MSS.EUR.D.1163/15.

73. Gregory and Natu, *The Burden of the Indian Tariff*, pp. 44–6.

74. For a list, see A.H. Hanson, *The Process of Planning: A Study of India's Five-Year Plans 1950–1964* (Oxford, 1966), pp. 37–40. Some of these were projects previously begun, but were later integrated within the framework of post-War reconstruction planning.

75. See Andrew Land, Rodney Lowe, and Noel Whiteside, *The Development of the Welfare State 1939–1951: A Guide to Documents in the Public Records Office* (London: HMSO, 1992), pp. 3–5.

76. The first meeting of a Reconstruction Committee of Council was held on 23 June, 1941. See Proceedings, in the papers of Sir Theodore Gregory, Economic Adviser to the Government of India, IOR: MSS.EUR.D.1163/4, ff. 3–12.

77. Lt Gen. Sir Thomas Hutton, 'The Planning of Post-War Development in India', *Asiatic Review XLIII* (April 1947), p. 130.

78. Note by Kingsley Wood, 14 March 1942: L/F/7/2861: f. 247.

79. Memorandum by Secretary of State for India: Secret: War Cabinet, 1 August 1942. L/PO/2/16.

80. Recorded by Wavell in his diary: Penderel Moon (ed.), *Wavell: The Viceroy's Journal* (London, 1973), p. 12, entry for 27 July 1943.

81. Sir Jeremy Raisman, Finance Member of the Government of India, had suggested to the War Cabinet early in the course of the discussions that the best way 'to mitigate the consequences of India's growing sterling balances at the end of the war' was to set up a reconstruction fund with part of the sterling balances which would be used to import capital and consumer goods into India. Minutes of War Cabinet meeting, 1/8/1942, copy in IOR: L/PO/2/16. City newspapers began to see the balances as 'a pent-up demand for the products of our export industries', *News Chronicle*, 22 September 1942, quoted in Amery to Kingsley Wood, *TP III*, Doc. 14. Meanwhile, J.B. Taylor, Governor, Reserve Bank, was warding off a possible 'embarrassing resolution' from his Indian colleagues by 'emphasising [the] importance and value of sterling for post-war re-equipment and industrial expansion of India'—a goal ardently desired by Indian business interests and, therefore, a good carrot to dangle. Linlithgow to Amery, telegram, 3 October 1942, *TP III*, Doc. 56.

82. Amery to Wood, 7 August 1942, L/PO/2/16.

83. Margin note in Treasury copy of above letter, quoted in Chatterji, *Trade, Tariffs and Empire*, p. 479.

84. 'In this country it is universally agreed that we are not going to go back, as we did after the last war, to the old financial standards of what we can afford or not, but that we must, as in the war, go ahead doing all the reorganisation work we believe to be necessary and let the problem of financing it solve itself.' Linlithgow's alarmed response, in his margin note, was 'Good Lord!'. Amery to Linlithgow, 27 May 1942, MSS.EUR.F.125/11, (*TP II*, Doc. 95).

85. East India Association, Discussion: 'India and Democracy', Tuesday, 14 October 1941, opened by Sir George Schuster, *Asiatic Review*, Vol. XXXVIII No. 133 (January 1942), p. 6. Schuster lauded the Government of India's step in enlarging the Viceroy's Executive Council to eight Indian and four British members. See also Guy Wint and George Schuster, *India and Democracy* (London, 1941).

86. Darling, Ahmednagar, to Guy Wint, Akbar Road, New Delhi, 16 January 1940, ff. 91–5, Item 6, Box LXI, Darling Papers, CSAS.

87. See Darling's record of his interview with L.S. Amery in June 1940 (written out on 17 April 1944); and Darling to Amery, 18 August 1941, ff. 98–9 & 100, respectively, Item 6, Box LXI, Darling Papers, CSAS. Darling was sent a brief reply by the India Office: the Secretary of State was 'trying to get a few days in the country'; he was not ignoring Darling's letter but was unable to comment at that moment. Clauson (?) to Darling, 21 August 1941.

88. This was after one attempt to gain Indian support for the war effort—the Cripps Mission proposals, offering limited participation of Indians in

government and post-War Dominion status and the right to secede from the Empire—had failed.

89. Minutes of War Cabinet meeting, 24 August 1942, copy in IOR: L/E/8/2527: f. 358. Present at the meeting were Attlee (in the chair), Sir Stafford Cripps, Sir John Anderson, Anthony Eden, Oliver Lyttleton, Ernest Bevin, Sir Kingsley Wood, Leo Amery, Viscount Cranborne, and Sir Archibald Sinclair. A week later, another cabinet minute proposed bringing the idea to the Government of India's notice. Minutes of War Cabinet meeting, 31 August 1942, copy in IOR: L/E/8/2527: f. 351. Present, in addition to the above, were Churchill in the chair, S.M. Bruce, Herbert Morrison, A.V. Alexander, Sir James Grigg (former finance member of the Government of India), Brendan Bracken, Sir Orme Sargent, Sir Wilfrid Freeman, and Lt Gen. A.E. Nye. Sir John Anderson, former governor of Bengal, was absent. It is slightly unclear how exactly the problems of the Quit India Movement, described by Linlithgow as 'by far the most serious rebellion since that of 1857, the gravity and extent of which we have so far concealed from the world for reasons of military security' (Personal telegram to Churchill, via India Office, 31 August 1942, MSS.EUR.F.125/158—*TP II*, Doc 662, p. 853), and the Japanese aggression were expected to be solved by such means.

90. Note by Croft to Anderson, India Office, 27 August 1942, IOR: L/E/8/2527, f. 357.

91. For a curious version of this argument, see IOR: L/E/9/435, file entitled 'Labour: Unemployment: International Labour Organisation Unemployment Convention 1919. Denounced by the Government of India 16.4.38'. The Convention was denounced on the grounds that since the provinces were now responsible for such things as unemployment, the Government of India could not adhere to such a convention. A Minute by the Economic and Overseas Department of the India Office dated 6 April 1938 noted 'it was doubtful policy to rely publicly on formal arguments open to dispute, when the obvious practical motives for denunciation were in fact generally known ... The Govt. of India ... are clutching at a constitutional pretext to get them out of an embarrassing situation ...'.

92. Note by Croft to Anderson, India Office, 27 August 1942, IOR: L/E/8/2527, f. 357.

93. Sir Atul Chatterjee, quoted in Minute by Croft, 18 September 1942, IOR: L/E/8/2527: f. 308.

94. Sir Ramaswami Mudaliar, (in England as the Government of India's representative to the War Cabinet) quoted in Note of Meeting at the India Office with regard to Sir Stafford Cripps' proposals. IOR: L/E/8/2527: ff 314–15. Section 93 was the section of the Government of India Act of 1935 which enabled provincial governors to rule in the provinces in the absence of elected ministries, this becoming necessary in 1939 when the Congress ministries resigned as a result of Linlithgow declaring war on India's behalf without reference to Indian opinion.

95. He referred in this connection to the Congress' pamphlet on 'National Debt', 'brought out some years back'. This almost certainly refers to a pamphlet prepared for the Second Round Table Conference, authored mainly by the Gandhian, J.C. Kumarappa, and repudiating a large part of the Indian 'national' debt as properly belonging not to India but to Britain. See the copy in IOR: L/I/1/149.

96. Mudaliar to Linlithgow, 2 October 1942, IOR: MSS.EUR.F.125/30. *TP III*, Doc. 53.

97. Amery to Cripps, 2 October 1942, IOR: L/E/8/2527: f. 299.

98. IOR: L/E/9/2527: ff. 278–80, 23 October 1942.

99. Amery to Cripps, 2 October 1942, IOR: L/E/8/2527: f. 299.

100. IOR: L/E/9/2527: ff. 278–80, 23 October 1942.

101. Bevin to Amery, 21 September 1942, IOR: L/E/9/2527: f. 270 and enclosed censorship excerpt, f. 271.

102. Bevin was already the author of a scheme for training skilled Indian labour in Britain in order to provide specialized manpower otherwise lacking in India for the war economy. This scheme came to be known as the 'Bevin Scheme' and the trainees 'Bevin Boys'. For details of the scheme, see IOR: L/R/5/291: Government of India Departmental and Miscellaneous Histories of the War: Labour Department: Note on 'Bevin Training Scheme'.

103. Raghabendra Chattopadhyay has attributed the proposal to Cripps' efforts to make amends for his failed Mission: 'The Idea of Planning in India'. This seems a rather narrow view to take; Cripps was known to be committed to Indian independence and was close to socialist circles in India.

104. See Partha Sarathi Gupta, *Imperialism and the British Labour Movement*, pp. 10–13 and passim.

105. Note by R.N. Gilchrist, India Office, 31 August 1942, IOR: L/E/8/2527: ff. 354–5.

106. Draft telegram, Amery to Linlithgow, IOR: L/E/8/2527: f, 349.

107. The Royal Commission on Labour in India's Report of 1931.

108. Draft telegram, Amery to Linlithgow, IOR: L/E/8/2527: f. 349.

109. Amery to Linlithgow, 1 September 1942, IOR: MSS.EUR.F.125/11. *TP II*, Doc. 673.

110. Gilchrist's note, 31 August 1942, IOR: L/E/8/2527: ff. 354–5.

111. Note by Sir Stafford Cripps, 2 September 1942, IOR: L/E/8/2527: ff. 339–41.

112. Note by Sir Stafford Cripps, 2 September 1942, IOR: L/E/8/2527: ff. 339–41.

113. Note by Sir Stafford Cripps, 2 September 1942, IOR: L/E/8/2527: ff. 339–41, paras 2–3.

114. Note by Aubrey Dibdin, Assistant Secretary, Economic and Overseas Department, India Office, to Croft, n.d., IOR: L/E/8/2527: f. 331.

115. Hubback to Monteath, India Office (Secret), 25 September 1942, IOR: L/E/8/2527: ff. 318–9.

116. Churchill suggested to Cripps and Amery that Bevin, Minister of Labour, and Wood, Chancellor of the Exchequer, should join them in a preliminary survey: Prime Minister's Personal Minute to Cripps, Lord Privy Seal, and Amery, Secretary of State for India, 20 September 1942, IOR: L/E/8/2527: f. 307.

117. Note by W.D. Croft, 11 September 1942, IOR: L/E/8/2527: ff. 332–6.

118. This echoes his 1938 paper. See above.

119. Note of meeting on Social and Economic Reconstruction in India, 23 and 24 November 1942. IOR: L/E/8/2527: ff. 243–4. *TP III*, Doc. 210. Those present included W.D. Croft (in the Chair), Sir Theodore Gregory, Sir Malcolm Darling, Sir Frederick Leggett, and Jack (Ministry of Labour), A.D.K. Owen (Lord Privy Seal's Office), Aubrey Dibdin (India Office).

120. Cripps to Amery, 15 December 1942; enclosure dated 10 December 1942, IOR: L/E/8/2527: ff. 231–40. *TP III*, Doc. 276. This document came from the Lord Privy Seal's Office; soon after this Cripps was shifted to the Ministry of Aircraft Production.

121. Secretary of State's note on Social and Economic Policy for India, 21/1/1943, L/E/8/2527: ff 221-6.

122. Amery to Linlithgow, 2 March 1943, MSS.EUR.F.125/12 *TP* II, Doc. 556. Discussions were now no longer confined to official circles; industrialists were being given a glimpse of what their future standing in India might be, and McGowan showed a good understanding of the political correctness required of British industry working in India after the War. In this he had good precedent to go by. Sir Edward Benthall, Senior Partner of Bird-Heilgers, Calcutta, and now a member of the Viceroy's Executive Council, had come to the conclusion at the time of the Round Table Conferences that European business in India, by virtue of its having claimed special safeguards as an Indian minority would need to accommodate more Indians on its companies' boards and in European-dominated chambers of commerce. See Benthall Papers, Box II, passim.

123. Enclosed in letter, Linlithgow to Amery, 2–4 May 1943, MSS.EUR.F.125/12, (*TP III*, Doc. 681).

124. Jenkins to Laithwaite, Personal Secretary to the Viceroy, 26 April 1943, enclosed note, IOR: L/E/8/2527: ff. 110-113.

125. Hutton to Laithwaite, Reconstruction Committee of Council, 27 and 28 April 1943, MSS.EUR.F.125/138 (*TP III*, Doc. 672).

126. IOR: L/E/8/2527: ff. 286–96.

127. Moon (ed.), *Wavell: The Viceroy's Journal*, p. 10, entry for 5 July 1943.

128. In a long letter to Amery, Linlithgow had also raised a large number of mainly technical and administrative, but also cultural, objections to Cripps' Note, also however, outlining the administrative framework being evolved in India to tackle such problems at the time. Linlithgow to Amery, 14 September 1943, MSS.EUR.F.125/14 (*TP IV*, Doc. 113).

129. Linlithgow to Amery, telegram, 16 July 1943, dealing with social policy.

Note for Wavell's, Amery's, and Mudaliar's eyes only. IOR: L/E/8/2527: ff. 106–7.

130. See Bhattacharya and Zachariah, "A Great Destiny".

131. The proceedings of the Reconstruction Committee of the Viceroy's Executive Council, of the Planning and Development Department which followed it, and the details of the debates—and projects—of post-War reconstruction planning can by followed in detail in the files of the Government of India Finance Department's Planning Branch, Planning-I, Planning-II, and Planning-III Branches dated 1944–1946 at the National Archives of India; in the Governor-General's Fortnightly Reports to the Secretary of State, reprinted in the *Transfer of Power* volumes; and in the papers of Sir Theodore Gregory, Economic Adviser to the Government of India, IOR: MSS.EUR.D.1163.

132. See Penderel Moon (ed.), *Wavell: The Viceroy's Journal* (London, 1973), pp. 46–77, entries for 1 January 1, 1944 to 30 June 1944; *TP* Vol. 4, chapter four of Summary of Documents, pp. (lv)-(lxx), documents relating to the period June 1943 to August 1944. It was only by claiming that the famine was damaging public morale and was, therefore, harmful to the war effort that some (inadequate) relief by way of supplies could be secured.

133. B.H. Baden-Powell, *The Land Systems of British India* (three volumes, Oxford, 1892).

134. Major J.C. Jack, *The Economic Life of a Bengal District* (Oxford, 1916); Malcolm Darling, *The Punjab Peasant in Prosperity and Debt* (Oxford, 1925); *Rusticus Loquitur, or the Old Light and the New in the Punjab Village* (Oxford, 1930); *Wisdom and Waste in the Punjab Village* (Oxford, 1934); Frank Lugard Brayne, *Better Villages* (Oxford, 1937).

135. See Malcolm Darling, *The Punjab Peasant*; *Rusticus Loquitur*; *Wisdom and Waste*; *At Freedom's Door* (Oxford, 1949).

136. See Clive Dewey, *Anglo-Indian Attitudes*, in which he views the Raj as providing a 'vast stage' which was essential to the 'full development of the middle-class mind', opportunities which they could never have had at home (p. ix). Dewey does not altogether engage with these attitudes as self-justificatory or self-delusory structures of thought; he regards the success or failure of civilians' 'improving' urges as the key to their attitudes or approaches to Indian society; of his two main protagonists, exemplars of the two poles between which the ICS veered, he sees Frank Brayne as arrogant and 'belligerent', therefore, a failure, and Malcolm Darling as a relative success, 'so sensitive to Indian feelings, so appreciative of Indian institutions, so averse to social tension' (p. 14). Dewey attributes the failure of Brayne's experiments in rural development to Brayne's arrogant and patronising attitude towards the natives, and his failure to take account of local conditions. He contrasts this approach to that of Darling who, being less aggressive and arrogant in his approach was, therefore, less patronizing (Dewey does not claim that Darling was much more successful than Brayne at achieving his goals). This is not borne out by my reading of Darling's views

on the Indian village and its development: Darling was gentler, but equally patronizing. See below.

137. Philip Mason, *A Shaft of Sunlight*; Penderel Moon, *Strangers in India*; Michael Carritt, *A Mole in the Crown*. This transformation is discussed explicitly in Penderel Moon's *Strangers in India*; and in Michael Carritt's memoirs: *A Mole in the Crown*. Carritt's move from ambivalent liberalism to communism must, however, be treated as an exception as far as the ICS is concerned; it was easier for most civilians to accommodate less complete changes in their own attitudes, which did not involve abandoning all of their previous points of orientation, and did not completely undermine their commitment to their imperial tasks.

138. For a vivid account of the life of a Bengal ICS officer in the 1930s, see Carritt, *A Mole in the Crown*. For an exploration of the experiences of the ICS in district administration (including accounts of several Indian ICS men), see Roland Hunt and John Harrison, *The District Officer in India 1930–1947* (London, 1980).

139. See, for instance, Sir Geoffrey de Montmorency's Note in NAI: 15-I-F, (1930).

140. Private letter, Lord Irwin (Viceroy) to Lord Birkenhead (Secretary of State for India), 14 October 1926, IOR: L/PO/1/18(i), 'Royal Commission on Agriculture in India: Correspondence', f. 21.

141. Mason, *A Shaft of Sunlight*, pp. 76–7. For Brayne's views, see Brayne, *Better Villages* (Delhi, 1937); Dewey's *Anglo-Indian Attitudes* deals with Brayne's work and views in great detail. An hierarchy of terms seems to appear in Sir Sikandar Hyat Khan, Premier of the Punjab under provincial autonomy, in his foreword to Frank Brayne's *Better Villages*: *Rural Uplift* has come to occupy a prominent place in the programme of *rural reconstruction*. This is as it should be. The experience of rural organisation all the world over has emphasised the necessity of *planning out an all-comprehensive rural programme*.' Sir Sikandar Hyat Khan, 'Foreword', to Frank Lugard Brayne, *Better Villages* (Second edition, Delhi, 1938), emphases mine. In this formulation, 'rural uplift' appears to be a sub-set of, and less ambitious than, 'rural reconstruction'. But the terms are often used to imply each other, with the older terminology to an extent coexisting with the new.

142. D. Spencer Hatch, *Up from Poverty in Rural India* (Oxford University Press, 1932); Lord Willingdon's 'Foreword', p. ix.

143. Hatch, *Up from Poverty in Rural India*, p. xi; emphasis in original. Hatch was associated with the YMCA's rural reconstruction projects in south India.

144. D. Spencer Hatch, *Further Upward in Rural India* (Madras, 1938), p. 7.

145. Hatch, *Further Upward in Rural India*, p. vii. Hatch's quest was undertaken 'through Indian primeval jungle armed only with a pocket camera, a New Testament, and an inquiring mind, accompanied by my wife who was the first woman of her race to walk that trail'.

146. Francis Younghusband, Chairman, Indian Village Welfare Association,

preface to C.F. Strickland, *Indian Village Welfare Association; Review of Rural Welfare Activities in India, 1932* (London, 1932), p. 5.

147. Strickland, *Review of Rural Welfare Activities in India, 1932*, p. 7.

148. 'Rural Reconstruction is a phrase originally coined by the Y.M.C.A., and for the last twenty-five years the Association has pioneered this form of service'. National Council, Y.M.C.A. India, Burma and Ceylon, *The Y.M.C.A. at work in India, Burma and Ceylon*, pamphlet, (Calcutta, n.d., but after 23 September 1940): the pamphlet notes on p. 4 that on that date the YMCA Union and Hostel for Indian Students in London was 'demolished by a German bomb'], p . 2.

149. Strickland, *Review of Rural Welfare Activities in India, 1932*, p. 30.

150. Strickland, *Review of Rural Welfare Activities in India, 1932*, pp. 30–1. On Sriniketan, see Sugata Dasgupta, *A Poet and a Plan (Tagore's Experiments in Rural Reconstruction)* (Calcutta, 1962); Uma Das Gupta, 'Rabindranath Tagore on Rural Reconstruction: The Sriniketan Programme, 1921–41', *Indian Historical Review* Vol. IV, No. 2 (January 1978). Tagore's views on rural reconstruction were never adopted in a major way outside Tagore's own circles, and although P.C. Mahalanobis, to provide one notable example, had been peripherally involved with Sriniketan, Tagore's ideas did not enter the mainstream of 'development' debates in India, although they shared some characteristics, such as the focus on moral uplift. There were also, however, significant exceptions: Tagore had warned of the dangers of a combination of 'oppression and patronage' which he felt had destroyed the villagers' self-respect and self-reliance under British rule, and which should not be replicated in Indians' attempts at rural reconstruction: Dasgupta, *A Poet and a Plan*, pp. 20–1. 'You must not insult the villagers with your help, nor must you make use of them to indulge your own feeling of superiority when you don't really want to help them', Tagore had told Leonard Elmhirst, the first director of Sriniketan's Institute of Agriculture, in 1924. Quoted in Leonard Elmhirst's 'Foreword' to Dasgupta, *A Poet and a Plan*, p. (ix).

151. This has been noted before. See Dewey, *Anglo-Indian Attitudes*; see also Gerald Studdert-Kennedy, *British Christians, Indian Nationalists and the Raj* (Delhi, 1991), on Brayne pp. 135–42. Of the non-official initiatives which attracted favourable attention, Sriniketan was one which had a certain attraction for Christians—C.F. Andrews, for instance, was associated with it, and Leonard Elmhirst was a former student of theology who had almost entered the Church: Dasgupta, *A Poet and a Plan*, p. 14. J.C. Kumarappa, the secretary of Gandhi's AIVIA's and its most effective organizer and propagandist, was also a Christian and had been an accomplished lay preacher before joining the Gandhians, in which capacity he continued to put his scriptural knowledge to good use: he combined a Christian theological world view with Gandhi's teachings to articulate a philosophy of the Gandhian village movement. On J.C. Kumarappa, see Chapter 4 of this volume.

152. Studdert-Kennedy, *British Christians...*, p . 135.
153. See, for instance, Malcolm Darling, Finance Commissioner, Lahore, to Viceroy-designate, Linlithgow, 10/1/1936, ff 83-6, Item 6, Box LXI, Darling Papers, CSAS. Darling suggested the government set up a fund to finance the cooperative movement, and consult 'a few Indians with strong rural ties' in this connection. 'It might also be politic', he wrote, 'to state that any organisation engaged in *bona fide* village welfare work may receive assistance from the fund. This would conciliate the Congress party, for they would take it as a hint that Gandhi's organisation would get assistance, as I think it should, if it works on non-political lines'. George Schuster's approval of Gandhi's anti-industrialization position has already been noted.
154. Datta was national secretary of the YMCA for India, Burma and Ceylon from 1919 to 1927, and represented the Indian Christians in the Indian Legislative Assembly from 1924 to 1926 and at the Round Table Conference in 1931. He was also associated with the Forman Christian College, Lahore, from 1909, as lecturer in history and biology, and from 1932 to 1942 as principal. See biographical note, IOR: MSS. EUR.F.178.
155. Gandhi to Datta, 14 December 1934, circular letter, IOR: MSS.EUR.F.178/ 30, f. 56, and Datta's acceptance letter to Gandhi, 17 December 1934, IOR: MSS.EUR.F.178/30, f. 67.
156. Dewey, *Anglo-Indian Attitudes*; P.H.M. van den Dungen, *The Punjab Tradition* (London, 1972).
157. Circular letter from Departmental Secretary, Mohammad Ashraf, dated 23 May 1936, file on Correspondence by Political and Economic Information Department of the All-India Congress Committee, AICC Papers, NMML, 26/1936, f. 17.
158. H.P.V. Townend, CIE, ICS, Rural Development Commissioner, Bengal, to Ashraf, dated 7 August 1936, AICC Papers, NML, 27/1936, f. 41.
159. H.P.V. Townend, to Ashraf, dated 7 August 1936, AICC Papers, NML, 27/ 1936, f. 41.
160. See IOR: MSS.EUR.B.402, 'Village Uplift Scheme': containing pamphlets published by the anti-revolutionary and officially inspired Agra District League, presented to John Henry Darwin, ICS, UP, 1909–37, and Collector of Agra, 1930–4.
161. Milton Israel, *Communications and Power*, pp. 41–3; Peter D. Reeves, 'The Politics of order: "Anti-Non-Cooperation" in the United Provinces, 1921', *Journal of Asian Studies*, Vol. 25, No. 2 (1966). The former draws mainly on the latter, while highlighting the propaganda aspects of the Aman Sabhas. Propaganda was disseminated in the UP mainly by village schoolmasters, though in Bengal, Punjab, and the Central Provinces it was felt at the time that schoolmasters were more likely to be opponents of the government. Bengal and Punjab also opposed the suggestion that *maulvis* be used to disseminate propaganda among Muslims, on the grounds that the Khilafat agitation had already claimed the loyalty of maulvis. Milton Israel, *Communications and Power*, p. 43.

162. Strickland, *Review of Rural Welfare Activities in India, 1932*, p. 10.
163. Peter Reeves, 'The Politics of Order', pp. 272–4. See figures provided in *Anti-Revolutionary League, Agra: Constitution—Aims and Objects* (Agra, n.d.), p.26, in bound volume entitled 'The District League, Agra: Publications', MSS.EUR.B.402, IOR. Under the heading 'No. of persons who came forward willingly to have the agitators convicted' is a blank space.
164. *Anti-Revolutionary League, Agra: Constitution—Aims and Objects* (Agra, n.d.), p. 1. Compare the above with the following excerpt from an Aman Sabha leaflet distributed as part of the anti-Non-Cooperation campaign of the UP government in 1921: 'Can you do without—1. The railway trains? 2. Irrigation from canals? 3. The letters, money orders and parcels that you send through the post offices? 4. Telegraph office? 5. Government hospitals? 6. Schools and colleges? 7. Just and impartial courts? 8. The advantage of peace and order in this country? If you cannot, then understand it and tell your neighbours and pray God that such a just and well-organised Government might always remain over us'. Quoted in Peter D. Reeves, 'The Politics of Order', pp. 266–7.
165. On the importance of the games ethic in the imperial imagination, see J.A. Mangan, *The Games Ethic and Imperialism: Aspects of the Diffusion of an Ideal* (Harmondsworth, 1985).
166. *Anti-Revolutionary League, Agra: Constitution—Aims and Objects*, p. 2.
167. B. R. Yadav, *Anti-Revolutionary League, Agra: Constitution—Aims and Objects*, p.
168. *Publicity Office, Agra: Report, March 1931 to March 1933* (Agra, n.d.), p. 1. B.R. Yadav was district publicity officer, Agra.
169. 'A Village Uplift scheme was prepared and a thousand copies were published in Hindi and some 200 copies in English. Each Sir-Panch [village headman] was supplied free with a Hindi copy and English copy [sic] has been sent to each Officer in the District'. B.R. Yadav, *Publicity Office, Agra: Report, March 1931 to March 1933*, p. 3.
170. The importance of the idea of India being a country of 'little republics' has been noted before; the argument was explicitly stated by Charles Metcalfe in the debates over the East India Company's Charter in 1854, and became an influential part of arguments widely divergent in content and intention. See John Matthai, *Village Government in British India* (London, 1913); Sidney Webb, 'Preface', to John Matthai, *Village Government in British India*; Karl Marx, 'The British Rule in India', *New York Daily Tribune*, 25 June 1853, (written during the debates in the Commons on the fate of the East India Company's charter), reprinted in Karl Marx and Friedrich Engels, *On Colonialism* (Moscow, 1959); M.K. Gandhi, *Hind Swaraj*, bibliography; Henry Maine, *Ancient Law* (London, 1861); *Village Communities of the East and West* (London, 1871). On Maine, see J.W. Burrow, *Evolution and Society* (Cambridge, 1966), pp 137–178; on Gandhi (and his admiration of Tolstoy), see Anthony Parel, 'Introduction' to M.K. Gandhi, *Hind Swaraj and other*

writings (Cambridge, 1997). See also Louis Dumont, 'The "Village Community" from Munro to Maine', *Contributions to Indian Sociology,* Vol. ix (1966); Clive Dewey, 'Images of the Village Community: a Study in Anglo-Indian Ideology', *Modern Asian Studies,* Vol. 6, No. 2 (1972).

171. Clive Dewey has written at some length on the assumptions, methods, and failure of Brayne's experiments. Dewey, *Anglo-Indian Attitudes.*

172. B.R. Yadav, *Village Uplift Scheme Introduced in Agra District* (Agra, n.d. but c. 1932), p. 3.

173. B.R. Yadav, *Village Uplift Scheme Introduced in Agra District,* p. 3.

174. B.R. Yadav, *Village Uplift Scheme Introduced in Agra District,* pp. 4–25.

175. B.R. Yadav, *Village Uplift Scheme Introduced in Agra District,* p. 25.

176. For instance, in 1936, when Darling was finance commissioner, Lahore, he wrote to the new Viceroy-designate, Lord Linlithgow, with the outlines of a proposal which he said he had been attempting to pursue for some time. This was to the effect that before the new Constitution was inaugurated, a gesture of goodwill would be helpful in order to help the 'experiment' succeed. To this end, 'England should return to India as a free gift the £100 million given her during the great war, or at least as much as has actually been paid: the sum, I am told, is £70 million'. The annual interest on this amount, about three crores of rupees, should 'be devoted to the improvement of the Indian peasant'. Darling referred to the general feeling 'amongst thoughtful Indians' that not nearly enough had been done by the government in the past to improve the condition of the peasantry. There was a strong desire to remedy this. 'Gandhi's village campaign is evidence of this in the political sphere'; Sir John Anderson in Bengal had expressed his determination to do something to improve the Bengal peasantry's condition and had been praised for this, and Sir James Grigg's Budget announcement of a sum of one crore rupees for the strengthening of the cooperative system had ' excited an interest and satisfaction quite disproportionate to the size of the grant'. Darling urged that 'as the administrative links between the two countries are loosed [sic], good will will become a more and more valuable asset', and that the apparently large sum of £70 million should be viewed as well spent in this context. The best effect, he added, would be obtained if the announcement was made when the Constitution was launched, and kept secret until then. Darling added a more directly remunerative consideration: 'If the village standard of living can be appreciably raised over a wide area, considering the millions involved, this might have a most beneficial effect upon British exports. from this point of view alone, the gift might well prove a first class investment'. Darling to Linlithgow, 10 January 1936, Box LXI, Item 6, ff 83-6, Darling Papers, CSAS. (Schuster and Amery, it might be recalled, used a similar line of reasoning). Linlithgow replied that this was now the provincial governments' concern; that the British Treasury would be unwilling to provide the money, but that he had been thinking of giving ministers under the new system 'a little financial rope in order that they may justify themselves

before their constituents'; if any money should become available, 'at least a part of it might find its way to the rural population'. Linlithgow to Darling, 27 January 1936, Box LXI, Item 6, ff. 87–8, Darling Papers, CSAS.

177. Darling was a close friend of E.M. Forster and at the fringes of the Bloomsbury set. See Dewey, *Anglo-Indian Attitudes*.

178. Darling Papers, CSAS, Box 1, 28.7, 'Memo. of talk with Keynes (8 February 1934)'. The *General Theory* was published in 1936.

179. Darling, *Wisdom and Waste*, pp. 340, 342–4.

180. Darling, *Rusticus loquitur*, pp. 332, 334, 336. See also Malcolm Darling, 'The Peasant Strength of India, *Asia* magazine, March 1941, p. 120, where he points to the dispossession of landlords as a distinct possibility.

181. Dewey, 'Editor's Introduction' to Darling, *The Punjab Peasant*, p. xxiii.

182. Darling, *Wisdom and Waste*, p. 317.

183. Darling, *Wisdom and Waste*, p. 322. This is in line with Dewey's comment that Darling was 'ambivalent' towards the moneylender who was after all someone who saved on behalf of the whole community the 'one thrifty person among a generally thriftless people'. Dewey, 'Editor's Introduction' to Darling, *The Punjab Peasant*, p. xxi.

184. R.H. Tawney, *Religion and the Rise of Capitalism* (first published London, 1926; originating in the Holland Memorial lectures at King's College, London, in 1922). Darling presumably read the 1926 edition; he cites pages 31 and 39. Tawney himself drew on the work of Max Weber, which he claimed was not then widely known in the English-speaking world: Tawney, *Religion and the Rise of Capitalism* (Harmondsworth, 1977 edition), pp. (ix)-(x), reprint of Tawney's Preface to the 1937 edition.

185. Malcolm Darling, presidential address on 'The Relation of Economics to ethics', Papers Read and Discussed at the Eleventh Conference of the Indian Economic Association held at Lucknow, January 1928, *Indian Journal of Economics*, Conference Number, Vol. VIII, Part 3 (January 1928), pp. 477–90.

186. Darling, 'The Relation of Economics to Ethics', pp. 492–5; J.M. Keynes, *A Short View of Russia* (1925), p. 25, quoted in Darling, 'The Relation of Economics to Ethics', p. 492.

187. Darling, 'The Relation of Economics to Ethics', p. 496.

188. Darling did not see himself as an opponent of capitalism. His criticisms of capitalism were far from systematic, and informed by a general sense of the injustice of starvation and a faith in the moral values inculcated by cooperation. On Marxism, he appears not to have found it necessary to disagree with Keynes, who 'was not a Marxian—he found it impossible to read Marx. A friend had marked for him passages of importance, but they were so dull and so turgidly involved in the economic doctrines of 1840 that he had found it quite impossible to get through Das Capital [sic]. He doubted whether many Communists had read him. When I said that it sounded as dull as the Koran, he agreed that it was just that'. Darling, 'Memo of talk with

Keynes (8 February 1934)', Item 28.7, Box I, Darling Papers, CSAS. It is unclear from this passage as to whether either Keynes or Darling had read the Koran.

189. Darling to Linlithgow, 10 January 1936, Box LXI, Item 6, f. 83, Darling Papers, CSAS.

190. Malcolm Darling, 'The Peasant Strength of India, *Asia* magazine, March 1941, published from New York for an American audience, p. 119.

191. Malcolm Darling, 'The Peasant Strength of India', p. 119. The hazards of democracy in India, especially for illiterate peasants, was a theme which greatly concerned Darling as well as other British administrators.

192. For a study of this see Rothermund, 'The Great Depression and British Financial Policy in India, 1929–1934'.

193. Malcolm Darling, 'The Peasant Strength of India', p. 120.

194. Darling, 'The Peasant Strength of India', p. 122.

195. Darling, 'The Peasant Strength of India', p. 120. He, however, claimed that landlord–tenant difficulties had not significantly affected the country as a whole due to the prevalence of peasant proprietorship, but where they had arisen, they had been the most difficult to deal with—a case, at best, of projecting the Punjab situation onto the whole of India.

196. Economic historians have noted this phenomenon—the main security on loans being land, and the produce from land being worth very little, lending ceased—or repayment of loans was demanded in gold. There was a large-scale export of gold during the Depression, largely after sterling went off the gold standard but the rupee remained pegged to sterling. This meant an effective rise in the price of gold outside India, which made it profitable to sell gold. There has been some debate among economic historians whether the large-scale gold exports, which incidentally enabled the Government of India to balance its books (Rothermund, 'The Great Depression and British Financial Policy in India, 1929–1934') were distress sales of hoarded gold in the countryside or profit sales by business interests; the two views are not mutually exclusive, distress sales making their way to the hands of various exporters who then sold abroad for a profit. Keynes wrote to Darling in 1932 that he agreed with him that the phenomenon of gold exports was 'a combination of the premium on gold and the impecuniosity of the producers'. Keynes, from 46 Gordon Square, Bloomsbury, to Darling, in Rawalpindi, 6 June 1932, f. 36, File 2, Box LXIV (A), Darling Papers, CSAS.

197. Darling, 'The Peasant Strength of India', p. 120. These difficulties were 'not likely to be mitigated by a democratic constitution with periodic elections'.

198. Darling, 'The Peasant Strength of India', p. 122.

199. Darling, 'The Peasant Strength of India', pp. 120–21.

200. Darling, 'The Peasant Strength of India', p. 121. Emphasis mine.

201. Darling, 'The Peasant Strength of India', p. 122.

202. Malcolm Darling, 'The Peasant and Politics', presidential address, in *The Indian Society of Agricultural Economics: Proceedings of the First Conference,*

Delhi, February 24th and 25th, 1940 (Delhi, 1940), pp. 7–23. The article for *Asia* effectively comprises excerpts from this article.
203. Item 28.6, Box 1, Darling Papers, CSAS; Malcolm Darling, *At Freedom's Door* (London, 1949).
204. Item 28.6, Box 1, Darling Papers, CSAS. emphasis mine.
205. Linlithgow to Darling, 13 March 1936, ff. 89–90, Item 6, Box LXI, Darling Papers, CSAS.
206. '...at the first possible opportunity a small committee of educational experts should be sent to Russia to learn the secret of this notable achievement (in achieving high rates of literacy) and to guage how far Russian methods can be applied with advantage in India.' Sir Malcolm Darling, 'The Indian Peasant in the Modern World', *Asiatic Review*, Vol. XXXVIII, No. 133 (January 1942).
207. Sir Malcolm Darling, 'The Indian Village and Democracy' *Journal of the Royal Society of Arts*, Vol. XCI, 6 August 1943, p. 493.
208. Malcolm Darling, *At Freedom's Door* (Oxford, 1949), pp. 12–13.
209. Philip Woodruff, *The Men who Ruled India, Part II: The Guardians*, p. 338. Woodruff (the pen name of former civilian, Philip Mason) is here speaking of, and for, the British members of the service; although he goes on to point out that by the end of the War the Service was almost half Indian (p. 339), it is doubtful that he meant to say the Indian members of the Service doubted that there could be a place for them in the new scheme of things.
210. Moon drafted the Report of the Advisory Planning Board of Jawaharlal Nehru's interim government in 1946, and was a secretary to the Planning Commission in the 1950s. See Moon Collection, MSS.EUR.F.230/19, IOR.
211. The specific events leading up to Moon's resignation were not mentioned in polite company, but the resignation attracted much attention, and caused a good deal of consternation in official circles at the time. See the biographical note introducing the Moon Collection, IOR: MSS.EUR.F.230. Moon's letters to his father in 1943 provide some clues as to other lines of disagreement. In a letter dated 31 January 1943, he writes regarding 'food difficulties out here. These are, in my opinion, to some extent due to the incompetence of the Govt. of India'. Certain remarks made regarding the treatment of political prisoners in this letter were deleted by the Censor. Two letters dated 16 May 1943 and 23 May 1943 talk about Moon having resigned, but provide no details as to why (presumably these would have been deleted if he had—all letters in this file are marked 'Opened by Examiner', and some have bits cut out, whose subject is difficult to ascertain). See MSS.EUR.F.230/18, IOR.
212. Moon, *Strangers in India*, p. 32.
213. Carritt, *A Mole in the Crown*, p. 4.
214. Moon, *Strangers in India*, p. 14.
215. Moon, *Strangers in India*, pp. 14–15.
216. This is an image Moon also uses himself: see *Strangers in India*, p. 33.
217. Moon pressed this analogy of parasitism, of the Britain–India relationship as

the moneylender–peasant relationship, further: the period between 1860 and 1900 saw the 'triumph of a parasitic class ... We fostered parasites; and, what is worse, we ourselves at the same time began to become parasitic.' Moon, *Strangers in India*, p. 35. On p. 33 he also argued that the 'foreign conceptions' of the British had led to the ascendancy of the moneylender—early rackrenting by the British and British-created landlords weakening the peasants; later legislation could not solve the problem. Moon wasted little space on the British claim that the use of British credit by the Government of India was essential for India's progress: 'a debtor can hardly feel that his interests are entirely safe when exclusively in his creditor's hands'. Moon, *Strangers in India*, p. 35.

218. This line of argument was also taken up by Moon elsewhere; but he found a convenient resolution for it. In a speech delivered sometime during the War, before an audience of predominantly, if not exclusively, Englishmen, Moon discussed Englishmen, the Empire, and the social background they came from. The Englishman, he wrote, is mentally lazy; intellectual exertion on his part is not encouraged. Why, despite this, are the English people able to rule not only themselves but their Empire? Moon sees possible good in English 'mental lethargy', whose corollary, according to him, is 'easy-going tolerance'. The occasional genius is allowed to flourish as a 'crank'; when in a crisis he is required, he exists. Also, 'statesmanship is the art of the second best': logical consistency with stated principles never really bothered the English. But the principal reason for English imperial success lies elsewhere: 'For the last 234 years they [the English] have enjoyed the inestimable advantage of having the assistance of the Scots. The inefficiency of the English throughout the world, and their (often) gross mental incapacity has been largely neutralised by the hordes of hungry, ambitious, uncouth but efficient Scotsmen, who ever since the Union in 1707 have poured forth from their gloomy towns and barren mountains into the English-speaking world and ended largely by dominating it'. MSS.EUR.F.230/40, IOR, speech beginning 'If I were an orthodox Englishman, I should have refused to give this talk', pp. 1–5.

219. Moon, *Strangers in India*, p. 5.
220. Moon, *Strangers in India*, pp. 5–6.
221. Moon, *Strangers in India*, pp. 5–6.
222. IOR: MSS.EUR.F.230/47, f. 1.
223. IOR: MSS.EUR.F.230/47, f. 2.
224. IOR: MSS.EUR.F.230/47, f. 4.
225. IOR: MSS.EUR.F.230/40: Text of All-India Radio Broadcast on 25 January 1941, Lahore Station, 8.15 p.m.; pp. 1–3.
226. IOR: MSS.EUR.F.230/40: Text of All-India Radio Broadcast, pp. 4–5.
227. IOR: MSS.EUR.F.230/40: Text of All-India Radio Broadcast, pp. 6–7.
228. IOR: MSS.EUR.F.230/40: Text of All-India Radio Broadcast, pp. 7–8.
229. Moon, *Strangers in India*, pp. 41–42.
230. Moon, *Strangers in India*, p. 43.

231. For a slightly contrasting view, see Malcolm Darling's review of *Strangers in India* in the *Asiatic Review* of 1945, pp. 107–109.
232. Moon, *Strangers in India*, reviewed by Darling, *Asiatic Review, 1945,* p. 107.
233. Moon papers, IOR: MSS.EUR.F.230/30, letter from Malcolm Darling, 28 May 1944; he added, 'I love the smell it all has of the earth', and 'I am telling everyone to read it—including E. M. Forster'.
234. *Asiatic Review, 1945,* p. 108.
235. Moon, *Strangers in India,* p. 107. Quoted by Darling, *Asiatic Review, 1945,* pp. 108–9.
236. Moon, *Strangers in India,* p. 194. Quoted by Darling, *Asiatic Review, 1945,* pp. 108–9.
237. *Asiatic Review 1945,* p. 109.
238. *Asiatic Review 1945,* p. 109; and Moon, *Strangers in India,* p. 194, quoted by Darling, *Asiatic Review, 1945,* p. 109.
239, Moon, *Strangers in India,* chapter three.
240. Moon, *Strangers in Inda,* pp. 38–41; see also Penderel Moon, *The Future of India* (London, 1945), pp. 44–54.
241. Darling, *Wisdom and Waste,* pp. 11, 13.
242. Darling, *At Freedom's Door.* The image of Arthur Young was one he was fond of invoking; see also Darling, *Rusticus Loquitur,* p. x.
243. Literally, 'servants of God'; organization in the North West Frontier Province led by Khan Abdul Ghaffar Khan, an ally of the Congress and sometimes referred to as the 'Frontier Gandhi'.
244. Darling, *At Freedom's Door,* p. 15.
245. Darling, *At Freedom's Door,* pp. 29–30.
246. Darling, *At Freedom's Door,* pp. 30, 300.
247. Darling, *At Freedom's Door,* pp. 312–13; Sidney Webb, quoted from Webb's preface to John Matthai, *Village Government in British India.* (London, 1913), p. 19. This was a book which Darling took extremely seriously. At a meeting of the India section of the Royal Society of Arts on 2 April 1943, he said, 'The British Government has done much for local self-government in India, but until recently very little for village self-government. It did nothing to protect the old village panchayat against the disintegrating forces of modern life. It was hardly even aware of its existence until 1915 [sic], when Matthai's book "Village Government in British India" appeared and it was not until after the last war that the first Panchayat Act was passed'. Sir Malcolm Darling, 'The Indian Village and Democracy', *Journal of the Royal Society of Arts,* Vol. XCI, 6 August 1943, p. 488.
248. Darling, *At Freedom's Door,* p. 348.

4

The Debate on Gandhian Ideas

This chapter seeks to examine the ways in which Gandhian ideas on India's future socio-economic order, centred on the self-sufficient, or nearly so, village, were sought to be justified by Gandhians before an audience of intellectuals who were the main protagonists in debates on 'development' in the 1930s and the 1940s. This was a period of relative marginalization of Gandhian ideas in the Congress and, more generally, in the Indian nationalist movement. The chapter traces the origins in earlier debates of some of the ideas brought into play in such justifications, and how they were sought to be expressed in terms of the general concerns with 'development' which were being articulated at the time by intellectuals. In so doing, it examines the ideas of Mohandas Karamchand Gandhi, who remained, throughout the period, a pre-eminent moral and political leader despite the rejection of his ideas in many circles, and with the interpretation of Gandhi on the subject of a desirable socio-economic order for India provided by J.C. Kumarappa who, as secretary of Gandhi's All-India Village Industries Association (AIVIA), conducted most of its propaganda and publicity drives.

Gandhi's ideas, as they were extended and popularized in this field (with regard to a desirable socio-economic order), were not part of an alternative discourse separate from British imperialist or 'Western' discourse or, indeed, from nationalist replies from within that discourse (which, as I have observed, shared some of the beliefs and/or discursive conventions of imperialist arguments but reworked them into quite different arguments). Nor were they in some sense more 'popular'. On the contrary, they were variations on those replies, elitist in origin and didactic in intent and tone.

Gandhian ideas have been seen by many later commentators as subordinate to, or less important than, the much discussed debates on socialism, capitalism, and industrialization which have been taken to be at the core of Indian debates on 'development'; and indeed were at the core of debates in the field of 'development economics' until quite recently, when ideas of 'sustainable development', environmentalism, and decentralization pushed previously marginalized ideas, among them Gandhian ones, back into centrestage. Consequently, much attention has been claimed recently by 'Gandhian economics' which, since the late 1960s or the early 1970s has continued to find supporters.[1] Current alternative positions, however, in seeking to recover marginalized ideas of development such as the Gandhian, often conduct unhistorical readings based on present day concerns and, thereby, attribute to those ideas meanings which they could not have had in their contemporary context.[2]

The main outlines of what has come to be known as 'Gandhian economic thought' are well known—a decentralized, village-based economic order which was as self-sufficient as possible, of rural small-scale agriculture, and industries which employed low technology—but the neatness and consistency of this position is more the contribution of later writers than of Gandhi himself.[3] Gandhi's several versions of his anti-machinery doctrine show that they were modified over the years to accommodate the use of some machinery. In 1924 Gandhi claimed he was not against all machinery, but was against the 'craze' for labour-saving devices while men went about unemployed. He called the Singer sewing machine 'one of the few useful things ever invented'; and when it was pointed out to him that these machines had to be made in factories with power-driven machinery, Gandhi replied that this was true, but he was 'socialist enough to say that such factories should be nationalised, State-controlled'.[4] In 1933 Gandhi praised the Nazis for reviving village industries and for de-mechanizing certain industries to create more employment, arguing that even a technically advanced country such as Germany recognized the need for limiting the use of machinery.[5]

Another aspect of Gandhi's thinking on the economic order which has not received attention from his retrospective supporters is his idea of the 'trusteeship' role of the wealthy: the rich would hold their wealth in trust for society in general, for which they would be expected, according to Gandhi's argument, to feel a moral responsibility.[6] This lack of attention is understandable; if the latter is treated together with the former, it is difficult to construct of 'Gandhian economic thought' the alternative to capitalism which many of its supporters claim for it.

'Gandhian economic thought' must, therefore, be recognized as a gradual and retrospective creation. Aspects of it were defined and articulated first as a political weapon against the economic domination of Lancashire, with precedents in the Swadeshi movement following the first partition of Bengal in 1905; other aspects were connected to Gandhi's concern for the moral and ethical education of Congress members and the Indian people; further aspects were articulated later, partly in response to the growing critique of Gandhi's ideas of village industries and 'constructive work'. The debate on Gandhi's ideas of a village-centred social, political, and economic order as a possible path to Indian 'development' began in earnest from the 1930s, and grew through the 1940s, and after his death. By the Second World War, these ideas seemed to have been successfully marginalized, but they came together in different forms after independence, with Acharya Vinoba Bhave's Sarvodaya movement claiming surprising converts, possibly the most surprising being one of Gandhian ideas' most articulate critics, Jayaprakash Narayan.[7] The forms in which post-Independence incorporations of economic and social ideas referred to as 'Gandhian' took place could, however, only partially be attributed to Gandhi—such as, the incorporation of Gandhi as a central legitimizing icon in 'community development' schemes in the 1950s.[8]

The 'Gandhian' approach, in its own time, concentrated not on the details along which to work out practical economics, 'picturesque descriptions of such things as sanitary devices, sinking and cleaning of wells, utilisation of waste, hygienic precautions to be taken etc.'. These were considered necessary; but 'much more important is the spirit of the approach'.[9] This chapter examines the manoeuvres and strategies of argument adopted in attempting to clear a discursive space for Gandhian ideas from the 1930s. In dealing with the arguments thus put forth as 'manoeuvres' or 'strategies' I do not mean to suggest that these were merely strategic ploys; they were, most of them, part of a larger world view, whose rationale and philosophical underpinnings needed to be explained before the more specific ideas that followed could persuasively be put forth.

In dealing with the strategic placement of Gandhian arguments, I argue that contrary to many interpretations, contemporary and hostile, present day and favourable, Gandhi and the Gandhians did not operate through claims to being anti-modern. They claimed, on the contrary, to offer solutions which were more modern than industrialization-based models of society, and to challenge the criteria of modernity which they saw as being somewhat uncritically borrowed from the 'West'. They based themselves on an equation of socialism and capitalism, both being 'Western' systems, as systems which paid too much attention to material needs, consequently neglecting the moral and ethical basis for society. This basis was sought in certain aspects of 'traditional' Indian society, which often meant a creative borrowing from and reinterpretation of 'Hindu' traditions as being 'modern' before the 'West' was 'modern'.

It was not possible, however, to base an argument at the time on a rejection of 'modernity'. Unlike in much present day writing, in which 'modernity' and the 'West' are equated and regarded as negative (this equation being projected into the past), 'modernity' was viewed as extremely empowering, and carried with it extremely positive connotations for a people called 'primitive' and 'backward'. The terms of the 1930s and 1940s—the modern, modernizers, modernity; Western, the West, and so on—were generally assumed to be intelligible in similar terms to the audiences before whom they were placed. They did not need to be defined; precision might perhaps weaken their effectiveness. In the political discourse of the time, their emotive significance had already been well established; of the two sets of terms, the first was desirable, the second to be avoided. A legitimate position, therefore, had to be based on something which was 'modern', but not 'Western'.

A major, if not the decisive, role in this process of formulating 'Gandhian economic thought' in these terms was played by J.C. Kumarappa. Kumarappa's major statement of the philosophy of the village movement was formulated in a book entitled *Why the Village Movement?*.[10] According to Kumarappa this was meant to clarify the ideals of the All-India Spinners' Association and the AIVIA;[11] the book, nonetheless, grew with each subsequent edition, addressing wider debates on socialism and capitalism, nation building, centralization, development, and planning, as they emerged.[12] This book largely succeeded in being an annotated commentary, from a Gandhian perspective, on development debates in India in the 1930s and the 1940s. Kumarappa was the best possible commentator among the Gandhians, given his early training in economics and finance and his consequent ability to place his arguments in the conventionally respected language of economics.[13] But it was a lot more than that as well; in it, Kumarappa undertook the rather ambitious project of enunciating an entire social philosophy on which his economic arguments were to be based. *Why the Village Movement?* is, after *Hind Swaraj*, the closest example we have to a manifesto of Gandhism. Kumarappa could be expected to interpret Gandhi to middle-class audiences and seek to persuade them with intellectual tools readily assimilable to mundane, rational thinking; he elaborates a series of arguments with a keen sense of the specifics of the issues with which he has to contend, centralizing, communist, socialist or capitalist, This chapter, consequently, deals in some detail with the social and intellectual genealogy of Kumarappa, his relationship with Gandhi, his writings, and the reception or potential impact of his writings.

In the sections that follow I attempt the following: to place Gandhi in the political and socio-intellectual currents of the times; to examine the positions being articulated in opposition to Gandhi and the consequent need for a further effective intervention in the debates on Indian 'development' from a Gandhian perspective; to examine that intervention; and to place the position so articulated in the perspective of the positions against which it contended.

Placing Gandhi

Gandhi has often been seen as standing outside the main currents of political debate in colonial India. Thus, while imperialists and nationalists both spoke of Indian 'backwardness', Gandhi apparently refused to join a debate with the colonial government on terms he understood to be their own terms: the solution to problems of 'backwardness' was to reject definitions of 'backwardness' which depended on a conception of 'civilisation' based on making 'bodily welfare the object of life',[14] founded on material rather than spiritual values. One of the ways in which the Gandhian attack on development through industrialization functioned was through an equation of industrial modernity with the 'West', which by implication or by direct accusation could be considered alien, immoral and culturally disruptive. Although this could remain, in Gandhi's own writings, within a universalist rather than a nationalist particularist philosophical position (the 'West' had deviated from its own spiritual roots, and, could potentially return to them and, thereby, overcome its spiritual degradation)[15] this distinction could, nonetheless, be lost in dissemination. Gandhi's interventions, therefore, tended to operate within a recognized convention of political argument in colonial India, in terms of a simple distinction between 'East' and 'West'.

It has also been said of Gandhi's writings and statements that they were essentially moral in character; though Gandhi was capable of putting forward arguments in which his idea of the village as economic unit was defended on essentially economic grounds—the wisdom of village industries in a largely agrarian economy with an abundance of under-employed labour—this was not his main argument. According to this view, it was only reluctantly that Gandhi expressed himself in terms of capitalism, socialism, law, and so on; but the terms of the debates on 'development' that emerged strongly from the 1930s forced him occasionally to do so. Here, this was in terms of the possibility of applying 'our own distinct Eastern traditions' in finding a 'solution to the question of capital and labour', or to the organization of the national economy around village-centred production by self-sufficient small producers.[16] Otherwise, Gandhi is said to have conducted a 'total moral critique of the fundamental aspects of civil society', of the 'dubious virtues of modern civilisation', without an appeal to history or precedent, outside 'the bounds of post-Enlightenment thought'.[17]

Starting from this point, Gandhian ideas, economic or otherwise, can be seen in several ways: as a more 'authentic' articulation of the Indian situation, through a critique of 'post-Enlightenment modernity' and its socio-cultural standards, and the reading of Gandhian ideas as 'cultural resistance',[18] an 'alternative vision'. They may also be seen as emanating from the debate within 'Hindu' tradition regarding the need to revitalize Hindu society and to defend it against colonial assaults;[19] or as a necessary stage in nationalist thought, its 'moment of manoeuvre', in which decrying the 'modern' (colonial capitalism) serves to consolidate the 'national' and pave the way for (Indian) expanded capitalist production, 'the development of the thesis by incorporating a part of the antithesis'.[20]

If viewed retrospectively, or from present-day perspectives, Gandhian ideas might indeed be interpreted as serving any or all these purposes. Whether he stood outside 'the bounds of post-Enlightenment thought' (an ambiguous phrase, since post-Enlightenment thought can be interpreted as thought which rejects some of the Enlightenment's tenets—illustrating some of the dangers of the prefix 'post-') or appealed to history and precedent only in exceptional circumstances seems more doubtful.[21] There are other interpretations as well, matters not being made much easier by his refusal to be consistent and his 'aphoristic' language.[22] It seems unproductive to quibble about the essential character of Gandhian thought; nor does it seem possible to arrive at a consensual description of Gandhism; instead, an attempt to unravel its specific meanings in relation to different contexts and audiences might prove to be more meaningful. Perhaps the strength of Gandhi's language was the multiple interpretations to which it could lend itself: it could acquire different meanings to different audiences—the Gorakhpur peasantry, Marwari businessmen, or militant Chitpavan Brahmins.[23]

This seems also to have been Gandhi's intention (he presumably recognized this as his strength); he was capable of switching register quite dramatically, arguing from several different standpoints. It is, therefore, better to recognize the equivalence of moral and political arguments in Gandhi's thought;[24] and, moreover, the strategic nature of Gandhi's uses of these arguments, switching 'abruptly ... from a religious idiom to a secular humanist one';[25] or indeed to the idiom of scientific expertise. The strategic placement of an argument within a discourse from which it was most likely to be effective was a consideration which often played an important role in Gandhi's thinking; he was prone to asking advice on the technical aspects of economic problems from businessmen before writing articles in which they would appear transformed into his characteristic style of presenting ethical dilemmas.[26]

Gandhi's own mysticism on economic matters has, unfortunately, often been mistaken for a mysticism of approach rather than of rhetoric. Gandhi was fully aware of the need for straightforward rational approaches to such matters; and although he did not usually take such a line himself in a sustained argument (perhaps he felt this would undermine his position as a spiritual leader), he believed it was important that somebody should. Gandhi, consequently, made certain demands on his authorized interpreters, demands which were rather empiricist in their approach to the problems of persuasion. Dissatisfied with one of the latter's efforts, Gandhi wrote sternly to Kumarappa in 1941,

> Your article on industrialisation I consider weak. You have flogged a dead horse. *What we have to combat is socialisation of industrialism.* They instance the Soviet exploits in proof of their proposition. You have to show, if you can, *by working out figures* that handicrafts are better than power driven machinery products. You have almost allowed in the concluding paragraphs the validity of that claim.[27]

The Political Context

'Modernist' debates regarding models of 'development' explicitly positioned themselves against Gandhian ideas. 'Socialist' alternatives for India began to be confidently articulated and presented to professional and intellectual audiences from the 1930s; socialist and communist activity previously having been mainly confined to organizing the urban working class. A less than systematic engagement with the possibilities opened out by the Russian Revolution for oppressed peoples had also begun among nationalist leaders, but this fell well short of an understanding of or sympathy with the goals of early Bolshevism.[28] The 1930s saw a second wave of socialism. The period after 1931 was one of intense soul-searching and the quest for alternative tactics and ideology to the

Gandhian within the Congress and among Congress sympathizers, as a consequence of Gandhi's tendency to order retreats, and of the anticlimax of the 1931 Round Table Conference. There was, gradually, a turn to socialism among a small but articulate group within the Congress—less through a thorough theoretical understanding, or through actual work among the peasantry, rural agricultural labour or the urban working class, than through an admiration of the most spectacular achievements of that other 'backward' country emerging from backwardness—an empowering experience—the Soviet Union. This was a late wave, corresponding to the news of Soviet miracles and the good press the Soviet Union was beginning to get even among the respectable left in Britain.[29]

Capitalists, who often cast themselves as inheritors of the traditional economic nationalist positions of opposition to government economic policies,[30] also failed until quite late to articulate their vision of a future Indian economy and society—possibly deliberately. As G.D. Birla pointed out, it was not a good idea for businessmen themselves to come up with a defence of capitalism, it looked too much like self-interest.[31] Moreover, a far more effective justification of capitalism was provided by Gandhi himself, through his theory of the 'trusteeship' of business which was, for Gandhi, perfectly compatible with his dislike of capitalism: the possessing class, Gandhi argued, held property in trust for the nation and for their less fortunate fellow beings, and they had a duty to use their wealth for the common good.[32] It was, therefore, useful for businessmen to restrict themselves to a more limited agenda of stressing the need for 'national' enterprise—thereby shifting the confrontational aspects of the debate outwards, directing them against colonial rule and, thereby, claiming allies on the basis of business demands being national ones—rather than turning the matter into an internal quarrel as a defence of Indian capitalism against either 'Gandhism' or 'socialism'.[33] As for the contradiction of claiming to be supporters of Gandhi and at the same time being large-scale machinery users, this was a dichotomy to be lived with. As Birla, the businessman who was perhaps closest to Gandhi, put it, the Mahatma was his spiritual leader, but as a businessman there were certain things which he simply had to do although he knew Gandhi did not approve.[34]

Gandhi's success in turning the Congress into a mass movement notwithstanding, many of his ideas were accepted by his political associates as politically expedient rather than out of conviction. Gandhi's frequent retreats, at times when mass movements seemed to be gathering pace and showing signs of independence from his leadership, were also prone to demoralize or disillusion some members.[35] Many of his ideas regarding the economic and social organization of a future India seemed particularly clouded in moral rhetoric and were regarded as far from practicable as the basis of national economic policy, although a 'constructive programme' of spinning and weaving *khadi* could be accommodated without much trouble. With the advent of a strong school of thought which regarded planning for industrialization as the basis for national development, opposition to Gandhi's economic ideas grew more explicit. This coincided, from the mid-1930s, with Gandhi's own relative eclipse in national politics. In 1934, after the anticlimax of the Gandhi-Irwin Pact, the failure of Gandhi to secure any gains from the Round Table Conference, and the failure of the second Civil Disobedience Movement, a group of younger Congressmen, who had been doing some serious rethinking decided to make explicit their socialist approach to politics and society and their differences with Gandhian politics. They still stressed the need to remain within the Congress, the most important anti-imperialist platform in the country, and the priority as the demand for independence from imperialism, but declared their goal of campaigning for a more socialist orientation, the mobilization of peasants and workers and an eventual goal of socialism after the immediate goal of freedom had been achieved.[36] Jayaprakash Narayan advocated left unity, anticipating the Comintern's United Front line, and urged socialists of all kinds to enter the Congress to strengthen its left wing.[37] Meanwhile, Gandhi retired from active membership of the Congress and declared it to be his intention to concentrate on 'constructive work' for the uplift of the masses. This did not mean that he was a peripheral figure in politics: on the contrary, he often crucially intervened, staking his personal integrity and image against those he considered recalcitrant or opposed to what he felt desirable.[38]

This was the background against which the great debate on Gandhian economic ideas took shape: the disillusion with, and self-imposed exile of Gandhi, and (against the backdrop of the Great Depression, the collapse of prices and consequent impoverishment of peasants) the great excitement caused by the economic successes and technological progress of the 'backward' Soviet Union. In this context Gandhi's statements about the importance of 'constructive work' in the villages and the immorality of machine civilization were often met with impatience. Socialists attempted both to bring Gandhi round to their point of view and to point out the flaws in his arguments so as to wean away his supporters and to gain more supporters themselves. Implicitly or explicitly, it was recognized by socialists that the main obstacle to a wider acceptance of (or, at least, a wider sympathy with) socialist principles, was Gandhi's insistence that socialism and capitalism were both foreign solutions to Indian problems; both were materialist and based on the violence of machinery. Capitalists, meanwhile, were able to hide behind the rhetoric of Gandhism.

As a result a great many socialists who attacked Gandhian positions were convinced that the route to an attack on Indian capitalism lay through a weakening of the Gandhian position. However, many who approached the problems of 'development' from a more technological perspective also attacked Gandhi, with arguments which were sometimes not clearly distinguishable from the socialists' arguments. Of this latter group, many were not opposed to or were supporters of private enterprise, although some thought of themselves as socialists. The organized critique of Gandhian ideas was thus conducted both by socialists and by those who considered themselves men of science; for reasons mentioned above, capitalists felt it desirable to pull their punches, reserving their energies to combat the socialist strand of thought. Those businessmen not explicitly 'nationalist', or only contingently so, also refrained from entering this debate with any intensity.[39]

Against Gandhi

The main lines of criticism of Gandhi were on the lines of his ideas inadvertently serving capitalism by providing legitimation for the capitalists through the idea of the 'trusteeship' role of the wealthy; that his ideas were 'backward' and not conducive to modern life; and that contrary to Gandhi's claims, they were not 'indigenous'. On this last point, unlike the other points, it was his opponents who felt more defensive. Gandhi's claim that his opponents' positions were not in keeping with Indian traditions or conditions; that they were 'Western', was the main strength which Gandhian arguments could rely on, as it drew on old anxieties regarding cultural disruption or what constituted legitimate borrowings from the 'West'.[40] The response of 'modernisers' to accusations of 'Westernisation' or a lack of respect for 'tradition' was based on a strategy which claimed that there was nothing wrong with the principles of science and the benefits of technology on which industrialization was based per se; if it appeared that they were not universally valid, this was due to their misuse, which had distorted the results obtained. In the hands of a nationalist government with due regard for Indian conditions they could be put to the best possible use.

The Gandhian voice seemed to represent an unfortunate commitment to 'backwardness' —it was admitted by 'modernisers' that village industries might have a place in an economically rational scheme to provide employment at the local level, and for this purpose might even be worthy of government protection, but, as the journal *Science and Culture* put it, to place a commitment to 'the philosophy of spinning wheel and bullock cart' at the centre of national economic life could only be a denial of the progress of science, of the 'techniques of modern civilisation'.[41] This was an unviable approach '[i]f India is to grow into a powerful world-entity like the U.S.A., Soviet Russia, and the countries of Western Europe ... A nation, however great its moral and spiritual qualities may be, can not hope to win battles with bows and arrows against tanks and artillery. In this world of strife and competition, if a nation wants to survive, it must develop the latest techniques of civilised existence'.[42] This, it might be noted, was a view of the state and of state power being conflated with the nation.

This was, moreover, a scientist's or a technologist's critique; it assumed a good deal in terms of the transformative capacity of technology. The Congress Socialists' critique was more subtle, and took Gandhian ideas more seriously, while still maintaining a strong polemic against them. The CSP were always careful to preface their criticism of Gandhian ideas with the assertion that they had no doubts as to Gandhi's own good intentions—it was merely the logic of his ideas that they questioned. Asoka Mehta, addressing the Gandhian question of whether machines caused unemployment, accepted that this was indeed the case in many countries of the world at present, but concluded that this was only the case under capitalism—'the logic of capitalism demands an army of unemployed as its reserve force, and it will not eliminate it'. Under socialism, 'there will be planned economy and work will be so evenly distributed that all will have their share of work and leisure'.[43] This rebuttal was conducive to confusions on an important point: planning under private ownership of technology could also lead to the replacement of workers by machines. Mehta had made the point clear elsewhere, when he argued, describing the initiatives of the New Deal, that planning under capitalism merely strengthens capitalism.[44] In the above passage, it was possible to interpret planning and socialism as somehow necessarily connected. This was a conflation of terms often made, with a planned economy and a large state sector being allowed to masquerade as socialism.

Another point of necessary attack on Gandhian ideas was on the claim that it presented a truly 'indigenous' solution. While pointing out that the logic of Gandhi's ideas often was of great help in justifying capitalists, the

CSP maintained that Gandhi was not a supporter of capitalism. Jaya Prakash Narayan, while accepting this, expressed himself forcefully in a rather polemical piece of writing. Pointing out that Gandhi's idea of the 'trusteeship' of the wealthy was not 'indigenous', he quoted William Godwin's *Political Justice*: 'The most energetic teachers of religion ... have taught the rich that *they hold their wealth only as a trust* ... The defect of this system is that they rather excite us to palliate our injustice than to forsake it'.[45] Narayan continued, in ironic mode:

He [Gandhi] says: "The Ramarajya of my dreams ensures the rights alike of the prince and the pauper". This is the keynote to the entire philosophy of Mahatma Gandhi. ... Even in his *dream* Ramarajya there will be paupers.
A Ramarajya of paupers and princes! Why not? How else will the noble soul get an opportunity to practise deeds of high-minded philanthropy and thus prove the Hindu conception of human nature![46]

A two-part article in the *Congress Socialist* by Nirmal Bose, a writer sympathetic to Gandhi, and not himself a socialist, examined Gandhi's ideas and asked the question, 'Is Gandhi a Nationalist?' (referring to the Hindu chauvinist Madan Mohan Malaviya's newly-formed party within the Congress, and excluding from its ambit socialists and Gandhians), coming up with interesting answers.[47] The Nationalists, according to Bose, wanted to build up a state which would 'primarily protect and foster the industries and the culture of India'. Gandhi, on the contrary, 'does not divide the human race into classes or nations. For him, humanity is one. In this respect, his sympathies are more with the Socialists than the Nationalists'.

But Gandhi is not a Communist ... Gandhi is in fact a philosophical anarchist. But as a practical idealist, he aims at building up little village states, as well as a feeble confederation of them in the form of a centralised State. That requires a certain use of violence, which he thinks, is unavoidable under the circumstances. He is eager to drop even that centralisation as early as possible. As such, Gandhi's Varnashrama, in its practical form, is another form of Socialism, but approaching Anarchism more closely than most prevalent forms of Socialism. It approaches Kropotkin's idea of an anarchistic socialism more closely than anything else'.[48]

This was a more gentle engagement with Gandhi than the more direct assaults on his ideas often found in socialist circles and elsewhere; it seemed to make Gandhism intelligible within (though not compatible with) the framework of socialist thinking, assimilating it to debates with which a reader of past and present socialist debates would be familiar, in particular the Narodnik–Marxist debates in Czarist Russia. In such a view, although Gandhi was regarded as wrong, he represented a stage through which many Marxists had passed.

Gandhi, according to this argument, had been appropriated by the Nationalists largely against his better judgement.

Time and again, the nationalists gave promises of support to Gandhi and wrenched out from him victories on their own behalf. Gandhi had to support the fostering of the mill-industry, disapprove of movements against the propertied classes as such, state that a rich man could become a trustee on behalf of the poor; but deep down he knew that trusteeship was a legal fiction necessary for an approximation in practice as long as the masses were not strong enough to bring the rich to their senses through non-co-operation. These leases of Gandhi to the capitalists did not form part of his creed; they merely represented Gandhi in retreat and, to that extent, the stabilisation of capitalism in India.[49]

Bose believed, however, that 'Gandhi's alliance with the nationalists was now at an end with the formation of the AIVIA, far closer to Gandhi's own heart than anything he had done before, which represented Gandhi's 'anarchistic socialism', and which Bose described as 'an experiment in the theory of Varnashrama made suitable to modern conditions'—he did not address the charge that the AIVIA was not 'modern'. Despite this, and despite his claim of Gandhi's affinity to socialism, Bose was not optimistic about an alliance between Gandhians and socialists—he dismissed such hopes as unrealistic; instead, he foresaw the probability of 'competition' between 'Gandhi's village organisation' and socialism—he referred to the two as 'Socialism both of the Gandhian and the Communistic type'.[50] This expression separated Bose from the socialists—few socialists would have accepted that a Kropotkinist view was compatible with theirs—intelligible, perhaps, but not compatible. Moreover, his interpretation of Gandhi as anti-capitalist depended on dismissing Gandhi's 'trusteeship' ideas as an inessential and irrelevant part of Gandhi's political creed. This was something many socialists wanted to believe; Gandhi's own good intentions were to be separated from the logic of his ideas and from the uses to which they could be put.

Gandhi's Earlier Intervention

The difficulties faced by contemporaries in the 1930s in placing Gandhi's ideas in the intellectual landscape of their time should not be taken to imply that Gandhi was so exceptional as to be unclassifiable. The key to the understanding of Gandhi's ideas is hinted at by the interpretations, both contemporary and retrospective, which placed him in a late nineteenth century context. This context has so far never been effectively analysed. Raghavan Iyer makes several remarks in passing, in what is essentially a sympathetic account of Gandhi's moral and political thought, which provide important directive guidelines: Gandhi's formative years were before his years in India (he returned to India from South Africa at the age of 45, in 1914); and he 'was more at ease with writers of the late nineteenth century ... than with twentieth-century thinkers like Freud'.[51]

Gandhi's main political statement in coherent form was the text which continues to be regarded as his political manifesto, *Hind Swaraj*. Over the years, Gandhi continued to defend this text as the key to his ideas.[52] *Hind Swaraj* was first published in South Africa in the Gujarati section of *Indian Opinion* in two instalments, on 11 and 19 December 1909. It was first published in book form in January 1910, and in English (the translation being Gandhi's own) in March 1910, the first Indian edition not appearing before 1919.[53] Although written in his South African period, it intended to address Indian audiences concerned about the state of India and of the correct path to be taken by nationalism in the context of the issues thrown up by the then ongoing *Swadeshi* Movement; and from the political commentary it provided along with its attempted philosophizing, it was apparent that Gandhi felt the need to address these general concerns. The historical context he provides in the text suggests this (and would have been taken for granted by his readers at the time).[54] However, *Hind Swaraj* did not reach India till 1919—it was banned as seditious by the Government of India in 1910[55]—and perhaps missed its chance to make its most profound impact. Although many read it in the 1920s as a manifesto of the Non-Cooperation Movement, this was in many ways a matter of strategy rather than conviction.[56]

At a time when the burning issues, in the aftermath of the first partition of Bengal in 1905, related to what constituted a swadeshi approach to politics and society—'constructive *swadeshi*', as one historian put it[57]— 'national' committees and bodies of various kinds strongly debated what constituted appropriate borrowings from the 'West', and how to indigenize them. Gandhi's was an extreme position on the question of the acceptability and possible assimilation of cultural borrowings. His position on those debates as to how far 'Western' science, technology, or education was relevant to India was to reject all of modern industrial civilization. His resolution of the problems of how to arrive at a pure nationalism, without the distortions caused by machinery and modern civilization (which had tainted the spiritual nature of the West's own Christian traditions), fit closely with the discussions on the nature of technology and science, of the East and the West, which had been taking place from the late nineteenth century among intellectuals and practitioners of science, though they were usually resolved differently. There was a perceived need for reconciliation of science as 'Western' and science as 'Eastern' or 'universal'[58]—a reconciliation which was sometimes effected in strange ways: in his later life, Bankimchandra Chattopadhyay was to claim that he found Darwin's theory of natural selection close to the Hindu concept of trinity; Ramendra Sunder Trivedi concluded his discussion on Darwin by saying that ultimately the world is *Maya*.[59] Gandhi, however, came up with a position of stronger rejection than anyone else of the dangers of modern civilization, which in *Hind Swaraj* is still identified closely, though contingently, with 'Western' civilization.

Ironically, in doing so, he often drew far more strongly on so-called 'Western' trends than many of those who sought to direct and guide the discussions which crystallized around the Swadeshi movement. Gandhi was an up-to-date and subtle user of various eclectic elements from 'Western' learning in his own philosophy. His European and North American influences have been traced in some detail by now.[60] Two aspects of these influences need to be highlighted, however. First, Gandhi's attraction to anti-industrialization and anti-technology ideas needs to be seen against the background of late nineteenth and early twentieth century reactions to industrialization, critiques of or discomfort with capitalism and market forces among thinkers in the 'West'—important to the understanding of Tolstoy, Thoreau, Edward Carpenter, or Ruskin, for instance. Second, many of Gandhi's other sources were equally inflected with British writings on India from the mid-nineteenth century or earlier, either directly or at second hand; and as a corollary to this, it needs to be noted that his interest in the philosophy and practices of 'Hinduism' and of 'Indian tradition' were also directed by his encounter with the 'West', and by 'Western' interest in 'Hinduism'. A good example of the second point is Gandhi's reading of Henry Maine's *Village Communities of the East and West*, included in the short bibliography of *Hind Swaraj*. Maine's comparative jurisprudence, which Gandhi came across in the course of his legal training, drew on the former's Indian experiences and on accounts of the 'Indian village community' which had been influential in early Orientalist accounts.[61] Gandhi was far from being the only Indian to come up with a romanticized account of 'village India'; the rural community ordered as an ideal and harmonious society, and the consequent privileging of an indigenous past shorn of colonial impurities appears, for instance, in the works of Radhakamal Mukerjee and Radhakumud Mookerji.[62]

But there is, of course, a further twist to the debates on the 'East' and the 'West' in this tale. The debates with which Maine was concerned—the origins of the Teutonic Mark and the Russian *Mir*, could, he felt, be illuminated by a study of the Indian village community, already shown to be closely related to a common 'Aryan' past through the comparative philology begun by William Jones, and popularized, in the Oxford of Maine's day (Maine himself was at Cambridge), by Max Mueller.[63] This academic debate, transported to Russia, became the scholarly basis of 'populism', to use a somewhat inadequate translation, which today means something quite different, in the Narodnik movement. This, ironically, spawned its own debate on the 'East' and the 'West': in this case, the Russian East had to avoid employing non-indigenous categories imported from the developed West.[64] There was thus a certain circularity of arguments: Tolstoy, familiar with the Russian debates, and glorifying his peasants, would have had access to the same intellectual source-material which debated the question of the East and the West with such vigour in different contexts. Upon reading Gandhi's *Hind Swaraj*, which the latter had sent him as a token of respect for his spiritual and intellectual influence, Tolstoy wrote in his diary, 'Read Gandhi about civilisation, wonderful'.[65]

Of the corollary to the second point, that Gandhi returned to his version of 'Indian tradition' through his agonized encounters with England, evidence can most directly be sought in his own story of his 'experiments with truth'. In Pretoria in 1893, he did 'not know much of Hinduism', and knew 'less of other religions', but he intended to rectify this error through study.[66] In London, he was introduced to what was later to be his main source of religious and philosophical inspiration, the *Bhagavad Gita*, by the Theosophists, and the first version he read was Sir Edwin Arnold's translation, *The Song Celestial*, though he was acquainted with the *Ramayana* through his family tradition.[67] He read, in South Africa, Max Mueller's *India—What Can it Teach Us?* and the Theosophical Society's translations of the *Upanishads*; also Edwin Arnold's *Light of Asia*, Washington Irving's *Life of Mahomed and his Successors* as well as 'Carlyle's panegyric on the prophet', and a book entitled *The Sayings of Zarathustra*.[68] His nationalist sympathies were acquired and philosophically moulded, by his own account, through very specific experiences: in South Africa; his initial contacts were with the Meman community from his native Porbandar; by extension he came to see the unity of Indians, but (perhaps in keeping with the spatial delinking of life in South Africa) his nationalism never extended as far as the Kaffirs.[69] His own attempts at 'playing the English gentleman', which he so successfully ridiculed later, tell a familiar tale of Indian attempts to conform to European civilizational values.[70] Gandhi carried his renunciation of these attempts to their extreme logical conclusion; true civilizational values were not to be found in 'modern civilisation'—therefore both India and Britain should reject it and return to their respective spiritual roots. The reason for highlighting these arguments is to stress the point that for Gandhi, as for many professionals and intellectuals in colonial India, the route to a discovery of India lay through Britain. To read Gandhi as an outsider to 'colonialist discourse' (as many do now) is to miss the point which Gandhi himself tried extremely hard to make: it is through indirections that he found his directions. This, it might justifiably be said, was the keynote of his intellectual and spiritual quest, of whose validity he sought to convince others.

I have argued so far that Gandhi's claims to 'indigenism' have been overdrawn. Gandhi, far from refusing to engage with 'Western' intellectual traditions, had himself had a long, intense and painful period of engagement with 'Western' values. Through this engagement he had negotiated a personal identity, and begun to discover and elaborate a moral, social, and, ultimately, political philosophy for Indians who sought to overcome both physical and mental colonialism. At a more distant level, and through his engagement with the writings of thinkers involved in a romantic rejection of capitalism, based on a rejection of materialistic values and a privileging of rural life, he appears to have absorbed and internalized Orientalist writing on India and, in particular, on the ancient Indian village republic, in some cases at second remove.[71]

It may also be argued that Gandhi himself played on a theatrical imagery of the quintessential Eastern holy man in his political style of functioning: the 'fakir', with powers beyond the comprehension of the European mind,[72] was a useful image to project before his imperialist opponents, his life and person thereby standing as evidence of the real possibilities of opposing colonialism. It was also an image that the Congress deliberately set out to create for Gandhi in the 1920s: Jawaharlal Nehru, then a loyal follower of Gandhi, and other Congress leaders, addressed the peasantry and told them that not all men in saffron were holy men: the real holy man was Gandhi; consequently, it was Gandhi who ought to be obeyed.[73]

But while this was important in his style of political functioning, it was hardly useful in an argument regarding how best to order the economic life of a country, which had to persuade quite a different audience. This is where Kumarappa came in; addressing the strategic problems of persuading an educated middle-class audience of the validity of Gandhi's economic ideas for India. Personal conviction being taken for granted, how could the ground best be laid for the communication of ideas to which the intellectual environment of the time was sceptical, if not downright hostile? This called for an intervention of an altogether different order, so as to claim for Gandhi's ideas a relevance in the political and intellectual environment of the 1930s.

Gandhi's Economic *Avatar* and the Coming of J.C. Kumarappa

By the 1930s, Gandhi was aware that the battle for 'his' way—that of the village community, decentralized village-based production, and economic self-sufficiency of the locality—would also have to be fought on a measurable and 'scientific' basis: on the basis of arguments which were communicable and persuasive also on grounds recognized by contemporaries as economic-rational. This was especially so as he knew he was seeking to communicate with the professional intellectuals who were the main advocates of allegedly 'Western' perspectives on development. And as mentioned earlier, there was among them a trenchant opposition to Gandhian ideas, expressed sharply and polemically, and using all the fora at their disposal; much of the criticism was directed at the implications of these ideas: their role in—indirectly—legitimizing capitalists; and the retrogressive nature of his ideas from the point of view of science and/or socialism.

However, Gandhi's economic ideas as a critique of industrialization-as-modernity were not particularly accessible to the people concerned with national development except when interpreted as a kind of modernity. Thereafter, there would, at least, be common terms on which to argue.

At the same time, Gandhi could not be seen to be arguing in such a manner as to treat the moral or ethical arguments as secondary; and also to be too explicitly against his, and the nationalist movement's, main financiers, the capitalists, who had gained legitimation through his 'trusteeship' theory. The main bulk of the 'economic' logic against 'Western' economic systems was provided, therefore, by Gandhi's main deputy in this regard, Kumarappa. 'Gandhian economic thought' was largely Kumarappa's creation; this was cemented as a concept even more after Gandhi's death, when Gandhi himself could make no more interventions.

Kumarappa adopted many of Gandhi's own ideas deriving from 'Hinduism' and Gandhi's debates with 'Hindu' tradition, especially regarding the allegedly moral basis of caste categories, though he systematized them more than Gandhi himself did; but as a Christian Kumarappa adapted these arguments to his interpretation of Christianity as well; and they fit.[74] The moral colouring to Gandhian economic thought, it could, therefore, be argued, was compatible with a vision of God and religious belief, irrespective of particular faiths. Yet Kumarappa used the 'Hindu' version far more than he used the Christian, unless he was specifically addressing Christians, in the knowledge that the Hindu appeal was likely to be wider. It is perhaps a pity that there was no one to provide a version of 'Gandhian economics' compatible with Islam.

The Uses of Economic Argument

A brief digression may be in order here, to demonstrate the use of apparently economic arguments to justify a position which might otherwise be interpreted as moral, communitarian, or obscurantist. In the course of defending the village-oriented economic order, the defence of the cow became an important project. That this was a divisive and potentially explosive project was evident. The attempted creation, from about the late nineteenth century, of a specifically 'Hindu' identity around the issue of the cow and its protection, and the assertion among Muslims of their cultural right to kill cows, is now well known.[75] The issue of the cow was one of the crucial issues regarded as 'communal' and potentially explosive, and was not useful in securing adherents to the nationalist cause among Muslims and other minorities. On the other hand, a great many nationalist leaders who did not see themselves as 'communal' were keen to defuse the issue by finding a way to argue against cow-killing, some feeling strongly themselves that this should be prevented; Gandhi himself was one of them.[76] A version of this argument was also inserted into ideas of a humane, village-based economic and social order, with an economic twist to them.

If the argument against cow-slaughter was framed in economic terms (which, the public was often being reminded, was a neutral, technical, and therefore non-communal way of looking at things), the emotionally-charged problem could be dealt with at a more rational level. In 1927, for instance, a book published from Madras examined the economic validity of the argument for cow-protection. The author wrote, he said, as an economist, through which discipline the truth of the matter could be arrived at; the disturbing business of cow-protection riots could be avoided through an economic understanding of the issues involved. The arguments he used were conventional: the importance of the cow in the agrarian economy of India. The optimism of the position is notable in its belief that the problem could be solved through rational arbitration within the rules of the discipline of economics, whose jurisdiction he did not question. The title page stressed that the author was a Fellow of the Royal Economic Society, London.[77]

Most of the arguments in this genre backed an anti-cow-slaughter position. This also became one of Gandhi's approaches to the argument. Situating himself in an argument made about 'national wealth', Gandhi introduced and personally endorsed a number of books published about the cow, several of them from publishers controlled by Gandhian organizations. 'Those who are interested in the preservation of the priceless wealth of India in the shape of the cow through constructive means will find much food for thought in the following well-written pages', he wrote in 1930 in his foreword to one such book.[78] The book itself, though claiming a 'scientific' approach, and providing tables and large quantities of facts and figures, usually from government sources such as the Indian Industrial Commission, the Royal Commission on Agriculture in India, and the Punjab Board of Economic Enquiry, occasionally lapses into a straightforward appeal to sentiment or morality. In one example, this is from a 'humanitarian' point of view (a passage which quotes from the *Brahma Purana* on the virtues of nursing sick cattle in their old age rather than selling them to others who will slaughter them, an argument dangerously close to arguing against selling old cattle to Muslims); in another, the Mughal Emperor Akbar's tolerance in forbidding cow-slaughter is held up to testify to his wisdom. The examples work in a different tone as well; in another passage a livestock officer's testimony before the Royal Commission on Agriculture in India, and Bhishma's views as retold in the *Mahabharata* are both cited as expert opinions— Bhishma having 'realised intuitively what modern science discovers by experiment'.[79]

Another such detailed study, written about twelve years later, ran to two large volumes, and was less eclectic in its selection of sources.[80] In the foreword, Gandhi commended the author, Satish Chandra Dasgupta, as 'one of the first and best pupils of the late lamented Dr P.C. Ray', and the book 'to the lover of the cow as also to every one who would learn that the slaughter of cattle for food is a pure economic waste'; he called the cow the 'Mother of Prosperity'.[81] The work was clearly positioned primarily as a 'scientific' book both by Gandhi and by Dasgupta; Acharya P.C. Ray was widely recognized as a figure who had stood for both science and swadeshi, and was a heroic public figure to whom both a lay public and a scientific community could relate.[82] Dasgupta engaged in a long debate against some of the findings of the Royal Commission on Agriculture in India, which had misled 'the scientific men and the economists'; consequently, he had 'had to quote expert opinion' for the 'findings' he had arrived at.[83] A long section on pharmacology in the second volume, essentially a veterinary tract, betrayed the author's background in chemistry; the drugs he prescribes include 'indigenous' herbs, but far from giving them primacy, he treated them as supplementary—hardly in keeping with Gandhi's *Hind Swaraj* position that 'to study European medicine is to deepen our slavery'.[84] Yet such argument was not to be considered merely scientific: 'The book is no mere collection of formulae for feeding a cow, or directions for obtaining the utmost milk from a cow. Cow-keeping is a *yajna*, and I have tried to show why and how it is so'.[85] The cow, if 'lifted from its downtrodden condition' by the 'constructive workers in the village', would prove a 'most responsive animal'; and, more importantly, the uplift of the cow would 'amount to lifting the nation'.[86]

The tone as well as some of the content of Dasgupta's work matches that of a good deal of the writing of Kumarappa who, by this time, was the established public face of the Gandhian constructive movement.[87] The message is clear: the movement for a village-based social and economic order was morally the correct choice for India; but if the question of the correct social and economic order were addressed scientifically, it would be found that the village-based social and economic order would also be the economically correct choice for India. This was constantly reiterated by Kumarappa in his speeches and articles. But beyond this congruence of the moral and the practical, there was the need for a deeper philosophical argument, on which to base the moral order.

Addressing the Intelligentsia

If Gandhism had a weakness, it was that its appeal to the urban professional middle classes and intelligentsia was limited. Gandhi's own appeals to the inherent instincts of the peasants (which he, nonetheless, sought to define, control, and direct to his own satisfaction) deprived many intellectuals of their perceived role in directing the nationalist movement. When dealing with matters of 'development', such ideas were at their weakest: it was important to convince the main protagonists in the debate—intellectuals—that Gandhian ideas deserved a hearing. But the moral rhetoric used by Gandhi was not particularly useful in this regard; though, of course, the ideas of the 'modernisers' also drew on moral principles, the rhetoric was predominantly that of economics, science, and rationality, moral principles being regarded as secondary, merely reinforcing arguments whose validity had already been established. Consequently, in order to effectively join this debate, Gandhism required translators who could dress Gandhian ideas in appropriate forms. Gandhi himself was not particularly well suited to the task; by his own admission, he knew very little about economics, and it was widely felt that he was rather too dependent on the views of industrialists in this regard.[88] It may be suspected that he knew more than he was willing to let on; nonetheless, he preferred to allow his disciples to interpret his economic ideas on his behalf; he was prepared to endorse these views as compatible with his own.

Kumarappa was the most original and interesting of Gandhi's authorized interpreters. Born in 1892, the ninth of ten children, the grandson of a priest, he was himself a devout Christian and an accomplished lay preacher. He wanted to be an engineer, but ended up as an accountant, completing his training in chartered accountancy in London; in 1927, he was invited by his elder brother J.M. Kumarappa (then known as John J. Cornelius) to come to New York. Having arrived in the USA, he obtained a BSc from Syracuse University in business administration, and then an MA in public finance from Columbia University in 1927–8, under the supervision of E.R.A. Seligman[89] (among whose students was B.R. Ambedkar)[90], where he did 'excellent work in the general field of Economics' and wrote 'an unusually able essay on "The Public Finance and Poverty of India"'.[91] The lineage of Kumarappa's choice of subject was rather respectable: finance was a subject which provided, within the framework of the academic discipline of economics, an ideal starting point for a critique (or defence) of the British government in India. An extremely respectable line of Indian academics and political activists wrote on public finance in India.[92]

Kumarappa was a late convert to nationalism, apparently arriving at his views on British exploitation of India in the course of his study of Indian public finance. Thereafter he turned his back on his 'upbringing on English model', as one of his biographers puts it (the similarity of this tale of renunciation with Gandhi's narrative of his own renunciation of English values is notable),[93] met Gandhi (on 9 May 1929), began to wear khadi, and along with his brothers adopted the Hindu family name 'Kumarappa', changing his name from Joseph Chelladurai Cornelius to Joseph Cornelius Kumarappa on 10 May 1929. He remained a bachelor all his life. From 1935 till his death in 1955 he was at the head of Gandhi's AIVIA; in 1938–9 he was involved in conducting an industrial survey of the North West Frontier Province and the Central Province and Berar. As member of the Nehru Committee in 1947–8 he helped formulate the 'Economic Policy of the Congress in Free India'; and was chairman of the Agrarian Reforms Committee of the AICC from 1948–50.[94] He was also a member of the Congress' National Planning Committee which came into being in 1938, but resigned after seven months, as he felt nothing particular could be gained by remaining a member of a body committed to large-scale industrialization.[95]

The Gandhi-Kumarappa partnership began in 1929, when Kumarappa returned from the USA and was searching, as suggested by Professor Seligman, for a publisher for his manuscript on public finance. He was told that this was a subject in which Gandhi might be interested; Gandhi should be given a first look at it before it was submitted to another publisher. Accordingly, he wrote to Gandhi of his manuscript, which he said 'attempts to trace how the Government Policy of Taxation has impoverished and lessened the productivity of the masses during the last hundred years'.[96] Gandhi was, indeed, interested and said that he proposed to publish it as a series in *Young India*.[97] He also asked Kumarappa whether he would be willing to undertake a rural survey for him in Gujarat for the Gujarat Vidyapith, as Gandhi found Kumarappa's approach to economics to be 'almost exactly the same as his'.[98]

It took slightly longer for Kumarappa to become a full-fledged disciple; he had, for instance, a few misgivings about Gandhi's penchant for vows. In 1930, he wrote, in a passage notable for its views of moral evolution:

I believe, spiritually and morally all men are not alike. A few are advanced, but most are mainly followers of leaders. We in different stages need different methods of guidance and leadership. I believe this is acknowledged by most religions and especially by Hinduism which approve [sic] of idolatry for those who are at the *lower end of the scale*. If I mistake not, you yourself are not averse to the use of idols by those who are unable to conceive God without material representation. Just as idols are means by which we seek to attain an end and help out those in the *lower stages of development* so are vows means by which leaders strive to hold up the highest resolve [in] the actions of their followers.[99]

The Church, he added, used vows as 'concessions to the weakness of man', which 'find no place in Christ's teachings'. A man should instead rely on 'the higher law of inner voice or his ideals', otherwise he was in danger of being degraded 'to the position of an automaton'. He stressed that he was not criticizing Gandhi's own vows, but 'the effect it will have on the ignorant masses'.[100] Gandhi's reply clarified, 'The vow I am thinking of is a promise made by one to oneself'. Jesus Christ, he added, 'was pre-eminently a man of unshakeable resolution, that is, vows. His yea was yea for ever'.[101] This was apparently convincing; in later years Kumarappa was to get extremely close to equating Gandhi with Jesus— the apotheosis of the Protestant idea of a personal God.[102]

Kumarappa provided for the Gandhian position all the necessary heavy artillery of a political economy education. He was an able pamphleteer not merely on the Gandhian position; he was the main author of the Congress' report on debt repudiation which was to be the basis of the Congress' position at the Round Table Conference in 1931.[103] During the War he voiced nationalist concerns over inflation, the sterling balances and the Bretton Woods Conference in extremely effective polemical pamphlets which managed to simplify complex problems to communicate with a general public.[104] But his main vocation remained the promotion of the ideal of the village movement.

Kumarappa's Village Movement

Kumarappa, beginning his manifesto *Why the Village Movement?* with a narrative of the evolution of the species and of man, sought to establish the basis for two 'types' which were crucial to his arguments: the 'pack type', who 'unite for aggression' (and are usually 'carnivores'); and the 'herd type' who gather together for safety (and are generally 'vegetarian').[105] Good and bad, desirable and undesirable, in this classificatory scheme, correspond to the 'herd' and 'pack' types, respectively.[106]

Evolution, Economics, and Civilizations

Civilized man's economic organizations still bear marks of earlier forms— the 'herd type' and the 'pack type'. The latter is characterized by a short-term outlook; central control and the concentration of power 'in the hands of individuals or small groups in a personal way' (as opposed to the impersonal); rigorous discipline; 'disregard of the welfare of the actual workers or contributors to the success of the organisation'; the '[s]uppression of individuality of the worker and a spirit of intolerance either in competition or in rivalry'; concentration of benefits among a limited few 'without reference to the altruistic value of service rendered'. Its motive force is 'the prospect of obtaining gains' and its activities 'generally radiate from a limited geographical area such as cities'.[107]

Having proceeded to set up the 'pack type' as a particularly unpleasant and undesirable one, Kumarappa needed only to characterize the forms of economic organization he was opposed to as 'pack type' organizations. Kumarappa was perfectly aware that he had to come up with an argument that undermined the sanctity of the generally held standards set by 'economics' and 'science' (the two terms considered to be intimately linked). Some of the images called upon to describe 'pack type' organizations were reminiscent of existing socialist and communist ideas: capitalism having reduced social relations to a cash nexus, the idea of alienated labour, and the ideal of individual freedom within a consensual community. At the same time, as further reading makes clear, Kumarappa intended these remarks to be a prelude to his attack on the Soviet system, which he also classified as 'pack-type', and bracketed in the same category as capitalism—for Kumarappa, as for many contemporaries whose ideas he opposed, an attack on the Soviet system constituted an attack on socialism.

The advantages of 'herd type' social organizations were: a long-term outlook; social control, decentralization and distribution of power being 'impersonal'; 'directed by a consideration of certain set ideals and social movements'. The object of all this was 'to satisfy needs judged from an altruistic point of view' (the community being, presumably, the custodian of the 'altruistic point of view').[108] The 'herd type' meets Kumarappa's 'test of civilization':

We must bear in mind that the true test of civilisation is not our material possessions or our manner or mode of life but the thought we bestow on the well-being of others. In predation, which is really barbarism, we cannot expect to find any civilisation, for true culture shifts the emphasis from 'rights' to 'duties'.[109]

On this basis, Kumarappa proceeds to approach the description of 'Western' and 'Eastern' economic organizations. 'Western' economic organizations, predictably, are of the 'pack type'. There follows a bit of European history, in which Western economic organizations are classified, 'according to the personnel of the central controlling group', into five groups: 'the dynasty of might, the dynasty of finance, the dynasty of the machine, the dynasty of labour, the dynasty of the middle classes'. The 'masses, whether of the West or of the East, are of much the same kind' and are, therefore, not a basis for classification.[110]

Kumarappa's classificatory system is based on the assumption that the economically dominant group controls military and political power—a familiar and unobjectionable assumption to his audiences. Yet given that his arguments hinge on a distinction between the West and the East, it is rather elitist that he does not attribute to the 'masses' any capacity for cultural or other differences based on their 'Easternness'.

The first three dynasties—of might, finance, and the machine—taken together, are considered 'capitalist' by Kumarappa; and a combination of the first two—of might and finance—give rise, according to him, to 'Imperialism'. The middle classes' struggle to seize power, represented by Nazism and Fascism, is also described as being 'based on much the same lines as capitalism'.[111] The classification of communism or the dynasty of labour as 'pack type' seems not to be quite so self-evident, so Kumarappa explains:

Most of the characteristics of the other organisations are represented, *viz.* centralisation of control and power, rigid discipline and suppression of the individual in regard to production and distribution. Whatever good may have been obtained or envisaged by the directing body giving primary consideration to the needs of the community and not so much to the amount of profit obtained, yet the organisation too is a sectarian or class organisation run by the proletariat with special privileges attached to the sect in power.[112]

There are certain features common to all these 'pack-type' organizations which Kumarappa tars with the same brush. All of them are 'city-centred' and will lead to the 'degeneration of the producing masses because no initiative is left to them, their functions being merely one of carrying out higher orders'. Kumarappa sees symptoms of this degeneration in the high incidence of 'nervous diseases' in the USA and the consequent 'clamour for "leisure" ... under their system, leisure is a necessity as their organisation is unnatural'. Consequently, the worker is led to 'resort to drink and other vices'.[113] Leisure, according to Kumarappa, is unnecessary if the worker has a rewarding life; all that is needed is a 'rest period' between spells of work.[114]

Under capitalism, 'every individual gets an opportunity to exercise his talent and energy as he likes', though this may be 'at the cost of injuring society'. Communism takes things to the other extreme: the profit motive is done away with, individualism is suppressed, and 'a small idealistic group plans the work for the nation'. Under both systems 'human values are not fully taken into account ... We have no right to look upon the common run of human beings, as either gun-fodder as under capitalism, or a cogwheel in a machine as under communism'. Both capitalism and communism, Kumarappa claimed, failed to bring out the best in individuals, and both had led to 'group violence'; while under imperialism this violence was 'directed towards foreigners and strangers', communism directed it internally 'in order to suppress the bourgeois class'.[115] He conceded that '... a certain amount of violence will always be involved in any state control, but what matters is the degree and the spirit behind what appears to be violence. Even a loving father chastises his child ... If the Government is truly democratic the Government will represent the people. In such a Government any regulatory functions that require violence, will be self-inflicted and so it is nothing more than self-discipline'.[116]

It is in the Eastern civilizations, such as India and China, and Japan before she chose to imitate the West, that one finds 'agricultural civilisation influencing economic organisation'.

Such civilisations are the results of philosophical and conscious social planning. The Western systems are haphazard growths without any thought behind them. In this sense the West can hardly be said to have a civilisation at all. It is more a refined barbarism.

The only exception to this in the Western world is Soviet Russia, 'the first attempt at a well-planned society in the West with a sociological philosophy, good or bad, behind it'. But this system shares with other Western, 'pack-type' forms of social organization, the common characteristic of 'aggression for economic purposes'.[117] In the political sphere, too, this is reflected in the West's lack of 'true democracy': what exists is a system which 'masquerades under the cloak of parliamentary organisation in which real power is vested in a group or in a single dominating personality'; and in religion, even a tolerant religion such as Christianity came to vest power and authority in a single person or institution.

By contrast, in India 'village republics managed their own affairs' which continued undisturbed 'even when foreign invaders came'; and in religious life a 'tendency to decentralise the form of worship and views in regard to the Godhead' resulted in 'extreme tolerance'.[118] Oriental systems achieve regulation and decentralization of power by 'hitching the economic machinery either to civil laws or religion or superstition'. Kumarappa conducts a defence of the joint family system, the 'division of labour by caste', and the 'method of distribution to artisans of a share in the products of agriculture'.[119]

Kumarappa conceded that 'exploitation was not altogether absent' in these 'old systems'; but 'the purpose of the organisation' was to minimize such exploitation by erecting 'social barriers' to it. And although they were admitted to be incapable of 'bearing the strain put on them by the tremendous expansion in the field of economic activity', and were now 'decadent', Kumarappa stressed the necessity of modelling 'present-day production' on similar principles: 'a system of economic production best suited to modern conditions and capable of working satisfactorily in India, if industrialisation is not to bring with it all the evils attendant on its development in the West'.[120]

Kumarappa had an ingenious interpretation of the *varnashrama* (the caste system): people in society could be divided into four groups: the idealistic, taking a 'long-range view of life'; the altruistic, whose somewhat narrower view 'is still beyond the span of their own life'; the materialistic; and, finally, 'those who follow in a rut without much imagination'. These corresponded, respectively, to the *brahmin, kshatriya, vaisya,* and *sudra,* respectively. These categories were, therefore, not dependent on birth; nor, indeed on occupation, but on motives:

For example an electrician who lives to explore the possibilities of the science without any regard to personal gain is a Brahmin. One who learns the science with the object of helping to industrialise his country and thereby raise the economic standards of his people is a Kshatriya. He who takes contracts or deals in electric supply or goods in consideration of material gain is a Vaisya. But the man who wants to enter the Government electrical department because of the permanency of tenure, economic security and a pension is a Sudra.[121]

In much the same manner, a brahmin or kshatriya by birth could degrade himself by acting contrary to the principles of his caste. The caste system, therefore, '[p]runed of all extraneous growth', is 'graded on a cultural standard of values almost unknown to money economy. Material considerations sink into insignificance when human needs claim our attention. Duty and not our rights determines our position in society'.[122]

Similarly, 'forms of human activity' can be classified, according to dominant motive forces, into four schools: The first, the economy of predation, is the 'lowest type', with life being 'on an animal plane'. The next, the economy of enterprise, ('laissez-faire' and the 'capitalist mentality'), stresses the exercise of the rights of the individual in a 'self-centred' manner. The 'economy of gregarianism' acknowledges certain ties between man and man, but includes imperialism, fascism, nazism, communism and socialism, in that '[t]he higher cultural values are forgotten and man is to live by bread alone'. All these are based on short-term interests: those of the individual's lifespan or that of a group or nation, therefore, are 'economies of transience' and are correspondingly characterized as sudra (predation); vaisya (the 'economy of enterprise and imperialism'); and kshatriya (nazism and communism), where 'individual interests are sacrificed on the altar of altruism'.[123]

The fourth school, the 'economy of permanence', is, however, 'Brahmanical in its idealism and conception. It is an attempt to get into alignment with the order that prevails in the universe and work in unison and in tune with the Infinite. It is the highest evolution man is capable of'. Principles of economics are framed therein 'in the perspective of eternity': a sparing use of natural resources, the consumption of labour and materials readily creatable by man rather than the drawing on exhaustible resources; and, consequently, an emphasis on distribution.[124]

This view of varnashrama as determined by good intentions and spiritual qualities was not always consistently maintained by Kumarappa; elsewhere, he argued that the caste system constituted 'Indian planning'— it was 'functional planning as opposed to production planning. Under this each person has a definite function to perform taking into consideration his inborn qualities, his environment and his training'. The caste system had now, he admitted, 'gone to seed' in becoming hereditary.[125]

Science, Economics, and the Eastern Modern

The ideas outlined above were the basis for all the distinctions, definitions, and characterizations which the author sought to make in the rest of the book. It is significant that Kumarappa found it necessary to set up this elaborate structure on which to build his arguments. That he was not merely tilting at windmills is evident when his seemingly abstract polemic is viewed against the backdrop of the arguments he sought to oppose.

Apart from positioning his arguments as a better alternative to communism or socialism and, consequently, as an 'Indian', 'non-violent' socialism, Kumarappa was also involved in addressing the arguments of science. Kumarappa's principles were far from self-evident given the prevailing intellectual and economic environment. The desirability of industrialization did not need to be established on theoretical grounds, the possession of power and affluence being so clearly with the industrialized nations. Kumarappa could not, however, be seen to draw merely on extra-economic or moral arguments, given the 'technical' or 'scientific' terms of the debates he sought to enter. He had the dual task of establishing that what he believed was morally correct was also economically rational, in order to establish the validity of his claim that an economics informed by the ethical and moral concerns he articulated was also viable. Conceptions of science were, therefore, brought in to reinforce ideas of the wisdom of the East and the need to 'regain the principles that guided our forefathers'.[126]

Thus, principles of economics framed 'in the perspective of eternity' alone can 'lead to the peace and prosperity of the human race and to a life of peace and goodwill based on culture and refinement'. It is because of this that the 'science' of economics must be studied 'from objective standards' and its application approached 'in relation to laws that govern the universe' rather than to 'man's needs of the moment'. This will '...give expression to a mode of life very different from what is considered "modern" in the West ... The "Modern" world is of Iron and Steel. We cannot afford to draw on our inheritance too freely and extravagantly ... Strange as it may seem the mud huts of India belong to the Economy of Permanence while the steel and concrete sky scrapers of New York are symbols of the Economy of Transience'.[127]

Kumarappa thus sought to establish the practicability of the village-based economy on the basis of the scientific wisdom of the principles of economics on which it rested. This was not a rejection of 'modernity'; Kumarappa challenged the basis of generally accepted yardsticks of 'modernity', claiming to establish a case for a better yardstick in the consideration of a longer time frame: 'the perspective of eternity'. Far from rejecting conceptions of 'modernity' and, consequently, of 'science' or 'economics', Kumarappa therefore sought to persuade his readers that his standards of 'modernity', 'science', and 'economics' were better than those which had currency.

Practical Arguments

This is evident in his other writings. In many of his articles he argued strongly that science and technology should be placed at the disposal of village industries, and denied the charge that the AIVIA was 'against human progress'. The idea that the village should be self-sufficient should not, he argued, be taken to imply that the artisans should be left to themselves: a *chamar*'s expertise in leather-working should not be restricted by the older technologies of tanning to which he was accustomed; rather, the assistance of scientific research should be available to him. Science should, however, be put to such correct uses, to transform the 'crude village economy'. 'We want to yoke science to human progress,' Kumarappa wrote. 'Today, science is being prostituted', its use 'denied to the masses'; it needed to be harnessed to village problems.[128] Stating his economic programme in a speech at Sir M. Visvesvaraya's Mysore Swadeshi Exhibition in 1936, he asserted:

(1) supply preceding demand is unnatural and leads to imperialism. (2) Production of goods without reference to the market leads to competitive increase of supply. (3) capitalistic production causes deterioration in the personality and the character of the masses engaged in machine feeding. (4) It is not possible to give gainful occupation to crores of people by industrialisation with large scale industry.
The obvious conclusions are: we have to follow demand and produce goods by decentralised methods and not standardise consumption unless we wish to standardise people.[129]

In such practical argument, however, the ethical underpinnings had to be accepted for the argument to retain its persuasive power. This is more explicit in another example: Kumarappa stressed the need for alerting consumers to their social responsibility: the urban buyer had it in his hands to alleviate the condition of the poor villager. Buyers influenced employment patterns and methods of production; therefore, they should not buy foreign or machine-made articles.[130] In *Why the Village Movement?* the buyer's duty is assigned to women:

The present system of production does not take into consideration the role that is assigned to women by nature. It will be generally admitted that by their very make up they are the custodians of a nation's culture and project into the future the achievements of the present generation. In primitive times consumption was controlled by women, while supplies were in the hands of men ... In the language of economics the woman was the creator of demand and the man's place was that of the supplier.[131]

In India, which was a 'herd type' 'Eastern' culture, women still looked after the home and made decisions which created demand. It followed that women could make or mar a nation's economic life; if uneducated, they would make ill-informed buying decisions, and if educated to 'consumers' duties', they would not fall 'an easy prey to psychological suggestions made by advertisers'.[132] Education, therefore, was Kumarappa's suggested insurance against the proverbial frailty of women.[133]

Kumarappa was at times prone to draw conclusions incommensurate with his observations, or to make implausible claims. In 1946, with India threatened with further food shortages, he made the point that '[t]he basic cause of food shortage is the departure from the village-economy of self-sufficiency'—he did not consider whether in such a situation of self-sufficiency the cities might starve instead.[134] In 1935, he observed that the true Swadeshi spirit which had been engendered by the partition of Bengal in 1905 had now been 'diverted into a support of large-scale industries in India to the exclusion of village crafts which were slowly dying out'.[135] A few years later, he argued that the idea of swadeshi in Bengal had been 'purely political, that is, Indian made articles as against foreign made goods'. It was Gandhi who had, according to Kumarappa, discerned 'that the downfall of India was due more to economic causes than political ones and he bravely shouldered single-handedly the burden, ridicule and ignominy of the charkha movement'.[136] This was an important step towards the reinvention of Gandhi as an economist, at least of a kind.

Conclusions: Statement, Communicability, (Mis?)readings

There are many discrepancies, inconsistencies, and incoherent passages in Kumarappa's arguments, which are not even internally consistent. One of the main opponents in *Why the Village Movement?* is an imagined communism which Kumarappa seems to have read a little about—in Columbia as part of his MA course, as well as afterwards—but had little direct experience of.[137] The ideal state, in his view, would inflict 'discipline' on itself. This self-disciplinary 'violence' is acceptable, he writes, because if a government is 'truly democratic', it 'will represent the people'; this violence is as a 'loving father chastises his child'. Kumarappa stops short of saying that the state will be the people: at best, it can be a sort of extended patriarchal family. He also frankly admits that existing ('Western') states are characterized by the nature of their leadership, and do not in any sense arise organically from society: the 'masses' are the same, Eastern or Western. But his envisaged alternative can think no further than a loving, decentralized patriarchy. This might even be read as a pre-conscious fascist argument, though Kumarappa would probably have been horrified by such a reading.

The defence of caste in terms of its 'directing the various units of economic activity'—as a mechanism for redistributing wealth, preventing falling prices, as a guarantor of subsistence and an obstacle to exploitation—is vulgar economism of a kind most 'Western', by his standards. Again, Kumarappa's (and Gandhi's) argument about the spiritual basis of caste was not particularly appealing at the time. A brahmin might

degrade himself, but no one had any difficulty distinguishing the spiritually
poor brahmin from the spiritually rich Sudra, the consequences for acting
contrary to one's caste being quite different in the two cases. (It must be
pointed out that Kumarappa's interpretation of Gandhi's views on caste,
in seeking to be consistent, was more dangerously appropriable than
Gandhi's less consistent pronouncements. In some cases, Gandhi took
caste to be a spiritual state, by doing which he disarmed high-caste claims
to being automatically superior; in other cases he denounced caste as
having no basis in true religion or in true Hinduism.)[138] Kumarappa's claim
to study economics 'in relation to laws that govern the universe' is
strongly reminiscent of Stalinist dialectics—history and society follow
universal laws that cannot be influenced by human beings or their
conscious behaviour. Kumarappa, therefore, gets entangled in the positions
he seeks to oppose.

But the defects in his arguments are not the point of this analysis. How
if at all was his persuasive strategy meant to work? What ideas did they
link up with? The main link in Kumarappa's assimilation of the Gandhian
moral discourse with the developmentalist modern one, was the distinction
between East and West. This distinction had been used in various ways
in constructing a rationale of 'difference' in both colonial and nationalist
arguments. In nationalist versions, the West is generally spiritually inferior
though materially superior (an argument with which not all colonialists
were uncomfortable); in the Gandhian version material superiority is
devalued by an assault conducted on the basis of that spiritual inferiority,
enabling the East to claim an overall superiority. Gandhi, at least by the
1930s, claimed that his was not a critique of 'Western' culture or religion,
'only a critique of the "modern philosophy of life"; it is called "Western"
only because it originated in the West'.[139] Kumarappa maintained this
distinction; yet he went a step further, using Gandhi's ideas in seeking to
detach modernity from the West and claim it for the East: the former's
'modernity' was only apparently so, as he sought to demonstrate in his
descriptions of the 'transience' of Western economic organizations or of
the 'barbarism' of Western civilization.

Kumarappa's strategies of argument were substantially different from
that of Gandhi's. He made a very definite appeal to history and the
process of evolution of human societies—although there was not much
historical evidence in it that would be accepted according to the
contemporary standards of the discipline. Although in a number of his
other writings, he also claimed a more spiritual and religious sanction for
this 'Gandhian' order in the Christian scriptures, this was largely before

Christian audiences, who Kumarappa had made it his personal task to wean away from collaboration with British rule in India.[140] For general audiences, while discussing the desirability of contending visions of the future development of India, he stuck to less directly religious arguments.

In doing so he was less mystical than Gandhi. Those attracted by Gandhi's moral ideas were often frustrated by the 'exceedingly elusive' nature of his economics,[141] and were constrained to sift through his numerous writings and statements to put together a coherent version. Kumarappa's success lay in his preserving a strong moral content— which, though as much Kumarappa's own as Gandhi's, was compatible with the latter's—while presenting economic matters in such a way as to bring Gandhian ideas into the field of everyday rational discourse, as well as to attempt to fit this moral and economic world view into 'modern' clothes. Kumarappa's writings presented Gandhian ideas in terms of economics, science, socialism, and modernity—terms which, by the 1930s, were crucial to nationalist formulations of 'development'.[142]

Kumarappa's (and Gandhi's) project was in this regard not fundamentally different from that of the 'modernisers': both were engaged in contesting the link between the West and the 'modern'. The latter, as I have said before, stressed the universal character of the 'modern'—and/or, in the version provided by *Science and Culture*, the connection, albeit indirect, of that modernity to the East, where originated 'all those arts and crafts which are responsible for the greatness of the present European civilisation'.[143] Kumarappa, similarly, claimed that a 'science of economics' based on 'Eastern' principles was better deserving of the term 'modern'. Kumarappa's was still the more ambitious project, conducted as a defence of principles, institutions, and customs especially considered opposed to the modern, rather than following the simpler path.

Kumarappa's version of Gandhism fitted more easily into the political discourse of the time. Given the fundamental importance to nationalists of the project of 'modernising' India through economic development, while at the same time appearing to be carving out a path different from that prescribed by colonialism,[144] there was a need to break the link between 'Westernisation' and 'modernity'.[145] It was not desirable to claim that the principles on which Indian development was to be based, despite their 'Western' origins, were perfectly relevant to India— nationalists could not afford to be seen as plagiarist.[146] This would have been seen as a surrender to the British imperialist view of Indian nationalism: nationalists belonged to a tiny elite of Westernized, English-educated urban professionals and intellectuals cut off from the 'real'

India, creatures of Macaulay's Minute. This, it might be said, was one of the vital points regarding Indian nationalist thought: 'derivative' or not, whether it succeeded in being different or not, it sought to be different.[147] But it had to seek to be so without seeming to fit British descriptions of 'backwardness'. The search by Indian nationalism for resources of resistance to British rule had long included claims to a better, more civilized, glorious past before British rule. These claims often leaned heavily on early British and European scholarship on the Indian past;[148] yet they did not consciously or directly do so. Kumarappa's appeals to 'regain the principles that guided our forefathers', to 'the perspective of eternity' and to rather selective 'Eastern principles' are not incompatible with his claims to defending a 'modern' position. Kumarappa was, therefore, drawing on a long-standing conventional framework of argument in which nationalist thought sought to be different by claiming a longer tradition, counterpoising Indian antiquity to that of Europe's classical antiquity; recovering the original nature of a now decadent varnashrama; or claiming that Eastern civilizations were 'the result of philosophical and conscious social planning' as opposed to Western systems' 'haphazard growths', were all ways to claim that India was modern before anyone else. This was not an unique claim, but one he shared with predecessors (in, for instance, the Arya Samajists' 'back to the Vedas' ideology, or Rammohun Roy's quest for a more rational religious faith in the ancient scriptures) as well as contemporaries and near-contemporaries.[149] Kumarappa's version of 'Indianness' or 'Eastern wisdom', as opposed to 'Westernisation' thus had something in common with other arguments which similarly looked for solutions to economic or social problems which could either be regarded as 'Indian', or at any rate not un-Indian.

This indicates not a separate trajectory, but a similarity in strategies of argument and possibly also similar anxieties shared by Indians under colonial rule. For some, the modern was more appealing for its being universal, fears regarding 'culture' or 'Indianness' being secondary; for others, modernity was more comforting if it could be Indian. This provides a reminder of the dual purpose which nationalist developmental ideas had to serve: to be modern, not backward (in answer to colonial claims) as well as to be Indian, not Western (in answer, once again, to colonial claims of the progressive aspects of colonial thought, as well as in response to Indian accusations or fears of loss of 'culture'). It is within this shared framework of anxieties and aspirations that the particular manoeuvres of Gandhian ideas were situated.

The question regarding Kumarappa's success or failure in communicating and propagating his ideas, therefore, rests on the persuasive capacity of his ideas within this framework, as possible resolutions to the given problems; in other words, Kumarappa's version of Gandhism fits more easily into the political discourse of the time, but did it actually succeed in making a significant impact on it? It must be said that these manoeuvres were not in the first instance very successful. More philosophically and psychologically satisfying resolutions were available elsewhere, which were also backed by the endorsement of present successes and by the prospect of similar success in India. Although Kumarappa was well within the parameters of conventional nationalist thinking in arguing a case for 'Indian' solutions, he was, as a consequence of his Gandhian training, often arguing a by then not entirely attractive case, which had been resolved and was, therefore, considered relatively uninteresting. By the 1930s, when Kumarappa was writing, questions of whether technology, machinery or 'socialism' could be regarded as 'Indian' or not, had been resolved in other quarters in ways that largely assuaged the anxieties (though some residual anxieties remained) and expressed the aspirations of a leading section of the nationalist intelligentsia: science and technology, though perhaps at present a 'Western' import, were universal achievements, worthy of emulation.[150]

Attacks on the Gandhian position, moreover, continued to base themselves mainly on Gandhi's, rather than Kumarappa's pronouncements— one of the drawbacks of the Gandhians' great dependence on Gandhi's unquestioned moral stature as a leader and, consequently, the great importance attached to his own statements by both opponents and allies. One critic, dismissing Kumarappa's intervention, called the philosophy of the AIVIA a 'cloak of tattered patches', which added to elements of Ruskin, William Morris, Proudhon, Bakunin, and Tolstoy 'an added dose of economic potion poured into it by Mr Kumarappa at the behest of the Bombay Congress—and produced practically to order as a swadeshi alternative to the imported ideas of socialism'.[151]

The tone of this criticism implied that Kumarappa's economics was an ill-conceived front: it was not proper economics at all. Critics continued to stress the fact that Gandhi had no answer to questions of economic exploitation, and the theory of 'trusteeship' came in for much ridicule. Although Kumarappa underplayed the trusteeship idea in his version of the argument, he also avoided questions of ownership of property; and as Gandhi continued through the 1930s and 1940s to make public statements, Kumarappa's special version of Gandhism was often undermined. For instance, Kumarappa claimed that khadi was more expensive because 'there is a greater degree of distribution of wealth included in the price while the apparent cheapness of imported mill made articles is due to a small share in the booty of the manufacturer and his government'. He, therefore, claimed that the urban consumer had a duty to buy khadi, and that Gandhi 'has often repeated that Khadi sales is his barometer'.[152] But Kumarappa's efforts to establish that khadi was economically viable if people took their duties as consumers seriously were undermined by Gandhi's statement, in 1945, that khadi should not be sold, but should only be given in exchange for yarn. This would ensure that the wearing of khadi would maintain its moral meaning, and that spinning would be a universal training in truth and non-violence; for only those who actually spun yarn would then have yarn to exchange for khadi. 'If hand-spun yarn cannot represent non-violence why should I not retrieve the error while I am still alive and save the wood used in the Charkhas?'[153] This was a difficult situation for the AIVIA and for Kumarappa. Although Kumarappa himself had written widely on the dangers of a money economy which forced peasants to exchange goods that they needed themselves for money which they needed for other purposes,[154] he had barely begun to find wider markets for khadi among people who would not spin themselves. Gandhi's statement effectively undermined his claim that a Gandhian economic order was economically viable. With no clear signal emerging, it was difficult to provide an unambiguous message.

There was also a problem of how to read the message which Kumarappa did provide. Hostile readings of Gandhi's ideas as anarchist were, of course, quite common; a more positive reading was provided in 1949 by R.B. Lotvala, a retired anarchist, of the Libertarian Socialist Institute, Bombay, on the basis of conversations with Kumarappa's brother. Lotvala summarized the Gandhian position as follows:

(1) India being an agricultural country, priority should be given to rural development.
(2) Decentralisation.
(3) Man should be non-economic.
(4) State being a class organisation to be replaced by voluntary cooperative associations.

Lotvala said that both men had agreed that these were 'predominantly Anarchistic ideas'; and added, 'Fundamentally, Anarchist position is humanistic and so man has been made herein the centre of all rational and moral values. Gandhism is very near to it.' He regretted that the Congress government had drifted from Gandhism and was 'merged [sic] in power politics', while it was 'exploiting the name of the Mahatma to stabilise its position'.[155] In a later letter, Lotvala wrote:

I appreciate the work you are doing. But mere writing to the Press or the literature of the type that you bring out will not be sufficiently effective as long as the capitalist system is not replaced by some other social system as would bring about equality of income, opportunity and even status. Fundamental values underlying capitalist system which are based on adoration of money economy as understood and taught by orthodox economists and acted upon by the government should change.

He added that a dependence on 'change of heart' was not enough; 'the truth must be based on scientific inductive research, to be verified on "a priori" method'. Although Gandhi had made great efforts to revive the *charkha* and handicrafts, 'as relations of forces, psychology and environments were against his program[me], he could not succeed in spite of vast energy and money spent after it'.[156] Lotvala had put his finger on the main problems: the hostile reception of Gandhian ideas was partly due to the environment; but also that the 'Gandhian' position did not seek to overthrow capitalism, and could at best be an enclave within it, composed of morally correct, by their own standards, individuals. At the same time, Lotvala's reading indicated the possibilities for selective and creative readings of 'Gandhism', incorporating particular aspects of it. As for the equation of Gandhism with anarchism, Kumarappa seems to have been an agnostic; earlier, he had replied to a hostile critic that he (the critic) would 'search in vain for authorities in Western text books', unless he recognized that the 'Village Industries Movement is an outcome of a desire for non-violence and truth in the economic sphere'. He admitted that 'certain aspects of our reasoning can be paralleled from anarchists and others but that is not sufficient cause to hang us'.[157] Apparently, the description of Gandhians as 'anarchists' could be negative when coming from a hostile critic, and positive, or at least neutral, when coming from a friendly critic.

More serious confusions of reading were also possible. Kumarappa's writing, in seeking to situate itself within a specifically 'Indian' ethos, could lend itself easily to slippages into a culturally defensive, parochial Hindu elitism, or to crudely obscurantist celebrations of a cultural identity which combined Gandhism with varying degrees of religious bigotry or sectarian triumphalism. One correspondent, a Brahmin by the name of T.V. Narayanaswami Iyer, wrote to Kumarappa in May 1947 in praise of *Why the Village Movement?* and paraphrased it in his own terms:

It [the book] is an unparalleled exposition of the truths of the ancient religion of India. The teachings of the great Rishis Vyasa and Valmiki are there in the English form. I also find same terms Varnashrama Dharma Swadharma. Self discipline and mass welfare. Truth is greatly stressed and non-violence still greater. The Ancient religion of India is a composition of Politics & Economics which is eternal and has got only one interpretation. Islam Christianity and other religions are only diluted forms of this ancient religion ... The caste system is no more than party systems which exist today. That party which observes most strictly the eternal principles are held high and the others a little below.[158]

The confusion of 'Hindu' with 'Indian' was, of course, not peculiar to Kumarappa; much has been written on the effects of early British imperialist accounts in privileging an ancient 'Hindu' civilization in India, and representing an Islamic period in India as a dark age of violence and oppression from which British rule rescued India.[159] For those who did not altogether accept this schematic partition of Indian history, there was a tendency to reject the idea of a British rescue from tyranny by a description of British rule itself as tyranny; but many of these rejections sought their intellectual resources in the same ancient and classical splendour that was the 'Hindu' India of the Orientalist imagination. A search for truly Indian values worthy of being upheld and carried forward to an age of renewal in independent India, therefore, often depended on accounts of such an ancient civilization. These, unfortunately, slid all too easily into an idiom which imagined India as Hindu.[160]

Iyer's view of a desirable India, taking off from Kumarappa's statements, was that true religion comprised spiritual, moral, and material aspects. Islam and Christianity, in his view, had 'diluted the eternal principles of Brahmacharyam & chastity'. He approved greatly of the AIVIA's paying 'greater attention to the spiritual and moral aspects before entering with full vigour in the material aspect'. He went on to wax lyrical on the subject of how 'village industries & village panchayats flourished in times past'. As symptoms of present decay, he pointed to '[t]he cow sacrifice by Muslims, the selling of vast numbers of cows by Hindus to agents of Slaughterhouses, the class distinction in railway carriages & steamers, the food and drink consumption and the manner of living by the people of High & Low rank'. He wrote at length on the dangers of the loss of the spirit of *brahmacharya*—a word which, it ought to be noted, has connotations of learning and spirituality as well as of celibacy:

Islam lured away the Kshatriya spirit in the land with their woman [sic] and brought down both their downfall [sic]. The English lured away the brahmanic spirit of the land with their Gold and brought down both their downfall [sic].

Woman & Gold are the negative aspects that attract irresistibly the positive in man and he has to struggle hard to extricate himself out of them and Seek the negative within himself.[161]

Man, Iyer explained, could only be complete unto himself if he contained both positive and negative aspects within himself; this could only happen in the spiritual sphere.

Although such interpretations were not particularly useful in shedding light on a project for the future of India, they also indicated the weaknesses of Kumarappa's playing on anxieties related to the 'West'. It might be argued that Iyer's pouring out his heart to an imagined sympathetic fellow-believer in Kumarappa can hardly be blamed on Kumarappa. On the other hand, Kumarappa's position certainly opens up the discursive space for such an interpretation as Iyer's within the framework of respectable argument. Nothing in Iyer's paraphrase is actually said in Kumarappa's book; but all of Iyer's premises can easily be found in the writing of Kumarappa, and in the writing of other Gandhians: the interpretation of *varna* as the 'brahmanical spirit' or the 'Kshatriya spirit', cow-killing as wrong, or celibacy as desirable. The rest might be extrapolation from what he saw as first principles, driven forward by goals and moulded by anxieties peculiar to him or more widely shared; and in the context of the 1940s, with anxieties regarding religious, regional, national, or other identity corresponding with political uncertainties and forcing those who were uncertain about such choices into making choices, they were more widely shared.[162] This was precisely what 'modernisers' of the Visvesvaraya, Meghnad Saha, and Nehru kind sought to avoid: the implications of arguments which drew on 'tradition' and derided 'Western' modernity were capable of being bent to obscurantist and reactionary arguments, regardless of the intentions of the originators of the argument. Ordinarily, without being linked to conceptions of civilisation and spirituality rather than religion, such a reading would be dismissed as 'communalism' and therefore, as illegitimate. When combined with the justificatory power of an argument endorsed by the Mahatma himself, such views could more comfortably stake their claim for inclusion in the mainstream.

Moreover, Kumarappa, unlike Gandhi, was not particularly careful about ensuring that such readings were avoided. A furious letter from one N.C. Bedekar in Aurangabad, written in 1948, objected strongly to Kumarappa's reply to a question on whether volunteers of the Rashtriya Swayamsevak Sangh (RSS), a Hindu paramilitary organization, could be of help in promoting constructive work. Kumarappa had apparently replied in the affirmative and had 'showered praise on the R.S.S. volunteers and even encouraged them to carry on their activities, which have been professedly antinational & communal in character in face of Govt. opposition & restriction on their activities'. Bedekar found this particularly objectionable in the light of the RSS' dangerous role in the communal violence and propaganda leading up to and after the partition of India in August 1947.[163] Kumarappa's reply seems in retrospect to be either extraordinarily naive or deliberately disingenuous. He wrote:

All I said were generalisations to which no exception can be taken. If there were young men of ideals, renunciation and firmness of purpose, *wherever we may find them*, they will be of invaluable use to our motherland at this time to build up our nation, if they are properly directed.
I am not concerned with Government policy towards the R.S.S. nor do I know what it is. So it will be futile my writing about it.[164]

This reply seems all the more extraordinary because, by the time this correspondence took place in late 1948, the RSS' active involvement in the assassination of Gandhi, on 30 January of that year, was well known. However, neither correspondent specifically mentioned it.

Despite these peculiarities, however, there were aspects of Kumarappa's interpretation of Gandhi which were clearly more accessible than his justifications in terms of caste or Indianness. Ideas of avoiding class struggle or relying on the goodwill and cooperative spirit of the propertied classes, as well as the significance of opposition to capitalism by advocating responsible buying and careful use of impermanent resources found other formulations. These were individual elements in an unstable and ultimately less than coherent system of thought. As individual elements, however, they were useful in other combinations, especially when they could be associated with the legitimating icon of the Mahatma, and could become free-floating elements in political debates which reappeared at various times in various combinations to justify diverse projects.

Gandhian arguments have, in recent times, been supported for being more culturally sensitive and less elitist than those of the 'socialists' in India, or even claimed by 'socialists' as a form of culturally sensitive and participatory 'socialism'. This view is not borne out by the writings of Gandhi or the Gandhians. Gandhians took upon themselves the task of convincing the 'masses' of what was good for them, and the right to guide the 'masses' to the correct moral and material goals. The execution of this task was to be accomplished at a local level rather than at a centralized level, but this was, nonetheless, to be done based on principles laid out by right-thinking, spiritual Brahmins, and not necessarily or even primarily on precedents derived from local practices—which makes Gandhians' claims, or later academics' claims on their behalf, to cultural sensitivity or anti-elitism seem rather dubious. On the contrary, they shared with more mainstream nationalists similar concerns with directing and disciplining the activities of the ordinary Indian in desired directions.

Endnotes

1. See, for instance, E.F. Schumacher, *Small is Beautiful* (London, 1973); Madhav Gadgil, 'On the Gandhian Economic Trail', *Gandhians in Action* (April–June 1994); or various statements by Medha Patkar on behalf of the Narmada Bachao Andolan.
2. For instance, Gadgil, 'On the Gandhian Economic Trail'; Madhav Gadgil and Ramachandra Guha, *Ecology and Equity: The Use and Abuse of Nature in Contemporary India* (London, 1995), especially, pp. 38–9, 188; Vasant Kumar Bawa, 'Gandhi in the Twentieth Century: Search for an Alternative Development Model', *Economic and Political Weekly*, Vol. XXXI, No. 47, 23 November 1996, pp. 3048–49; various articles in the journal *Gandhi Marg*.
3. See the chapter on 'Gandhian Economics', in Bhabatosh Datta, *Indian Economic Thought: Twentieth Century Perspectives* (New Delhi, 1978), pp. 150–8, especially, p. 152; Ajit Dasgupta, *Gandhi's Economic Thought* (London, 1996).
4. Mahadev Desai, preface to M.K. Gandhi, *Hind Swaraj*, (revised new edition, Ahmedabad, 1939), pp. ix–x. in which he reprints a previous article from the *Harijan*.
5. *Harijan*, 27 October 1933, reprinted in *The Collected Works of Mahatma Gandhi*, Vol. LVI (New Delhi, 1973), pp. 146–8.
6. For an account of Gandhi's various elaborations of this theory, see Ajit K. Dasgupta, *Gandhi's Economic Thought* (London, 1996), chapter six.
7. On Vinoba Bhave, see Shriman Narayan, *Vinoba: His Life and Work* (Bombay, 1970)—Shriman Narayan, formerly Shriman Narayan Agarwal, (and author of the 'Gandhian Plan' of 1944—he later dropped his caste name), was himself a Gandhian; consequently, this is an insider's biography. For Jayaprakash Narayan's own account of his move from socialism to Gandhism, see Jayaprakash Narayan, 'Letter to PSP Associates', 25 October 1957, reprinted in Jayaprakash Narayan, *Towards a New Society* (New Delhi, 1958).
8. See Benjamin Zachariah, *Nehru* (London, 2004), pp. 194–8.
9. J.C. Kumarappa, 'The Economy of the Cross', a summary of three addresses to the Mid-India Conference of Christian Students at Nagpur, 5–7 November 1942, reprinted in *Christianity: Its Economy and Way of Life* (Ahmedabad, 1945), p. 1.

10. J.C. Kumarappa, *Why the Village Movement? (A plea for a village-centred economic order in India)*, (fifth edition, Wardha, 1949; first edition, 1936) [hereafter, referred to as Kumarappa, *Village Movement*].

11. Preface to the first edition, reprinted in Kumarappa, *Village Movement*, p. (iii).

12. The second edition in 1937 added material on 'Barter Exchange', 'Education for Life', 'Democracy in the Orient', and 'Centralisation and Decentralisation'. The third, in 1939, added a chapter on 'Surveys and Plans'; the fourth, in 1945, added material on 'Schools of Economics', 'Peoples' Income', 'Moral Issues of Riches', 'Non-violent Standards of Life', and 'Planned Economy'. The book was also translated into several Indian languages.

13. See my point in Chapter 1 of this book on why economics became important as the terms which served to frame arguments, but was seen to include, or to need supplementing by, important non-economic issues. See, also, Chapter 2 on 'moral and material progress' and its importance in British, nationalist, and (the apparent exception) Gandhian conceptions of development; and Chapter 3 for its operation in imperial arguments.

14. M.K. Gandhi, *'Hind Swaraj'*, chapter VI, p. 35, in Anthony J. Parel (ed.), *Gandhi: Hind Swaraj and Other Writings* (Cambridge, 1997).

15. As has been pointed out, for instance, by Partha Chatterjee, *Nationalist Thought and the Colonial World: A Derivative Discourse?* (London, 1986), p. 93, and Parel, 'Introduction', in *Gandhi: Hind Swaraj*, p. xlvii.

16. Partha Chatterjee, *Nationalist Thought*, p. 112.

17. Partha Chatterjee, *Nationalist Thought*, pp. 93–4, 99.

18. See, for instance, Ashis Nandy, *Tradition, Tyranny and Utopias: Essays in the Politics of Awareness* (Delhi, 1987).

19. See Bhikhu Parekh, *Colonialism, Tradition and Reform: An Analysis of Gandhi's Political Discourse* (New Delhi, 1989).

20. Partha Chatterjee, *Nationalist Thought*, pp. 50–2; for the exposition, see chapter four, pp. 85–130.

21. Partha Chatterjee, *Nationalist Thought*; Partha Chatterjee, 'Gandhi and the Critique of Civil Society', in Ranajit Guha (ed.), *Subaltern Studies III* (Delhi, 1984).

22. Gandhi's own word for his language, quoted in Partha Chatterjee, *Nationalist Thought*, p .85.

23. See Shahid Amin, 'Gandhi as Mahatma', in Ranajit Guha (ed.), *Subaltern Studies II* (Delhi, 1983); G.D. Birla, *In the Shadow of the Mahatma: A Personal Memoir* (Bombay, 1968); Tapan Ghose, *The Gandhi Murder Trial* (New York, 1973).

24. As, for instance, implicitly, in Raghavan Iyer, *The Moral and Political Thought of Mahatma Gandhi* (New York, 1973); and, more explicitly, in Ajit Dasgupta, *Gandhi's Economic Thought*.

25. Ajit Dasgupta, *Gandhi's Economic Thought*, p. 103. Dasgupta observes many such shifts, but does not read them as particularly significant in strategic terms.

26. For instance, he asked Thakurdas about aspects of business views on the British government's 'scorched earth' policy when Japanese invasion was anticipated in 1942. See Thakurdas Papers, NML, File 279 Part I, ff. 12–14, Thakurdas to Gandhi, 12 March 1942, responding to Mahadev Desai's request for Thakurdas to write to Gandhi on his views on 'scorched earth', and Gandhi's version, *Harijan*, 22 March 1942, copy in Thakurdas Papers, File 279 Part I, f. 60.

27. 'Bapu' to 'Ku', 12 August 1941, J.C. Kumarappa Papers (JCK), NML, New Delhi. Subject File No. 5, f. 75. Emphasis mine. Significantly, Gandhi did not phrase the intended project in terms of the need to combat the use of machinery, as he was conventionally wont to do, but in terms of the need to combat the 'socialisation of industrialism'—not 'industrialism', but the 'socialisation' thereof. This was certainly an engagement with issues thrown up by the 'Enlightenment'.

28. See, for instance, Karuna Kaushik, *Russian Revolution and Indian Nationalism: Studies of Lajpat Rai, Subhas Chandra Bose and Ram Manohar Lohia* (Delhi, 1984), pp. 38–86, on Lala Lajpat Rai. Lajpat Rai was impressed by the Russian Revolution but remained an Arya Samajist, with the Hindu overtones which went with being a member of that organization.

29. Many people cited accounts such as Sidney and Beatrice Webb, *Soviet Communism: A New Civilisation?*, two volumes, (London, 1935). The Government of India initially contemplated banning the book in India, but decided against it. See IOR: L/P&J/12/493.

30. For an account, see Bipan Chandra, *The Rise and Growth of Economic Nationalism in India* (Delhi, 1966).

31. See Birla's letter to Thakurdas regarding the 'Bombay Manifesto' against Nehru's socialist pronouncements, quoted in Bipan Chandra, 'Jawaharlal Nehru and the Capitalist Class, 1936', *Economic and Political Weekly*, Vol. X, No. 33–35 (August 1975), p. 1319. This is not to suggest that businessmen steered clear of political issues: see Claude Markovits, *Indian Business and Nationalist Politics* (Cambridge, 1985).

32. See Ajit Dasgupta, *Gandhi's Economic Thought*, chapter six, on the Gandhian theory of trusteeship.

33. See Chapter 5 of this book, for further discussion.

34. Birla, *In the Shadow of the Mahatma*, p. xv.

35. For Gandhi's retreats, see, especially, Sumit Sarkar, 'The Logic of Gandhian Nationalism: Civil Disobedience and the Gandhi–Irwin Pact (1930–31)', *Indian Historical Review*, Vol. III, No. 1 (1976).

36. See CSP manifesto, reprinted in *Congress Socialist*, 29 September 1934.

37. See Jayaprakash Narayan, *Why Socialism?* (Benares, 1936). Narayan also advertised the Marxist and Leninist approaches of the CSP, which was far from true of all its members, but was *believed* by a large number of members, at least at the time, to be an accurate way to describe their politics.

38. For instance, he crucially intervened to disarm Subhas Bose as Congress

president in 1939. On the 'Tripuri crisis', see Sumit Sarkar, *Modern India 1885–1947* (Madras, 1983), pp. 372–5.

39. For the distinctions between groupings of businessmen vis-a-vis nationalism, see Claude Markovits, *Indian Business and Nationalist Politics*.

40. Such anxieties have been chronicled for earlier periods—see, for instance, Sumit Sarkar, *A Critique of Colonial India* (Calcutta, 1985); Partha Chatterjee, *The Nation and its Fragments: Colonial and Post-colonial Histories* (Princeton, 1994), especially, pp. 6–7 on the 'cultural' sphere of 'nationalism'; Dhruv Raina and S. Irfan Habib, 'Bhadralok perceptions of Science, Technology, and Cultural nationalism', *Indian Economic and Social History Review*, Vol. 32, No. 1 (1995); Dhruv Raina and S. Irfan Habib, 'The Unfolding of an Engagement: The Dawn on Science, Technical Education and Industrialisation', *Studies in History*, Vol. 9, No. 1, (January–June 1993); and Ashis Nandy in some of his early essays—see, Ashis Nandy, 'Sati: A Nineteenth Century Tale of Women, Violence and Protest', in Ashis Nandy, *At the Edge of Psychology: Essays in Politics and Culture* (Delhi, 1980) (Nandy's interpretation is based on what current psychotherapy and social work terminology might refer to as 'reactive ethnicity'—he does not use the term—and his writing indicates that he is possibly suffering from it himself). There are disagreements as to the significance to be attributed to the trends referred to—but the evidence points clearly to anxieties related to disruption of a world and a world-view by British colonial rule, and the search for a world-view compatible with new conditions of existence and with the newly-available intellectual tools as well as what was understood of the old.

41. *Science and Culture* Vol. IV, No. 10 (April 1939), pp. 534–5. One of the stronger advocates of 'modern' solutions to problems of Indian development was the journal *Science and Culture* ('A Monthly Journal of Natural and Cultural Sciences'), published from Calcutta, founded and edited by Meghnad Saha, eminent physicist and developmentalist.

42. *Science and Culture* Vol. IV, No. 10 (April 1939), editorial, p. 533.

43. Asoka Mehta, 'The Victory of Socialism over Romanticism', *Congress Socialist*, 3 February 1935.

44. Asoka Mehta, *Planned Economy for India?* (Bombay, 1935), a CSP pamphlet which contains the substance of his articles in the *Congress Socialist*; Mir Alam, 'India's New Deal', *Congress Socialist*, 3 February 1935, p. 15, which includes a review of M. Visvesvaraya's *Planned Economy for India* (Bangalore City, 1934).

45. Quoted in J.P. Narayan, *Why Socialism?* p. 86: JP's italics.

46. J.P. Narayan, *Why Socialism?* pp. 87–8.

47. Nirmal Bose, 'Is Gandhi a Nationalist?', *Congress Socialist*, 10 February 1935, pp. 14–16; and 'Is Gandhi a Nationalist: Alliance with the Socialists', *Congress Socialist*, 24 February pp. 6–8. For the views of the nationalists, see their pamphlet, Madan Mohan Malaviya and M.S. Aney, *The Congress Nationalist Party: What it Stands for: Why Every Indian Should Support It*

(Bombay, August 1934), IOR: P/V 119. The main plank of the Nationalists' programme was their rejection of Ramsay MacDonald's 'Communal Award', which they denounced as a British attempt to divide the Indian population, but then fell victim to that logic by asserting that 'Hindus' were not adequately represented considering the strength of their numbers. The Congress Socialists regarded the Nationalists as a 'communal' party: see *Congress Socialist*, 6 October 1934, p. 14. This usage of the term 'Nationalist' was an unusual and specific one: a 'nationalist' was generally considered to be someone who opposed British rule in India, by which meaning 'socialists' and 'Gandhians' were sub-sets of 'nationalists'. It is in the latter sense that I have used the term elsewhere in this dissertation.

48. *Congress Socialist*, 10 February 1935, p. 16.

49. *Congress Socialist*, 24 February 1935, p. 7.

50. *Congress Socialist*, 24 February 1935, p. 8. Looking at the future, Bose predicted: 'So far as Nationalism is concerned, there is no doubt that it will hardly be able to raise its head sufficiently as long as Gandhi is there to work against it. Devoid of any active programme, there is a likelihood that the two branches of Communalism, Hindu and Muslim, will now form a combine against Socialism both of the Gandhian and the Communistic type. But it will be a harmless organisation because it will have no path of direct action of its own. Only the more idealistically inclined nationalists will go over either to the side of Gandhi or the Socialists, and add some strength to those two causes'. This polarization did not take place.

51. Raghavan Iyer, *The Moral and Political Thought of Mahatma Gandhi* (New York, 1973), pp. 9–10, 14. Iyer's classification of Freud as a twentieth century thinker is interesting; most current studies treat the intellectual genealogy of Freud as a nineteenth century Viennese Jewish bourgeois one. Gandhi himself did on occasion refer to psychoanalysis.

52. See Anthony J. Parel, 'Introduction', in Anthony J. Parel (ed.), *Gandhi: Hind Swaraj and Other Writings* (Cambridge, 1997). As late as 1945, Gandhi stated that he stood by what he had written in *Hind Swaraj*: Gandhi to Jawaharlal Nehru, 5 October 1945 (in Hindustani written in the Roman script), Jawaharlal Nehru Papers JNP, NML, Correspondence, Vol. 26, f. 135.

53. See 'A Note on the History of the Text', in Parel (ed.), *Gandhi: Hind Swaraj*, p. lxiii.

54. This point has largely been missed by commentators—it is not mentioned, for instance, by Parel in any of his sections on the historical and intellectual contexts in his introduction—probably because Gandhi's text did not explicitly state its desire to intervene in these debates.

55. Parel (ed.), *Gandhi: Hind Swaraj*, Note 2, p. 5.

56. See, for instance, Naba Choudhuri, Cuttack, to Jawaharlal Nehru, 8 September 1933, JNP, Correspondence, Vol. 12, ff. 49–53: Gandhism, Choudhuri wrote, had 'now outgrown the personal moral ideas, prejudices

and Sanskaras of Gandhiji himself. Gandhism as a revolutionary method is quite distinct from Gandhism as a spiritual force for the moral upliftment [sic] of the human personality'. He believed in the value of Gandhism as revolutionary method, but rejected Gandhi's personal views (f. 49). Another more contemporary reading is S.A. Dange, *Gandhi vs Lenin* (Bombay, 1921)—which has been read as hostile to Gandhi by Anthony Parel (Parel (ed.), *Gandhi; Hind Swaraj*, pp. lviii-lix)—I read it, in fact, as a detailed analysis of the relative strategic value of a 'Leninist' and 'Gandhian' approach to political struggle in the specific case of India, with the tone as well as the content of the text by no means implying that the matter was decided.

57. Sumit Sarkar, *The Swadeshi Movement in Bengal 1903–1908* (Delhi, 1973), pp. 55–7.
58. For a more detailed discussion of this point, see Chapter 5 of this volume.
59. Deepak Kumar, *Science and the Raj 1857–1905* (Delhi, 1995), p. 195.
60. See, for a well-researched short account, Parel, 'Introduction', in *Gandhi: Hind Swaraj*, pp. xxxii–xlvii.
61. Parel, 'Introduction', p. xlii. On Maine, see J.W. Burrow, *Evolution and Society* (1970 edition; first edition Cambridge, 1966), pp. 137–87. Maine had outlined his first major contribution to his field, *Ancient Law*, before he had ever been to India; he elaborated these ideas in his *Village Communities of the East and West*, published in 1871, with his Indian experience behind him.
62. See, for instance, Radhakamal Mukerjee, *The Foundations of Indian Economics* (London, 1916); Radhakumud Mookerji, *Local Government in Ancient India* (London, 1919). An example of the overlapping of the imperial and national uses of the idea of 'development', appears in John Matthai's doctoral dissertation, at the LSE, under Sidney Webb, and published in 1915: John Matthai, *Village Government in British India* (London, 1915). Matthai was often cited by colonial officials: see Chapter 3 of this book—but what he claimed in his dissertation did not seem to be central to his own later thinking.
63. J. W. Burrow, *Evolution and Society*, (Cambridge, 1966), pp. 141, 148–9.
64. Burrow, *Evolution and Society*, p. 159; Clive Dewey, 'Images of the Village Community: A Study in Anglo-Indian Ideology', *Modern Asian Studies*, Vol. 6, No. 3 (1973); for a concise account of the Russian situation, in particular the Narodnik–Marxist divide, see Isaac Deutscher, *The Prophet Armed* (London, 1959), chapter 1. *Narodnaya Volya* defended the 'indigenous' *Mir* as the basis of action, and attacked the emergent Marxists as outsiders and Westernizers. The 'Marxists', on the other hand, referred to the *Mir* as a bulwark of absolutism; the emancipation of the serfs in 1861 had given the responsibility for periodic land redistribution to the *Mir*. Ironically, Marx himself seems to have tended towards accepting the so-called 'indigenist' and 'terrorist' position of Narodnaya Volya and was suspicious of the 'Genevans', as he called the *Cherny Peredel* group of Georgi Plekhanov, who called themselves 'Marxists'. Cyril Smith, *Marx at the Millenium* (London, 1996), pp. 52–9.

65. Tolstoy's diary, entry for 20 April 1910, quoted in Raghavan Iyer, *The Moral and Political Thought of Mahatma Gandhi*, p. 24.
66. M.K. Gandhi, *The Stories of My Experiments with Truth* (Harmondsworth edition 1982; first published in two volumes, 1927 and 1929, Ahmedabad, translated by Mahadev Desai), p. 121.
67. Gandhi, *The Story of My Experiments with Truth*, p. 77.
68. Gandhi, *The Story of My Experiments with Truth*, pp. 156–7.
69. See Maureen Swan, *Gandhi: The South African Experience* (Johannesburg, 1985); Dhruba Gupta, 'Indian Perceptions of Africa', *South Asia Research*, Vol. 11, No. 2 (November 1991), pp. 163–5. Gupta argues persuasively that Gandhi was not inclined to make an argument for equality of 'kaffirs' and Indians.
70. Gandhi, *The Story of My Experiments with Truth*, pp. 60–3.
71. I use the term in its pre-Saidian sense—to denote eighteenth- and nineteenth-century students of 'classical' India, though the post-Saidian meaning might also be useful here: see Edward W. Said, *Orientalism* (London, 1978).
72. That is, Orientalism in its post-Saidian sense—as a stereotype of the non-European in the European imagination. This was somewhat ironic, given that Gandhi had come to such stereotypes through his acquaintance with British thinking on the subject.
73. S. Gopal, *Jawaharlal Nehru: A Biography*, Vol. 1 (London, 1975), p. 53.
74. See Kumarappa, *The Practice and Precepts of Jesus* (Ahmedabad, 1945); and the essays collected in Kumarappa, *Christianity: Its Economy and Way of Life* (Ahmedabad, 1945).
75. See Gyan Pandey, 'Rallying Round the Cow', in Ranajit Guha (ed.), *Subaltern Studies II* (Delhi, 1983). Subho Basu, 'Strikes and "Communal" Riots in Calcutta in the 1890s', *Modern Asian Studies*, Vol. 32, No. 4 (1998) describes the importance for Muslim jute-mill hands of their perceived right to sacrifice cows, and their attacks on the police (though not on their Hindu fellow-workers) because of the police's attempts at preventing cow-sacrifice. In some circumstances it was possible to ensure that Muslims voluntarily gave up eating beef and killing cows out of solidarity with their Hindu brethren. In December 1919, in connection with the Non-Cooperation and Khilafat movement, the Muslim League asked its followers to give up sacrificing cows at Bakr-Id. Cited in Sumit Sarkar, *Modern India 1885–1947* (Madras, 1983), p. 196.
76. For a reading of Gandhi's opposition to cow-slaughter as an 'animal rights' argument, rather than an opposition dictated by Hindu reverence for the cow, see Ajit K. Dasgupta, *Gandhi's Economic Thought* (London, 1996), pp. 60–3.
77. L.L. Sundara Ram, *Cow Protection in India* (Madras, 1927).
78. M.K. Gandhi, Foreword to Valji Govindji Desai, *Cow Protection* (Ahmedabad, 1934). Note that Gandhiji's endorsement of the book is dated Sabarmati, 8 March 1930, four years before the book was finally published (by the

Navajivan Press, judging by its appearance and design, though the name of the Press, usually present in its publications, is missing here). The delay was presumably due to the Civil Disobedience Movement, the Round Table Conference, and the second Civil Disobedience Movement which intervened.

79. Valji Govindji Desai, *Cow Protection* (Ahmedabad, 1934), pp. 29–30, 101–2, 116.

80. Satish Chandra Dasgupta, *The Cow in India, Vol. I—Breeding—Dairy Industries* (Calcutta, 1945); *The Cow in India, Vol. II: The Body of the Cow—its Diseases and Treatment* (Calcutta, 1945). Both volumes were published by the Khadi Pratisthan, in May and September 1945, respectively.

81. M.K. Gandhi, Foreword, to Satish Chandra Dasgupta, *The Cow in India, Vol. I*, p. (i), dated Mahabaleshwar, 20 May 1945.

82. On P.C. Ray and his influence, see Chapter 5 of this volume. See also P.C. Ray, *Life and Experiences of a Bengali Chemist* (Calcutta and London, 1932), especially, pp. 129–151; and the somewhat ironically-titled *Acharyya Ray Commemoration Volume* (Calcutta, 1932), edited by Satya Churn Law, a *Festschrift* for the Acharya on the occasion of his seventieth birthday, published half a year late, but certainly during his lifetime.

83. Dasgupta, *The Cow in India, Vol. I*, p. (vii). Much of Dasgupta's opposition to the Royal Commission was due to the latter's recommendation that the buffalo was a more useful agricultural animal than the cow; Dasgupta argued strenuously against that position: chapter four, pp. 87–203. This caused Gandhi to emphasize, in his Foreword, that this argument was not intended to imply that the buffalo 'should be killed or starved out', merely that it should 'not be favoured at the expense of the cow'. Gandhi, 'Foreword', p. (i).

84. Dasgupta, *The Cow in India, Vol. II*, Part VI, pp. 291–316; Gandhi, *Hind Swaraj*, in Parel (ed.), *Gandhi: Hind Swaraj and Other Writings*, p. 64.

85. Dasgupta, *The Cow in India, Vol. I*, p. (vii).

86. Dasgupta, *The Cow in India, Vol. I*, p. (viii).

87. He was almost single-handedly editing as well as writing the AIVIA paper, the *Gram Udyog Patrika*, in its early years. Later on, Kumarappa's brother Bharatan Kumarappa was also a frequent contributor; when Kumarappa was in jail during the Quit India Movement, many of the articles were written by Vaikunth L. Mehta.

88. See Benthall Papers, Centre for South Asian Studies, Cambridge, Box II, file on 'Ghandi'; Dietmar Rothermund, *India in the Great Depression 1929–1939* (Delhi, 1992), p. 212.

89. McVickar Professor of Political Economy, Faculty of Political Science, Columbia University.

90. Seligman supervised B.R. Ambedkar's PhD thesis, later published as *The Evolution of Public Finance in British India: a Study in the Provincial Decentralisation of Public Finance* (London, 1925), and appears in the acknowledgements of Gyan Chand's *Essentials of Federal Finance: A*

Contribution to the Problem of Financial Re-adjustment in India (London, 1930), Preface, p. viii.

91. Seligman's recommendation letter, dated 29 January 1929, copy in JCK, NML, Subject File No. 1, f. 19.
92. See, for instance, K.T. Shah, *Sixty Years of Indian Finance* (Bombay, 1921); B. R. Ambedkar, *The Evolution of Public Finance in British India*; Gyan Chand, *Essentials of Federal Finance* and *Local Finance in India* (Allahabad, 1947); P.J. Thomas, *The Growth of Federal Finance in India: being a Survey of India's Public Finances from 1833 to 1939* (India Branch, Humphrey Milford, Oxford University Press, 1939).
93. See Gandhi, *The Story of My Experiments with Truth*, pp. 60–3. For Kumarappa's account of the beginnings of his own renunciation, see Kumarappa, 'Our meeting', n.d., p. 1–3, in JCK, NML, Speeches and Writings, Vol. VI, ff. 15–17.
94. Biographical details are taken from K. Muniandi, 'Kumarappa the Man', *Gandhi Marg*, Vol. 14, No. 2 (July–September 1992), pp. 318–26; and Devendra Kumar, 'Kumarappa and the Contemporary Development Perspective', *Gandhi Marg*, Vol. 14, No. 2 (July-September 1992), pp. 294–5, unless otherwise stated.
95. Kumarappa's reason for his resignation—its 'economic aspect'—was laid before the readers of the *Gram Udyog Patrika* in an article entitled 'Out of One's Element'. The priority for the AIVIA, as far as economic organization was concerned, was the creation of employment for the villages. This was also a correct approach for a country with an abundance of labour and a shortage of capital. The NPC did not appreciate this; instead, they 'seemed to think that all would be well as long as we produced large quantities of standardised goods'. *Gram Udyog Patrika,* September 1939, pp. 1–2.
96. Kumarappa, 'Our Meeting', p. 1; letter to Gandhi dated 22 May 1929 on letterhead 'Cornelius and Davar, Incorporated Accountants and Auditors', in JCK, NML, Subject File No. 5, f. 17.
97. It was serialized in *Young India* over November and December 1929 and January 1930, and published subsequently in book form by the Navajivan Press as J.C. Kumarappa, *Public Finance and Our Poverty: the Contribution of Public Finance to the Present Economic State of India* (Ahmedabad, 1930).
98. Kumarappa, 'Our Meeting', p. 2. The Gujarat Survey was published as J.C. Kumarappa, *A Survey of Matar Taluka (Kaira District)* (Ahmedabad, 1931); when it was reprinted in 1952—without revisions or modifications (Kumarappa's preface to the second edition, p. xi)—it was entitled, significantly, *An Economic Survey of Matar Taluka* (Ahmedabad, 1952).
99. Kumarappa to Gandhi, 25 October 1930, JCK, NML, Subject file No. 5, f. 1. Emphases added.
100. Kumarappa to Gandhi, 25 October 1930, JCK, NML, Subject file No. 5, ff. 3, 5.
101. Gandhi to Kumarappa, 31 October 1930, JCK, NML, Subject file No. 5, f.

5a. The translation of the original term into English, Gandhi said, had been inadequate; Gandhi had not read the translation. He added, 'A life of vow is like marriage, a[s] sacred[.] It is marriage with God[,] is dissoluble [sic] for all time. Come let us marry Him.' The equivalent Sanskrit term was *vrata*, a solemn resolve or a spiritual decision, according to Gandhi. [Raghavan Iyer transliterates this text as '...A life of vow is like marriage, a sacrament...': *The Moral and Political Thought of Mahatma Gandhi*, p. 82). On the wider parameters of Gandhi's views on the importance of vows, of Gandhi's statement on the connotations of the Sanskrit terms vrata and *yama*, and the debate with Kumarappa, see Raghavan Iyer, *The Moral and Political Thought of Mahatma Gandhi*, pp. 73–81, 164–7.

102. See Kumarappa, *The Practice and Precepts of Jesus*, especially, pp. 3–5. He prefaced his later remarks with the following contextualizing statement: 'It is a common practice among oriental teachers and devotees to identify themselves with the Godhead. This is never understood to signify an exclusive claim to divinity. The fourth gospel depicts Jesus in this mode throughout' (p. 3).

103. See 'Congress Select Committee, Report on the Financial Obligations Between Great Britain and India, official summary issued July 1931', copy in IOR: L/I/1/149. This argued that most of India's public debt was not really India's public debt but Britain's, as it had not been incurred in Indian interests or by a government which was Indian.

104. See Kumarappa, *Currency Inflation: Its Cause and Cure* (Wardha, 1943)—the title is loosely borrowed from the title of Edward Carpenter's book; his collection of essays on imperial wartime finance, Kumarappa, *Blood Money* (Wardha, 1948); and Kumarappa, *Clive to Keynes (A Survey of the History of our Public Debts and Credits)* (Ahmedabad, March 1947), respectively.

105. I have elaborated the details of Kumarappa's classificatory system elsewhere: Benjamin Zachariah, 'Interpreting Gandhi: JC Kumarappa, Modernity and the East', in Tapati Guha Thakurta (ed.), *'Culture' and 'Democracy': Papers from the Cultural Studies Workshops* (Calcutta, 1999). I shall outline the main points here.

106. Kumarappa, *Village Movement*, pp. 1–3.

107. Kumarappa, *Village Movement*, pp. 4–5.

108. Kumarappa, *Village Movement*, pp. 5–6.

109. Kumarappa, *Village Movement*, p. 3.

110. Kumarappa, *Village Movement*, pp. 7–8. Much of Kumarappa's attempted history of 'Western' economic organizations can be omitted; it is a confused and somewhat incoherent account, with several obvious inaccuracies in historical detail—Napolcon is in his account a feudal baron, for instance: '... what did Napoleon care how many of his soldiers he left dead on the way so long as he could get to Moscow?' is Kumarappa's example of feudalism. Kumarappa, *Village Movement*, p. 8.

111. Kumarappa, *Village Movement*, p. 10.

112. Kumarappa, *Village Movement*, pp. 9–10.
113. Kumarappa, *Village Movement*, pp. 10–11.
114. Kumarappa, *Village Movement*, p. 62.
115. Kumarappa, *Village Movement*, pp. 12, 15.
116. Kumarappa, *Village Movement*, p. 15.
117. Kumarappa, *Village Movement*, p. 16.
118. Kumarappa, *Village Movement*, pp. 18–19.
119. In the joint family competition is controlled and the weak protected through the 'equitable' sharing of the income of the earning members with non-earning members. The caste system 'aimed at directing the various units of economic activity in consonance with one another and safeguarding the community from overproduction', and payment in kind to artisans such as the carpenter, blacksmith, or chamar ensured everyone a 'minimum subsistence allowance', the underlying principles being 'the conception that work itself is a method of distribution of wealth', and that the community as a whole was 'a corporate unit', its parts akin to organs of the same body. Kumarappa, *Village Movement*, pp. 16–17.
120. Kumarappa, *Village Movement*, pp. 18–20.
121. Kumarappa, *Village Movement*, p. 22.
122. Kumarappa, *Village Movement*, pp. 22–3.
123. Kumarappa, *Village Movement*, pp. 25–9.
124. Kumarappa, *Village Movement*, pp. 27–8, 30.
125. Kumarappa, 'The Village in Our Economy'. Sent to *India and World Affairs*, n.d., ff. 95–6, Speeches and Writings in Bound Volumes, Vol. II, JCK, NML.
126. Kumarappa, *Village Movement*, p. 21.
127. Kumarappa, *Village Movement*, p. 28. Kumarappa elaborated these ideas in a later work: Kumarappa, *The Economy of Permanence* (Wardha, 1948). (Kumarappa recycled his writing a good deal. As he was also a prolific journalist, a great number of his articles also recycle earlier material; his main arguments remain simple, and the rest is elaboration from first principles.)
128. 'Place of Science in the Industrial Development of India: Inaugural lecture to the Science Association of Nagpur University at the Convocation Hall, by Sjt J.C. Kumarappa, Secretary, All India Village Industries Association', n.d., ff. 299–305, Speeches and Writings in Bound Volumes, Vol X, JCK, NML.
129. 'Summary of a speech delivered at the Mysore Swadeshi Exhibition of 30th May 1936 by Sjt. J.C. Kumarappa', ff 189–91, Speeches and Writings in Bound Volumes, Vol X, JCK, NML.
130. Kumarappa, 'Intelligent Buying', *Gram Udyog Patrika*, July 1941, reprinted in *Gram Udyog Patrika, Part I* (Madras, 1971), pp. 191–3; Kumarappa, 'Consumer's Duty', *Gram Udyog Patrika*, April 1946, reprinted in *Gram Udyog Patrika, Part I* (Madras, 1971), pp. 415–16; Kumarappa, *Village Movement*, chapter IX: 'The Place of Women', pp. 70–81.
131. Kumarappa, *Village Movement*, chapter IX: 'The Place of Women', pp. 70–1.

132. Kumarappa, *Village Movement*, pp. 70–3.
133. Women's education was considered especially necessary by Kumarappa for another reason: because women were 'the natural custodians of the generations to come'; at an early stage of a child's life, women were '[b]y temperament and natural endowment' better equipped to deal with it. Kumarappa, *Village Movement*, pp. 182. Such clearly ascribed roles for women were an essential part of the public statements of Gandhi or the Gandhians. J.B. Kripalani, while making a speech to popularize khadi, apparently told his audience that he could not understand why women complained that khadi saris were too heavy when they bore the weight of their husbands every night. This was reported to Nehru by a correspondent, who asked him whether this was not overstepping the limits of decent politics: M.N. Chadha to Jawaharlal Nehru, 13 October (1933?), JNP, NML, Part 1. Vol. IX, f. 129. (It might be noted in parentheses that Kripalani's missionary zeal also seems to have assumed the missionary position).
134. Kumarappa, 'Balanced Cultivation', *Gram Udyog Patrika*, June 1946, reprinted in *Gram Udyog Patrika, Part I* (Madras, 1971), p. 423.
135. Typescript of article, 'A Catechism on the All India Village Industries Association', *Contemporary India*, 29/6/1935, f. 9, Speeches and Writings in Bound Volumes, Vol. II, JCK, NML.
136. Outline of speech by Kumarappa on 'Gandhiji's Programme of Village Reconstruction', made at Jinnah Hall, [place not stated], 29 September 1941, f. 293, Speeches and Writings in Bound Volumes, Vol. X, JCK, NML.
137. See JCK: Notebooks, especially, Sl. Nos. (2), (4), and (10), NML. Kumarappa seems to have read a number of extremely eclectic critiques of capitalism; and his first encounters with the ideas of Soviet Marxism seem to have been through the accounts of Fabians. His notebook for 1936 contains notes from Sidney and Beatrice Webb's *Soviet Communism*, which he summarized in two pages, apparently without much interest in it—at a time when he had presumably already written much of *Why the Village Movement?* - Kumarappa, Notebooks, Sl. No. (4), pp. 55–6, JCK, NML. There is no indication that he had read much more than this, though he ought to have read a fair amount of J.A. Hobson, judging by the course outline provided by Seligman. See Kumarappa, Notebooks, Sl. No. (2).
138. See Dasgupta, *Gandhi's Economic Thought*, pp. 100–104.
139. Quoted in Partha Chatterjee, *Nationalist Thought*, p. 93 and Note 28, p. 126.
140. See Kumarappa, 'The Economy of the Cross', a summary of three addresses to the Mid-India Conference of Christian Students at Nagpur, 5–7 November 1942, reprinted in Kumarappa, *Christianity: Its Economy and Way of Life* (Ahmedabad, 1945), and other essays in that volume.
141. J.J. Anjaria, *An Essay on Gandhian Economics* (1944), quoted in Bhabatosh Datta, *Indian Economic Thought*, p. 158.
142. See Chapter 5 of this book.
143. *Science and Culture*, Vol. IV, No. 10 (April 1939), editorial, p. 535.

144. Partha Chatterjee, *Nationalist Thought*; *The Nation and its Fragments*, chapter eleven.

145. Rather than, as in the version provided by so much 'cold war' developmental rhetoric, maintain a distinction between 'tradition' and 'modernity', with the latter being identified by adherents of the former as 'Western'.

146. Even though, at the level of the particular, British precedent was regularly cited as a reason to introduce a particular measure in India, this was usually by way of accusing the British of inconsistency with proclaimed values.

147. I am referring here to work following from Partha Chatterjee's *Nationalist Thought*; the phrase 'derivative but different', Chatterjee's own, has become, in the work of some subsequent scholars, one which is regarded as an adequate summary of his views on the nature of nationalist thought in the colonial world—rather unfortunately, as it does no justice to the details of his arguments.

148. That is, 'Orientalists' in the pre-Saidian sense of the term.

149. The Indian case was perhaps not unique either; through the nineteenth century and into the twentieth, various nationalisms had claimed that their nation had always existed, while radical strands within them had been anxious to bury the unpleasant and undistinguished past.

150. See Chapter 5 of this volume.

151. P.S. Narayan Prasad, quoted in Kumarappa, 'Violence in Economic Activity', typescript of article for the *Harijan*, n.d., in reply to an article in *Twentieth Century* by Narayan Prasad, f. 56, Speeches and Writings in Bound Volumes, Vol. II, JCK, NML. The phrase 'at the behest of the Bombay Congress' was a reference to the Congress right, which was seen to be an ally of Indian big business.

152. Kumarappa, 'The Message of Khadi', *Gram Udyog Patrika*, April 1940.

153. M.K. Gandhi, 'Why Khadi for Yarn and Not for Money?', *Gram Udyog Patrika*, July 1945.

154. For instance, Kumarappa, 'A Stone for Bread', *Gram Udyog Patrika*, December 1942.

155. R.B. Lotvala to Kumarappa, 21 March 1949, ff. 1–2, Correspondence with Lotvala, JCK, NML. Lotvala is described by Sumit Sarkar as 'a millionaire with socialist leanings', who supplied Marxist literature to S.A. Dange's group of student radicals in Bombay in the 1920s—a connection which led to Dange's writing of *Gandhi vs Lenin* in 1921 (Sumit Sarkar, *Modern India*, p. 212). He was also extremely interested in eugenics, which he sought to promote in India: see Sarah Hodges, 'Indian Eugenics in an Age of Reform', in Sarah Hodges (ed.), *Reproductive Health in India: History, Politics, Controversies* (Delhi, 2003), pp. 123–4.

156. Lotvala to Kumarappa, 31 March 1949, f. 3, Correspondence with Lotvala, JCK, NML. Kumarappa had replied to Lotvala's earlier letter to say that he did not have the time to read Lotvala's writing.

157. Kumarappa, 'Violence in Economic Activity', typescript of article for the

Harijan, n.d., in reply to an article in *Twentieth Century* by Narayan Prasad,
f. 56, Speeches and Writings in Bound Volumes, Vol. II, JCK, NML.
158. Narayanaswami Iyer to Kumarappa, 11 May 1947, Subject File No. 12,
JCK, NML.
159. See Thomas Metcalf, *Ideologies of the Raj* (Cambridge, 1994), for a summary.
160. For an overstated case, which argues that all imaginings of India, except for
those of the communists, were 'religious nationalist', see Peter van der Veer,
Religious Nationalism: Hindus and Muslims in India (Berkeley, 1994); see
also my review of the book in *Modern Asian Studies*, Vol. 32, No. 1 (1998). A
tendency to see 'Hindu' India as an ancient and sophisticated civilization, in
opposition to British claims of Indian 'backwardness', I would argue, falls
short of constituting a religious nationalism. There were, of course, explicit
attempts to push forward the idea of an aggressively 'Hindu' and
exclusionary India, but these were by no means universally accepted even by
those who drew on the model of a glorious Hindu past.
161. T.V. Narayanaswami Iyer to Kumarappa, 11 May 1947, Subject File No. 12,
JCK, NML.
162. The contexts to the 'communalism' of the 1940s must be kept in mind here;
but rather than argue that there was such a thing as 'communal consciousness'
as a clearly defined and coherent world view, it is more plausible to argue that
a variety of factors contributed to a privileging of 'Hindu' or 'Muslim'
identities in the 1940s; and that this privileging was neither inevitable nor
immutable.
163. N.G. Bedekar, Aurangabad, to Kumarappa, n.d., but sometime in late 1948,
Subject File No. 12, JCK, NML.
164. Kumarappa to Bedekar, 6 December 1948, Subject File No. 12, JCK, NML.
Emphasis mine.

5

Development: Possible Nations

This chapter deals with ideas of 'development' which were encompassed within the framework of mainstream Indian nationalism—by which I mean those ideas which came to be generally acceptable at a national as opposed to a regional or local level. This principle of selection mainly privileges the views of intellectuals close to the Congress, but not exclusively so (many intellectuals and politicians outside the Congress shared many of the conceptions put forward by or through the Congress). The term 'nationalist' was also used at the time for any Indian who wanted the British to leave India; 'nationalism' was, therefore, a very broad church. I argue that it is necessary to look at conceptions of development as analytically distinct from conceptions of planning. Although they usually travelled in pairs from the 1930s onwards, to conflate them entirely is to confuse form with content.

It becomes apparent, once this necessary separation is made, that although the *language* in the 1930s was a peculiarly inter-War one (therefore using reference points which were general to the period—the Depression, the New Deal, fascism, the Soviet Union), it was grafted on to intellectual currents and concerns emanating from within India, incorporating within itself nineteenth and early twentieth century debates, and adapting them to the new context. A closer look, from this perspective, reveals a discourse of development which identified itself as 'socialism', but which was a mixture of three predominant elements: ideas of 'science', of economic and political 'socialism', and of 'national discipline'. This chapter will analyse these ideas, their intellectual antecedents, and the concerns and anxieties which drove them.

Middle-Class Intellectuals

The level of engagement of the professional middle classes with the problem of 'development', through which to articulate an identity for the proposed new Indian state, was extremely intense; this was a project intimately entwined with a number of other major themes close to the intellectual and psychological life of the professional middle classes under colonialism: progress, national self-respect, an escape from 'backwardness'. The middle-classness of development debates in India needs to be stressed; the conceptualization of the wider implications of 'development' in India was not a contribution of Indian big business, though they succeeded to a large extent in the post-Independence period in hijacking the main lines of development practice in India to suit their more limited ends.[1] The Gramscian concept of 'passive revolution' has been invoked as an explanation of this;[2] but such explanations do not resolve the question of intellectual leadership. It is doubtful, if we are to use Gramscian terminology, whether the Indian professional bourgeoisie— politicians, scientists, engineers or academics—who largely conducted the debates on 'development' among themselves, were the 'organic intellectuals' of the industrial bourgeoisie. If anything, many of the former were suspicious of or downright hostile to the latter, taking sides with state control or socialism. They were not 'organic intellectuals' of the working class, either, conforming more closely to what Gramsci called 'traditional intellectuals', though it is possible further to complicate matters and raise the question of where intellectuals created by colonial education to fill professions 'traditional' in the metropole might have stood in this scheme.[3]

These intellectuals, an articulate, multilingual, cultural elite, often highly educated and self-consciously cosmopolitan in outlook, dominated a good deal of the space of organized political activity, and especially the political philosophy behind it. This applied to politics of all kinds, from the 'left' to the 'right'; social origins were, consequently, not necessarily good indicators of political allegiances. The social circles in which the members of this class moved were small and closed; it was, therefore, not unusual for the same family to contain members of completely ideologically opposed political parties. Crossing the floor was not unknown, not necessarily as conscious acts of opportunism; personal connections often cut across party lines, and ideological crossovers were made smoother by these connections. What was common, then, to 'politics' as it was conceived at the time, was that it was the domain of this class. British complaints about middle-class agitators being a 'political class' who misled the otherwise loyal peasantry merged with that class' own perceptions about the importance of education and enlightenment in leadership. A corollary to this principle is that intellectual activity was related to, and essential to, politics. Those who were not active in the dangerous areas of politics often saw themselves as engaged, albeit indirectly, in the essentially political activity of providing the right intellectual materials necessary for national life.

Form and Content: Compromise Formulae, Divergent Goals

Before a discussion of the main constituent elements of the discourse is attempted, an outline of the form and range of discussions related to development is necessary. The most audible form taken by the demand for development in India in the 1930s was that of a demand for a planned economy. This has usually been associated retrospectively by later commentators with the rise of socialism in India; but a great deal of this had little to do with 'socialism' of any kind—a fact well known at the time.[4] N.S. Subba Rao, an economist, lecturing at the University of Madras in March 1933, commented that the phrase 'economic planning' was 'in danger of becoming a cliche, if indeed it has not become one already', not merely because of its overuse 'in the realms of economic fancy', but in practical affairs, 'like the character in Moliere's play, who was amazed to find that he had been speaking prose all his life without knowing it, statesmen and administrators and business men have been planning the economic life of the community in one aspect or other, at any rate in segments, without being aware of it'.[5] Subba Rao took pains to point out that planning did not necessarily imply socialism; nor was it merely a temporary measure to overcome the Depression. 'Discerning students of society saw the need for planning our economic life before either Russia began her tremendous experiment or the Depression had cast its shadow'.[6] Laissez-faire, to his mind, was already being abandoned by the beginning of the century, finally to be overcome by the Great War. Hopes of returning to pre-War 'normal' life now were vain, given that it was doubtful whether the period before August 1914 had not itself been the culmination of an extraordinary and abnormal period in world history. 'The automatic working of the economic machine, if it ever existed, had broken down, its self-regulating capacity, which had figured so largely in the talk and the writings of the day, was not to be discerned, and the operation of the invisible hand was no longer visible'.[7] Modern planning, he emphasized, could only be undertaken by the state, which could, 'as the agency of the community at large', safeguard consumers and labourers against the restrictive cartels and international agreements of business.

The present-day state, being democratic, need not be feared (Subba Rao was speaking in general here, with the tone implying the gap between the general principle and the Indian reality). State intervention should not be 'fitful or sporadic', because otherwise industry would not be able to accustom itself to state influence—intervention being both an ineffective and disturbing influence.[8]

While others discussed planning specifically in terms of socialist objectives and an independent India,[9] the demand for planning was often voiced in less politically adventurous circles in the form of an appeal to the government.[10] Sir M. Visvesvaraya had had a long and distinguished career as a civil engineer, winning accolades from the British government culminating in a knighthood, and had spent a long spell as Dewan of Mysore, one of the more 'progressive' of the native states, where he was involved with a number of development projects.[11] In his *Planned Economy for India*,[12] he offered his suggestions to the government to implement, since they 'appear to have been thinking in the same direction for some time now, though they have not been able to reach any practical decisions yet'.[13] If government action was not forthcoming, he believed it to be 'the duty of the leaders and economic experts in the country to advance their own independent proposals' to influence government policies on the one hand, and to stimulate private enterprise on the other.[14] Pragmatists like Visvesvaraya were even-handed in their appeals to those in power to take action, tempering their political assumptions to meet currently acceptable political conditions. In 1920, he had stressed 'loyalty to the Sovereign and to the British connection' as an aspect of the creation of an Indian ideal of citizenship.[15] In 1937, as provincial autonomy was inaugurated, and a year before the establishment of the Congress' National Planning Committee, Visvesvaraya urged the Congress, because it was now in government, to 'make up their mind as to the lines of national economic activity'. (Although the 'moral value' of khadi, prohibition, and other Gandhian measures would have a necessary and prominent place in reconstruction schemes, he wrote, the current situation of 'confusion' had to be cleared up.)[16]

Industrialists made similar demands on the government. At the annual meeting of the Federation of Indian Chambers of Commerce and Industry (FICCI) on 1 April 1934, various members, in their speeches, urged the government to take steps to set up a planned economy. Birla stressed the need for a substantial rise in the standard of living through coordinated, planned action, involving both government intervention and 'the co-operation of the people'. He did not 'charge the Government with utter inaction'; only with lack of coordinated schemes. Indian business, he stressed, did not 'aspire to build industries artificially on the strength of our export trade'. Industrial development had to 'depend entirely on the home market' and, consequently, on an increase in the purchasing power of the masses.[17]

Birla was also in close touch with British officials like Schuster and Lord Lothian, the latter formerly of the Round Table group, both believers in a more closely integrated 'Commonwealth'.[18] Birla also constantly pleaded for a less confrontational politics between the British government and Indian nationalists; and in private correspondence advised British officials to strengthen Gandhi's hand within the Congress instead of seeing him as an enemy. Gandhi, Birla said, was not an enemy of Britain but a friend; and if his just demands were accepted, it would be better in the long run than the alternative of rejecting them, which would simply strengthen the socialists.[19] Birla, like Schuster, believed that the interests of Britain and India could be adjusted to mutual advantage, but he was clear that as far as he was concerned this could only happen if adequate provision were made for the development of Indian business; if not, he would oppose the government—he was, for instance, opposed to imperial preference and to financial and commercial safeguards for British business in India on such grounds.[20]

None of this, however, could legitimately be voiced publicly if accusations from the left of capitalists merely being interested in feathering their own nests were to be avoided; and Birla recognized this.[21] In his public statements, therefore, it was more important to stress, in general terms, the overall importance of raising standards of living and purchasing power and its importance for industrialization.

On the ascribed causes of economic backwardness there was a strong nationalist consensus: it was caused by colonial rule. Emergence from colonial rule was necessary before India could emerge from backwardness. Consequently, mechanisms for international trade-sharing or imperial preference, mooted as possible solutions to the problems of the Depression, were treated in India with suspicion. Subba Rao, in his 1933 lectures, outlined a position to his students which, in far more moderate language, was in its essentials the position taken on economic matters by the post-Independence Indian state. Dealing with the question of national planning and wider proposals for international planning and economic co-operation, he supported the latter in principle, provided the mechanism for coordination and arbitration of conflicting interests existed.[22] However, he raised the crucial question of the role the 'backward' countries would play in this scheme of things. The economic life, 'both planned and unplanned', of the advanced countries, was 'based on the existence of backward countries which serve as markets for their industrial output and as sources of supply of foodstuffs and raw materials'. What, then, was a 'backward country'?

The feature that is common to them all is that they have not passed through the Industrial Revolution like the advanced Western countries. They have all been exploited by the advanced countries, but the usual term employed in this connection is 'economic penetration'.[23]

This relationship was undergoing a change. Recently, the tendency in Europe had been to develop agricultural as well as industrial self-sufficiency; 'a gap is, however, made in the wall of protection for the export of surplus industrial goods and imports of raw materials'. It had also been suggested that 'a revival of prosperity in the West may be sought by the development of Africa and China by Western capital'. But 'political pressure not infrequently accompanies foreign capital'.[24] Given this, India needed to depend as little as possible on foreign capital while passing through an industrial revolution of her own—'trying to catch up', as Nehru put it, with the advanced countries.[25] In Nehru's stronger language, '....the very basis of our Planning is a free India, democratically fashioned, where no external authority can interfere or obstruct the nation's work ... Political domination is patent enough, but a far more dangerous and insidious thing is economic domination. While the public can see and feel political domination, and therefore react to it, it is not so conscious of the economic stranglehold which throttles the life of the nation and prevents industrial and other growth'.[26]

Beyond these basic points, however, the consensus was more apparent than real. In this connection, it would be useful here to consider briefly the two initiatives which, in terms of their implications for the nature of a future India, attracted the most attention in the run-up to Indian independence: the National Planning Committee and the 'Bombay Plan'.

The Congress' National Planning Committee (NPC) was the culmination of the 1930s discussions on planning India's economy and her future. It owed its origin to the conference of provincial industries ministers at the beginning of October 1938, which passed a resolution to the effect that 'problems of poverty and unemployment, of national defence and of economic regeneration in general' could not be solved without industrialization, to which end a 'comprehensive scheme of national planning', providing for 'development of heavy key industries, medium scale industries and cottage industries', should be formulated. Initially a Planning Committee was to be appointed, thereafter to submit its report to the Congress Working Committee, and the All-India National Planning Commission. The latter, when formed, was to consist of one government nominee from each province or state, four representatives of FICCI, one of the AIVIA, and all the members of the NPC. It could appoint sub-committees of 'experts' for technical or financial advice.[27] Planning 'under a democratic system' was defined as 'the technical co-ordination, by disinterested experts, of consumption, production, investment, trade and income distribution in accordance with social objectives set by bodies representative of the nation'. It was, nonetheless, rather ambitiously to consider, in addition to economic matters, 'cultural and spiritual values and the human side of life'—of which more will be discussed later.[28] The NPC itself included industrialists, scientists, politicians, and academics.[29] In 1940, Nehru announced that Dr P.C. Mahalanobis of the Indian Statistical Institute, Calcutta, had agreed to examine all the sub-committees' reports 'from a purely statistical point of view'.[30]

The significant omission from these formulations was 'socialism'—an omission which was explicit and deliberate, for that was the one issue bound to divide the NPC, unless introduced in such a way as to have no specific meaning. If the latter, it could be used by capitalists as a harmless catchphrase and by Gandhians to describe their 'true' and 'indigenous' form of it. The composition of the NPC and its constituent sub-committees should have belied any hopes of socialist solutions: too many of them were either industrialists or were committed to private enterprise by conviction. This is not to suggest that 'socialism' was an altogether absent category in the NPC's debates. However, the 'socialist' aspects of the debates surrounding planning in the Congress circles responsible for the setting up of the NPC were deliberately downplayed in the NPC itself. To create common ground, the Congress left had to eat at least some of its socialist words. Referring to the Congress' May 1929 Resolution—the oft-quoted AICC resolution read 'in order to remove the poverty and misery of the Indian people and to ameliorate the condition of the masses, it is essential to make revolutionary changes in the present economic and social structure of society and to remove the gross inequalities'—Nehru admitted that it indicated 'an approval of socialistic theories', but he clarified that apart from this general approval and some further advances in subsequent resolutions, 'the Congress has not in any way accepted socialism'.[31]

Nehru, consistent with the coalitional nature of anti-imperialist politics, sought to provide space for the cooperation of businessmen. The

composition of the Committee was explained in 1939 by Nehru to its
Honorary General Secretary, K.T. Shah, a man who stood by his socialism,
thus:

The middle class is too strong to be pushed out and there is a tremendous lack
of human material in any other class to take its place effectively, or to run a
planned society... a premature conflict on class lines would lead to a break-up
and possibly to prolonged inability to build up anything.[32]

Nehru's use of the term 'middle class' here was ambiguous. The
'human material' of the middle classes at this time was not, in fact,
exclusively capitalist; socialists and communists in India were in a very
large majority of cases middle-class intelligentsia, and had more in common
with a Nehru than a Birla. K.T. Shah continued to provide a dissenting
voice, urging a concentration on socialist principles.[33] Moreover, Nehru's
concentration on compromise did not assuage the doubts of the non-
socialists in the NPC; as far as they were concerned, this was a socialist
forum to which they had been invited as outsiders.[34]

The sub-committees of the NPC were broadly in agreement regarding
the need for as great an amount of self-sufficiency as possible, especially
in 'basic' and 'key' industries—indicative of the consensus regarding the
connection between 'self-sufficiency' and 'planning', the connections
between 'self-sufficiency' and 'socialism' or 'planning' and 'socialism'
being more disputable. But loopholes were left for exceptions.[35]
Manufacturing industries were to be established in industrially backward
areas 'subject to economic considerations' allowing this. No unit was to
be 'so large as to be outside the reach of competition by smaller, but
economic units', the size of these economic units to be decided by
'qualified authority'.[36] The question of defining the role of the public and
private sectors was also a problem. It was agreed that existing private
plants producing heavy machinery should, if economically viable, be
encouraged to function. But in the 'transitional period'—a phrase which
became an ideal formula to achieve consensus—'the State may encourage
private capital' to start plants in the category of automobiles and light
mechanical industries, by guaranteeing interest over a period of years,
imposing heavy duties on foreign articles and other methods, 'provided
always that the State exercise rigid control of all such undertakings in the
interest of national planning'. It was stressed, however, that '[t]he State
referred to is the national free State of India, and not a State controlled
by foreign authority'.[37]

The question of nationalization rarely appeared unambiguously in the
resolutions passed by the NPC, indicating that disagreements in this

regard were significant but that attempts were being made to confine them to internal discussions of the sub-committees. The exceptions were in the declaration of all power and fuel resources to be national property, and the recommendation of state ownership, management, and control through Electricity Boards in order to keep electricity rates for domestic and industrial use low,[38] and the recommendation of abolition of intermediaries on land 'of the type of taluqdars, zamindars, etc.', who should be progressively bought out by granting 'such compensation as may be considered necessary and desirable'.[39]

Regarding labour, a set of guidelines was laid down on the basis of 'essential human standards': a 47-hour week and 9-hour day with no consequent reduction of earnings; the minimum age of factory workers was to be 'progressively raised to 15 in correlation with the educational system' (which recommended free and compulsory education until age 14). Improvement in health, safety, and night-work conditions, guaranteed minimum wages, housing, paid holidays, maternity benefits, workmen's compensation, equal pay for equal work by women, compulsory and contributory social insurance were also recommended. The difficulty of enforcing all this was implicitly recognized: 'In the event of an industry not being able to comply with these conditions, the State may protect, subsidise or take it over, if it is in the interest of the community to do so'.[40] How these terms were to be interpreted was left open.

The controversy between the advocates of mechanization and cottage industries took up a good deal of the NPC's energies. On the side of mechanization stood both capitalist and socialist opinion, against Gandhi's blend of the emotional appeal of khadi and a cottage-industries-oriented 'constructive programme'. Nehru tried to get round this problem by laying down a principle of no interference between large-scale and cottage industries, the latter to be supported by the state; in the event of competition between the two in a specific area, the large-scale industry should also be controlled by the state to prevent any conflict from arising. If this were done, 'co-ordination will be easy'.[41] Such optimism was not genuine; the prospect of, say, cotton-mill owners being dispossessed because of the need to 'co-ordinate' mill production with that of khadi could never have been bright. The final resolutions of the Rural and Cottage Industries Sub-Committee, arrived at after the resignation of its former Chairman, J.C. Kumarappa, urged that 'employment in the natural setting of the worker's own place of habitation combined with numerous physical, moral, material and other benefits': the opportunity for subsidiary earnings for the cultivating classes and the comparatively lower cost of living in rural areas were good reasons to promote cottage industries. Regarding their relative position vis-à-vis large-scale mechanized production in state policy, it was agreed that the Planning Authority should examine 'the relative economic and social value of the two methods of production', set up a permanent Cottage Industries Board for training workers and undertaking 'scientific and technical research', and protect certain cottage industries to neutralize disadvantages. But the question of the role envisaged for cottage industries in an independent India was left unanswered.[42]

As a document for determining an economic programme, the NPC's report was of little use, being clouded in compromise formulae which sought to maintain as high a degree of consensus as possible and, consequently, being unable to resolve any major questions. Regular meetings ceased with the arrest of Congress leaders during the Second World War.[43] Although the NPC continued formally to remain in existence through and after the War, businessmen, many of whom had been on the NPC, decided that they needed to start a committee of their own, not least the better to defend capitalist interests. These they saw as under threat in the NPC, a body which did not adequately represent their interests, and left vital questions open rather than solve them to their satisfaction. The intellectuals, on their part, were thinking far beyond the narrow confines of a planning committee—this was evident from the NPC's discussions— and it was felt by industrialists that they needed to write their own plan. This they did in 1944.

The 'Bombay Plan' of 1944, authored by several prominent Indian businessmen, cutting across earlier divides,[44] began by acknowledging its debt to the NPC, 'to whose labours the conception of a planned economy for India is largely due'. Its objective, it was claimed, was to put forward, 'as a basis of discussion', a set of objectives regarding general lines of development and its demands on national resources. Politically, it made the assumption that there would be 'a national government' after the War with 'full freedom in economic matters'. The future government was to be on a federal basis, but central government jurisdiction on 'economic matters' should extend over the whole of India.[45] The reference to the NPC and a 'national government' asserted businessmen's nationalist credentials while, at the same time, the 'as a basis of discussion' clause left doors open for the government, the latter already having in principle committed themselves to some form of national government. Although the 'maintenance of the economic unity of India' was considered essential to 'effective planning', 'this does not preclude the possibility of a regional grouping of provinces and States as an intermediary link in a federal organisation'.[46] This was a reference to the possibility of Pakistan which, at the time, was not seen necessarily to imply a complete division of India and Pakistan into separate states.[47]

The 'Bombay Plan' envisaged a doubling of the per capita income in 15 years, which would, allowing for population increase, amount to a trebling of the national income. The initial stages would give attention to the development of industries for power and capital goods, with the ultimate objective of 'reducing our dependence on foreign countries'.[48] A qualification was to be made for essential consumption goods, which could be produced by small-scale and cottage industries, which would then not only employ people but reduce the need for expensive machinery purchases. There was an attempt to define a minimum standard of living and public health, and special attention was paid to maternity and childbirth, education and literacy.[49] 'Basic industries' were power, mining and metallurgy, engineering, chemicals and fertilizers, armaments, transport, and cement—'the basis on which the economic superstructure envisaged in the plan would have to be erected'.[50] The need for self-sufficiency in food was stressed, and cooperative farming was recommended as a solution to the problem of fragmentation of land holdings—to achieve which 'some measure of compulsion appears to be desirable'.[51] Regarding finance, the Plan envisaged the use of hoarded wealth in gold, which would be available for capital investment due to the faith in a national government, India's favourable trade balance, the sterling balances (to be utilized for 'importing the capital goods required at the beginning of the plan'), foreign borrowing, especially from the USA, and creating money 'to increase the productive capacity of the nation'—planned inflation.[52]

The second part of the Plan essentially concerned itself with drawing boundaries beyond which the state would not be permitted to encroach upon private enterprise's territory.[53] Private enterprise, 'in spite of its admitted shortcomings ... possesses certain features which have stood the test of time and have enduring achievements to their credit ... we think it would be ... a mistake to uproot an organisation which has worked with a fair measure of success in several directions'. Although the acknowledged aim of policy was a 'reasonable standard of living' and 'gradually to reduce the existing inequalities of wealth and property and to decentralise the ownership of the means of production', it was stated that 'total abolition of inequalities, even if feasible, would not be in the interest of the country'.[54] The Plan recommended a steeply graduated income tax— with adequate remission granted for asset depreciation and income reinvested on industrial and agricultural production. The precondition was a 'national government': 'it is a dangerous thing to vest large powers of taxation in a foreign government bred in traditions of imperialist exploitation'.[55] It also saw the need for a 'comprehensive scheme of social insurance'—but recognized its unfeasibility until full and stable employment had been achieved—'until the risks insurable are reduced to manageable proportions'—and until individual incomes had risen to be able to meet the contributions required by such a scheme.[56]

The role of the state was to 'exercise in the interests of the community a considerable measure of intervention and control'. But despite an 'enlargement of the positive as well as the preventive functions of the State', democratic ideas required the 'assent of the community', and a 'surrender' of freedom could only be demanded for 'well-defined ends'. Moreover, the modification of laissez-faire and the move towards state intervention had transformed capitalism to the extent that 'the distinction between capitalism and socialism has lost much of its significance from a practical standpoint':[57] in other words, we are all socialists now. The Plan then proceeded to distinguish between state ownership, management, and control. The last was the most important 'from the point of view of maximum social welfare', and it was accepted that this was 'bound to put important limitations on the freedom of private enterprise as it is understood at present'. Such control was necessary for enterprises under state ownership, public utilities, basic industries, monopolies, or those using scarce natural resources. State ownership of enterprises important to 'public welfare or security' was recognized as necessary, but all state-owned ventures need not be under state management; moreover, if private finance 'is prepared to take over these industries', they could do so, although state control should remain.[58] Regarding matters such as agriculture, solutions suggested were more desultory and less well-thought-out: agriculture was less directly the problem of the authors. But a certain deference for property had to be observed if the sacrosanct nature of their own property was to be recognized. Regarding land tenure, it was argued that in effect, the occupancy tenant was the proprietor of the land as various tenancy acts had already 'deprived the zamindar of a considerable part of his proprietary right'. The ryotwari system, which collected revenues directly from the cultivator, was recommended to be introduced in place of zamindari, as the Floud Commission on Bengal had already recommended (this was a safe authority to cite), but a 'gradual application of this recommendation' was urged, with stress on compensation payments by the state.[59]

These two documents share a similar language and, consequently, seem to share a similar set of concerns. These similarities have resulted in assumptions being made about the similarity of the two projects, matters being further complicated by the appearance, also in 1944, of the Government of India's *Second Report on Reconstruction Planning*, which read much the same, paraded its nationalist credentials, and spoke of nationalization, basic industries, and industrial development.[60] Yet it would be mistaken to conclude, especially given what is already known from other sources about the divergent aims of the groups concerned, that there were no significant differences among the various groups responsible for the National Planning Committee Report, the 'Bombay Plan', and the *Second Report*, whether the conclusion drawn from it be that the Congress' 'socialism' was actually 'capitalism', or that a new phase of 'constructive imperialism' was beginning at the end of the Empire.[61] The claims being negotiated are relatively clearly visible. The NPC attempted to negotiate a compromise among private enterprise, Gandhians and socialists; this need probably originated from the realization that no single group within the Congress or within Indian nationalist politics could at the time stake a claim to power on its own. The 'Bombay Plan', in a much more straightforward manner, tried to protect private capital against encroachment from socialism of a radical or moderate kind, defending private capital by incorporating weakened strains of apparent socialism into itself. The Government of India's *Second Report*, clearly the interloper, attempted to incorporate and appropriate nationalist sentiment at a time when its position was particularly precarious and its need to win the War dominated its considerations. The question which, therefore, arises is why they shared a similar language.

It is evident that the NPC was the master-project in terms of legitimacy: it was a *national* committee, which had been positioned as a major step forward for the 'nation'. Dr Syed Mahmud, Development Minister of the recently-elected Congress government of Bihar, said of the Industries Conference which made the decision to set up the NPC that it 'should be regarded as a turning point in the history of India'.[62] Subhas Chandra Bose, who was then Congress President and had taken the initiative in appointing the Committee, announced that 'Planning is to improve the well-being of the community by intensifying economic development in an ordered and systematic manner'.[63] Although much of the enthusiasm for the setting up of the NPC came from the left wing of the Congress, in including members of different political beliefs, scientists, businessmen, and opposition politicians who were willing to cooperate,[64] the NPC's credentials as a body representing the national movement as a whole, and not just a sect or group thereof was enhanced. Indeed, the inclusiveness of the NPC was allegedly not confined to its members; its debates were phrased as public debates, envisaging the participation of the 'public':

In this work that we are doing we require of course the fullest intelligent co-operation of the public and the press. Ultimately it is not the Committee that will decide the future of India or of its political or economic organisation, but the people of India who will take the final decision. It is for them, therefore, to pay attention to what this Committee is doing. Perhaps one of the most important and desirable consequences of our work is to make people think of planned work and a co-operative society. This thinking has been too rare in the past. In order to reach the public the obvious medium is the Press.[65]

Moreover,

The task of the National Planning Committee is, in effect, never completed, for it goes on with the life and progress of the nation. But ... this edifice will serve as a secure foundation to build upon ... [T]he future of the community, that is, of all of us who live in India and have the future of India at heart, is intimately involved in the measures that will have to be taken before long in this country in the political, economic, and social domain.[66]

Such a project, in its sheer grandeur, dwarfed anything else on offer in terms of imagining the future. It was impossible to improve upon this armed with mere economics; in a sense the vagueness and indecision of the NPC's economic proclamations was irrelevant.

The NPC's definition of its work deserves quoting in full:

Planning under a democratic system may be defined as the technical co-ordination, by disinterested experts, of consumption, production, investment, trade and income distribution in accordance with social objectives set by bodies representative of the nation. Such Planning is not only to be considered from the point of view of economics and the raising of the standard of living, but must include cultural and spiritual values and the human side of life.[67]

It would appear from the phrasing of this document that 'disinterested experts' were not to be trusted with 'social objectives' (possibly *because* they were 'disinterested'?); these were to be 'set by bodies representative of the nation'. The 'disinterested experts' would then come in to execute the project, 'cultural and spiritual values' and all. But this apparent distinction was actually unclear in the perceptions of the members who controlled the Committee. In this scheme someone had already been cast as 'bodies representing the nation': the NPC itself, and its sub-committees. However, the basis of the representativeness of such bodies, in the conception of its organizers and members, seems unclear; most members were nominated by a committee, or coopted by that committee (the NPC) which had itself been nominated by a committee (the Industries Conference), which perhaps was in some way representative because the governments its members represented had been elected (though on a limited property franchise).[68] Nomination proceeded on the basis of some claims to familiarity with the subject under discussion: 'expertise' of some kind, rather than representing a particular constituency.

The logical conclusion to be drawn from this was that those NPC members who directed the proceedings believed themselves to be both 'experts' and representative. Yet there was a tension between the two principles; the 'representativeness' came from appeals to the 'public and the press' to follow the debates (the press readily responded to the appeal): these were important matters, which the NPC was discussing on behalf of the 'public', so the public should 'pay attention'. A circular argument lay implicitly behind this conception: the NPC members were 'experts' and could, therefore, represent the public; the public, by paying attention, and absorbing the debates, would become enlightened as well as make the 'experts' more representative. In practice, as I have argued earlier, the 'public' was narrower than the public envisaged by the publicists.[69] Moreover, not all the 'experts' were considered 'representative': although compromise formulae were put forward by the left in the NPC, in particular by Nehru as chairman, it was clear who was leading discussions and who was following: businessmen participated as 'experts', but not as representative 'experts'.[70]

Businessmen, on their part, were involved in fighting a rearguard action to prevent the 'socialist' atmosphere of late colonial debates on development from going too far for their liking. It was this rearguard action which required them to come up with their own plans dressed up as socialism; and to search for ideas which were realistic enough to concede some ground to 'socialism'—mainly in rhetorical terms, or in versions diluted enough to be easily combated through the space left for private industry.[71] Industrialists were thus seeking to narrow definitions of 'development' to the merely economic—if they had to blur the wider issues and plead their case in terms of economic efficiency, this narrowing was their best chance. But they had, at least to a certain extent, to participate in the ethical and philosophical debates of the times to show that there were indeed shared concerns between businessmen and other thinkers on the subject.

This explains why the 'Bombay Plan' was phrased as socialism of a kind; a clear case of tailoring a project in part to fit the available normative language, rather than instrumentally tailoring the normative language to the project.[72] In this, the compromising tone of the NPC was particularly useful; the NPC had itself skirted delicately round the question of socialism, in order to avoid conflict; it had certainly not endorsed capitalism (in the political discourse of colonial India, there was no one, by the 1930s, who could hope to be taken seriously as a supporter of capitalism). It had not altogether ruled it out, however, and referred frequently to the value of 'national enterprise'. The 'Bombay Plan' could, therefore, seek to claim a genealogy in the NPC, and could perhaps even go further in endorsing 'socialism' than the NPC had. The question was 'how far socialist demands can be accommodated without capitalism surrendering any of its essential features'.[73]

Lineages

I shall return to this question later; the point to be made here is that by the 1940s the contours of a conventional normative language in which contenders for legitimacy on the Indian political scene had to speak were already visible; which raises the larger question as to how it came to be so. The overall context within which these debates operated, and the lineages of nationalist intellectuals' concern with 'development' need to be outlined here. These lineages were discernible in the large penumbra of ideas which surrounded the debates of the NPC and its various sub-committees, as well as in prior and subsequent writing. The NPC succeeded in drawing together various strands of thought relating to India's future and crystallizing them around the large project of setting before India its potential future.

'Socialism'

From about the end of the 1920s, mainstream Indian nationalism had begun to look more closely at socialism. Nehru expressed his socialist opinions strongly and freely, and in 1929 and 1931 the Congress had come up with resolutions expressing approval for the reordering of society on more radical lines; in the 1930s Nehru, as Congress President, and the most articulate spokesman barring Gandhi for the Congress, succeeded in alarming a number of people with his socialist rhetoric. In 1934 the socialists within Congress organized themselves into the Congress Socialist Party. There was both an element of fear and an element of excitement in all this: the old guard in the Congress saw impending disaster in class wars to follow from the stirring up of working class antagonisms; younger elements, disappointed at the retreats and reversals of Gandhian Congress politics, were looking with renewed interest at alternative forms of society, and especially at the great experiment in social engineering represented by the Soviet Union, which had managed to avoid the most pressing problem of the time, one which had perplexed and weakened the greatest of the world's powers: the Great Depression.

The CSP claimed to set 'before the masses' the goal of '[t]he attainment of Independence and the establishment of a State in which power shall rest in them and which would work for the restless elimination of those who exploit them. It is the ambition of the party to make of the masses a conscious solid phalanx by dispossessing them of their tribal and communal selves, and arousing in them the sense of class-solidarity which their class-interest demands of them.'[74] The Congress, as constituted in 1934, would not accept socialism, composed as it was of heterogeneous elements and people with divergent aims and interests, wrote Narendra Dev. The CSP's task, through 'patient and hard toil for many years', was to achieve this conversion of Congress to socialism; to achieve the fundamental aim of setting up a socialist state, certain secondary aims assumed present importance. These were the development of the anti-imperialist struggle within the Congress; and the organization of peasants in their own unions on the basis of an economic programme, and 'assisting as auxiliaries in the organisational work of labour unions'; as far as labour was concerned there were already 'veteran labour leaders' with 'a rich experience of labour organisation'; but as far as the peasantry was concerned, the CSP could 'act as principals'.[75]

Many members of the CSP were Marxists from outside the Communist Party, claiming explicitly to adopt a Marxist programme and framework of analysis.[76] It was claimed that the CSP sought to win over those who were 'objectively anti-imperialist'[77]—peasants, workers and petite-bourgeoisie. The only force capable of fighting imperialism were the masses, because they were not dependent on imperialism themselves, while the Indian bourgeoisie 'is not in a position to play a revolutionary role' due to its close ties with and dependence upon imperialism.[78] Development planning occupied an important position in the CSP programme, in what was seen as a specifically socialist form.[79] The national struggle, it was claimed, was a struggle '... for executing and completing the task of the bourgeois democratic revolution ... in fighting its own battle the bourgeoisie also fights the battle of the masses, in so far as bourgeois democracy consists in releasing the forces of production from the strangle-hold of feudalism.

But the united front of the bourgeoisie and the masses, whom it exploits, is largely held together by national idealism, whose function it is to hide the naked reality of class struggle under the cover of the unities of race, language, culture, tradition, historical memory, government etc..'[80]

Some of the writing in the first issue, equating social democracy with Fascism, and calling Leon Blum and the Second International all kinds of names, echoed the Comintern line of the time.[81] At the same time, the CSP differed from 'orthodox communists' in wanting also to mobilize the petite-bourgeoisie in unison with the proletariat; and anticipated the Comintern in advocating a 'united front' line before the latter did. The CSP defence of this strategy was direct: the petite-bourgeois, during the Depression, due to the peculiar development of class problems in Indian society—a semi-developed industrial capitalism—were a disillusioned class due to large-scale unemployment; some sections of them— like the working class—suffered. 'They become revolutionary and, according to the leadership offered to them, they are capable of being either on the side of Fascism or of Socialism.'

In short, we have here a large influential, because politically-minded, class, vehemently critical of present capitalism, in part at least socialistic in its attitude. Today this class is not Fascist ... But it is potentially revolutionary and is yearning for a more intelligent economic system. It is easily misled by Fascism's all-embracing appeal...[82]

At the same time, socialism ought not to turn into 'a mild and compromising affair'; this would 'frighten one's friends rather than one's opponents'—and was the 'fatal defeat of Macdonaldism', as well as of the Social Democrats in Germany.[83]

The dangers of fascism were stressed; the Depression had 'persuaded the Indian bourgeoisie to think of economic planning, which must take on a fascist or semi-fascist character, so long as private property in the means of production is not abolished'.[84] It was noted with distaste that some Indians were attracted to fascism; at the LSE Students' Union election 'a wealthy Indian student stood on the Fascist ticket ... Of course he was trounced by the United Front candidate—but the fact that he stood on the ticket is significant and we must not miss its import'.[85]

The attempt of the CSP to address itself to the petite-bourgeoisie might have also been one of the consequences of the experiences of many of the CSP's members within the Congress, both in their pre-socialist and socialist days. It was realized that there was no point relying on peasants and workers in order to move the Congress leftwards; even though some of the peasants and workers were primary members, they were not particularly politically aware, (peasants were loyal to Gandhian 'romanticism'; the primary membership had in any case little influence on the Congress' organizational or strategic machine, the Congress Working Committee, or the AICC. The intellectual appeal of socialism as a coherent system of thought, through which the future 'development' of India was to be conceived, had to depend, more or less, on a strata of membership capable of assimilating its arguments—that is to say, to the 'traditional intellectuals'. It is to this element in Congress that the CSP addressed its political philosophy perspective.

Marxism was not, however, the only road to Congress socialism. For others, the route to socialism lay through less stringently Marxist perspectives, a route which led past what might be called a vague Fabian socialism to more radical ideas and, it might be added, back again. This route has been traced for Nehru, the most influential of the 'socialists' in mainstream Congress politics, from his most radical phase in the mid-1930s,[86] to a commitment to 'development' with most of the socialism left out.[87] Nehru was considered one of theirs by the CSP, although he never joined them and on many a crucial issue deserted the left. The Indian left seemed to maintain a romantic relationship with Nehru, convinced of his good intentions: 'He was our beautiful but ineffectual angel, beating his luminous wings largely in vain'.[88]

Bishweshwar P. Sinha, member of the CSP, traced his own path to socialism through Bertrand Russell, Harold Laski, J.A. Hobson, and G.D.H. Cole and his attraction to the ideas of the Fabian Society; but these ideas 'proved too tame for an Indian who had played with fire in India'. Sinha, a former Gandhian, believed that Gandhi's essentially religious appeal had to be replaced with a more realist approach; Gandhi's 'rural romanticism', he accepted, had 'a certain purificatory value for the higher and middle classes, but they leave the masses cold'. After his Fabian phase he was a supporter of the Independent Labour Party (ILP) platform of James Maxton and Fenner Brockway—'a middle path between Labour Party gradualism and communist catastrophe', thus yielding to a position of greater tolerance for communists and a united front.[89] Nehru's pronouncements on socialism also tended to emphasize his dislike of the absence of democracy in Soviet-style socialism, in which he, nonetheless, saw much he could admire.[90] Minoo Masani, who more than any other socialist travelled the road determinedly in the opposite direction,[91] remembers being influenced in his teens by the writings of H.G. Wells and Bernard Shaw; and was 'greatly moved by that anthology of the literature of protest through the centuries put together by Upton Sinclair, *The Cry for Justice*;[92] he was later a student at LSE.[93]

Nehru, as I have already indicated, was an important link figure in debates on 'development', and in politics in general, his strategic position in the nationalist movement ensuring his crucial role in the transmission of ideas.[94] By virtue of family tradition as much as by virtue of political conviction, he had been inducted into politics at a reasonably high level, beginning as a close follower of Gandhi's.[95] In the 1930s, his professed left-wing ideas made him the focal point of various elements within the Congress searching for an alternative model of leadership to the Gandhian, of limited and controlled struggles, which these elements saw as feeding into the legitimizing of Indian capitalists while failing to serve the interests of the masses.[96] Partly because he was already an important and influential member of the Congress, those who believed that the anti-imperialist struggle ought not to be split prematurely, but carried out through the Congress, felt that Nehru was ideally suited to be their spokesman: his voice already carried weight within the Congress, and it was felt for that reason that no one else could present the left's arguments within the Congress with as much effectiveness as he.[97] The decision of the left to work with and through Nehru in the Congress turned out to be, in retrospect, a mistake on their part. Not only did he let them down in many crucial situations, but, because he was given the status of the spokesman of the left (both by the left itself and the right), he spoke with more authority and legitimacy than he might have done, had he been seen as speaking merely for himself and not carrying the Congress left with him.

The status given to Nehru within socialist circles as spokesman and transmitter of ideas could be from the perspective of strategic expediency, with a certain scepticism as to the stability or reliability of his socialism: as Abdur Rahim, then the President of the Bengal Labour Party, wrote to Nehru in 1933: 'I have read, will soon re-read, your brilliant exposition of our plight in your "Whither India"'.[98] He stated this to be an improvement on Nehru's general equivocation and his 'giving into [sic] Gandhiji'. With *Whither India*, Nehru had redeemed himself: Rahim, before reading it, 'had decided no more to burn incense to a leader whose feelings were so correct, but actions halting'.[99] Others were more optimistic: Jayaprakash Narayan enunciated much of his strategy for the Congress Socialists within the Congress on the basis of 'what Pandit Jawaharlal should do'.[100] If he was to be the carrier of left ideas into the core of the Congress, as many hoped, Nehru also had to be educated. One such educator of his leader, Cedric Dover, CSP member, invited Nehru, when the latter was in London in 1936, to come to a meeting with Paul Robeson, Erskine Caldwell, and others.[101] He also sent Nehru reading lists.[102]

Outside socialist circles, among those looking for a new direction, it was often to Nehru that they appealed for advice—given his undoubted importance in the Congress as a whole—on questions of where the Congress was going. One correspondent wrote, asking for a clear lead from Congress:

As it is, at present a great many people think that the Congress will either voluntarily hand over the country to the 'capitalists', or will be befooled by them into doing so. On the other hand, a great many persons, possessing property, even very limited, are very afraid that the unknown bogey called 'Bolshi' will capture the Congress & tear the shirts off all the property owners' backs & the bread off all their childrens' mouths; and so on.[103]

Nehru wrote a long reply: of his own views, he wrote, 'Briefly they are socialistic and my interpretation of history is what is commonly called the Marxist view. That view limits private property but of course some private property still remains'. Nehru tried 'to lay stress on the economic side and world events are gradually forcing people to think on those lines.' 'People talk of not encouraging class war-fare but the whole world to-day is based on domination of one class by another. To recognise this is to recognise an obvious fact ... Facts will not fit in with our theories. It is for our theories to fit in with the facts as they are.'[104] He added, in a passage notable for its ability both to reject a conception of the strong leader and reinstate it at the same time:

The so-called modern view is to lay greater stress on the social group and its organisation, hoping that a better environment will produce a better individual. Of course... the individual and the social group act and re-act on each other. It is a question of stress. Always the method of securing wise and unselfish legislatures has been a vital problem. Plato as you know wanted philosophers to be rulers. *The difficulty has been to find a method of picking out these supermen and placing them in seats of power.* Much will depend on the objective that one aims at. Even apart from this it is an extraordinarily difficult thing to get the right man at the top ... Ultimately, one can only rely on a sufficiently enlightened wide-awake public opinion.[105]

All one has to do, then, is to educate public opinion to recognize the right leaders when they see them. Yet it is the leaders themselves who educate public opinion. Another circular argument has developed here, similar to that of the representative experts: leaders enlighten the masses the better to recognize the leaders: the better to praise and anoint them.

Nehru did not reject the idea of Plato's philosopher–ruler, an idea which, it should be noted, was also a favourite of the ICS in its heyday[106]—if only they could be properly selected. It needs to be said that this was no sleight-of-hand intellectual sophistry; these implications seem to have been quite opaque to the intellectual elite who cast themselves as enlightened leaders. This is very far from an ideal of popular participation in government.[107]

While Nehru's position as spokesman and leader continued to be important, socialists were to be increasingly disillusioned with his inaction and desertions at crucial moments. By 1938, ironically the year of the establishment of the NPC, and Nehru's appointment as its chairman by a Congress president elected largely on the support of the Congress left, even the most optimistic were beginning to be sceptical of Nehru's commitment; Jayaprakash Narayan wrote to Nehru:

... if you will excuse me for saying so, it would be unfair of you, who are naturally used to doing things on a grand scale, to noncooperate with the efforts of Socialists in India just because they are puny as compared with those of older and wider organisations. We are, I think, not unjustified in expecting that, if you will not fully identify yourself with us, you will, as a socialist, at least help us in doing well the little we may undertake to do.[108]

Nehru himself represents, however, the complex lineages of what was within his circles called socialism, and believed to be socialism, but which carried traces of other influences which coexisted in dissociation or contradiction with many Indian socialists' (to themselves) consistent socialism; it might justifiably be said that Nehru's confidence in socialism of the kind he professed in the early 1930s merely disintegrated earlier than that of his comrades.[109] It was, of course, difficult to hold the various strands together consistently, in a project which was expected to leave nothing untouched by its project for change.[110] Yet Nehru's confusions, because they emanated from a source accustomed to dealing in imperatives and certainties, and a source expected to provide a leading voice, had consequences more than private. It was often Nehru's personal influence which had led his colleagues to socialism. His Congress colleague Syed Mahmud had written to Nehru in May 1935:

My mind is confused & I do not really know what line of action to take. In your own inimitable way you expressed a desire, more than once, that I should become a socialist. It is enough for me & emotionally speaking I am already one but you yourself will not like it. You will wish me to grasp it intellectually ... You can still carry the Mahatma a long way on your road, so I feel. Don't you?[111]

Syed Mahmud was an old friend of Nehru's, and had grappled with the question of the suitable political path for India before. In 1923, for instance, he had written to Nehru:

By the way, have you read 'Dorian Gray'? If not, please do so now ... They say it is an immoral book. But those who find ugly meaning, to quote Oscar Wilde's own words, in beautiful things are corrupt without being charming. After reading this book, I think, you will feel young. I should like you to feel young. It is as necessary for an individual as for a nation to feel young in order to do anything good or great. Mussolini has made the Entire Italian nation to feel and act as young.[112]

In the 1930s the attraction of fascism for India was still strong, though not mainstream; the CSP's fear of the dangers of people getting misled by fascism was not unrealistic. As far as many Indians were concerned, as a strong and self-reliant form of nationalism, fascism had its merits. It had been put to Nehru in 1936:

... on your Socialism, there is one question I should like to ask you: why do you stop with it, why don't you go on to the next step, Fascism, and be done with it. Of course, Fascism is a reaction against Socialism, just as Socialism is a reaction against Capitalism. I shall put it in Hegelian terms: Capitalism is the thesis, Socialism is the antithesis and Fascism is the synthesis. That is how the world movement is working itself out: here in India, the word will be Nationalism, the only difference I can see ... you will end up as Mussolini or Hitler, not as Lenin: and on the whole I prefer you to be Mussolini, though I do not hide myself from the fear that it may be a Hitler.[113]

Nehru's reply: 'Have you gone so far astray as to think in terms of Fascism? ... I agree that Lenin is much beyond reach but why this fall to Mussolini or Hitler? Politics apart, I dislike the vulgarity of Mussolini as well as the Fascism in Germany. Why does Fascism breed such crude types, or is it the crude types that beget Fascism?'.[114]

The one thing that Nehru did know extremely clearly was that he was unequivocally opposed to fascism.[115] He was, nonetheless, in demand as a potential ally of fascist regimes. Nehru complained in 1936 to one of his communist friends that 'The Duce is evidently interested in me. Yesterday the Italian Consul at Lausanne travelled up here to give me Signor Mussolini's personal message of sympathy and condolence'—upon his wife's death in a Swiss sanatorium.[116] Two letters from one Hans Georg von Studnitz in 1938 to Nehru are interesting: one invited him to visit 'the new Germany' to clear up 'misunderstandings';[117] the other, written on 5 September 1938, expressed the hope that 'the actual European crisis' would not prevent Nehru from visiting Germany.[118] Nehru, in Europe at the time, wrote a number of articles for his paper, the *National Herald*, on the dangers of fascism, of appeasement of fascism, and of impending war.

As to his socialism, he was often less clear. One crucial instance of uncertainty was the 1939 Congress presidential elections, when the left, for the second time running, had succeeded in electing its candidate, Subhas Chandra Bose, as president. The right opposed Bose and refused to accept his Working Committee, creating a crisis; Gandhi intervened, and Nehru sided with the right; after which, the Congress Socialists, having given the matter much thought, decided not to split the Congress, and abandoned Bose as well.[119] In the acrimony that followed, in which Subhas Bose justifiably felt that Nehru had betrayed him, Nehru wrote to Bose, on the tenth page of a long letter:

Am I a socialist or an individualist? Is there a necessary contradiction in the two terms? Are we all such integrated human beings that we can define ourselves precisely in a word or a phrase? I suppose I am temperamentally and by training an individualist, and intellectually a socialist, whatever all this might mean. I hope that socialism does not kill or suppress individuality; indeed I am attracted to it because it will release innumerable individuals from economic and cultural bondage ... Let us leave it at this that I am an unsatisfactory human being who is dissatisfied with himself and the world, and whom the petty world he lives in does not particularly like.[120]

Writing to J.C. Wedgwood, an old English acquaintance and member of the House of Commons, from Dehra Dun district jail two years later, in April 1941, he seems to have done a little more thinking.

I hate anarchy of all kinds, of the mind, the body, and the social organism. I dislike a mess, and my own predilection is entirely in favour of order. And yet there are worse states than that of anarchy and disorder, and in this mad world of ours, the choice often lies between evils.[121]
No, I am not a communist, nor indeed do I belong to any other 'ism'. Having failed to find anchorage in religion, I refuse to give up my mental freedom in favour of amy dogma or binding creed. Yet I believe in the socialist structure; it seems to me inescapable if the world is to survive and progress.[122]
These last five years ... have had a powerful effect upon me, and my mind's assurance about the future of humanity has been considerably shaken.[123]

He spoke of Indian culture, of its resilience over thousands of years— 'a stability and a continuity'.

The new culture and civilisation that will come will (or I hope it will) produce a classless society & will make Brahmanas and Kshatriyas of all of us wherever we may be.[124]

This usage is particularly interesting—echoes of Gandhi's (and Kumarappa's) argument on the moral basis of true caste seem to appear here. It was a moment of weakness; the image is not regular Nehru; and these doubts were not expressed in public. Nevertheless, a few months later, Nehru was still writing in terms of the antiquity and resilience of Indian civilization: 'British rule in India is after all just an episode in our long history, a very unsavoury episode, I think'.[125] This could sound like Moon's reflections on the legacy of British rule in India: in Moon's case British ineffectiveness rescued them from having committed too much evil, in Nehru's case it was also comforting.

Gandhi had written to Nehru in 1934, 'You have no uncertainty about the science of socialism but you don't know in full how you will apply it when you have the power'.[126] Gandhi perceptively wrote to his Quaker friend, Agatha Harrison, in 1936 after Nehru's 'I am a socialist' speech to Congress, which so alarmed moderates and businessmen:

His address is a confession of his faith. You see from the formation of his 'Cabinet' that he has chosen a majority of those who represent the traditional view i.e. from 1920. Of course the majority represent my view ... But Jawaharlal's way is not my way. I accept his ideal about land etc. But I do not accept practically any of his methods. I would strain every nerve to prevent a class war. *So would he, I expect.* But he does not believe it to be possible to avoid it. I believe it to be perfectly possible if my method is accepted.[127]

Here was a paradoxical socialism; one not readily recognized as such except by name, a personal quest at least as much as a political direction. The emotional bonding with socialism which affected these colonial intellectuals was built on a fair amount of romanticism, and a good deal of eclecticism; it drew strongly on elements of British anti-colonial politics which themselves drew on romantic strains.[128] Yet it also sought to claim for itself links with scientific thought. The references to Fabian thought which were current at the time were not in any way systematic or respectful of the integrity of the original idea borrowed; it may, however, be said that Fabianism as an intellectual tool facilitated, when required, a distancing of oneself from the revolutionary left while still maintaining a claim to 'socialism'; and, possibly more importantly, justifying a socialism brought about by an elite who were great believers in science.

Science

In India, these claims to science had lineages of their own which also strongly entered the picture—longer lineages, in fact, than 'socialism'. In the course of the insistence on the need to industrialize—a call which went back to the nineteenth century—a great deal of attention had been paid to the lack of technology and technological skills in India. The main concern with the teaching of science was centred in imperial discourse around its clearly practical applications—the promotion of engineering colleges being one such area. The debate around 'technical education' was also a strong strand in British India, merging with the demand for industrialization; while for the Indian side of the argument, this was to be combined with constructive government activity, a protective tariff policy, and genuine fiscal autonomy, it was often the limit to what the government was willing to do. Nevertheless, in connection with 'development' it was urged that science should be put to the service of industrial research and technical training of scientists who would, thereafter, serve industry—a phenomenon, it was claimed by opponents of the government, which was well known in Britain and other industrialized nations. Nationalists were quick to blame government policy for the inadequate promotion of industrial research or technological training.[129]

In the course of these debates, scientists were increasingly being cast as the most potentially influential group in a new India; they were increasingly being included in discussions on developmental matters as 'experts'; and a number of them had already begun to take this role extremely seriously, carrying the message of the importance of science to a wide and constantly increasing readership among the educated middle classes. Journals which catered to a general middle-class readership carried articles on the importance of science, on occasion discussing complicated concepts in various branches of science taking for granted the interest of its readership in these matters;[130] a scientific journal could cater to a general interested readership beyond the scientific community, carrying articles on the intricate details of electronic engineering, statistics, or physics problems alongside news of the latest developments in Sigmund Freud's work in Vienna and the successes of the Soviet industrialization programme.[131]

The connection between 'development' and science was an obvious one if 'development' was intended to privilege industrialization and increased agricultural production; but 'science' also carried wider connotations of 'rational', and 'progressive' activity. These connections were self-evident for many of the personnel who came to be closely associated with the planning of such industrialization, men who were closely involved in the practice of 'science'. Meghnad Saha, physicist, of Presidency College, Calcutta, and Imperial College, London, was author of a scheme to dam the river Damodar, and a member, from 1938, of the

Congress' NPC, and on the Sub-Committee for River Training and Irrigation, and the Sub-Committee for Power and Fuel.[132] P.C. Mahalanobis, Presidency College, Calcutta and King's College, Cambridge, physicist-turned-mathematician-turned-physicist-turned-statistician-turned-developmentalist, a relative latecomer to debates on Indian 'development' (although he had been a close member of Rabindranath Tagore's circle, and peripherally connected with the Sriniketan experiment in rural development), and later to be author of the eponymous 'Mahalanobis Model' of development planning, set up the Indian Statistical Institute at Presidency College, in a corner of the physics department. Both were close associates of Satyendranath Bose, Einstein's sometime collaborator—and had worked together with him on a book on relativity.[133] This was a social and professional circle which had begun closely to associate science, development, and modernity: Saha set up the monthly journal of the Indian Science News Association, *Science and Culture*, to promote a 'scientific' approach towards problems of development and national progress, and did a great deal of writing for it himself; Mahalanobis and Saha were regular contributors to the annual Indian Science Congresses; both Saha and Mahalanobis had worked on the problem of floods in the Damodar valley in the 1920s and 1930s.[134] Sir M. Visvesvaraya, highly successful former civil engineer and government servant, and author of several books on developmental schemes, was one of the vice-presidents of Mahalanobis' Indian Statistical Institute for a while; and Saha, Visvesvaraya, and Mahalanobis were all involved in the Congress' NPC, though Mahalanobis more peripherally: he wrote to Nehru in 1940 suggesting that he examine all the reports of the NPC from a 'purely statistical point of view'.[135] Visvesvaraya shared a similar belief in science and its transformative powers,[136] though perhaps it would be more accurate to call him a technologist, for he believed in applied science, certainly for 'backward' countries. For many, then, science was interpreted as technology; and those who believed that there was more to science than technology also placed a high premium on the importance of technology in the progress of the nation.[137]

'Economics' was, of course, (and still is) billed as a science itself; and the educational and intellectual antecedents of Nehru, a BA in natural sciences from Trinity College, Cambridge, with Fabian connections, left-wing links, and strong sympathies—for a period—with 'scientific socialism',[138] Jayaprakash Narayan, whose American education had brought him in touch with the Communist Party of the USA;[139] or Minoo Masani, LSE student with Labour Party and ILP experience to go with the

Fabian connections of LSE life,[140] contained strong doses of scientific optimism—science as a panacea for most ills, scientific socialism in varying proportions, and a belief in progress, the possibilities of social change.

The claim to 'science' fell short of a well-worked-out philosophy of science, however; the belief in the capacities of applied science to change existing conditions was built on a conception that it was the use of technology which marked out the 'advanced' from the 'backward' societies.

...if we take the motor car industry as an index of civilised existence, the U.S.A. stands easily first, with over 30 million cars in use; about one man in five possesses a car, *i.e.*, every family possesses a car. ... in India, there is one car for every 2300 persons. This figure gives an appalling picture of the low index of civilised life in India....[141]

'Civilisation' here is understood in material terms, apparently opposed to the more abstract connotations of 'culture'; but still carrying with it the idea of being opposed to 'barbarism', or 'backwardness', in much the same sense as Kumarappa uses it in his 'test of civilisation', which I have referred to earlier. This distinction does not seem to have been rigorously maintained, the existence of the two terms being useful to distinguish one from the other in the same space.[142] Certain aspects of 'culture', according to this view, needed to be jettisoned:

... if this country is ever to enter the path of progress, her younger generations must be cut adrift from many medieval ideas and traditions which are instilled into their minds in the name of religion, philosophy, custom, tradition or history. Only a good dose of scientific education can undo the evil influences to which young minds are subjected.[143]

Or as Jawaharlal Nehru put it:

...I realised that science was not only a pleasant diversion and abstraction, but was of the very texture of life, without which our modern world would vanish away. Politics led me to economics and this led me inevitably to science and the scientific approach to all our problems and to life itself. It was science alone that could solve these problems of hunger and poverty, of insanitation and illiteracy, of superstition and deadening custom and tradition, of vast resources running to waste, of a rich country inhabited by starving people.[144]

The 'science alone' part is surprising—possibly meant for his specific audience of scientists, possibly a rather revealing Freudian slip. Those with socialist sympathies were not usually willing to claim that science was an apolitical practice, merely that it could be a search for universally relevant knowledge if it was freed from its bondage to capitalism.[145] As an editorial in *Science and Culture* put it in 1938, 'It is true that the Industrial Revolution in Europe caused great social dislocation and political unrest, but this was due to the fact that the discoveries of science were first utilised by capitalists, for the sake of private gain...'.[146] Nehru was not a particularly reliable guide to the consensus among socialists or the scientific community, despite being a facilitator of communication and organization. He wrote in 1939, in reply to a letter by one Ahmed Bashir, Secretary of the Majlis Kabir Pakistan of Lahore, in which the latter had urged him to accept the partition of India:

Perhaps it is true, as you say, that I look at the facts from the Westerner point of view, though I have not divorced myself from facts in India. I move about the country a great deal and see vast numbers of people in the villages and in the towns. Nevertheless it is true that my outlook on life and politics is what might be called scientific.[147]

Here Nehru collapsed the categories 'scientific' and 'Western'; the latter term, one most often used as abuse in colonial India, was appropriated by Nehru as a positive trait. This was far from what Indian scientists perceived themselves as doing; and Nehru himself did not consistently make this equation, usually stressing the universal rather than the 'Western' aspects of science. A closer analysis of these slips would require a closer study of Nehru's psychological history, which is not of primary importance to this argument; it must be said, however, that the anxiety recurrent in Indian political discourse of the time, of the need for 'Indianness', is encountered again here, with the distinction between 'Eastern' and 'Western' ways of thought and action remaining crucial. This theme, which dominated earlier political debates, and survived notably in the Gandhian position, tended to be used by the right wing of the nationalist movement to delegitimize its leftist opponents.[148] Nehru's own tracing of the trajectory of his 'discovery of India' was more honest than most who sought to claim the necessary 'Eastern' authenticity: he found the east via the west.[149]

What is important to note is that science as a world view was also often explicitly set out in opposition to Gandhian ideas.[150] Yet in such an attack the main target was not Gandhi's search for an 'Indian' solution, but his ideas' alleged lack of modernity. Science was not to be regarded as outside the Indian cultural framework:

It is probably not so well known that the East has originated all those arts and crafts which are responsible for the greatness of the present European civilisation. It was in the East that copper was first discovered from its ores and used to replace tools made from stones. The East has used bronze which is far superior to copper for offence, defence, and work, upto 1200 B.C. It was again the East which first showed that iron by special treatment could be converted into steel, a product far superior to bronze for fighting and tool making. Even the use of mineral coal originated in the East.[151]

This rather ingenious reversal of arguments turns the problem on its head: European civilization having borrowed from the east, the east is entitled to reclaim the fruits of its own achievements. Science, thereby, performs its rightful duty in developing a modern India whose modernity is her own, not plagiarized.

There are lineages to these arguments which need to be entered into, which might explain the engagement with science in a colonized country as well as the confidence with which the arguments on 'development' were being raised in this period. 'Science' as a universal framework, with a capacity to legitimize the work of the colonized and to create equality between the colonized and the colonizer—'progress' in science as being neutral and universal—was a powerful ally to claim in colonial India. This was one ground on which a claim could be made to counteract the attitude towards 'nativeness' and consequent difference—an attitude which had given rise to colonial perceptions of its own superiority. The universality of this dynamic—a downtrodden group's need for legitimating criteria, its escape from negative placings of itself—the scientist as scientist, not as native, Jew, or Negro—has been discussed in different contexts.[152] At the same time the scientist was an Indian scientist—the Indian part of it was relevant, not in Indian science being separate from 'Western' science or science as a whole, but in that Indians could contribute as equals in the scientific world.[153] If there was an initial anxiety involved in practising a science seen as 'Western',[154] by the 1930s, anxieties arising from being an 'Indian' practising 'Western' science hardly arose in a significant manner; if they had once existed, resolutions to the arguments had been found; the confidence in the practice of modern science was widely accepted.

Initially, the teaching of science had been strongly linked to inculcating modern values in the Indian.[155] Modernity was linked, in the colonial project as well as in much of Indian resistance to that project, to an attempt to impose 'Western' values on Indian society. From the middle of the nineteenth century to the first decades of the twentieth century there had been lively debates, mainly in Bengal, as to the relevance of science and the need to negotiate an 'Indian' version of science and scientific practice. These acquired immediacy in the period surrounding the Swadeshi movement and the corresponding demand for 'national education'.[156] The resolution of this debate seems to have been achieved through a conception that the technological achievements of 'Western' science needed to be appropriated so that a national programme of industrialization could be launched; this despite the material nature of 'Western', 'natural science'-based civilization, as opposed to the moral civilization of India; for without industry Indian sovereignty could not be realized.[157]

Crucial links in such a resolution were found in the rediscovery for India of an ancient past of scientific practice. Acharya Prafulla Chandra Ray, of Bengal Chemicals and Swadeshi fame,[158] a larger-than-life figure who became a major inspiration behind Indian science, wrote a two-volume *History of Hindu Chemistry* challenging the idea of science as the achievement of 'Western' thought alone.[159] He was himself a major influence on Brajendranath Seal, philosopher and educationist, incidentally the man who introduced a young Mahalanobis to practical statistics,[160] and the future vice-chancellor of Visvesvaraya's creation, Mysore University. Seal's treatise on *The Positive Sciences of the Ancient Hindus*.[161] originated in his contribution to the second volume of Ray's *History of Hindu Chemistry*, which he enlarged and recast for publication.[162]

This tendency was not unlike Gandhi's argument on the purity and beauty of village life, reaching backwards to a better, golden age—with the consequent implication that to relive that golden age in the present constitutes liberation. Ray was a complex figure who managed to combine an insistence on the virtues of practical science, technology, and entrepreneurship with his support for Gandhian ideas (he had actively campaigned for khadi in the 1920s in connection with the Non-Cooperation Movement, and was a believer in a moderate version of Gandhi's anti-machinery doctrine) even as many of his students and fellow-scientists rejected Gandhian views sharply and found themselves closer to views on socialism and science of the Nehruvian kind.[163] Ray was extremely eclectic in his choice of influences and his views of past and future; in a most un-Gandhian manner he attributed the 'intellectual renaissance in Bengal' to the efforts of Rammohun Roy and Thomas Babington Macaulay, and agreed with James Mill that the 'Hindu' mind was capable of great metaphysical subtlety but deficient in practical skills.[164] Three years later, he used the same Minute of 1835 as a quote beginning a chapter dealing with the Bengali's imitative tendencies: adopting European dress, customs, manners, and consumption patterns, embodied in tea, tobacco, and automobiles: the Macaulay's Minute-led process, he implied, had gone too far and in the wrong directions.[165] He also maintained respect for

Mussolini, quoting him on the inadequacy of university learning and the need for actual experience, alongside Ramsay Macdonald and Lord Haldane—a reminder of the coexistence of often contradictory ideas among Indian thinkers on 'development' problems at the time.[166] While some of his contemporaries slid into sectarian arguments (sometimes uncritically) in unearthing a glorious 'Hindu' past and lamenting the onset of decline with Muslim invasions,[167] Ray was able to avoid a situation in which his historical quest turned into ancestor-worship and sectarianism.[168]

The links of the 1930s scientists with these earlier debates were direct: Ray, for instance, was still alive and well, and a major influence on Saha and his associates, of whom not a few had been taught by Ray at Presidency College. The tentativeness of the earlier debates on the validity of science for India had now been overcome, not least because of the recognition which had been achieved on the world stage by Indian scientists, such as Ray, Jagadish Chandra Bose, and later Satyen Bose, Saha, and C.V. Raman, and the erosion of some of the discrimination in terms of employment suffered by Indian scientists in earlier years.[169] It was possible in the 1930s to argue with far greater confidence that science, if not a universal philosophy, was certainly not to be regarded as outside the Indian cultural framework; for it was in the 'East' that 'all those arts and crafts which are responsible for the greatness of the present European civilisation' had originated.[170] With these tools, the professional middle classes were to conceptualize their project of 'development' for India: scientific research and technology would serve together to further the much desired cause of industrialization, through which the nation would emerge from backwardness.

Morality, Modernity, National Discipline

Much less self-conscious and explicit than conceptions of socialism and science was the tendency to think about development and progress in terms of national discipline. It was thought necessary and desirable to make explicit certain connections between projects of economic regeneration and development and the wider process of 'nation-building'.[171] Such connections were explored in the writings and speeches of several proselytizers closely associated with ideas of 'development' in India. This could be made clear in the course of discussions whose sphere of competence might logically have excluded these ideas. The way to nationhood, Gandhi had pointed out in *Hind Swaraj*, lay through moral self-improvement; despite disagreements in other fields, many on the side of 'modernisation' would have agreed with this. Gyan Chand, an economist from Patna University, and later closely associated with Indian planning as an admirer of China, put the issue squarely before his readership:

India's political freedom ... cannot come to us as a gift of the gods. No nation deserves to be free without strenuous exertion or great sacrifices ... we should have a right sense of values ... the leaders of national life have to cultivate, in some measure, the quality of seers and look ahead for inspiration. It is necessary for right thinking and action that our gaze should be fixed on the India of our hopes and aspirations; and the proposals for the solution of our national problems bear the impress of coming events.[172]

These 'leaders of national life' who were cast as 'seers' were essentially men such as Gyan Chand himself; though this was perhaps an unintended meaning. He made no apology for dealing with such issues in a book about federal finance: federalism was a way of ordering the state, in which there was a need to negotiate multiple loyalties, perhaps multiple patriotisms. The issue of federal finance was, therefore, connected with the question of distribution of resources and the harmonization of these loyalties therefrom. 'Indian history is, if we read it aright, an experiment in nation-making without stamping out differences'; it was necessary 'that in our nation-building we should work for a synthesis which makes this diversity an organic part of our common life'. This made the wider philosophical issues regarding identity, differences, and the harmonization thereof through 'the Indian view of life which postulates the necessity of difference' not unrelated to federal finance: it might be called 'the metaphysics of federal finance'. A federal state is 'an intermediary stage in the political development of a people, and a device by which the way is prepared for a stable and lasting unity on the basis of strong national spirit'.[173] This equation of national values and national morality with the 'political development of a people'—on the basis of *deserving* freedom (once again, echoing Gandhi, but also, perhaps, imperialist ideas of progress towards self-government)—carried with it an implicit corollary: the people of India had to be made worthy of that freedom. This could only be done through ordered, disciplined progress.

One of the most articulate and prolific of the public figures who built a career on advocating 'development', and the most insistent advocate of national discipline as a means to national efficiency was Sir M. Visvesvaraya, a man generally acknowledged in the official genealogies of development planning in India as an influential early pioneer, and a man who was in 1938 considered an automatic choice for the NPC.[174] Visvesvaraya combined a very successful personal career with an obsessive and energetic advocacy of what he saw as a project for national regeneration. As a talented student, he had won a Government of Mysore scholarship to the College of Science at Poona; from March 1884 he became assistant engineer in the Bombay Public Works Department. A very able engineer, well regarded by his British employers, he rose in the ranks to just below Chief Engineer of Bombay Presidency—that post was reserved for Englishmen, so he resigned in 1908. He was Chief Engineer and then Dewan of Mysore from 1909 to 1918, during which he undertook a number of schemes, irrigation and hydroelectric projects, (he had achieved great success in the field of irrigation engineering), industries, and education; the princely state of Mysore became, under his influence, an attractive field for private investment by Indian businessmen.[175] The founding of Mysore University in 1916, as an Indian-run competitor of what was seen as the colonial government-controlled Madras University, was among his notable achievements, recognition for which was difficult to secure at first; eventually this was achieved through Visvesvaraya's own influence and his ability to recruit academics like Brajendranath Seal, M.S. Subba Rao, K.T. Shah, Sarvepalli Radhakrishnan, and Radhakumud Mookerji. Special emphasis was placed on technical education (unsurprisingly); agriculture was taught as a science; in addition, other agricultural and commercial schools were opened by him.[176] Visvesvaraya was also an extremely influential public voice. In large measure as a result of his career and earlier successes, he commanded a ready audience on matters related to economic life, national regeneration, industrialization and nation-building—his every publication and public statement would receive extensive coverage in regional and national newspapers, political journals, and specialist literature.[177]

'Industrial life', according to Visvesvaraya, 'connotes production, wealth, power and modernity'.[178] There is nothing tongue-in-cheek about this statement. Visvesvaraya was quite clear about this; he had visited Japan in 1898 when the Japanese were attracting great attention as late industrializers; he visited several industrialized countries over the years, studying various industries and advocating solutions for India from these examples.[179] Visvesvaraya was convinced that a good deal of the problem of lack of modernity and power could be solved from the perspective of national discipline. The main deficiency in national life, in Visvesvaraya's opinion, was illiteracy, keeping the people ignorant of 'scientific practices and modern methods'. This was due to 'the absence of an active State policy to abolish illiteracy and to train people to lead orderly and disciplined lives'.[180] He emphasized the need for cooperative credit societies, cooperative farming and marketing, and diversity of occupations, in which connection he recommended compulsory mass education in the three Rs plus practical training in agricultural operations, cottage industries, smithy, carpentry, accounting, etc.. Calling for the promotion of rural, cottage, and home industries, he noted their decline 'under the stress of Western civilisation' and that 'no modern or organised methods' had emerged as replacement.[181] He was, nonetheless, an ardent advocate of large-scale industries, which he had actively promoted in his capacity as Dewan of Mysore. The role assigned to labour, meanwhile, was to refrain from participating in or assisting, even 'involuntarily', strikes or agitations which might 'kill the goose that lays the golden eggs'. As industry expanded, wages and the standard of living would go up 'automatically'. Only after this could labour 'assert itself and claim many of the privileges conceded in industrially developed countries'.[182]

The connection between national discipline and national regeneration or nation-building was the most important aspect of the problem of Indian development to Visvesvaraya. In 1920, writing in the context of what he saw as an opportunity for nation-building provided by the Montague–Chelmsford reforms, he spoke of the necessity of 'nation-building' and 'Indianisation'—a term used in imperial documents to imply the gradual handing over or opening of higher posts in administration and government to Indians, but to Visvesvaraya used by analogy with 'Americanisation', the process by which immigrants to the US were assimilated. Indianization was '[t]he process of unifying the tastes and mentality of a population differing in race, religion and language, by means of education and training'.[183] Visvesvaraya was clear that an idea of Indian citizenship had to be created—a citizenship that was to be 'purposeful, progressive and self-respecting'. The 'Indian mind' had to be 'familiarised with the principles of modern progress'.[184] This quest also had personal implications for Visvesvaraya; India had to join 'the rest of mankind'; at present, he felt a 'feeling of humiliation' at the 'low international standing' of his country.[185]

Propaganda which sought to teach the masses to lead disciplined and more modern lives could overcome this problem.[186] In 1931, Visvesvaraya stressed the need to 'improve the working efficiency of the villager' through a system of 'home discipline to train the body, the mind and the character of the villager and to educate him in practices of self-reliance and self-help'.[187] The idea of 'citizenship training' runs through his work, the need for it arising from the basic fact that 'India is inhabited by people in all stages of civilisation from the primitive to the most advanced'.[188] Special efforts were required 'to raise every class of people in the scale of economic civilisation', otherwise 'national progress as a whole is bound to be retarded'.[189] Economic progress, in Visvesvaraya's view, would lead the process of national progress as a whole; though the latter included 'political, social and cultural' progress.[190] 'The public should be induced and trained to make up their mind to work harder, more methodically and in clear cooperation with their neighbours'.[191]

By 1934, he was able to draw upon a far more authoritarian rhetoric in his search for national discipline: he stressed the need for military training and conscription 'to introduce the much-needed elements of regularity, method, and discipline into the daily life of the Indian population'. He quoted Roosevelt on the need for moving 'as a trained and loyal army willing to sacrifice for the good of a common discipline'.[192] He noted, citing a Fascist manifesto, the establishment in Italy of 'leisure time' institutions which 'promote the better enjoyment of the free time of workers of all classes with the object of raising their intellectual, moral, physical and social status in accordance with a policy of enhancing national values'.[193] He added, 'What has gone wrong with the Indian population is that their collective will power is feeble ... In countries like Germany and Japan and generally in most European states, a determined effort is made by the Governments concerned to promote the physical and economic efficiency of their citizens ...'.[194]

From Visvesvaraya's point of view, with the emphasis on 'development' and 'modernity', an urging of the adoption of programmes which could have been labelled fascist was as straightforward a choice as a resort to Soviet examples; and he certainly did not see himself as a socialist.[195] In the same year he wrote to Gandhi, 'I feel that in this machine age, we should not hesitate, except in temporary situations, to utilise mechanical power to the utmost limit that circumstances permit ... I am enclosing an extract from a speech by the Russian leader J. Stalin ...'.[196] This equivalence of choices was also a not uncommon strand among some Fabians, a group that had influenced Indian socialists to a greater or lesser extent over the years, and whose ideas also had their influence on non-socialist ideas of 'development' in India—as another approximately equivalent choice in arguments which justified 'development'. Visvesvaraya would not have been unaware of this; in January 1933 he had been at a party in honour of George Bernard Shaw and his wife; Shaw had been interviewed by the correspondent of the *Hindu* and was quoted as having said 'I am a Communist'. When asked to elaborate, Shaw reportedly said that 'there must be a government either of the Mussolini kind or of the Lenin type. Democracy was all sham. The Parliament was very irresponsible, and it should go. It was a talking institute. There must be dictatorship'.[197] This apparently struck a chord for Visvesvaraya: in his clipping of the report, he had marked the bit concerning the irresponsibility of Parliament; he was in the habit of marking significant passages in his papers and newspaper clippings.[198]

The impetus to the adoption of the last point about parliaments might seem strange in the Indian context, given that parliaments in any but a caricatured sense had never existed in colonial India. But it becomes less opaque if it is related to the project at hand. It seemed to many at the time that the primary requirement for a vision of the future was that it provided an escape from imperialist domination through a claim on India's part to 'modernity'. The tension between this claim to 'modernity' and the socio-cultural behaviour of the masses, which only reluctantly lent itself to being called 'modern', created a barrier which needed to be bridged, producing in some minds schemes to 'modernise' people who did not meet the standard: cultural and spiritual values were to be made to conform with the demands of 'modernity'. This was an urgency shared with the socialists:

The Congress Socialist Party sets before the masses a clear goal. The attainment of Independence and the establishment of a State in which power shall rest in them and which would work for the restless elimination of those who exploit them. It is the ambition of the party to make of the masses a conscious solid phalanx by *dispossessing them of their tribal and communal selves*, and arousing in them the sense of class-solidarity which their class-interest demands of them ....[199]

The raising of moral questions regarding 'development' was quite the norm rather than the exception; and there was a definite equation made between a morally correct being and a disciplined being. Once again, Gandhi's writings come readily to mind; P.C. Ray's memoirs also succeed powerfully in stressing the possibilities of disciplined, hard work by using his own life and work as an example, as well as the numerous uplifting examples of the life and work of other historical and contemporary figures: Ben Franklin, Oliver Cromwell, Mustapha Kemal Pasha, Mahatma Gandhi, G.D. Birla, Nalini Ranjan Sarkar, Thomas Lipton or Thomas Bata, Mussolini, and Masaryk.[200] The main point running through these examples was that a university education is useless unless physical hard work and discipline become part of daily life; the latter makes the former relatively unnecessary.

There was also a trend towards conceiving the national state as a body, a physical entity composed of morally and physically healthy citizens. The General Education Sub-Committee of the NPC proposed a compulsory social or labour service to make all young men and women between the ages of 18 and 22 contribute a year of 'national disciplined service in such form and place, and under such conditions as the State may prescribe in that behalf [sic]'. It, moreover proposed to fix general norms of physical fitness which were to be adhered to.[201] The Sub-Committee on Population, while stressing the need for birth control as well as 'self-control', spoke of the need for removing the barriers to intermarriage 'for eugenic and other social reasons'.[202] In 1938, the NPC's Sub-Committee on 'Woman's Role in Planned Economy' was able to come up with the following resolution:

The health programme of the State shall aim at the eradication of serious diseases, more especially such as are communicable or transmissible by marriage. The State should follow a eugenic programme to make the race physically and mentally healthy. This would discourage marriages of unfit persons and provide for the sterilisation of persons suffering from transmissible diseases of a serious nature, such as insanity or epilepsy.[203]

In a project which, in the words of the NPC, involved not just the 'technical co-ordination, by disinterested experts' of aspects of economic life 'in accordance with social objectives set by bodies representative of the nation', but simultaneously 'cultural and spiritual values and the human side of life',[204] it was a short step to the conceptualization of the custodians of the national entity as an enlightened elite who were entitled to conduct the ordering of a nation to their own liking, if not in their own image, through 'development'.

Once again, there are lineages of these ideas which need to be taken into account. Nationalist debates in India had long been concerned with questions of how to overcome the stigma of being a backward nation—to this end various forms of education and discipline had been advocated. These debates were incorporated into later discussions on development. Socialists were perhaps more stringent about their selection of methods and examples through which to achieve this dispossession, and would certainly have taken much trouble consciously to maintain a distance from what they saw as fascist ideas; but the project is, nonetheless, recognizable. However, it was also possible to be influenced by contemporarily available metaphors of national purification and health, discipline and control, many of which were authoritarian in nature, and were not necessarily seen as fascist; such influences cut across political lines. Moreover, as is evident from several instances provided above, fascism was not necessarily discredited in Indian eyes in the 1930s, linking up with Indian concerns with creating an efficient and disciplined nation in the process of nation-building: 'merely an aggressive form of nationalism'.[205] And there was less than an intellectually rigorous and consistent engagement with the origins of the ideas borrowed for Indian use.

The language of race efficiency and eugenics was also much used in connection with national discipline. Once again, this had not clearly been discredited as Nazi or fascist until carried to its logical conclusions by the Nazis during the Second World War; in the 1920s, Fabians discussed 'socialist man'; and socialists as well as liberals spoke of improving the human stock;[206] Keynes had toyed with eugenics in his writings on mathematics and economics.[207] In India too, there was a strong confusion among terms like 'race', 'nation', and 'civilisation', often used interchangeably, for instance, in the tendency to speak of a 'Hindu nation' or a 'Hindu race'.[208]

In part this can be seen as a problem of translation, both linguistic and cultural: linguistically to discover equivalent terms in Indian languages for those in English, and vice-versa; and culturally to map Indian concerns onto debates current in British and European contexts. This cultural translation had important political motives, in a public sphere dominated by the British colonial state: political arguments in colonial India were necessarily interventions into arenas structured by the British colonial power; an intervention which was to be effective had to appeal to principles which the colonial power recognized as valid and, therefore, was forced to rebut. This meant that an idea which had already secured political and/or academic respectability in Britain was particularly useful in arguments put forward in India: the credibility of the idea on which the argument was to be based had already been established. The confusion of 'race' and 'nation' can similarly be observed in contemporary perceptions regarding language, culture, and race. The distinction was never quite clear to the Theosophists, who played a crucial role in the rediscovery of Hinduism in India as well as provided echoes of recognition for predecessors of the Nazis with their theories of Aryan supremacy.[209] Moreover, the temptation in India to claim a similar racial origin to rulers who claimed racial superiority was particularly strong, although one consequence of this manoeuvre was to deny such resources to those among Indians who could not claim an 'Aryan' origin.

Not all these strands found their way into the work of the NPC, or more generally into the conceptualization of development planning: crucially, 'race efficiency' was a relevant category, but not as a sectarian category; rather, 'race' in the NPC's debates appears as an approximate synonym for 'Indian national', having shed its 'Aryan' or 'Hindu' connotations. Thus, in the attempt to conceptualize a disciplined 'national' entity which would achieve a shared goal of 'development', the meaning of a potentially divisive categorization such as 'race' was turned to imply solidarity and collective effort.

The routes to such semantic shifts were not always straightforward. One strange trajectory was that of the statistician, Mahalanobis.[210] Although closely associated with Presidency College, and the circles which discussed the role of science in the development of national life, he was a relative latecomer to the concerns which his colleagues articulated.[211] Much of his first published work, in the 1920s and the 1930s, related to anthropometrics, eugenics, and race.[212] Mahalanobis' interest in statistics was channelled in these directions as a consequence of his working with Dr N. Annandale, then Director of the Zoological and Anthropological Survey of India, on some of the latter's anthropometric data.[213] This was the sort of problem to which the young discipline of statistics was being applied, especially through the work of Karl Pearson, socialist and Galton Professor of Eugenics at University College, London, with which these early writings engage.[214]

At first Mahalanobis maintained his distance from the project in which he was involved, absolving himself of responsibility for the conclusions.[215] Annandale clarified that he was 'doubtful about the value of bodily measurements taken on the live person', and 'suspicious that there was some fallacy in the whole method'.[216] Although the general conclusions bore out Annandale's doubts, the relevance of the category of race itself was not questioned,[217] and Mahalanobis stated in his definition of terms, following Pearson's 'Coefficient of Racial Likeness': 'By "race efficiency", I would denote stability, combined with capacity to play a part in the history of civilisation'.[218] In later writings, Mahalanobis overcame his diffidence and entered the debates in earnest. In particular, he attempted, through statistical analyses of anthropometric material, to modify the work of H.H. Risley on the *Castes and Tribes of Bengal*.[219] By the time he became involved with national planning, possibly through the influence of his colleagues,[220] this strand was no longer particularly important to him.

The term 'race' can be read, as used in debates on development, as a red herring; it was a term which did not properly denote the idea which it conventionally implied in European contexts at the time. More relevant was the need for national discipline, a factor agreed upon by intellectuals across political barriers. The 1920s, in the aftermath of the Great War and the Montague–Chelmsford Reforms, saw a focus on a rhetoric and practice of 'nation-building'; this process of 'nation-building' was seen as necessary in advancing towards self-government. Imperialist arguments stressed the need for a period of 'nation-building' before India could qualify for self-government.[221] Although nationalists denied the need for a period of qualification they, nonetheless, believed that a greater sense of national solidarity and discipline had to be created. A number of initiatives for creating this sense of solidarity were already in existence: social service organizations, 'constructive Swadeshi' measures, religious reform movements; Indian appropriations of that specifically imperialist organization, the Boy Scouts; paramilitary 'Hindu' outfits like the RSS; and the Congress' own volunteer corps. Some of these groups were explicitly Hindu, sectarian, and violent;[222] others less so, or not at all. Explicitly sectarian arguments were, however, not acceptable in a programme for national development, which was expected to carry the whole nation with it; if a sectarian argument had to be made to appear legitimate, it had to be framed within the rhetoric of economic need (as in the case of arguments for cow protection as preservation of national wealth),[223] or national solidarity, in which a sectarian argument operated by blaming an opposing sect of itself being sectarian, and of breaking the rules of national solidarity.

Many of these movements stressed discipline, physical fitness, skill in the martial arts, the ability to use weapons, and obedience to a leader, in different combinations. This was not necessarily seen as a commitment to militarism: it was a question of discipline and of mass mobilization rather than of violence. Such mobilization, it was felt, could bring those groups which had so far remained outside the mainstream, into the nationalist movement—into which category, for instance, women might be placed. In 1938, Subhas Bose wrote to a woman who told him of her desire to serve the country through a women's welfare organization that she had set up, advising her to 'give physical training to younger women. They have to learn lathi and dagger play etc.' in order to defend themselves.[224] It was in this context—of both mobilization and control of mass participation in politics—that Mussolini's success in Italy was interpreted—as a version of what Indian nationalists hoped to achieve with the Indian masses, and as a particularly effective form of nationalism.[225] It needs to be remembered that Mussolini's Fascists were, in the 1920s, regarded by many as a progressive force—Bernard Shaw's confusions have been noted in this connection. Moreover, the need for such discipline could be stressed for its own sake, or in terms of its necessity for the running of a future state.

The problem of how to deal with workers was influenced by this tendency: a directly socialist vision would place them at the centre of that vision. But such socialism as the mainstream debates were willing to accommodate agreed that this would have had to be in accordance with the need for national discipline and efficiency. A relative consensus on this existed across political tendencies. Strikes were a betrayal of the work and discipline ethic; and work was morally uplifting.[226] Particularly in rural areas, India had the advantage of possessing 'a large store of cheap and docile labour'.[227] This force had to be drawn upon for industrialization. As for the organized workforce, quite logically, men like Visvesvaraya, and the men who framed the Bombay Plan, felt that workers should avoid conflict with management—strikes killed golden-egg-laying geese, and so on.[228] The Congress' NPC, however, shared similar views, though apparently approaching the problem from a different perspective: since capitalists were productive 'human material', in Nehru's words, they ought not to be dispossessed in a hurry if productivity and industrialization was the goal (although they were not to be given control of 'key' industries unless they controlled them already). In such a scenario, workers were owed certain trade-union and welfare rights—better working conditions and hours, promises of health insurance, better safety conditions at work, maternity benefits, and a wide range of housing and transport facilities—greatly exceeding, in their scope, existing conditions, and influenced by socialist principles. In return, they were supposed not to disturb the 'industrial peace' too frequently and to submit conflicts to procedures of arbitration.[229] Here, however, the need for discipline and efficiency was stressed: trade unions were entrusted with the responsibility 'to keep the workers mobilised, disciplined, and efficient; provide for their comfort, welfare and education; secure justice; administer their several funds ... [;] suggest lines for new legislation or executive orders on problems arising from the daily experience of workers, and do all other things that concern the worker's employment efficiency, discipline and welfare'.[230] The hierarchy of priorities is clear: mobilization, discipline, efficiency; then welfare and justice—a curious role for a trade union.

Connections

The coupling of conceptions of order, progress, reason, science, discipline, held together by a general concern with the need to escape from backwardness, is evident in the debates on 'development' discussed above. The common assumption, shared among protagonists who approached 'development' through 'science', 'socialism', or 'national discipline'—approaches which were interlinked, though not congruent—was a faith in directing expertise, shared among all advocates of 'development' towards 'modern' goals.

'Expertise' was also strongly linked to the claims of technology, properly utilized in the service of national progress; whatever the wider parameters of 'development' might require, it was generally agreed that a necessary component of 'development' would be the technology to overcome backwardness. A variety of positions shared the initial premise of the need for technology within a shared project of industrialization-as-modernity. These positions tended to share a common insistence on the need for a disciplined national life and disciplined masses—which, in implying the need for standards of such discipline and the goals which such disciplined life should seek to attain, tended in turn to privilege a directing elite of 'experts' who could set such standards. 'Technology' was itself also the stable remnant of various strains of thought once the connection between the 'science' and 'socialism' strains was disrupted. 'Expertise', thus conceived, was not simply technical expertise, but also an expertise of morality and values—implicitly claiming for the class of intellectuals the central role in deciding how the 'nation' was to be made, and the consequent right to direct other classes.

'Technology' and 'expertise', then, tended to become the terms of reference which were acceptable to all concerned, unattached to questions such as the relationship between private capital and the state, the necessity of land reforms or the nationalization of industry. They became the compromise formulae for debates which were politically difficult; socialists could believe that in an imperfect world they were in some sense building socialism through technology, capitalists were not unhappy with the benefits obtained therefrom; and scientists and engineers became a new priesthood.

But this resolution of debates was not perfect. In public rhetoric, it is certainly possible to trace a strong appeal to the political neutrality of 'technical' solutions. Equally important to public standards of legitimacy were claims to socialism (loosely interpreted as conducting policies for the benefit of the people), and to the solidarity of the nation in disciplined, collective progress. These strands appeared in various arguments in differing proportions and combinations, but they together provided the language in which public debates on legitimate political action had to be phrased.

The slippages of meaning which led to the loss of the 'socialism' from the 'science and socialism' equation can be well illustrated in the writing of A.K. Shaha, scientist and 'scientific socialist', the man who claimed to have persuaded Subhas Bose, Congress President at the time, to set up the NPC, and a member of the NPC. Shaha had been one of the Soviet Union's 'technical experts' himself before returning to India in the late 1930s. Shaha, author of *Flameless Combustion Process in Industry* (in Russian) and *Lectures on Fuels and Furnaces*, and with a host of academic degrees to his name,[231] was by the time of his return a firm admirer of the Stalinist approach to 'development'; in a book written in 1948,[232] he dwelt on the similarities between Russia and India in terms of the 'psychological make-up of the nation concerned ... or so-called national culture', many of which were worked out in chapters written by his Russian wife, Tatiana Shaha-Sedina.[233] His advocacy of solutions were in terms of technology alone, the indigenization thereof through importing prototype machines, the patents of most of which had lapsed, and copying them—legally—and the suggestion that 'German experts' be imported into India.[234] There is nothing in the book about the philosophy or aims of socialism, and Soviet ideas of planning and industrialization were sought to be sold to his readers through inspiring examples— Gosplan and the role of the scientist in 'the birth of the world-known and much celebrated Stakhanov's movement whose influence upon the development of the country's Industries, Agriculture and almost ever branch of social life', will 'go down as a most glorified [sic] page in the history of the period'.[235] This was high Stalinism at its best: '"Industry and technique solve all problems," rightly said Comrade Stalin'.[236]

This was also an underlying problem of the intensity of the urge to 'development' and the deeply felt necessity that this could be achieved, in fact had been achieved quickly. The Soviet Union was a role model in this respect not merely for socialists; there were also, even in the mid-1930s, a number of socialists who were beginning to have their doubts about the moral credentials of Stalinism to speak as and for socialism. But these doubts were suppressed.[237]

There was also another problem which had to be thought through: the position of business in national life. If socialists positioned themselves as organizers of industrial and agricultural labour, at the same time as having a short-term programme for the defeat of imperialism, how did they stand on the question of indigenous capital, especially in terms of the need to have a macrosocial view of India? In practice, and certainly as regards wider perspectives of 'development', a capitalist's demand was a national demand, 'progressive' in that indigenous capitalism was preferable to both imperialism and indigenous feudalism. This was reflected in the ambivalence of socialists in attempting to distinguish between business as national industry and businessmen as capitalists. This ambiguity among left thinkers was a source of strength for the right, and for industrialists; in 1938 Jayaprakash Narayan complained to Nehru, 'We are faced today with the real danger of Indian industry being made a synonym for Indian nationalism'.[238]

This phenomenon could also be the unintended result of 'scientific' solutions. There were adherents of technological solutions who thought of themselves as socialists as well as scientists, of course; Meghnad Saha counted himself as one of them. He was a firm believer in the principle that the true emancipation of science and its use for the betterment of society was possible only under socialism. Yet, in practice, he was confined to recommending solutions to limited problems arising within the framework of colonial or indigenous capitalism. At the same time, the linkages between business and science were facilitated by intermediaries such as Visvesvaraya, who was convinced of the necessity to industrialize and less committed to questions of social organization in terms of capitalism or socialism. These linkages worked in curious ways: in Visvesvaraya's crusade for the setting up of an automobile industry in India, one of his main allies was Meghnad Saha's journal, *Science and Culture*. Visvesvaraya was also operating through the industrialist, Walchand Hirachand, whose reputation as a defender of the rights of Indian shipping had won him his nationalist credentials,[239] and negotiating with the Government of Mysore for land and a collaborative venture on the project. Saha, whose dislike for businessmen was well known, defended the project on the grounds of the need to lift India to a higher plane of technological existence.[240] Visvesvaraya, who had less qualms about businessmen, provided the principled assault on the government for its obstructive tactics, through his organisation, the All-India Manufacturers' Organization, arguing that it was short-sighted and malicious of the government to refuse to grant permission to set up an industry which would, in addition to building up Indian industry, be so useful to the war effort.[241] This strand was used strongly by Hirachand to justify the importance of his venture; it was somewhat ironic that through all this he never succeeded in learning to spell Visvesvaraya's name.[242]

The Uses of a Language of Legitimacy

The working of the elements of this language of legitimacy needs to be dealt with briefly, by way of conclusion. As the politics of the War and of approaching independence unfolded, serious divergences of opinion were papered over and held together by this language—a language which evolved as a means of sustaining communication among people who would otherwise not have had a common basis of communication.[243] By the mid-1940s, the conventions were in place; as political events speeded up, 'development' was discussed within these conventions.

Businessmen were quite successful in manipulating the practice of development planning in India. They played an extremely small role in the formulation of the ideas; when they did, it was according to terms of legitimacy already set; in order to make a valid intervention, they participated as intellectuals, or through intellectuals in their employ.[244] Yet their access to that class was limited: they were a different set of people from the intellectuals. They were confined to adapting to conceptions of development whose legitimacy had already been established, to find space for themselves in a framework which was ostensibly hostile to them.

With the coming of the Second World War, the circumstances in which discussions on 'development' had been carried out earlier changed drastically as the equations of the British–Indian economic relationship were recast, and the politics and practices of wartime production and mobilization came into play.[245] This was clearly recognized: 'the essential importance of the work of the N.P.C. has grown as the months have gone by. The coming of war and the possibility of vast changes in the political, economic, industrial and social domains, both in India and elsewhere, has made planning incumbent on us, so that we might fit in with these changes and take advantage of them for the advancement and greater well-doing of the Indian people. We have been charged with a task of the greatest significance for our country and we shall persevere with it'.[246] The Bombay Plan inserted itself into this context: with the NPC out of action, the Congress outlawed, and most of its leaders, including NPC members, in jail, another initiative was possible without seeming to invade the space of the former body.

The main objective of the Bombay Plan was obvious to the sponsors of the project: since it was reasonably clear that the government would soon be a national one, it would get round quickly to dealing with the problem of economic development. In the given anti-capitalist atmosphere worldwide,

...[t]he inevitability of a change in the direction of a socialist economy even in a country like India must now be recognised and leaders of industry would be well advised to take this into account and be prepared to make such adjustments as may meet all reasonable demands before the socialist movement assumes the form of a full fledged revolution. The most effective way in which extremer demands in future may be obviated is for industrialists to take thought while there is yet time as to the best means of incorporating whatever is sound and feasible in the socialist movement. One of the principal tasks of the Committee will therefore be to examine how far socialist demands can be accommodated without capitalism surrendering any of its essential features.[247]

This had to be done without seeming to attempt 'to vindicate capitalism as an institution but impartially to analyse capitalism with a view to determining what modifications are necessary to enable it to render the best possible service to the country'.[248]

The Bombay Plan was phrased in terms which could be said to emanate from the NPC, and was cast as the latter's successor. In this project the planners were fortunate in having on their payroll a former Congress Socialist as director of public relations ventures surrounding the Plan: Minoo Masani, having just left the Congress Socialists, combining a rather perceptive assault on Stalinism with an abandonment of his commitment to socialism and a recommendation of a closer look at Gandhian ideas in a more constructive light,[249] had just joined Tata Sons.[250] Masani was an adept publicist, succeeding even in turning the material of an economic plan into an illustrated children's book.[251] The Plan itself was largely the work of John Matthai, also an employee of Tata Sons and, it might be remembered, a former student of Sidney Webb at LSE, under whom he had written his doctoral dissertation on village government in British India—a much-cited work, which Matthai himself seems not to have considered too important to his own intellectual development.[252]

Perhaps more significant was the abandonment by the British government of the conventional imperialist defence of Empire, and dressing itself in nationalist colours. The politics of this abandonment is a story which can be told in some detail, but this must be done elsewhere; here an outline can be provided. During the War, the British Government of India began to speak of post-war reconstruction and development. With the significant shifts in the political equations as provided by the War, and the need to secure as much support from Indians as possible, the government was now concerned with appearing to be especially concerned with legitimate national aspirations, as the phrase went, in India. As a result, as with other things, post-war reconstruction had to be phrased in terms acceptable to nationalists. After the publication of the Bombay Plan, the Government of India decided to take a 'friendly' attitude to the Plan and to refrain from 'destructive criticism'.[253] The Information Department's unofficial note on the first part of the Plan, prepared in pursuance of the viceroy's request for the India Office to provide 'confidential guidance' to newspaper editors,[254] stated that, 'there can be no two opinions about the ideals aimed at in the Bombay Plan and there is no difference between Government and the authors in regard to the ultimate objectives.'[255] Soon afterwards, Sir Ardeshir Dalal, one of the authors of the Bombay Plan, was inducted into the Viceroy's Executive Council as member for the newly created Department of Planning and Development.[256]

The Second Report on Reconstruction Planning appeared to concede most of the nationalist demands on economic matters, including an interventionist and protectionist policy on the part of the government in order to encourage industrialization.[257] By this time, however, any proposal which had to be taken seriously had to appear to reject conventional imperialism, to dress itself in nationalist colours and, in addition, to concede socialism.[258] The rhetoric of the Second Report duly conceded all these things, as did the government's Statement of Industrial Policy in 1945.[259] Speakers in London at fora traditionally dominated by old India hands now spoke of the great achievements of Britain in leading India out of backwardness to both impending independence and development.[260]

In the short run, this argument cut no ice with Indians, who continued elaborately to contrast the practices of British rule during and after the War with this rhetoric of caring for Indian progress. As the formal Empire in India receded into the immediate past, however, the rhetoric of the 'Commonwealth' appeared alongside new measures to preserve the Sterling Area and the Empire Dollar Pool, and to coordinate Colonial Development, Sterling Area Development, and aid to the newly independent Dominions of India and Pakistan, the old Dominions, and the dependent colonies.[261] The rhetoric of equality and mutual aid could not altogether blunt the conflicts and hard bargaining around the rate of release of the sterling balances by Britain, but it, nonetheless, provided a context in which disagreements could be presented as details negotiated by people on the same side. As Nehru famously said of India's membership of the new Commonwealth, 'It is an agreement of free will, to be terminated by free will'.[262] Free will: this was an extraordinarily liberating phrase for a people colonized until so recently.

It was internally, among Indians, that the rhetoric of development and its constituent elements—science/technology, socialism, national discipline—had further consequences. Divergences in the nationalist consensus or, at least, the truce which had operated across divergent political tendencies as long as the British showed no signs of departing from India, began to develop serious cracks. Many on the left resented the collaboration of businessmen with British rule during the War, and accused them of subordinating national considerations to the lure of quick wartime profits. The businessmen used the stock argument of furthering the national interest through the development of national enterprise, and complained that the British had not encouraged the growth of new industries during the war; on the contrary, they had retarded it by refusing permission to begin new industries like the automobile industry, and preventing reinvestment of profits by imposing a punitive Excess Profits Tax.[263] This worked to a certain extent; at times it could work almost too well. Birla saw the war as a good opportunity to begin automobile production, just as Walchand Hirachand did. Hirachand, however, as I have mentioned, worked through his connection with Visvesvaraya and the Mysore Darbar. As the plan ran into government-led difficulties and obstructions, Birla, who had been a director in the original venture, opted out: he wrote to Hirachand that the delay was too great, Mysore was not a good location for an automobile factory (the original location was to have been Bombay), the prospects were too uncertain.

Besides, as I have told you, I am going ahead with my own project, quietly and without any fuss or propaganda. I cannot therefore conscientiously participate in your project.[264]

When, eventually, Birla clinched a deal with Lord Nuffield, he had broken the rules of nationalist solidarity, and the press rapped him on the knuckles for it. One editorial called the deal 'shady and sinister', and declared:

If the economic future of the country is to be safeguarded[,] public indignation must be roused against the sinister deal with foreign capital.
Have the Birlas entered into an *entente* with foreign capital just when the National Planning Committee has expressed itself against such a course?
It is deplorable that Birlas who are so closely associated with the Congress High Command should be involved in such a sinister and shady deal.[265]

It was definitely safer, as the Bombay Plan had done, to remain within the accepted conventions of a little socialism, technology and expertise, national solidarity and national discipline, especially if the 'socialism' was not particularly damaging. And the limits of socialism were still set by the limits of 'national' demands, as long as the British remained in India. There were enough voices critical of the Bombay Plan in both its details and its implications, notably in that it was not actually socialist. Even the Communist Party of India (CPI), in its criticism of the Bombay Plan, used as its yardstick of criticism the deviations of the Bombay Plan from the aims set out by Nehru to the NPC. The CPI's interpretation of the NPC was more consistent and without the contradictions of the NPC's debates; its point was that the Bombay Plan was not even the 'national' plan envisaged by the NPC; and its message was 'Go back to the National Planning Committee'.[266] Businessmen continued to be afraid of a left-wing wave, both within and outside the Congress, even as they learnt to utilize the language.[267] In 1950, Birla published the first of the books through which he sought to provide himself with good credentials as a nationalist and as a planner.[268]

Political discourse in India under British rule was greatly dependent on the oppositional category of imperialism for its coherence and its emotive significance. Towards 1946–7, when transfer of power was a definite reality, the Congress began to suffer a very genuine crisis of identity, and many members were worried by the decline in the quality of the Congress membership. J.B. Kripalani wrote to Dharmraj Kulkarni soon after Independence complaining of the 'traditional shoe-licking and back-biting tendencies that we see in the rank and file of the Congress today'.[269] An agonized debate on the future of the Congress began. *Purna Swaraj*, the avowed objective of the Congress, having been achieved in effect (although Dominion Status continued until 1950), a new orientation was required. As a platform geared to fighting imperialism but being united on little else, a crisis of identity was not far away. This took the form of a debate as to whether the Congress should now be a party, not a platform   questions that had been raised earlier in the context of 'groups' within the Congress, this being largely a concern of the Congress right wing which was uncomfortable with the presence of the CSP within it. Eventually, these debates led to the expulsion of the Hindu Mahasabha, a sectarian organization whose ideas went against the avowed creed of the Congress, whereas the CSP programme had nothing directly against the Congress creed. Now, with independence achieved, a new role had to be found; Gandhi's idea that the Congress should dissolve itself, its aims having been achieved, was discussed but found to be uncomfortable. Ram Manohar Lohia argued in 1947 that power could only be transferred to the Congress because no other party was capable of receiving it. The question now to be answered was 'what next?'.[270] Interestingly, the socialists seceded from the Congress at about this time.

'Development' was one theme which could provide a solution. The problem was that the parameters of such development had not been altogether resolved. Jhaverbhai Patel, a Gandhian, asked why even

Congress Governments had not adopted the Constructive Programme, especially its economic part.[271] His answer was 'lack of conviction on the part of all concerned': the government felt people were not interested and did not benefit because the progress made would be ineffective and impractical. 'The masses,' he said, 'frankly see no better prospects in the adoption of the programme. They have seen that even where people have taken all the items of this programme there is hardly any appreciable change in their life or circumstances ... By experience they have come to regard this programme as associated with some sentiment or other of Gandhiji, but hardly one which can bring them economic relief in adequate measure.'[272] Having said this, Jhaverbhai failed to resolve the dilemma he set up for his readers. The problem, he stressed, was that the Constructive Programme was not understood; mass support was essential. He regretted that there was no 'antimaterialist front' left in the Congress.[273] It is unclear as to whether he thought such a front would solve the problem, given that he did not seem to think the programme worked particularly well.

The Socialist Party, having dropped the word 'Congress' from its name, came up with its programme at this point:[274] 'The Socialist Party believes that, where democracy and civil liberties are in existence, the transition to socialism must be peaceful and through democratic means'. There was much emphasis on the 'transition period'—to 'a society in which all are workers—a classless society', in which human labour would not be subject to exploitation for private profit, and all wealth would be 'truly national or common wealth'. The transitional period, however, was essential, because '[a] socialist society is not created in a day'.[275] For the transitional period, it would have to be the Constitution that would provide: 'The Constitution should provide, through the creation of *statutory bodies*, such as Economic Councils and Planning Commissions, for the reorganisation and development of economic life on the basis of social ownership and control of the means of production'; and 'a strong federal centre', without 'any diminution of the inherent freedom and autonomy of a unit to push forward, without let or hindrance, its program [sic] of social, cultural and economic advancement in pursuance of the mandate of the people'.[276] 'There should be a Social and Economic Council at the centre as well as in the units authorised to plan economic and social measures, investigate and examine economic, social or other schemes or matters referred to it and generally advise the Governments on matters requiring special or expert information.' 'These Councils should be constituted on a functional basis and should provide representation among others to scientists, engineers, physicians and surgeons, educationists, lawyers, political and administrative experts, business, economic and agricultural experts and to trade unions, co-operatives, peasant organisations and other similar bodies.'[277] Technical solutions, administered by statutory bodies, economic councils, planning commissions would lead to technology-driven, technocrat-run socialism.

This would require a 'reform of the system of administration'. 'Clean, conscientious public service is one of the essentials of sound democracy. Every effort must, therefore, be made to root out corruption from the public services. This cannot be done unless the public also cooperates. Members of the public are today as much responsible for the rampant corruption as the corrupt public servants. Ultimate purity of national life depends upon the purity of the individual citizen.'[278] The moral rhetoric of purity takes over again. We are quite far away from socialism in this passage. Instead we have morality, moral discipline, purity, cleanliness.

This was almost the moment at which the old boundaries of 'Gandhian' and 'left' had begun to dissolve within the old Congress circles. Minoo Masani had paused briefly in his rightward drift to consider the possibilities of a democratic socialism which drew on Gandhi rather than Marx.[279] The old CSP had always had a close relationship with Gandhi, whom they greatly respected; and many Congressmen had agonized over the prospects of converting Gandhi to socialism; others had sought to separate Gandhism in terms of theoretical implications, tactics, or revolutionary potential from the limits that Gandhi put on the use of his political methods. Gandhi's insistence on public morality had always had echoes in various areas. Ram Manohar Lohia, in jail during the war, had put his mind to exploring the possibilities of Gandhism;[280] Jayaprakash Narayan was to follow in 1957.[281] The consequences of these shifts resolved themselves in the 1950s; their effect on public rhetoric was simply to reintroduce as a central element the suppressed element from the earlier debates: the anxiety regarding an 'authentic' form of politics. Now outside the Congress, 'socialism', which had been declared foreign by Gandhi, could, indigenized by the introduction of Gandhism and stylistically revamped by the ascetic figure of Vinoba Bhave roaming the countryside in search of alms in the form of land, shift the pressure of foreignness onto the communists, cast as agents of a foreign power.[282] The Congress, which continued to claim socialism as its own goal after the secession of the socialists, incorporated Gandhi as a crucial icon in its 'Community Development' schemes.[283]

With the certainties of the years of British rule—racism, exploitation, subordination—ended, a realignment of politics was necessary. This realignment was, however, conducted with a set of ideas and a language of legitimacy which was not simply the legacy of, but, in fact, better suited to, an era of direct imperialism. But that story must be told elsewhere.

Endnotes

1. Contrary to the assertion of Medha Malik Kudaisya, 'The Public Career of G.D. Birla, 1911–1947', unpublished PhD dissertation, University of Cambridge, 1992, and to a certain extent Raghabendra Chattopadhyay, 'The Idea of Planning in India, 1930–1951', unpublished PhD dissertation, Australian National University, Canberra, 1985.

2. Partha Chatterjee, *Nationalist Thought and the Colonial World: A Derivative Discourse?* (London, 1986); Raghabendra Chattopadhyay, 'The Idea of Planning in India'; Partha Chatterjee, *The Nation and its Fragments: Colonial and Postcolonial Histories* (Princeton, 1994); and others, after Antonio Gramsci, 'Notes on Italian History', *Selections from the Prison Notebooks* (London, 1971).

3. For a discussion of intellectuals and their social role, see Antonio Gramsci, *Selections from the Prison Notebooks* (London, 1971), pp. 5–18. The Gramscian debate is concerned with who leads the revolution, passive or otherwise, or movement of emancipation otherwise defined; the leadership question itself, as far as India is concerned, has been somewhat diverted by the debate over whether businessmen benefitted from the post-Independence order of things, despite the claims to socialism of nationalist politicians, or not. This chapter makes it clear that leadership of the nationalist movement was provided by the 'traditional intellectuals'—who have been influentially described in the Indian context as a separate class by Pranab Bardhan, *The Political Economy of Development in India* (Oxford, 1984).

4. The *Congress Socialist* ran several articles on non-socialist planning measures, for instance.

5. N.S. Subba Rao, *Some Aspects of Economic Planning: Sir William Meyer Lectures, University of Madras, March 1933* (Bangalore, 1935), pp. 2–3.

6. Subba Rao, *Economic Planning*, p. 10.

7. Subba Rao, *Economic Planning*, p. 13. This seems to echo quite closely some of Keynes' remarks in *The Economic Consequences of the Peace* (New York, 1920). This is not surprising as it was one of the most well received books of the post-First World War period, and would definitely have been read by Subba Rao as an economist. For the impact of the *Economic Consequences*, see D.E. Moggridge, *Maynard Keynes: An Economist's Biography* (London, 1992), pp. 319–47.

8. Subba Rao, *Economic Planning*, pp. 16–19.

9. See below.

10. S.C. Mitter, *A Recovery Plan for Bengal* (Calcutta, 1934), was dedicated to Sir John Anderson, then governor of Bengal, and based on the assumption

that the government would undertake economic planning. The book included a message of appreciation from Rabindranath Tagore commending Mitra's services to the nation, and another by Acharya P.C. Ray.

11. See M. Visvesvaraya, *Memoirs of My Working Life* (Bombay, 1951); Dietmar Rothermund, *India in the Great Depression 1929–1939* (Delhi, 1992), p. 173. Dhruv Raina, 'Visvesvaraya as Engineer-Sociologist and the Evolution of his Techno-Economic Vision', National Institute of Advanced Studies, Bangalore, published lecture, 2001.

12. M. Visvesvaraya, *Planned Economy for India* (Bangalore City, 1934), outlining a ten-year plan for India.

13. M. Visvesvaraya, *Planned Economy*, preface. See also p. 354, where he refers to two of Willingdon's speeches to the Legislative Assembly in this connection, the second in January 1934.

14. M. Visvesvaraya, *Planned Economy*, p. 366 and preface.

15. M. Visvesvaraya, *Reconstructing India* (London, 1920), pp. 284–6.

16. M. Visvesvaraya, *Nation-Building: A Five-Year Plan for the Provinces* (Bangalore City, 1937), p. 2. He also argued that the provincial governments should 'be less critical of British economic interests in the country', because the 'economic strength which can be built up with proper constructive policies, and with British co-operation, if it can be secured, is bound to be substantial'. Visvesvaraya, *Nation-Building*, p. 14. In 1944, he no longer claimed this non-confrontationist approach, and took the position that a national government was essential if anything constructive had to be done—the British government was deliberately obstructive of Indian efforts to industrialize. M. Visvesvaraya, *Reconstruction in Post-War India: A Plan of Development All Round* (Bombay, 1944), pp. 10–15, 49. This last scheme of Visvesvaraya's shared the political assumptions of the 'Bombay Plan', and backed its recommendations—for which, see below.

17. G.D. Birla's speech, at the Annual Session of FICCI, Delhi, 1 April, 1934, reprinted in Birla, *The Path to Prosperity: A Plea for Planning* (Allahabad, 1950), pp. 14–23; also quoted in Raghabendra Chattopadhyay, 'The Idea of Planning', p. 65.

18. On the Round Table group, see Frederick Madden, 'The Commonwealth, Commonwealth History, and Oxford, 1905–1971', pp. 9–24, and Deborah Lavin, 'Lionel Curtis and the Idea of the Commonwealth', both in Frederick Madden and D.K. Fieldhouse (eds), *Oxford and the Idea of the Commonwealth* (London, 1982). On Lothian's connections with the Round Table, see J.R.M. Butler, *Lord Lothian (Philip Kerr) 1882–1940* (London, 1960), pp. 35–60; for a list of Lothian's articles for *Round Table*, see pp. 323–5. On Leo Amery's contacts with the Round Table group, see William Roger Louis, *In the Name of God, Go! Leo Amery and the British Empire in the Age of Churchill* (New York, 1992), p. 37.

19. See, for instance, Birla, *In the Shadow of the Mahatma*, letter to Samuel Hoare, 14 March 1932, pp. 50–3; conversation with the Bengal Governor,

John Anderson, 10 April 1932, pp. 55–6; interview with Home Member, Sir Henry Craik, 30 June 1935, pp. 144–5; Birla to Purshotamdas Thakurdas, 16 May 1932, in Purshotamdas Thakurdas Papers, NML, File 107 Part II, f. 665.

20. See Basudev Chatterji, 'Business and Politics in the 1930s; Lancashire and the Making of the Indo-British Trade Agreement, 1939', *Modern Asian Studies*, Vol. 15, No. 3 (1985).

21. Bipan Chandra, 'Jawaharlal Nehru and the Capitalist Class, 1936', *Economic and Political Weekly*, Special Number, Vol. X, Nos. 33–35 (August 1975), p. 1319.

22. Subba Rao, *Economic Planning*, pp. 24–8.

23. Subba Rao, *Economic Planning*, pp. 37 and 39.

24. Subba Rao, *Economic Planning*, pp. 41–2; 48. Subba Rao suggested that for the success of planned economies, an increasing self-sufficiency of large areas and the 'formation of regional groups' was required, along with regulation of population sizes in both the advanced and the backward countries. 'Only in these ways will the element of *conflict between the White and the Coloured races,* whether the economic life of the communities is planned or unplanned, be eliminated'. Subba Rao, *Economic Planning*, pp. 51–2. Emphasis mine.

25. Quoted in Partha Chatterjee, *Nationalist Thought and the Colonial World: A Derivative Discourse?* (London, 1986), p. 158; and in Partha Chatterjee, *The Nation and its Fragments: Colonial and Postcolonial Histories* (Princeton, 1993), p. 202.

26. Chairman's [Nehru's] note of 1 May 1940 to the NPC, in K.T. Shah (ed.), *Report: National Planning Committee* (Bombay, June 1949), [hereafter, *NPC Report*], p. 120.

27. *National Herald*, 5 October 1938.

28. *NPC Report*, p. 10.

29. The members of the NPC were Nehru (Chairman), Sir M. Visvesvaraya, Sir Purshotamdas Thakurdas, Meghnad Saha, A.D. Shroff, K.T. Shah (Honorary General Secretary), A.K. Shaha, Nazir Ahmad (of the Technological Laboratory, Bombay), V.S. Dubey (of the Benares Hindu University), Ambalal Sarabhai, J.C. Ghosh (Director, Indian Institute of Science, Bangalore), Radhakamal Mukerjee (Lucknow University), and the labour leader, N.M. Joshi. Copy of membership list in Walchand Hirachand Archives, File No 48, Part I, f. 139, NML.

30. *NPC Report*, p. 119, Nehru's note of 1 May 1940.

31. See *NPC Report*, pp. 35–7: Chairman's Note on Congress Policy, 21 December 1938.

32. Nehru to K.T. Shah, 13 May 1939, quoted in Raghabendra Chattopadhyay, 'The Idea of Planning', p. 106.

33. See Shah, *National Planning, Principles and Administration* (Bombay, 1948).

34. This impression is borne out by a study of the ways in which the committees worked; and comes across from the above statement itself: 'too strong to be

pushed out', implying that otherwise they might have been 'pushed out'. See also the reports of the sub-committees, *National Planning Committee* series, published between 1946 and 1949 by Vora & Co, Bombay.

35. It was agreed that 'all machinery required in India should be made in India except in very special cases where this may not be considered absolutely necessary and economically feasible'. Sub-Committee on Engineering Industries including Transport Industries: *NPC Report*, p. 134.
36. Manufacturing Industries Sub-Committee, *NPC Report*, p. 139.
37. Sub-Committee on Engineering Industries including Transport Industries: *NPC Report*, pp. 135–6.
38. Interim Report: Power and Fuel Sub-Committee, *NPC Report*, pp. 167–71.
39. Land Policy, NPC Sub-Committee, *NPC Report*, pp. 208–10.
40. Sub-Committee on Labour, *NPC Report*, pp. 153–7.
41. *NPC Report*, p. 102: Nehru's address, 12 February 1940.
42. *NPC Report*, pp. 225–30.
43. *NPC Report*, p. 10.
44. The distinction between the 'moderate' and 'Congress' wings of Indian big business follows that of Claude Markovits, *Indian Business and Nationalist Politics*; see his Introduction.
45. Sir P. Thakurdas, J.R.D. Tata, G.D. Birla, Sir Ardeshir Dalal, Sir Shri Ram, Kasturbhai Lalbhai, A.D. Shroff, and John Matthai, *A Brief Memorandum Outlining a Plan of Economic Development for India* (Bombay, January 1944) (hereafter, 'Bombay Plan'), Introduction.
46. 'Bombay Plan', Introduction.
47. The Cripps Mission's formula had been post-War Dominion status with the right of secession for individual provinces, regions or groups, but some sort of centre to which the constituent units adhered was still envisaged. This possibility was still being discussed as late as 1947. See Ayesha Jalal, *The Sole Spokesman: Jinnah, the Muslim League and the Demand for Pakistan* (Cambridge, 1985), pp. 70–1, 77–81, 252–4.
48. 'Bombay Plan', pp 1–6.
49. 'Bombay Plan', pp. 7–20.
50. 'Bombay Plan', p. 25.
51. 'Bombay Plan', p. 31.
52. 'Bombay Plan', pp. 44–50.
53. Sir P. Thakurdas, J.R.D. Tata, G.D. Birla, Sir Shri Ram, Kasturbhai Lalbhai, A.D. Shroff, and John Matthai, *A Plan of Economic Development for India, Part II: Distribution: Role of the State* (Bombay, December 1944) (hereafter, 'Bombay Plan II')—this was written minus Sir Ardeshir Dalal, who had by this time been appointed Member for Planning and Development in the Viceroy's Executive Council.
54. 'Bombay Plan II', pp. 1–5.
55. 'Bombay Plan II', pp. 20–2.
56. 'Bombay Plan II', p. 19.

57. 'Bombay Plan II', pp. 23–5.
58. 'Bombay Plan II', pp. 27–32.
59. 'Bombay Plan II', pp. 15–6.
60. Government of India, Planning and Development Department, *Second Report on Reconstruction Planning* (New Delhi, 1944).
61. Raghabendra Chattopadhyay, 'The Idea of Planning'; C.A. Bayly, 'Returning the British to South Asian History: The Limits of Colonial Hegemony', *South Asia*, Vol. XVII, No. 2 (1994), p. 17.
62. *National Herald*, 12 October 1938.
63. Subhas Chandra Bose, *Amrita Bazar Patrika*, 24 December 1938, quoted in Bidyut Chakrabarty, 'Jawaharlal Nehru and Planning, 1938–41: India at the Crossroads' Modern Asian Studies, Vol. 26, No. 2 (1992), p. 279.
64. The Bengal government, run at the time by a Krishak Praja Party–Muslim League coalition, sent a representative, Abdul Rahman Siddiqui: *NPC 2*, p. 3. For the Krishak Praja Party, and the nature of relations between it and the Muslim League, see Shila Sen, *Muslim Politics in Bengal 1937–1947* (New Delhi, 1976).
65. Nehru's statement to the Press, May 15, 1940, *NPC 2*, p 74.
66. Chairman's [Nehru's] Statement to the Press, 1 July 1940, *NPC 3*, p. 37.
67. *NPC Report*, p. 10.
68. The 1935 Government of India Act extended the franchise from 6.5 million property-owning adults to 30 million. In practice far fewer voted. Separate electorates and reserved seats also complicated matters. See Sumit Sarkar, *Modern India*, pp. 336–7; Reginald Coupland, *India: A Re-Statement* (London, 1945), pp. 141–6.
69. See Chapter 2 of this volume.
70. As I have mentioned earlier, Indian businessmen were generally cast as self-interested and rather cynical operators, in both imperialist and socialist discourse; they were, according to the terms of the discourse, illegitimate participants in arguments about what was good for the 'nation'. This is a similar point to that made by Birla himself, in his oft-quoted remark about businessmen needing to rely on the right wing of the Congress to represent them, because it looked 'crude' for businessmen to represent themselves (see Bipan Chandra, 'Jawaharlal Nehru and the Capitalist Class, 1936', p. 1319). Yet some of their activities could be presented as legitimate 'national' enterprise: I will return to this ambiguity below.
71. This point was made by Amiya Bagchi, 'Private Investment and Partial Planning in India', unpublished PhD dissertation, University of Cambridge, 1963—plans were wreckable through the space left for private industry, who could control production decisions better than the government could.
72. See Quentin Skinner, 'Language and Social Change', in James Tully (ed.), *Meaning and Context: Quentin Skinner and his Critics* (Cambridge, 1988), p. 132.
73. Purshotamdas Thakurdas Papers, NML, File 291 Part II: Post-War Economic Development Committee, ff. 265–6.

74. 'Ourselves', in the inaugural issue of the *Congress Socialist*, Saturday, 29 September 1934, p. 2. (The CSP was founded in May 1934).

75. Narendra Dev, 'The Task Before Us', *Congress Socialist*, Vol. I, No. 1, Saturday, 29 September 1934, pp. 2–3.

76. See Jayaprakash Narayan's statement of objectives and strategy on behalf of the CSP, published in a book aimed at Congress workers: Jayaprakash Narayan, *Why Socialism?* (Benares, 1936).

77. Narayan, *Why Socialism?* pp. 154–60.

78. Narayan, *Why Socialism?* pp. 136, 143.

79. Narayan, *Why Socialism?* pp. 28–9; 32–62.

80. Amarendra Prasad Mitra, 'The Communal Problem and the National Movement', *Congress Socialist*, Vol. I, No. 1, Saturday, 29 September 1934, p. 6. He characterized the Congress as a 'Hindu bourgeois party'; such unities as were stressed by Congress did not exist as common between Hindus and Muslims, alienating the Muslim bourgeoisie, and leading to 'Muslim national idealism': pp. 6–7.

81. See Ashit Mukerjea, 'Social Democracy = Fascism', *Congress Socialist*, Saturday, 29 September 1934, pp. 10–11. The similarity is illustrated by the 'crossovers' of Oswald Mosley, and earlier Benito Mussolini; also by the Cripps tendency in the British Labour Party. Mukerjea speaks of 'Social Democratic betrayal and treachery, particularly from 1914 onwards', and calls it 'the pathmaker for the advance of Fascism and Imperialist War'.

82. Letter to the editor from Asit Mukerjea, Calcutta, 4 October 1934, *Congress Socialist*, 6 October 1934, p. 16.

83. Letter to the editor from Asit Mukerjea, Calcutta, 4 October 1934, *Congress Socialist*, 6 October 1934, p. 16.

84. Amarendra Prasad Mitra, 'The Communal Problem and the National Movement', *Congress Socialist*, Saturday 29 September 1934, p 7

85. *Congress Socialist*, 10 March 1935, p. 10. Fascism was not considered a great danger in India, certainly by the communists. Although certain people were influenced by its ideas, the CPI's interpretation of the Comintern's 'United Front' policy was as a united front against imperialism rather than fascism, which it stated was unimportant in India. In this, as I have mentioned, they had been anticipated by the CSP.

86. Nehru's closeness to Marxism at this time has been much commented upon. In October 1933 appeared his three articles collectively called *Whither India?*, thereafter, published in pamphlet form, which was seen by many at the time as his manifesto. Reprinted in S. Gopal (ed.), *Selected Works of Jawaharlal Nehru*, Vol. 6 (Delhi, 1974), pp 1–16. This sought to answer the vexing question of what was to come after independence—a question which exercised a great many people at the time. These questions were often put directly to Nehru, and the questions are often more revealing than the answers he sought to provide.

87. Partha Chatterjee, *Nationalist Thought*, chapter five.

88. Hiren Mukerjee, *The Gentle Colossus* (Calcutta, 1964; new edition Delhi, 1986), pp. 222–3.
89. 'Why I am a Congress Socialist'—one of a series of articles of the same title—*Congress Socialist*, 10 March 1935, pp. 5–6. It is interesting that he speaks of the communists in terms of tolerance, not partnership. This foreshadowed later debates in the CSP when it was felt that the communists were taking over the CSP (the Communist Party, then outlawed, was operating through the CSP as members). This caused some consternation as far as some members of the CSP were concerned; the key arguments were that communists were loyal to the Soviet Union at the expense of Indian interests, or for those who were not Marxists such as Masani, the feeling that they were being marginalized in their own party. See Minoo Masani, *Bliss Was It in That Dawn...* (New Delhi, 1977), pp. 89–123.
90. See, for instance, Jawaharlal Nehru, *An Autobiography* (this edition New Delhi, 1982; first edition London, 1936), p. 361: 'I had long been drawn to socialism and communism, and Russia had appealed to me. Much in Soviet Russia I dislike—the ruthless suppression of all contrary opinion, the wholesale regimentation, the unnecessary violence (as I thought) in carrying out various policies. But there was no lack of violence and suppression in the capitalist world, and I realised more and more how the very basis of our acquisitive society and property was violence'.
91. For landmarks in Masani's rightward drift, see M.R. Masani, *Socialism Reconsidered* (Bombay, 1944); and his own account in M.R. Masani, *Against the Tide* (New Delhi, 1981).
92. Minoo Masani, *Bliss Was It in That Dawn...*, p. 11.
93. Masani, *Bliss Was It in That Dawn...*, pp. 19–25. This self-drawn intellectual genealogy of CSP members almost adds credence to the claim, often made by Gandhians, that socialism was outside the framework of 'Eastern' thought, barring the appearance of Gandhi himself in the genealogy—unless it is remembered that Gandhi's own intellectual genealogy was not very 'Eastern', though he did not choose to highlight it: see Chapter 4 of this book. Once again, this draws attention to the misphrasing of the question of ideological influences in terms of 'Western' and 'Eastern'; it is the transpositions and crossovers across those barriers, as ideas are applied in different contexts, which need to be studied.
94. See Chapter 2 of this book.
95. When he entered the political scene in the 1920s, and through his personal battles with his father, Motilal Nehru, he found an alternative father figure in Gandhi, who not only nurtured the young Jawaharlal politically, but encouraged him to assert his independence against his father. For a good assessment of Nehru's tendency to accept the position advocated by the Congress right due to his adoption of Gandhi as a father figure, see Michael Brecher, *Nehru: A Political Biography* (London, 1959), pp. 2–3.
96. This position is stated most clearly and coherently in Jayaprakash Narayan,

Why Socialism? The theme appears regularly in the pages of the *Congress Socialist*, the weekly organ of the CSP.

97. Until the Comintern changed its line to introduce the United Front line, the communists stayed aloof from this idea. Thereafter, the CPI being illegal, (banned in consequence of the Meerut Conspiracy Case), communists often operated from within the CSP, which became an umbrella organization of the left, though not without tensions.

98. In 1933, Nehru published *Whither India?*, which was his long-awaited statement of his position, appearing before the formation of the CSP, serialized in the press, including the British-controlled *Statesman* of Calcutta. In it he outlined, in basic terms, his approach to politics and economics, and what he envisaged to be the desired direction of a future India. He received several calls for clarifications after this. Nehru replied to the effect that he wanted to keep the public statement simple and non-academic but was willing to discuss things in more detail later. See Gopal (ed.), *The Selected Works of Jawaharlal Nehru*, Vol. 6, pp. 17–32.

99. Abdur Rahim to Nehru, 26 October 33, JNP, NML, Vol. 1, f. 24

100. Jayaprakash Narayan, *Why Socialism?*, pp. 19–21. This section was published in the *Congress Socialist* of 24 February 1935, pp. 5–8, prior to the publication of the book, under the title 'What Must Pandit Jawaharlal Do?'.

101. Dover to Nehru, 'Sunday' (1936), JNP, NML, Vol. 18, f. 123.

102. He recommended that Nehru read George Padmore's *How Britain Rules the Blacks*—Dover to Nehru, 16 May 36, JNP, NML, Vol. 18, f. 115. Also, had Nehru read (1) Stalin's *Marxism and the Colonial Question*: 'This book, with its very intimate meaning for us, should be read by every Congressman'. (2) Dimanstein's *The Soviet State and the Solution of Problems of Nationality*; (3) Palme Dutt and Bradley's *Indian Politics*; (4) Wang Wing's *The Revolutionary Movement in the Colonial Countries*; (5) Jackson's *Dialectics: The Logic of Marxism*: 'Like Stalin's, a "basic" book of great importance to us...'. Dover said he would try to return to India in winter— '... when I do come I promise wholehearted service, apart from the creation of a Eurasian alliance in the anti-imperialist struggle' (Dover was a Eurasian, or an 'Anglo-Indian'). Dover to Nehru, 18 May (1936?), JNP, NML, Vol. 18, ff. 125–7.

103. Babu Bhagavandas to Nehru, 16 September 33, JNP, NML, Vol. 7, f. 251.

104. Nehru to Babu Bhagavandas, 23 September 1933, JNP, NML, Vol. 7, ff. 259–61.

105. Nehru to Babu Bhagavandas, 23 Septemeber 1933, JNP, NML, Vol. 7, ff. 263–5. Emphasis mine.

106. This principle was nominated as the unifying factor which defined the ICS ethos in Philip Mason's paean for British rule in India, his two-volume study of *The Men Who Ruled India* (London, 1965), written under the pseudonym Philip Woodruff.

107. It might be added that this was also quite far from what many, both at the time

and retrospectively, would be willing to call a 'Marxist view' of history, unless it be seen as a rather caricatured simplification of the idea of the Bolshevik 'vanguard', as expressed in Stalin's leadership cult.

108. Jayaprakash Narayan to Jawaharlal Nehru, Calicut, 23 November 1938, f. 58, JNP, NML, Vol. 54. Narayan had been particularly close to Nehru, and addressed him as 'bhai' (brother).

109. Narayan moved on in the 1950s, coming close to the Gandhians and to Vinoba Bhave. See below.

110. As Nehru declared, in his message to the Indian Science Congress' Silver Jubilee Session, 'Life is one organic whole and it cannot be separated into watertight compartments'. *Science and Culture,* Vol. III, No. 7, January 1938, p. 350.

111. Syed Mahmud to JN, 5 May 1935, JNP, NML, Vol. 97, ff. 141–2.

112. Syed Mahmud to JN, 30 November 23, JNP, NML, Vol. 97, f. 128.

113. George Joseph to Nehru, 18 July 1936, JNP, NML, Vol. 37, ff. 57–8.

114. Nehru to George Joseph, 7 August 1936, JNP, NML, Vol. 37, f. 59.

115. He usually expressed his opposition to fascism in terms of grounds more substantive than its vulgarity. This was usually in terms of the political realities of fascist depredations—Abyssinia, Spain—see his newspaper articles for *National Herald,* copies in JNP, NML, Writings and Speeches: National Herald Editorials, Sl Nos. 10–20.

116. Nehru to Amiya Chakravarty, 4 March 1936, Montreaux, JNP, NML, Vol. 11, f. 189.

117. von Studnitz to Nehru, 25 June 1938, JNP, NML, Vol 97, ff. 28–30.

118. von Studnitz to Nehru, 5 September 1938, JNP, NML, Vol. 97, ff. 31–2. This was during the Czechoslovak crisis.

119. On the Tripura crisis, from two points of view, see Subhas Chandra Bose to Jawaharlal Nehru, 28 March 1939, reprinted in Sisir Kumar Bose and Sugata Bose (eds), *The Essential Writings of Netaji Subhas Chandra Bose* (Delhi, 1997), pp. 237–45, and Nehru to Bose, 3 April 1939, JNP, NML, Vol. 9, ff. 193–211, also reprinted in Sisir Kumar Bose and Sugata Bose (eds), *Netaji Collected Works, Volume 9: Congress President: Speeches, Articles and Letters, January 1938–May 1939* (Delhi, 1995), pp. 217–32. Bose's long correspondence with Gandhi on the subject of the 'stalemate' (Bose to Gandhi, 25 March 1939, in *Netaji Collected Works 9,* p. 127) is also reprinted in this volume (pp. 126–82, letters and telegrams dated 24 March 1939–6 May 1939). An account is also provided in Reba Som, *Differences Within Consensus: The Left and Right in the Congress, 1929–1939* (London, 1995), pp. 240–60. Whether Bose was any more stable as a leftist than Nehru is, of course, debatable, given his early attraction to fascism and his later attempts to achieve Indian independence through the assistance of the Axis powers. In 1937, he had, however, specifically rejected fascism in an interview with Rajani Palme Dutt of the CPGB, claiming that his initial attraction for fascism was due to his not having known enough about it. See below. For a critical,

though ultimately sympathetic, account, which absolves Subhas Bose of being a fascist despite his Second World War exploits, on the grounds of naivete and ignorance, see Gautam Chattopadhyay, *Subhas Chandra Bose and the Indian Communist Movement* (Calcutta, 1975). But see, also, below, on the subject of national discipline.

120. Nehru to Subhas Bose, 3 April 1939, JNP, NML, Vol. 9, f. 211.
121. Nehru to Subhas Wedgwood, 23 April 1941, JNP, NML, Vol. 103, f. 31.
122. Nehru to Wedgwood, 23 April 1941, JNP, NML, Vol. 103, f. 32.
123. Nehru to Wedgwood, 23 April 1941, JNP, NML, Vol. 103, f. 32.
124. Nehru to Wedgwood, 23 April 1941, JNP, NML, Vol. 103, f. 33.
125. Nehru to Wedgwood, 21 November 41, JNP, NML, Vol. 103, f. 34.
126. Gandhi to Nehru, 21 January 1934, JNP, NML, Vol. 24, ff. 2–3.
127. Gandhi to Agatha Harrison, 30 April 1936, copy in JNP, NML, Vol. 24, f. 55. Emphasis mine. What both Gandhi and Nehru did have in common, along with a great many other Indian intellectuals and politicians of the time, was the ability to project their own anxieties and uncertainties onto the 'nation' as a whole, to make virtues of these anxieties and, therefore, to come to prescriptive conclusions for the nation on the basis of these anxieties. The anxieties were, to some extent, shared, though with clear variations in different fundamental social groups. Their resolution, through these personal projections by national leaders, were channelled in particular directions, ruling out some other resolutions.
128. See Stephen Howe, *Anticolonialism in British Politics: The Left and the End of Empire 1918–1964* (Oxford, 1993). Howe points out that many of the strands of anti-colonial politics in Britain originated in romantic identification with downtrodden peoples rather than in critiques of imperialism or capitalism (p. 34).
129. See Bipan Chandra, *The Rise and Growth of Economic Nationalism in India: Economic Policies of Indian National Leadership, 1880–1905* (fifth edition, New Delhi, 1991; first published New Delhi, 1966), pp. 76–81.
130. For instance, the *Modern Review* and the *Prabashi* in Bengal.
131. One of the stronger advocates of 'modern' solutions to problems of Indian development was the journal *Science and Culture*, which called itself 'A Monthly Journal of Natural and Cultural Sciences', published from Calcutta, founded and edited by Meghnad Saha. Scientists subscribed to it, (see Bhatnagar to Saha, 12 December 1935, Meghnad Saha Papers, NML, correspondence with S.S. Bhatnagar); but among its supporters could be ranked other middle-class intellectuals; Shyama Prasad Mookerjee wrote to Saha in 1936, 'It will be a great pity if Science and Culture has to be discontinued for want of funds and Bengali enterprise. We must devise a way out of this possibility'. S.P. Mookerjee to Saha, 28 October 1936, Meghnad Saha Papers, NML, correspondence with S.P. Mookerjee.
132. Ravindra Chandra Ray, *Colonial Economy: Nationalists' Response* (Varanasi, 1996), p. 74. See also *National Planning Committee: Power and Fuel*

(Bombay, 1947); *National Planning Committee: River Training and Irrigation* (Bombay, 1947).

133. Mahalanobis' official biographer describes the three as co-authors of a book on relativity: see Ashok Rudra, *Prasanta Chandra Mahalanobis: A Biography* (Delhi, 1996), p. 199. This is not quite accurate: it was a book of translations of papers from the original German, the translations having been done by Saha and Bose, with Mahalanobis providing a 'historical introduction'. M.N. Saha and S.N. Bose (transl), *The Principle of Relativity: Original Papers by A. Einstein and H. Minkovski. With a Historical Introduction by PC Mahalanobis* (Calcutta, 1920). (This is also the place to acknowledge the inadvertent factual error—reflecting the hazards of secondary sources—in my review article: Benjamin Zachariah, 'The Development of Professor Mahalanobis', *Economy and Society*, Vol. 26, No. 3 (August 1997), p. 438, in which I cite Rudra's error. I owe the correction to former students of P.C. Mahalanobis in his *avatar* as a physics teacher, who cast doubts on Mahalanobis' capacity to understand Einstein's work on relativity.)

134. A.C. Mukhopadhyay, 'A Brief Account of PCM's Work on Meteorology and Flood Control and Irrigation', in Ashok Rudra, *Prasanta Chandra Mahalanobis: A Biography*, p . 160.

135. Raghabendra Chattopadhyay, 'The Idea of Planning', p. 118.

136. See M. Visvesvaraya, *Reconstructing India* (London, 1920); *Planned Economy for India* (Bangalore City, 1934); *Memoirs of My Working Life* (Bombay, 1951); see also the extensive press clippings of matters related to his career kept by Visvesvaraya, in the Visvesvaraya Papers, microfilm, NML.

137. Although the importance of technology was strongly argued by *Science and Culture*—as well as by Visvesvaraya in all his speeches and writings (see also Visvesvaraya Papers, NML, microfilm)—there was also a sense that the connection between science and technology or industrial research could be pushed to extreme lengths. In 1940 Meghnad Saha wrote to his fellow scientist S.S. Bhatnagar, in connection with the proposed Scientific and Industrial Research Board to be set up by the government, that though such a board was necessary and, in fact, long overdue, it was necessary to make a distinction between scientific research and industrial research to avoid disappointing the public or inviting government accusations of making money. He cited the experience of the Indian Institute of Science, Bangalore, as an example, stated that many industries that needed setting up needed protection, not research, and added, 'I, as a scientific man [sic], do not wish to take upon myself the responsibility for which I am not fitted. Let it be thrown on the political and industrial leaders'. Saha to Bhatnagar, 29 March 1940, Meghnad Saha Papers, NML, correspondence with S.S. Bhatnagar, f. 7. Saha made the same point in writing to the government: Saha to Ramaswami Mudaliar, 20 March 1940, Meghnad Saha Papers, NML, correspondence with Ramaswami Mudaliar, ff. 7–11.

138. S. Gopal, *Jawaharlal Nehru: A Biography*, Vol. 1 (London, 1975).

139. G.D. Overstreet and M. Windmiller, *Communism in India* (Berkeley, 1959), p. 156.

140. Masani, *Bliss Was It in That Dawn...*, pp. 19–36.

141. *Science and Culture*, Vol. IV, No. 5 (November 1938), editorial, p. 256. Figures based on Sir M. Visvesvaraya's statistics—this editorial examines Visvesvaraya's two pamphlets, *Proposals for an Automobile Factory in Bombay*, Note I and Note II (Confidential), (Bangalore, 1938); the quote above is a paraphrase of Visvesvaraya. The editorial continues, 'We learn further from these pamphlets that 'Cheap Cars for All' is the latest watchword in Nazi Germany, which is contemplating the introduction of a People's Car, for the use of people with a monthly income of Rs 175/-p.m....'.

142. The distinction between 'culture' and 'civilisation' is often unclear or blurred in non-specialized modern usage. See Raymond Williams, *Keywords*, pp. 59–60, 90–93.

143. *Science and Culture*, IV, No. 1 (July 1938), editorial, 'The Next Twentyfive [sic] Years of Science in India', p. 2

144. *Science and Culture,* Vol. III, No. 7 (January 1938), Nehru's message to the Indian Science Congress' Silver Jubilee Session, p. 350.

145. Such views were also commonly expressed in the *Congress Socialist*. For some in the CSP, 'scientific socialist' politics implied that political practice as well as political understanding was a 'science' (although such rigid interpretations of 'socialism' were not universal).

146. *Science and Culture*, Vol. IV, No. 4, October 1938, editorial on the Wardha primary education scheme, p. 200.

147. Nehru to Ahmed Bashir, 26 December 1939. JNP, NML, Vol. 1, f. 87.

148. See Chapter 4 of this volume.

149. Nehru, *The Discovery of India* (Calcutta, 1946).

150. See Chapter 3 of this volume.

151. *Science and Culture*, Vol. IV, No. 10 (April 1939), editorial, p. 535.

152. Frantz Fanon made this argument about the tension between a (universal) metropolitan education and the inescapable particularities of 'negritude'—see Frantz Fanon, *Black Skin, White Masks* (London, 1980). The argument about tension between the Jew as a practitioner of science, claiming inclusion within the Christian/Aryan environment, and the Jew as Jew despite this claim, both excluded and excluding himself, has also been made: see, for instance, Sander L. Gilman, *Freud, Race and Gender* (Princeton, 1993). These questions are resolved in different ways by different commentators thereon; but this is not the place for me to enter into a discussion on the relative merits of these resolutions.

153. On the claims of imperialism to science, the use of apparently scientific arguments in the justification of imperialism, or the tendency of science to act as, and be seen as, an agent of imperialism, much has been written. For the Indian case, and on the debates surrounding the relevance and possibilities of an indigenized science, see, for instance, Deepak Kumar (ed.), *Science and*

Empire: Essays in the Indian Context (1700–1947) (Delhi, 1991); Deepak Kumar, *Science and the Raj*; Dhruv Raina and S. Irfan Habib, 'Bhadralok Perceptions of Science, Technology and Cultural Nationalism', *Indian Economic and Social History Review*, Vol. 32, No. 1 (1995); Dhruv Raina and S. Irfan Habib, 'The Unfolding of an Engagement: The Dawn on Science, Technical Education and Industrialisation', *Studies in History*, Vol. 9, No. 1, (January–June 1993), p. 15. See, in particular, Deepak Kumar's discussion of the contours of 'colonial science' as described by other writers, *Science and the Raj*, pp. 1–15.

154. Ashis Nandy puts it strongly: '... modern science which, though overtly universal, had come to acquire an essentially western culture over the previous three hundred years'; in a colonial society such associations 'were bound to make science a symbol of western intrusion': Ashis Nandy, *Alternative Sciences: Creativity and Authenticity in Two Indian Scientists* (Delhi, 1980; second editon, Delhi, 1995), p. 19. This is, of course, too strong a formulation, reflecting Nandy's own agreement with strongly 'culturalist' positions. (An interesting shift in meaning of the term 'culturalist' has come about over the last fifteen or so years; from being derogatorily applied to deviant Marxists to being happily accepted by defenders of essentialized 'traditions'.)

155. In this connection, see the debates surrounding the establishment of the Hindu College in Calcutta, and subsequently of the Presidency College of Bengal, and the strong emphasis on the teaching of science therein; for the highlighting of this argument, see Benjamin Zachariah, Subhas Ranjan Chakraborti, and Rajat Kanta Ray, 'Presidency College, Calcutta: an Unfinished History', in Mushirul Hasan (ed.), *Knowledge, Power and Politics: Educational Institutions in India* (New Delhi, 1998); see, especially, my sections on the Hindu College and on the relevance of the teaching of science.

156. See Ashis Nandy, *Alternative Sciences*; Sumit Sarkar, *The Swadeshi Movement in Bengal, 1903–1908* (Calcutta, 1973); Raina and Habib, 'Bhadralok Perceptions...'; Raina and Habib, 'The Unfolding of an Engagement'.

157. Raina and Habib, 'Bhadralok Perceptions...', pp. 106, 114.

158. P.C. Ray was an alumnus of Presidency College, Calcutta, and joined the staff of its chemistry department after returning from Edinburgh with a DSc in 1889. He established a strong tradition of research in chemistry at the college (during the period 1889–1916, 77 original research papers were published by him and his co-workers). He founded the Bengal Chemicals Swadeshi Works, which became celebrated in the period of the Swadeshi Movement as an exemplar of the possibilities of Indian entrepreneurship. Prafulla Chandra Ray, *Life and Experiences of a Bengali Chemist* (Calcutta, 1932); Sumit Sarkar, *The Swadeshi Movement in Bengal 1903–1905* (New Delhi, 1973), pp. 95, 125, 498–9; Zachariah, Chakraborti, and Ray, 'Presidency College, Calcutta: an Unfinished History', p. 332.

159. Prafulla Chandra Ray, *The History of Hindu Chemistry* (two volumes, 1902 and 1908). The influence of P.C. Ray was acknowledged by S.S. Bhatnagar in a letter to Meghnad Saha: 'the guiding spirit invisibly working within me has been Sir P. C. Ray.' He asks Saha to convey this to Ray—'I think it will please him to know that at least one amongst his chemical grand-children confesses where the source of inspiration lies hidden'. Bhatnagar to Saha, 13 October 1934, from University Chemical Laboratories, Lahore, Meghnad Saha Papers, NML, correspondence with S.S. Bhatnagar, f. 1.

160. Mahalanobis' own acknowledgement of this debt is cited by his biographer: Ashok Rudra, *Prasanta Chandra Mahalanobis: A Biography* (Delhi, 1996), pp. 127–8.

161. Brajendranath Seal, *The Positive Sciences of the Ancient Hindus* (London, 1915).

162. P.C. Ray, *Life and Experiences of a Bengali Chemist*, p. 163.

163. P.C. Ray, *Life and Experiences of a Bengali Chemist*, pp. 361, 387–8, 392.

164. P.C. Ray, *Life and Experiences of a Bengali Chemist*, pp. 140–2, 147. 'Macaulay's famous minute (1835) was in no small measure responsible for the intellectual renaissance of India, however much neo-Hindu revivalists may take offense at some of the passages in it' (p. 142). And (p. 147) where science should have flourished as a result of the 'ferment all around', '[u]nfortunately, the Hindu intellect, lying dormant and fallow for ages, was overgrown with rank weeds and brambles'.

165. P.C. Ray, *Life and Experiences of a Bengali Chemist*, Vol. II (Calcutta, 1935), pp. 333–43.

166. See P.C. Ray, *Life and Experiences of a Bengali Chemist*, p. 259.

167. 'On the 'Hinduness' of science and civilisation in India, and their decline from the time of the 'Muslim conquest', see P.N. Bose, *A History of Hindu Civilisation During British Rule*, Vol. 2 (Calcutta, 1894), and Vol. 3 (Calcutta, 1896); Benoy Sarkar, *Hindu Achievements in Exact Science* (New York, 1918), cited in Deepak Kumar, *Science and the Raj*, pp. 209–12. Such arguments are often dismissed as 'Hindu revivalist'; although they often were, the dismissiveness is unwarranted and retards a closer understanding of why they were so—they would merit closer attention on the grounds that they were often not directly or instrumentally sectarian or anti-Muslim; and they drew strongly on conventions of metropolitan academic writing in their references to and mixing of the categories of 'Hindu' and 'Aryan'—see, for instance, P.N. Bose, *A History of Hindu Civilisation During British Rule*, Vol. 1 (Calcutta, 1894), p. 20; Vol. 2, pp. 1–5. See also below, on race and national discipline.

168. It is impossible to do justice to P.C. Ray's work in a short summary; but see, for instance, his critical remarks on the close links of Hindu chemistry with medicine on the one hand, and with magic on the other: P.C. Ray, *History of Hindu Chemistry*, Vol. 1, p. (v). Ray's avoidance of this formula is particularly significant in that he was close to both Benoy Sarkar and P.N.

Bose: Bose had been his colleague at Presidency College (he was in the geology department) and Benoy Sarkar was prominent in the Swadeshi Movement, of which Ray's company, Bengal Chemicals, was an inspirational institution. See Deepak Kumar, *Science and the Raj*, pp. 209–11, 213.

169. On the subject of such discrimination see PC Ray, *Life and Experiences of a Bengali Chemist*, pp. 79–82.

170. Cited above: *Science and Culture* Vol. IV, No. 10 (April 1939), p. 535.

171. See, for instance, Visvesvaraya, *Nation Building: A Five-Year Plan for the Provinces*.

172. Gyan Chand, *Essentials of Federal Finance* (Oxford University Press, 1930), p. 1. Gyan Chand's footnotes are full of Harold Laski, G.D.H. Cole and H.G. Wells, as well as British constitutionalists like Bryce and Dicey.

173. Gyan Chand, *Essentials of Federal Finance*, pp. 1–5.

174. Among Visvesvaraya's publications were *Reconstructing India* (London, 1920); *Rural Reconstruction in India: An Outline of a Scheme* (Bangalore City, 1931); *Planned Economy for India* (Bangalore City, 1934); *Unemployment in India: its Causes and Cure* (Bangalore City, 1932; second edition 1935)—originating in an address delivered before the University Union, Bangalore, 8 September 1932; *District Development Scheme: Economic Progress by Forced Marches* (Bangalore City, 1939); *Reconstruction in Post-War India: A Plan of Development All Round* (Bombay, 1944).

175. See, also, Amiya Kumar Bagchi, *Private Investment in India*, on the attractiveness of the native states for Indian private investors. The Mysore goverment undertook several joint projects with Indian capitalists.

176. Biographical details are taken from M. Visvesvaraya, *Memoirs of My Working Life* (Bombay, 1951); Y.G. Krishnamurti, *Sir M. Visvesvaraya: A Study* (Bombay, 1941); V. Sitaramiah, *M. Visvesvaraya* (New Delhi, 1971); A.P. Srinivasamurthy, *Sir M. Visvesvaraya (A Brief Review of His Services)* (Bangalore, 1984); Shakuntala Krishnamurthy, *Dr Mokshagundam Visvesvaraya* (Bangalore, 1980); and Pandri Nath, *Mokshagundam Visvesvaraya: Life and Work* (Bombay, 1987). The last is the 'Indian tradition' version, published by the Bharatiya Vidya Bhavan, which casts Visvesvaraya as one who 'gave up the traditional ways of his ancestors and decided to pursue the "Modern" trend' but nonetheless did not lose his 'Indian tradition' - such as 'respect to one's elders'—playing his role 'in the upholding of "dharma" as only the Indian psyche can understand it'. It also stresses Visvesvaraya's Brahmin origins—the Mokshagundam Brahmins 'were fair, slender of build, endowed with a broad forehead and a sharp pointed nose—in other words—a fairly handsome lot!', Pandri Nath, *Mokshagundam Visvesvaraya*, pp. 1–3.

177. This is evident not only from a study of the vast amount of newspaper clippings related to his life and work that Visvesvaraya himself maintained—see Visvesvaraya Papers, microfilm, Reels 1–6, NML—but also from studies of journals such as the *Modern Review*, *Science and Culture*, or the *Congress*

Socialist. The last-named, although it shared Visvesvaraya's position on the necessity of industrialization, had many occasions to disagree with him, especially on the issue of his support for private capital, and took pains to refute him in great detail when it did disagree—comparable only to the space expended on refuting Gandhi or Gandhian positions.

178. Visvesvaraya, *Planned Economy for India* (Bangalore, 1934), p. 220.

179. Visvesvaraya, *Reconstructing India* (London, 1920); Visvesvaraya, *Memoirs of My Working Life*, (Bombay, 1951).

180. Visvesvaraya, *Planned Economy*, pp. 31–4.

181. Visvesvaraya, *Planned Economy*, pp. 38–9 and 48–9.

182. Visvesvaraya, *Planned Economy*, pp. 240; 242–3.

183. Visvesvaraya, *Reconstructing India,* pp. 284–6, chapter entitled 'Nation-Building'.

184. Visvesvaraya, *Reconstructing India*, Preface, pp. (v)–(vi).

185. Visvesvaraya, *Reconstructing India,* pp. 13–14, 325–6.

186. Visvesvaraya, *Reconstructing India,* pp. 295–9; 310–26.

187. Visvesvaraya, *Rural Reconstruction in India*, p. 15.

188. Visvesvaraya, *Nation-Building*, (Bangalore, 1937), chapter VI, 'Citizenship Training', pp. 38–9.

189. Visvesvaraya, *Nation-Building*, p. 39. The process of such training was also laid out: the 'ordinary citizen' was to be 'advised' by the 'leaders of the country' (who must first 'come to a proper understanding among themselves') to 'adopt a standard dress, a uniform language, besides certain well-recognised international habits and practices in matters pertaining to business, society, travel and self-defence'. Visvesvaraya, *Nation-Building*, p. 42.

190. Visvesvaraya, *District Development Scheme*, p. 60. In this vein, caste distinctions, 'communalism', and untouchability could be dealt with through economic progress. This was an idea which Visvesvaraya first advanced in *Reconstructing India* in 1920 (see, especially, pp. 8, 13–15)—and was in accordance with the views of Jawaharlal Nehru, expressed later, as Partha Chatterjee points out: *Nationalist Thought*, p. 141 and p. 163, Note 31. But Visvesvaraya believed that these other spheres should be separated, in plans for development or reconstruction, from the economic sphere, for reasons of efficiency. On this issue, he was to dissent from the terms of reference of, and probably for that reason eventually resign from, the NPC, which he felt tried to do too much. Walchand Hirachand Archives, File No 48, Part I, copy of Sir Purshotamdas Thakurdas' letter to Nehru, 15 June 1939, ff. 84–5. Thakurdas said that the NPC had been assigned too much work in two little time—he was supported in this view by J.C. Kumarappa, Sir M. Visvesvaraya, A.D. Shroff and Nazir Ahmed. "The somewhat superficial reports, which the Committees may make, may in some cases mislead the public, and, to that extent, may be injurious to the cause for which the National Planning Committee is set up.'

191. Visvesvaraya, *District Development Scheme*, p. 12.
192. '... because, without such discipline, no progress can be made, no leadership becomes effective'. Visvesvaraya, *Planned Economy*, p. 263.
193. Tomaso Sillani, *What is Fascism and Why?* (1931), cited in Visvesvaraya, *Planned Economy*, p. 260.
194. Visvesvaraya, *Planned Economy*, pp. 203; 205, 263. He also produced a set of 'Rules for Citizen Efficiency' (pp. 264–5).
195. Although Visvesvaraya filled his book with examples of Russian productivity which had 'freed the Russian peasantry to a full enjoyment of the advantages of modern culture and education', he was satisfied to try and appropriate the form, not the content, of Soviet planning. The Indian Plan's 'basic policy should be to encourage collective effort without interfering with individual initiative'. Communist 'doctrines' should be 'discouraged as unsuited to the present conditions in India'. Visvesvaraya, *Planned Economy*, pp. 8; 49–50. Capitalism's ills were acknowledged—unequal distribution of wealth despite benefits of promoting science and developing industries, facilitating the productive use of money and so on. As long as the question of equitable distribution of the profits of industries received increasing attention, it could be said that 'socialism is gaining ground'. Only the monopolies 'incidental to capitalism' should be minimised; wherever they are 'inevitable', 'modifications' might be made through legal enactments. Visvesvaraya, *Planned Economy*, pp. 237–43. The examples which India should follow, however, are on the lines of 'such capitalist countries as France and the United States'—or, in another example (p. 8), the USA and Turkey. In the USA, a 'new kind of State Socialism' is, under Roosevelt's National Recovery Act, 'being tried on a gigantic scale'.
196. Visvesvaraya to Gandhi, 20 November 1934. This was in response to Gandhi's request to him to be one of the advisers to the AIVIA in matters in which he possessed 'special knowledge': Gandhi to Visvesvaraya, 15 November 1934. Visvesvaraya said that he was willing to advise the AIVIA without being officially involved with it. He objected to Gandhi's views on machinery, and said that he would send him a copy of his book *Planned Economy for India*. Gandhi's reply acknowledged that the two held 'perhaps diametrically opposite views' and that the excerpt from Stalin had no appeal for him. He, nonetheless, acknowledged Visvesvaraya's 'love of the country'. Gandhi to Visvesvaraya 23 November 1934. These letters are reprinted in Shakuntala Krishnamurthy, *Dr Mokshagundam Visvesvaraya*, pp. 61–3.
197. *The Hindu*, 14 January 1933, report of a party for Mr and Mrs Shaw on 12 January 1933 hosted by one Atiya Begum, at which Visvesvaraya was present—he is mentioned in the report.
198. Clipping in Visvesvaraya Papers, NML, microfilm, Reel 6.
199. 'Ourselves', in the inaugural issue of the *Congress Socialist*, Saturday, 29 September 1934, p. 2. Emphasis mine.
200. P.C. Ray, *Life and Experiences of a Bengali Chemist*, pp. 211; 221–3; 273–4; 277–9; 286–7.

201. *NPC Report*, pp. 207–8.
202. *NPC Report*, pp. 148–9.
203. *NPC Report*, p. 114. At this time, Nehru was in Europe, establishing his solidarity with anti-fascist and socialist forces. See his regular contributions to the *National Herald* in that year.
204. *NPC Report*, p. 10, also cited above.
205. This was the phrase used by Subhas Chandra Bose in an interview with Rajani Palme Dutt of the CPGB in 1938. When Palme Dutt asked him to comment on his view of fascism in the light of his remarks on fascism in his book, *The Indian Struggle*. Bose replied:

My political ideas have developed further since I wrote my book three years ago.

What I really meant was that we in India wanted our national freedom, and having won it, we wanted to move in the direction of Socialism. This is what I meant when I referred to 'a synthesis between Communism and Fascism'. Perhaps the expression was not a happy one. But I should like to point out that when I was writing the book, Fascism had not started on its imperialist expedition, and it appeared to me merely an aggressive form of nationalism.

Subhas Bose, quoted from 'Report of an interview with R. Palme Dutt, published in the *Daily Worker*, London, 24 January 1938', reprinted in Sisir Kumar Bose and Sugata Bose (eds), *Netaji Collected Works, Volume 9: Congress President: Speeches, Articles and Letters, January 1938–May 1939* (Delhi, 1995), p. 2. The 'imperialism' of fascists did not prevent Bose from seeking an alliance with the Axis powers during the Second World War.
206. On the history of eugenics and its uses in political argument from the turn of the century onwards, see G.R. Searle, *Eugenics and Politics in Britain 1900–1914* (Leyden, 1976); Daniel J. Kevles, *In the Name of Eugenics: Genetics and the Uses of Human Heredity* (New York, 1985); Donald K. Pickens, *Eugenics and the Progressives* (Nashville, Tennessee, 1968), pp. 3–36, and, especially, pp. 23–36 on Francis Galton, the man who coined the term and was regarded as the founder of eugenics; on liberal and socialist interpretations of eugenics, see Marouf Arif Hasian Jr, *The Rhetoric of Eugenics in Anglo-American Thought* (Athens, Georgia, 1996), pp. 112–138. For an account of the German case, not limited to the Nazi period, see Paul Weindling, *Health, Race and German Politics between National Unification and Nazism* (Cambridge, 1989); on eugenics outside Europe and North America, see Nancy Leys Stepan, *"The Hour of Eugenics": Race, Gender and Nation in Latin America* (Ithaca, 1991).

On the continued respectability of eugenics in the 1930s, see Third International Conference on Eugenics, 1932, *A Decade of Progress in Eugenics* (Baltimore, 1934; reprint, New York, 1984). Progressives were well represented: one participant argued that 'fundamental economic forces' were at work which were 'quite beyond the control of us as eugenists'; that, unfortunately, 'Galton lived too early to appreciate the principle brought out by Marx' (H.J. Muller, of the University of Texas, 'The dominance of Economics over Eugenics', p. 139); but, nonetheless, saw a role for eugenics, in 'scientific birth control' and 'the actual increase of those having the more valuable genes', to which ends economic obstacles had to be removed (p. 140). He called for a 'revolutionary attitude towards women' and asked, 'Do male eugenists suffer from the illusion that most intelligent women love to be pregnant ... ?' (pp. 140–41). The economic system, he argued, 'acts to foil the true purposes of eugenics' by 'masking the genetic constitution of individuals and of vast groups through the gross inequalities of material and social environment which it imposes on them' (p. 141). But he agreed, 'That imbeciles should be sterilised is of course unquestionable' (p. 138).

Of particular interest in the Indian context is a paper by Henry E. Roseboom and Cedric Dover, 'The Eurasian Community as a Eugenic Problem', which cites P.C. Mahalanobis' 1922 work with Annandale on the Anglo-Indians, and his analyses of race mixture in Bengal (pp. 90–1), of which more below. Dover, an Eurasian and a member of the CSP, and one of Jawaharlal Nehru's self-appointed educators (see above), insisted (along with his co-author), on the one hand, that 'the problem of the Eurasian community, as the Simon Commission (1930) points out, is essentially economic' (p. 89), but on the other hand insisted that 'anthropometric study will demonstrate the physical equality of its members with those of any other community in the East, even if it does not suggest the possibility of the physical superiority under improved conditions. He argued for the influence of environment in addition to 'miscegenation' as influencing the 'characteristics of the community', appealed to a notion of 'hybrid vigour': 'a carefully nurtured hybrid is superior to either parent', advocated miscegenation—the 'development of mixed breeds' would also remove racial friction—and envisioned a future world of 'one composite race' (pp. 92–3).

207. On Keynes' encounters with the Galton Laboratory, see the public exchanges between Keynes and Karl Pearson (1857–1936, Professor of Applied Maths and Mechanics at University College, London; in 1911, upon Galton's death, he became Galton Professor of Eugenics, which he remained until 1933: see *DNB 1931–1940* (Oxford, 1949), pp. 681–4) in 1910 over a study of 'the influence of parental alcoholism on the physique and ability of the offspring', reprinted in *The Collected Writings of John Maynard Keynes*, Vol. XI (London, 1983), pp. 186–216—categories such as 'feeble-mindedness' and 'racial difference' in samples from Manchester and Edinburgh were hotly debated in terms of the representativeness of the sample—a debate which was given much of its heat because of its importance in connection with the claims of temperance reformers, but which was conducted in terms of the discipline of statistics. Keynes argued that the Edinburgh population in particular was of low quality, therefore, biasing the study: '... the authors are comparing drunken stock with *bad* sub-normal sober stock, and find, naturally enough, that there is not much to choose between them' (p. 195,

emphasis in original)—or in Pearson's paraphrase of his argument, that the Edinburgh sample was from 'an exceptionally "low grade" population in which "physical and moral squalor are rampant' (p. 205)—therefore, the differences in degeneracy between the alcoholics and non-alcoholics would not be significant. Pearson argued that the sample was quite representative. In this debate on the interpretation of figures, Keynes' absolute contempt for people from 'low districts' comes across clearly; neither Keynes nor Pearson questioned the validity of figures derived from measurements of Manchester and Edinburgh schoolchildren by an anthropometric committee. Keynes continued to take the categories of anthropometrics as valid, and discussed them in his Treatise on Probability (1921); his bibliography cites a good deal of Pearson's work: *The Collected Writings of John Maynard Keynes,* Vol. VIII (London, 1973), pp. 498–9.

208. In this connection, see Christophe Jaffrelot, 'The Idea of the Hindu Race in the Writings of Hindu Nationalist Ideologues in the 1920s and 1930s: A Concept Between Two Cultures', in Peter Robb (ed.), *The Concept of Race in South Asia* (Delhi, 1995); for the tendency to see caste in terms of race, and the importance of the category 'Aryan', in nineteenth and early twentieth century British colonial ethnography—and the tendency of India writers to absorb these then state-of-the-art academic concerns, see Susan Bayly, 'Caste and "Race" in the Colonial Ethnography of India'; on anthropometry and its colonial uses, see Crispin Bates, 'Race, Caste and Tribe in Central India: The Early Origins of Indian Anthropometry', both in Robb (ed.), *The Concept of Race in South Asia.* See also Carey Watt, 'Education for National Efficiency: Constructive Nationalism in North India, 1909–1916', *Modern Asian Studies* Vol. 31, No. 2 (1997), though Watt's concern is not with the significance of this confusion in terminology. That a concern with 'Hindu' nationhood tended to exclude or alienate minorities who could not be discussed in such terms has often been pointed out before, to the extent of having replaced the old nationalist tales of triumphant mass mobilisation interrupted by 'communalism' caused by British divide-and-rule strategies in many text-books. However, there is now a tendency to carry the argument too far in an opposite direction: namely, that *all* mainstream Indian nationalist ideologues leaned towards an exclusionary and consciously 'Hindu' movement, provoking necessarily separate minority, and especially Muslim, nationalisms: see Peter van der Veer, *Religious Nationalism: Hindus and Muslims in India* (Berkeley, 1994). Once again, those who used such arguments included some who built their solidarity around anti-Muslim sentiment, and others who sought to include Muslims and other minorities in their nationalism through various devices—the *Swadeshi* movement had appealed to the Muslims as brothers, using the *rakhi*-tying ceremony, usually performed by sisters on brothers, to indicate this tie. Rabindranath Tagore, who had been prominent in the Swadeshi movement, was later to realize the limitations of such strategies of creating cross-community

solidarities; others were less aware of this. Gandhi was later to use a strategy of coalition of specifically religious feelings in the Non-Cooperation/Khilafat Movement. See Sumit Sarkar, *The Swadeshi Movement in Bengal, 1903–1908*, pp. 287, 426; *Modern India 1885–1947* (Madras, 1983), pp. 196–7, 233–4.

209. See Norman Cohn, *Warrant for Genocide* (London, 1967), pp. 110–11; see, also, Gandhi's remarks on the sources he read on Hinduism, M.K. Gandhi, *An Autobiography, or The Story of My Experiments with Truth* (two volumes, Ahmedabad, 1927 and 1929; this editon Harmondsworth, 1982), pp. 76–7. See, also, the Theosophical Society's journal, *The Aryan Path*.

210. Mahalanobis, as mentioned before, was at the time only peripherally connected with the debates on Indian development planning—he offered to examine all the NPC's reports from a 'purely statistical point of view': see above.

211. Mahalanobis was at Presidency College from 1915 to 1948, teaching physics, with spells as acting principal, head of the Department of Physics, and principal. Employed as a physics teacher, he was far more interested in conducting his statistical research, the college playing host, in a corner of the physics department, to his statistical laboratory, which was later to grow into the Indian Statistical Institute. Indian Statistical Institute, *History and Activities, 1931–1963* (Calcutta, n.d.), pp. 1–11. His first encounter with the discipline of statistics was apparently through the journal, *Biometrika*, at Cambridge; on his return to India, Sir Brajendranath Seal, Professor of Philosophy at Calcutta University, asked him to work with some figures relating to Calcutta University examination results. Seal was himself acquainted with the statistical methods in use at the time, and gave Mahalanobis detailed guidelines on what to do, the latter's first encounter with actual statistical analysis. Rudra, *Prasanta Chandra Mahalanobis: a Biography*, pp. 127–8.

212. He kept extensive notes on race and anthropometry, and also took extensive head-length measurements of Bengalis by caste, from which data he published his articles. Trunk T-2, P.C. Mahalanobis Archive, Indian Statistical Institute, Calcutta.

213. Indian Statistical Institute, *History and Activities, 1931–1963*, p. 1.

214. Karl Pearson (1857–1936), sometime professor of applied maths and mechanics at University College, London, founded in 1901, along with Francis Galton, the journal, *Biometrika*. In 1911, upon Galton's death, he became Galton Professor of Eugenics, which he remained until 1933. Pearson was a barrister, and in his early years lectured on maths and physics, philosophy and medieval languages, and talked on Lassalle and Marx at revolutionary clubs in Soho on Sundays. See *DNB 1931–1940*, pp. 681–4, which, however, makes no references to Pearson's politics—for which, and for Mahalanobis' contributions to the field of population genetics, see R.L. Kirk, 'P.C. Mahalanobis and Population Genetics in India', *Samvadhvam:*

House Journal of the Indian Statistical Institute, Vol. 10, Nos. 1–4 (P.C. Mahalanobis Memorial Volume), December 1974.

215. 'I frankly confess that I know very little of anatomy. My work on the data supplied has been purely statistical'. P.C. Mahalanobis, 'Anthropological Observations on the Anglo-Indians of Calcutta, Part I: Analysis of Male Stature', *Records of the Indian Museum*, Vol. XXIII, April 1922, p. 7.

216. Annandale clarified that he meant Eurasians, as the new terminology agreed upon by the Government of India went, to avoid the derogatory connotations of the term 'Eurasian'. Annandale, Introductory Note, to Mahalanobis, 'Anthropological Observations on the Anglo-Indians of Calcutta, Part I', p. 1.

217. Annandale's note contains an involved debate on racial categories, relative purity of blood, 'civilised and uncivilised tribes', 'recent Negro blood', 'persons of mixed blood', and so on. Annandale, Introductory Note, to Mahalanobis, 'Anthropological Observations on the Anglo-Indians of Calcutta, Part I', p. 1.

218. Mahalanobis, 'Anthropological Observations on the Anglo-Indians of Calcutta, Part I', Appendix I: Note on Statistical Terms, p. 94.

219. P.C. Mahalanobis, 'Analysis of Race Mixture in Bengal', *Journal of the Asiatic Society of Bengal* XXIII (1927), pp. 301–33; Mahalanobis, 'Revision of Risley's Anthropometric Data relating to the Tribes and Castes of Bengal', (Abstract), *Proceedings of the Indian Science Congress (Nagpur)* 18, (1931), p. 411 (a version of this paper was published in the first issue of Mahalanobis' own journal, *Sankhya*, the journal of the Indian Statistical Institute, founded in 1933; *Sankhya* 1, 1933, pp. 76–105); Mahalanobis, 'Revision of Risley's Anthropometric Data relating to the Chittagong Hill Tribes' (Abstract), *Proceedings of the Indian Science Congress (Bangalore)*, Anthropology Section 19, (1932), p. 424; *Sankhya* 1, 1934, pp. 267–76; Mahalanobis, 'Analysis of Racial Likeness in Bengal Castes' (Abstract), *Proceedings of the Indian Science Congress (Calcutta), Anthropology Section* 22, (1935), p. 335. Risley wrote in the 1890s, and greatly annoyed many Bengalis by concluding that they were not Aryan but 'Mongolo-Dravidian'. See H.H. Risley, *The Tribes and Castes of Bengal: Ethnographic Glossary* (two volumes, Calcutta, 1891); Risley, *The Tribes and Castes of Bengal: Anthropometric Data,* two volumes, (Calcutta, 1891). Mahalanobis himself took a moderate line, arguing that 'social barriers and caste restrictions' had not succeeded in suppressing inter-mingling of the 'indigenous stock in Bengal with the north-east tribes and the aboriginal tribes from Chota Nagpur; as a consequence 'a larger Hindu Samaj has evolved which is not only not identical with the traditional society of Vedic or classic times but is in many respects even antagonistic. Sectarian obstacles have not proved insurmountable ...'. Mahalanobis, 'Analysis of Race Mixture in Bengal', pp. 322–3.

220. The only article on industry he wrote before the Planning Commission papers was one for Meghnad Saha's new journal, *Science and Culture*: P.C.

Mahalanobis, 'Application of Statistical Methods in Industry', *Science and Culture* 1 (1935), pp. 73–8. For details on the trajectory of Mahalanobis' career, see Benjamin Zachariah, 'The Development of Professor Mahalanobis', *Economy and Society* Vol. 26, No. 3 (August 1997).

221. See Chapter 2 of this volume.

222. For instance, the RSS: see W.K. Andersen and S.D. Damle, *The Brotherhood in Saffron: the Rashtriya Swayamsevak Sangh and Hindu Revivalism* (Boulder, Colorado, 1987).

223. See Chapter 4 of this volume.

224. Subhas Bose to Amita Purkayastha, 3 September 1938, reprinted in Sisir Kumar Bose and Sugata Bose (eds), *Netaji Collected Works, Volume 9*, p. 271. Translated from Bengali.

225. Several articles in the *Modern Review* in the 1920s, for instance by Benoy Sarkar, express this fascination. Acharya P.C. Ray, a professed Gandhian, quoted Mussolini: Ray, *The Life and Experiences of a Bengali Chemist*, p. 259. Rabindranath Tagore accepted an invitation from Mussolini to visit Italy in 1926, with Mahalanobis and his wife joining him as travel companions. (Mahalanobis moved on to London and from January 1927 spent some months at Karl Pearson's laboratory). Rudra, *Prasanta Chandra Mahalanobis: a Biography*, p. 106.

226. The Gandhians shared this position on the moral value of work: as S.N. Agarwal paraphrased it in 1944, manual labour was to Gandhiji 'the law of nature'; and Gandhi 'regards the cry for more leisure as dangerous and unnatural'. S.N. Agarwal, *The Gandhian Plan of Economic Development for India* (Bombay, 1944), p. 21. Kumarappa, it may be recalled, had similarly decried the need for leisure: Kumarappa, *Why the Village Movement?*, fifth edition, (Wardha, 1949), p. 62.

227. An official report framed by Sir M. Visvesvaraya and Pandit Hari Kishan Kaul in 1925, pointed out that there was 'a large store of cheap and docile labour' in India, and that 'in many parts of the country chronic under-employment is a marked characteristic of every day rural life'. As a source they cited Malcolm Darling's *The Punjab Peasant in Prosperity and Debt*. See *Report of the Indian Economic Enquiry Committee* (Calcutta, 1925), p. 6.

228. Visvesvaraya, *Planned Economy for India*, pp. 240; 242–3; P Thakurdas et al, *A Plan of Economic Development for India* (Bombay, 1944: two parts). In 1951, Visvesvaraya wrote in his memoirs, 'One common slogan of the West, the importance of which the Indian citizen has not yet sufficiantly grasped, is: 'If you do not work/ Neither shall you eat." Visvesvaraya, *Memoirs of My Working Life* (Bombay, 1951), p. 142. This was a line of reasoning which also entered Gandhian reasoning: S.N. Agarwal's 'Gandhian Plan' in 1944 had stated, quoting St Paul, unlike Visvesvaraya who did not provide a footnote, '"He that will not work, neither shall he eat"'. S.N. Agarwal, *The Gandhian Plan of Economic Development for India*, p. 21.

229. *NPC Report*, pp. 153–7. The discussions on labour had often taken strange turns—discussing the question of arbitration, the socialist, K.T. Shah, had at

one point said that 'in Planned Economy there should be no room for strikes and lock-outs'. Minutes of NPC meeting, 7 May 1940, at which the Labour Sub-Committee's report had been considered. Walchand Hirachand Archives, File No 48, Part II, f. 318, NML.

230. K.T. Shah (ed.), *National Planning Committee: Report of the Sub-Committee on Labour* (Bombay, 1947), Section IX: 'Workers' Organisation', p. 93.

231. 'A.K. Shaha, author of *Flameless Combustion Process in Industry* (in Russian) (Leningrad and Moscow, 1934); and *Lectures on Fuels and Furnaces* (in English) (Calcutta, 1944); BSc (Dacca) Aspirant (Moscow) equivalent to PhD, Candidate of Sciences (USSR) equivalent to DSc. Ex-foreign specialist invited by the Soviet government during the First and Second Five-Year Plans.' Title page, A.K. Shaha, *India on Planning: Planning for Liquidation of Unemployment and Illiteracy* (Calcutta, 1948).

232. A.K. Shaha, *India on Planning*.

233. The main constructive contribution of these chapters, apart from comparing Russian with Indian history (both in rather Stalinized versions), was a recommendation for the new Indian state of Stalin's position on the nationalities question: Tatiana Shaha-Sedina, 'The Problem of Nationalities', in A.K. Shaha, *India on Planning*, pp. 199–238.

234. Shaha, *India on Planning*, p. 140.

235. Shaha, *India on Planning*, p. 53.

236. Shaha, *India on Planning*, p. 108.

237. 'Is it any longer possible to doubt the fact of the rise of giant factories and fabulous production without capitalists and entrepreneurs, the rise of huge co-operatives and, most miraculously of all, the growth of collectivised agriculture? ... Regarding a detail of administrative policy, regarding a particular incident, regarding a Party-"purge", regarding many other things, not all unimportant, there may be mystery, uncertainty, doubt, but with regard to the major policies and achievements of the Soviet Government, it is not possible to be in doubt any more.' Jayaprakash Narayan, 'New Incentives', *Congress Socialist*, 30 December 1934, p. 15. When Masani broke this silence, he, rather ironically, drew strongly on a Trotskyist critique of Stalinism. Minoo Masani, *Socialism Reconsidered*, first part, 'A False Dawn', a savage indictment of 'Stalinism'—he used the term himself, once or twice, either while quoting Max Eastman (p 40) or himself, in conjunction with 'Hitlerism' (p. 43). At the same time, he sought to combine this with a trust in the virtues of the 'trusteeship' of capital and a sympathetic, though bastardized, version of Gandhism.

238. Jayaprakash Narayan to Nehru, 23 November 1938. NML, Vol. 54, f. 58. Despite its pledges to defend the interests of the masses, the Congress was being turned into 'a hand-maid of Indian vested interests'. This was made possible, he felt, by a 'vulgarisation of Gandhism' giving the new Congress the 'requisite demagogic armoury'. Narayan's views are corroborated by circumstantial evidence elsewhere: the trend he was describing, however, was

not avoided by the left-wing of the Congress, and was not purely dependent on an use of 'Gandhism'. In February 1929, after a long and serious strike at Tatas' iron and steel factory in Jamshedpur, lasting from February to September 1928, Subhas Bose criticized the union leader, Manek Homi, for his unwise actions—the survival of Tata's steel enterprise was important, for it was a 'public cause'. In 1937, with the Congress in power, the company invited Rajendra Prasad and Jawaharlal Nehru to arbitrate between the company and the Tata Workers' Union, at the time being run by a Congressman, Abdul Bari, who was 'gently chided' for his activities. Quoted in the official history of the Tata group of companies, R.M. Lala, *The Creation of Wealth: the Tata Story* (Bombay, 1981), pp. 120–1. Labour rights were apparently to be sacrificed to the need for national enterprise.

239. Amiya Kumar Bagchi, *Private Investment in India, 1900–1939* (Cambridge, 1972), pp. 210–11, 350–1. In this campaign, he had also used the historian Radhakumud Mookerji as an intellectual ally—Mookerji's *History of Indian Shipping* justified Hirachand's position by referring to India's glorious past of shipping and maritime commerce. See Radhakumud Mookerji, *A History of Indian Shipping and Maritime Activity from the Earliest Times* (London, 1912).

240. See Meghnad Saha, editorials in *Science and Culture*, in particular November 1938; the project also found a supporter in P.C. Ray, who wrote an open letter to Sir Richard Gregory, President of the British Association for the Advancement of Science, who had recently condemned fascism for putting science to anti-human uses. Ray wrote that it was not only fascism, but also imperialism which frustrated the 'human welfare' object of science. 'Industrialisation, which is essential for the prosperity and strength of a nation in the modern age, has been persistently opposed, and even recently the Government of India has refused to support the growth of an automobile industry in India ...'. Sir P.C. Ray, Open Letter to Sir Richard Gregory, President of the British Association for the Advancement of Science, *Hindusthan Standard*, 16 November 1941.

241. M. Visvesvaraya Papers, NML, microfilm; Visvesvaraya, *Reconstruction in Post-War India*, pp. 10–15; Visvesvaraya, *Indian Automobile Factory Scheme: Government of India's Obstructive Attitude* (Bombay, 1942), All-India Manufacturers' Organization pamphlet, copy in Walchand Hirachand Archive, NML, File 563, ff. 10–60; Sir M. Visvesvaraya's address to the AIMO, reported in the *Hindustan Standard*, 15 January 1942; news item, 'Visvesvaraya Exposes India Govt.'s Tactics', *Bombay Chronicle*, 17/7/1942.

242. He referred to the scheme as 'Sir Vishveshva Aiya's Motor Mfg. Scheme'. Letter to Lalchand Hirachand, 9 July 1939, Walchand Hirachand Archives, File No 552 Part I, Vol. II, f. 265, NML.

243. See Chapter 2 of this book.

244. See Chapter 2 of this book.

245. See Chapter 3 of this book.
246. Joint letter from Jawaharlal Nehru (Chairman) and K.T. Shah (Honorary General Secretary), NPC, to NPC members and chairmen and secretaries of sub-committees, *National Planning Committee, No. 2: Being an Abstract of Proceedings and other particulars relating to the National Planning Committee* (Bombay, May 1940), p. 13.
247. Purshotamdas Thakurdas Papers, NML, File 291 Part II: Post-War Economic Development Committee, ff. 265–6.
248. Purshotamdas Thakurdas Papers, NML, File 291 Part II: Post-War Economic Development Committee, f. 266.
249. Minoo Masani, *Socialism Reconsidered* (Bombay, 1944).
250. Purshotamdas Thakurdas Papers, NML, File No. 341, 'Bombay Plan 2/1/45-20/1/50'. Masani moved steadily rightwards, emerging as a key spokesman for the failed project of Indian liberalism in the Swatantra Party of the 1960s; his rhetoric began to take rather American free-market forms, eventually leading to a situation of his becoming the caricature of the capitalist stooge of his own polemical writing during his socialist days. For his own account of the drift, see the two volumes of his memoirs, Minoo Masani, *Bliss was it in that Dawn ...* and *Against the Tide.*
251. M.R. Masani, *Picture of a Plan*, (Bombay, 1944).
252. This was published as John Matthai, *Village Government in British India* (London, 1915). Webb's preface to this had been cited by Malcolm Darling in his parting advice to the new Government of India to place the peasant at the centre of its economic vision in *At Freedom's Door*: see Chapter 2 of this book.
253. Cipher telegram from Wavell, Viceroy, to Leo Amery, Secretary of State for India, 12 June 1944, f. 93, IOR: L/I/1/1061. Accordingly, the Economic Adviser, Sir Theodore Gregory, prepared detailed notes on the Plan. See IOR: L/I/1/1061, ff. 95–104 and ff. 27–29. These were intended not only to address 'fallacies and technical defects in economic and financial argument' but also to express agreement regarding general aims and objectives. Cipher telegram from Wavell to Amery, 12 June 1944, IOR: L/I/1/1061, f. 93.
254. See IOR: L/I/1/1061, f. 93.
255. Unofficial note on the Bombay Plan, IOR: L/I/1/1061, f. 105.
256. This department took over the job of coordinating 'post-war reconstruction and development' from the 'Inter-departmental Reconstruction Committee of Council'. See IOR: L/I/1/1129; Raghabendra Chattopadhyay, 'The Idea of Planning', pp. 178–242.
257. Government of India, Planning and Development Department, *Second Report on Reconstruction Planning.*
258. The public phrasing of the *Second Report* in such terms required that it be phrased in the most general terms possible. Finance Member, Jeremy Raisman advised Sir Ardeshir Dalal, the member for planning and development, to tread softly in what he said on financial matters on the grounds that

everything seemed uncertain during the war: Raisman to Dalal, Simla, 15 September 1944, NAI: 1(4)-P/45: 'Proceedings of the Reconstruction Committee of Council', ff. 58–61. The discussions on the preliminary drafts of the *Second Report* and the correspondence thereon show a concern with toning down the more categorical commitments contained in it to more non-committal forms (ff. 68–73). A Planning Branch memo dated 17 October 1944 on the *Report*'s commitment to meeting the costs of housing for workers suggested that the sentence 'should not be so categorical and should be more non-committal' (f. 73).

259. Government of India, Statement of Industrial Policy, 1945, copy in NAI: 8(5)-P/45, 'Planning of Industrial Development', ff. 119–27. The generalities of the Statement were bewildering even to those in the planning bureaucracy, one of whom described it as 'nebulous', 'redundant', being a repetition of the *Second Report*, 'not strictly accurate' and serving 'only to confuse the issue' (A.S. Lall, Deputy Secretary, Finance, to Additional Secretary, Planning, 11 October 1944, f. 2). Another said it betrayed 'loose thinking' and was 'vague' (V. Narahari Rao's memo dated 18 October 1944, ff. 7, 11). A European bureaucrat, C.E. Jones, seemed to understand the reasoning better when he wrote in response to these criticisms that the Statement was 'highly generalised in form and necessarily vague'—the vagueness being 'understandable' because the planning and development department was seeking 'to secure general agreement on the main features of their approach to the problem' (C.E. Jones' note, 19 October 1944, f. 12). A.S. Lall, however, in a note dated 30 December 1944, predicted that despite the planning and development department's appearing to 'set great store' by an 'unequivocal declaration' of its desire 'to do everything in its power to promote the rapid industrialisation of India', this would not help the government's public image; it would 'take not even the more intelligent industrialist to argue, and argue correctly, that such a statement means, and can mean, very little' (f. 19).

260. T. Hutton, 'The Planning of Post-War Development in India', *Asiatic Review*, Vol. XL, No. III, (April 1947).

261. See R.J. Moore, *Making the New Commonwealth* (Oxford, 1987); P.J. Cain and A.G. Hopkins, *British Imperialism: Crisis and Deconstruction, 1914–1990* (London, 1993), chapter eleven; Philip Joseph Charrier, 'Britain, India and the Genesis of the Colombo Plan, 1945–1951', unpublished PhD dissertation, University of Cambridge, 1995.

262. Speech in Parliament, 16 May 1949, reprinted in Jawaharlal Nehru, *India's Foreign Policy: Selected Speeches, September 1946–April 1961* (Delhi: Publications Division, Ministry of Information and Broadcasting, 1961), p. 135.

263. Walchand Hirachand Archives, NML, Files 47, 81, 101, 552–3, 556, 561, 563; Purshotamdas Thakurdas Papers, NML, file 235; G.D. Birla, 'India's War Prosperity a Myth', reprint from *Searchlight*, 1941, in Purshotamdas Thakurdas Papers, NML, File 175 Part I.

264. G.D. Birla to Walchand Hirachand, Calcutta, 14 May 1941, Walchand Hirachand Archives, IV (E) (ii), File No. 563, f. 158, NML.
265. *Hindusthan Standard*, editorial, 19 December 1945.
266. B.T. Ranadive, *The Tata–Birla Plan: Will it Work?* (Bombay, n.d.), pp. 9–12, 24.
267. See Homy Mody's response to the 'extremely radical' AICC economic programme of 1948, letter to Walchand Hirachand, 28 January 1948, Walchand Hirachand Archive, NML, File 81 Part II, ff. 551–3.
268. Birla, *The Path to Prosperity: A Plea for Planning*.
269. J.B. Kripalani to Dharmraj Kulkarni, 1 December 1947, AICC Papers, File G-6/1947-48, f. 43, in reply to Kulkarni's of 20/ November 1947, ff. 41–44.
270. Ram Manohar Lohia's note (1947) 'Fifteen-Point Note on Congress and the Socialist Party', AICC Papers, File 6/1947, ff. 467–477.
271. Note by Jhaverbhai Patel, undated, but after 1947, AICC Papers File 27 (Part I)/1947, ff. 101–119.
272. Note by Jhaverbhai Patel, AICC Papers File 27 (Part I)/1947, f. 101.
273. Note by Jhaverbhai Patel, AICC Papers File 27 (Part I)/1947, f .101.
274. Socialist Party programme, copy in AICC Papers File 27 (Part I)/1947, ff. 127–145.
275. Socialist Party programme, copy in AICC Papers File 27 (Part I)/1947, f. 127.
276. Socialist Party programme, copy in AICC Papers File 27 (Part I)/1947, f. 131.
277. This is already the 'experts' view of things. Socialist Party programme, copy in AICC Papers File 27 (Part I)/1947, f. 133.
278. Socialist Party programme, copy in AICC Papers File 27 (Part I)/1947, f. 135.
279. Minoo Masani, *Socialism Reconsidered*.
280. Ram Manohar Lohia, 'Economics After Marx', written in 1943, reprinted in Ram Manohar Lohia, *Marx, Gandhi and Socialism* (Second edition Hyderabad, 1978; first published 1963).
281. Jayaprakash Narayan, 'Letter to PSP Associates', Patna, 25 September 1957, reprinted in Jayaprakash Narayan, *Towards a New Society* (New Delhi, 1958).
282. On Vinoba Bhave, see Shriman Narayan, *Vinoba: His Life and Work* (Bombay, 1970); on the claim of Sarvodaya to being (p. 198) 'the only effective alternative to Communism and Marxism', see pp. 197–204.
283. See A.H. Hanson, *The Process of Planning: A Study of India's Five-Year Plans 1950–1964* (Oxford, 1966), pp. 419–21. The Community Development and National Extension movement was actually inaugurated on Gandhi's birthday, 2 October 1952 (p. 420).

Conclusions

'Development', in the India of the 1930s and the 1940s, stood forth as a category through which a variety of concerns related to the future of India were ordered, and was intimately connected with ideas of regeneration and progress. 'Development', therefore, involved agreement or disagreement about views of progress, about what constituted progress, and about who could claim to be legitimate agents of progress.

Catalysed by contemporary worldwide discussions about how to manage economies, how to industrialize quickly, and how to overcome economic catastrophe, discussions in the 1930s regarding the progress of India turned to envisaging comprehensive planned frameworks for a future Indian state and nation. These began to attract and incorporate originally separate concerns, whose protagonists were attracted by the comprehensive and ambitious possibilities of developing India, and the immediacy provided to the project in connection with imperial and world events which seemed to be transforming the present as well as possible futures.

To an extent, in being so incorporated, these earlier concerns were transformed as they were rephrased in the language of 'economics'. 'Economics' was a field in which imperialist arguments placed themselves; and it was this field which nationalists had to attempt to take. In the neo-classical stability of the pre-First World War years, this was less easy than when the assumptions of economics began to shift, the issue being forced in many parts of the world by the Depression—which made many non-socialists look more closely at the Soviet five-year plans. These moving boundaries of acceptable economics were also useful in India where the boundaries took extremely permeable forms: economics was to include moral, ethical, and cultural considerations, take truly Indian forms, and so on.

It was still important to call the bulk of this 'economics'. As political arguments in colonial India were necessarily interventions into political arenas structured by the British colonial power, an intervention, in order to be effective, had to appeal to principles which the colonial power recognized as valid; 'economics' was one such recognized set of principles. But the debates could now accommodate a wide range of concerns which were important to questions of progress, identity and self-respect, as corollaries or necessary adjuncts to the economic part of 'development'; and these concerns largely gave form and direction to the economic part.

The conventions of imperialist arguments were themselves changing in this period, however, and abandoning the more strongly held claims to superiority of expertise in governance. A new, less obviously objectionable justification for imperialism had to be found, in which claims to proper respect for Indian nationalist sentiment and 'legitimate' demands were to play an important role. In such formulations, certain aspects of nationalist demands were selectively admitted to be acceptable, as long as they were not held in 'extreme' forms. Many of the aspects that were admissible into imperialist arguments were, however, compatible with older visions of a benevolent imperialism, which a great many imperial administrators found difficult to abandon: thus, Gandhi's idea of the 'real' India as rural and non-industrial was attractive in that the Civilian also believed in the peasant whom he knew and administered, and thought of the urban Indian as inauthentic. Somewhat inconsistently in terms of logical argument, but equally consistent with the psychological impulses it satisfied, the projected departure of the British from India was depicted as the logical fruition of the British mission in India: not, as before, as the triumph of the illegitimate and inauthentic urban middle-class agitators, but as an act of supreme creativity: the British had made a nation of India.

Nationalist arguments, meanwhile, worked through an unstable resolution of the concerns with development, in terms of the importance of science and technology, of the need for government to express certain social concerns (called 'socialism', but whose criteria varied enormously), and of the need for 'national discipline', often expressed in terms of the moral unity of the 'nation'. Given the difficulties of coalitional politics against British rule, radical forms of 'socialism' were not particularly in evidence, though it was extremely important that various measures be referred to as socialist. Technical expertise and national discipline—the latter also implying the strong guiding hand of directing expertise—were equally important aspects of the conventions of legitimate political argument; these three recurrent themes appeared in various combinations.

A fourth theme, which could attach itself variously to arguments using any or all of the other themes, but which on its own was ineffective as a yardstick of legitimacy, was what might be called the 'indigenist' theme: to be legitimate, 'development' had to take an Indian, not a 'foreign' path. The themes were contained within a view of development-as-progress— which had to be 'modern' (implying a progress possibly universal in nature), but not 'Western'.

The Gandhian position, insofar as 'development' was concerned, appears in its eccentricity to be an exception to this general thematic map. But it is in important respects only apparently an exception. Its position of strength was with respect to the fourth, 'indigenist' theme. It sought to stress 'indigenous' solutions, within which paths to progress had to be negotiated—a problem which had greatly exercised the Indian nationalist imagination around the turn of the century. However, its construction of what was 'indigenous' was largely dependent on British constructions of an 'indigenous' India, now ironically internalized as an authentically Indian position. The successful disassociation, in the Gandhian position, of the categories 'Western' and 'modern', occurs not through a straightforward acceptance of the universality of the 'modern', but through the introduction of *separate criteria* of 'modernity'—criteria which were not 'Western', but truly Indian, but which, by implication, it would be desirable to make universally applicable. The criteria of 'modernity' had themselves to be tested by 'science' as well as 'morality', which were compatible. If these criteria were properly applied, the argument went, the Gandhians would appear as the true socialists, with science on their side. The Gandhians also held explicit views on the importance of moral discipline, in their equation between individual self-control and collective self-rule, which were, at least, as clear on the issue of the need for a leadership of directing experts (morally enlightened ones, in the Gandhian case) as other nationalists. It was these thematic similarities, it might be argued, which enabled Gandhian ideas to find their place in the rhetoric of development in the 1950s, despite the differences in more specific arguments with the 'Nehruvian' consensus.

By the 1940s, the nationalist arguments that used these themes, which had been crystallized in opposition to the conventions of imperialist argument, had begun to lose their opponent. As the conventions of imperialist arguments began to shift towards a more apparently nationalist rhetoric, particularly during the Second World War, many supporters of the idea of imperialism were able to reconcile their acceptance of nationalist positions on development with their faith in the progressive role of the British in India, now dissolved into a rhetoric of the partnership of free nations within a mutually beneficial Commonwealth. Nationalists could argue that this was an Indian achievement; imperialists could argue that it was a British one.

The building-blocks of these arguments, imperialist and nationalist, centralizing or decentralizing, socialist or capitalist, drawing as they did on a finite set of conventions, could be extremely similar, although they were pieced together into divergent, and often antagonistic, arguments.

This sharing of terminology or ideas should not seem too surprising: it was difficult, in colonial India, to access intellectual resources prior to or untouched by colonialism in order to make any argument. The recovery of an authentically 'Indian' past, for instance, was extremely dependent on the early work of European scholars discovering a glorious past for India: 'indigenous' intellectual materials, if they existed at this time, could not be recognized apart from their representation and refraction through British or colonial sources. There was, therefore, some amount of borrowing among later nationalists from the work of early Orientalists or British administrators; and later from official sources and reports. Thus, what was declared 'indigenous' might have been invented indigenism (Sir Charles Metcalfe's, Sir Henry Maine's, Karl Marx's, Gandhi's, John Matthai's, or Sidney Webb's 'ancient village republics'?); but, like Voltaire's God, was a necessary invention. The invention was put to different uses in different arguments—as it had been in previous times.

Some of this borrowing was strategic (not necessarily in the sense of the ideas not being believed by those who employed them in their arguments). As I have noted above, public arguments could be more effective if they employed metropolitan scholarship in their support. Therefore, the coalescing of debates on 'backwardness' around the conception of 'economic backwardness' was a consequence of 'economics' being accepted as a rational, scientific field, whose principles were acceptable to nationalists and imperialists alike, and upon which terms debate could be carried on. The major difference between the two groups of positions was in their interpretation of this backwardness: to nationalists it was contingent, removable through 'economic development'; to many imperialists the causes ran deeper—India was not a European country, her practices were not amenable to transformation to 'modern' forms.

More specific arguments could be built on particular uses of ostensibly metropolitan or other ideas; yet they were often used in such forms as to be unrecognizable except by name as having emanated from a particular source. It is necessary at times, therefore, to distinguish between a shared terminology and shared ideas: the same terminology could indicate a possible source of an idea in a borrowing from metropolitan or other contexts, but the refractions the idea underwent in the Indian context might have been extremely significant in shifting the meaning of the term, as used by Indians, away from the meaning it might have had in its original or conventionally understood context. The extreme eclecticism of such borrowings from other contexts and the juxtaposition of apparently incompatible ideas can often be understood in terms of these shifts in meaning.

In addition, some of the assumptions which the nationalists adopted from imperialist conventions of argument were implicitly absorbed without conscious borrowing. 'Moral and material progress', pinned together in imperial discourse, were also bound together in nationalist thought. Gandhian arguments tended to stress the moral aspects of progress, from which adequate material progress would follow; in most versions, 'modernisers' of various kinds agreed that though the material aspect was more of a tangible concern, moral progress would accompany the material. A version of this argued that progress towards more 'modern' forms of social life through material benefits accruing to the poorer sections of society would decrease the tendency towards pre-modern forms of behaviour—or at any rate that was what should happen.

Underlying unities of thought, however, are necessary as the grounds on which to disagree. This points to a shared discursive framework of late colonialism in India—which does not imply, therefore, that there was a substantial consensus operating in the political environment of late colonial India. It is important, therefore, to stress that there was a good deal of variety within a largely common discourse. It must be recognized that 'colonial society' was constituted by both the colonized and the colonizing—although apparently separate, and often explicitly in opposition to each other, they were in close interaction, responding to each other in a dialectical relationship, defining each other against each other.

Nor should this be taken to imply that such an explicitly oppositional framework was confined to situations in which the colonized and the colonizer confronted each other. The implicit existence of two publics in the colonial situation—a metropolitan and colonial pro-imperialist public and a native colonial public (not always anti-imperialist, but which had to be addressed with arguments different from those which would justify imperialism before the former audience)—required that even internal arguments among imperialists or nationalists had to take account of the effects of these arguments on the other public. This was a quasi-theatrical situation in which every argument had a hidden, implicit protagonist— arguments formulated internally took into account the potential effects of their consumption across the imperialist–nationalist boundary. This often took the explicit form of anticipating opposing arguments: 'the nationalists will argue...' or 'the government will say...' were phrases which often entered internal debates.

There were thus finite intellectual resources with which to construct different arguments. Each protagonist in the debate juggled the terms—which were common to the political and discursive framework in which the protagonists operated—in different ways to make specific arguments. To state the case in general terms, the common intellectual resource base was related to a shared and interconnected colonial public sphere and intellectual context—the specifics of particular colonies and the anxieties and aspirations of groups or classes therein providing the particular character and directions taken by specific arguments. In the case of India, there was a schematic predictability about the arguments concerned: in response to British claims of Indian backwardness, Indians claimed that they were not backward except economically, which was Britain's fault—progress had been retarded by British rule, and the task of Indians was to get rid of the British as a prerequisite for the achievement of modernity. The custodians of the national movement might debate what precisely the standards of such modernity were, but there was agreement that the British were responsible for India's lack of it. But these Indians, who spoke for Indians as a whole, agreed that *some* Indians were indeed backward. These backward Indians, the 'masses', had to be rescued from backwardness (the passive voice in which this claim was phrased often hiding the implicit assumption regarding who were to be the agents of such a rescue)—the British claim that Indians had to be rescued from backwardness being mirrored in Indian intellectuals' claims that the lower classes had to be raised to modernity.

It is too easy, as a consequence of these similarities, to read this externally and flatten the argument into a claim that imperialism and nationalism were equivalent and, consequently, to postulate a seamless continuity between empire and nation. This is a tempting short-cut; but such flattening, without any attempt to understand the conventions within which the political arguments under consideration operated, can only lead to misreadings, even in an attempt to study the intricacies of political strategy rather than an attempt to pay attention to the ideas which ordered such politics.

Existing studies have been unable adequately to explain, for instance, why imperialists, nationalists and capitalists appeared to adopt the same positions on development in the 1940s; they conclude, variously, that

'Nehruvian socialism' was not socialism at all (a conclusion possibly true in itself, but which tells us nothing about the standards by which 'socialism' was judged in that period, even if the author presents us with his own standards);[1] that capitalists were so enlightened and positive about their nationalism that they were willing to be socialists in that cause (and/or because this suited their 'class interest');[2] that in the context of the 1940s and the 1950s anyone who had been in charge of the Indian economy would have had a planned one (which evades the question of what sort of planned economy and what sort of social goals they might have had);[3] that national planning was simply an adoption of the wartime controls set in place by the colonial government (once again, there are similarities, but significant discontinuities and differences, not least in declared and actual goals);[4] or that a new era of 'constructive imperialism' was about to begin (which does not tell us much about what such 'constructive imperialism' might have meant to those who conceived it).[5] Some of these arguments are more evasive than others, which do try to provide a reading of the available evidence; however, if the conventions of argument remain opaque, so does the evidence. Unless it is understood that the shared terms were necessary conventions of legitimate politics, it becomes impossible to disentangle the positions; they appear to be the same, and are in danger of being read as actually being the same.

There is a rather damaging view that a 'history of ideas' (unworthy of study for its own sake) is fundamentally opposed to the study of 'political strategy'. This stems from an unnecessarily narrow and instrumentalist view of 'political strategy', and a consequent inability to see the strategic importance of ideas in political use (the strategic placement of an argument in the conventions within which it was most likely to be persuasive), as well as a refusal to acknowledge that a language that appears to be intelligible in familiar terms is not necessarily so.

The strategic uses of the conventions of political argument regarding 'development' might profitably be reiterated here. The appeal to purely 'technical' criteria was a favourite mode of argument in politics which sought not to foreground divergent political perspectives. Indeed, it was a very useful strategy to adopt in situations where an explicitly political argument would be discounted. Yet it must be stressed that this did not altogether succeed; for instance, economic criteria as technical criteria continued to be used in both imperialist and nationalist arguments, but as far as the colonialism-versus-legitimate-national-aspirations argument was concerned, imperialists charged nationalists with being suspect critics of government practices because they were biased and did not look at the economic arguments; and nationalists reversed the charges - this was an explicitly political perspective. It also, however, contained the danger of degenerating into a non-argument: nationalists could not have a correct and unbiased view of economics because they were nationalists, while imperialists could not have a correct view because they were imperialists.

The apparent depoliticization, therefore, should not be taken too seriously; it was used only as a temporary truce, to facilitate some sort of interface; opposing protagonists in the arguments usually acknowledged that differences sprang from divergent political perspectives. In the 1940s, differences were sought to be bridged not by appeals to better technical knowledge, but by claims to being on the same side politically: it was the imperialist side of the argument which adopted the conventions of the nationalist side. There could now be apparent agreement in many spheres regarding what constituted progress (though the good intentions of imperialists could be doubted), but not about who could claim to be legitimate agents of progress. Such agents, nationalists argued, could only be nationalists themselves.

Among nationalists, it is true, internal differences were often underplayed, for instance within the NPC in the late 1930s; in the 1950s, the claim made that the Planning Commission was, a body representing technical expertise and was consequently, beyond politics, was indeed 'used as an instrument of politics'.[6] But it must not be forgotten that claims to technical expertise could only operate as legitimate within a consensus which regarded socialism and/or national discipline as the legitimate desired goals. It was within these boundaries of legitimacy that politics was played out. It could, for instance, be claimed that 'socialism' could not be achieved without the required disciplined behaviour of the Indian citizenry. Or it might be claimed that extreme or excessive forms of socialism were incompatible with disciplined national life—this latter claim was more tentatively made, and was often accompanied by the claim that extreme socialism was not properly 'Indian'.

All this tended to privilege a professional directing elite which was to make decisions for the 'nation' as a whole: its social and political goals, its cultural standards, and so on—implying an expertise which went beyond merely technical matters, which sought to encompass both the moral and the material. Formal politics remained the domain of the urban middle-class intellectual; thinking about formal politics was similarly his domain even when he was not a politician. One consequence of this was that the 'masses' all too often entered the picture only as the somewhat abstract ultimate beneficiary, whose interests were claimed to be represented by various socialist parties or even capitalists, in an obligatory populist rhetoric, but whose active participation was hardly envisaged, except in the limited sense of producing the required effort and sacrifices for the success of 'development'—materials to be moulded to a project of development as fulfilment of self-respect for a colonial intellectual elite. This was one of the ambiguities of nation-building in India: those who sought to appropriate the responsibility of forging the nation were unacquainted with the human material available to them. The failure of the masses to conform to the norms of 'modernity' as defined by its leadership either placed them beyond the pale or prompted ardent efforts to teach them the correct modes of behaviour, efforts often not far different from the colonial-paternalist civilizing mission.

The curious point here is that the mixing of liberal, illiberal, and socialist idioms in thinking about 'development' in India—aspects of which were later to be rationalized and dignified as 'non-alignment' and the 'third path'—was to be called 'socialism'. If 'Nehruvian', (Congress) Socialist Party, communist, and capitalist (and more) versions of 'socialism' found space to coexist, it was precisely because a socialism rather nebulously defined (when defined at all) could mean different things to different people. It might be said in passing here that the communists had a more important role in public discourse in India than in most other countries never ruled by a 'communist' government. The leftward orientation of economic discourse up to the 1940s and for a good part of the 1950s was a part of the Marxist–Leninist lineage, even when espoused by 'moderate' Left tendencies like the (Congress) Socialist Party or appropriated by groups further right such as the Congress—now minus the socialists. Communists were often the driving force behind debates on 'development' in India even when they were not, or rather were not permitted to be, actual participants; their language being appropriated and thereby neutralized through being drained of any precise meaning.

The 'socialism' strand of argument remained so important a claim that, in the 1950s, all contending parties called themselves socialist—the Congress, the (formerly Congress) Socialist Party and, later on, its various fragments, the Communist Party, and the Gandhians—making for a very crowded left, a thinly populated centre, and an empty right, if the rhetoric is to be believed. In the 1950s all capitalists were socialists; in the 1960s, when the Swatantra Party was launched as a pro-private enterprise and largely capitalist-run party, an important section of Indian capital, led by Birla, decided to stay with the Congress.[7] The government and party of

Indira Gandhi, in the 1970s, effectively combined the rhetoric of discipline and socialism to create a temporary dictatorship, nationalizing banks and inserting the word 'socialist' (along with the word 'secular') into the preamble to the Constitution while taking the offensive first against communists and then against other political opponents. If this was at times a rather cynical use of the legitimating vocabulary, it also indicates the extreme importance of that legitimating vocabulary.

Endnotes

1. Raghabendra Chattopadhyay, 'The Idea of Planning in India, 1930–1951', unpublished PhD dissertation, Australian National University, Canberra, 1985.
2. Aditya Mukherjee, 'Indian Capitalist Class and Congress on National Planning and Public Sector, 1930–47', in K.N. Panikkar (ed.), *National and Left Movements in India* (New Delhi, 1980); Aditya Mukherjee, *Imperialism, Nationalism and the Making of the Indian Capitalist Class 1920–1947* (Delhi, 2002).
3. This is a view put forward by what seeks to be a standard textbook on the subject of Indian economic history: B.R. Tomlinson, *The Economy of Modern India, 1860–1970* (Cambridge, 1993), p. 173.
4. Dietmar Rothermund, 'Die Anfaenge der indischen Wirtschaftsplanung im Zweiten Weltkrieg', in Peter Habluetzel, Hans Werner Tobler, and Albert Wirz (eds): *Dritte Welt: Historische Praegung und politische Herausforderung: Festschrift zum 60. Geburtstag von Rudolf von Albertini* (Wiesbaden, 1983).
5. C.A. Bayly, 'Returning the British to South Asian History: The Limits of Colonial Hegemony', *South Asia*, Vol. XVII, No. 2, 1994, p. 17. The general contention of this essay, that an understanding of Indian history in the colonial period requires a better understanding of British history, is one with which I agree.
6. Partha Chatterjee, *The Nation and its Fragments: Colonial and Postcolonial Histories* (Princeton, 1993), p. 205.
7. On the Swatantra Party, see H.L. Erdman, *The Swatantra Party and Indian Conservatism* (Cambridge, 1967).

Glossary

Acharya	preceptor, professor, teacher, spiritual guide; title usually given to brahmins.
Akbar	Mughal emperor (1556–1605) to whom is attributed great wisdom and religious tolerance.
artha	money, wealth, politics, finance.
Arthashastra	laws relating to worldly matters; text attributed to Chanakya or Kautilya, according to legend, a minister at the court of Chandragupta Maurya, the first ruler of the Mauryan dynasty, ruling from Pataliputra; the term is often translated as political economy, economics, or politics
Ashoka	third ruler of the Mauryan dynasty, c.269–232 BCE, allegedly transformed by the horrors of war to a believer in non-violence, spiritualism, and the welfare of his subjects.
avatar	incarnation.
badmash	rogue, rascal, villain.
bania	trader, dealer, shopkeeper (often used pejoratively).
bhadralok	respectable person (Bengali).
Bhishma	character in the Mahabharata, the son of Santanu by Ganga, epitomizing wisdom, self-sacrifice, resolve, and determination
Brahma Purana	one of the eighteen *Puranas*.
brahmacharya	celibacy/ celibate; first stage of life, as a student, in the *varnashrama*.

brahmin — priestly caste, in the four-fold *varna* classification.

chamar — tanner/leather-worker, of untouchable caste status (often used pejoratively)

Chandragupta Maurya — first ruler of the Mauryan line, 4th–3rd century BC.

charkha — spinning wheel.

Chitpavan Brahmins — sub-caste of Maratha brahmins, formerly serving the Chhatrapatis, rulers of the Marathas, later a power in their own right as Peshwas, de facto rulers of the Marathas, and a caste closely associated with Indian nationalism as well as with sectarian Hindu politics in western India.

Civilian — member of the Indian Civil Service.

Commonwealth — term originating in the English Revolution (Civil War 1640); used in the twentieth century to refer first to the white possessions of the British Empire, which as Dominions had a higher status within the Empire than the dependent territories, and as part of the term 'Empire-Commonwealth' to refer to the British Empire as a whole; recast in 1949 as an association of apparently equal member states.

communal/communalism — pertaining to communities; used in India to describe sectarian tendencies.

criminal tribes — British Indian legal category: certain tribes were classified as inherently 'criminal'; often they were to be reformed through forced labour.

dacoit — bandit.

dharma — complex term usually translated as religion or faith, but also implying virtue, religious merit, duty, morality, righteousness, piety, law, justice.

District Magistrate — British Indian official in charge of the administration of a district and also acting as judge.

Fa-Hien	Chinese Buddhist monk and traveller who visited India in the fifth century CE.
gram udyog	village uplift.
Hiuen-Tsang	Chinese Buddhist monk and traveller who visited India in the seventh century CE.
Ibn Batuta	Arab traveller who visited India in the fourteenth century.
Jatakas	tales and traditions surrounding the life of the Buddha.
jati	caste, sub-caste, lineage, tribe, nation, species, class, variety, genus, birth, origin, descent, race, family, profession.
khadi	coarse hand-woven cloth.
khilafat	Caliphate.
kisan	peasant.
kshatriya	warrior caste, in the four-fold *varna* classification.
Mahabharata	epic poem.
martial races	British classification of 'races' in India as the basis for military recruitment.
marwari	trading and moneylending caste originally from western India, later also capitalists.
maulvi	Muslim religious scholar.
maya	illusion, deception.
mohalla	locality.
Montague–Chelmsford Reforms	the basis of the Government of India Act of 1919, named after the then Secretary of State for India, Lord Montague, and the then Viceroy, Lord Chelmsford.
panchayat	committee of five; allegedly the basis of village self-government in ancient India
patrika	newspaper.
Permanent Settlement	land revenue settlement established in Bengal in 1793 by Lord Cornwallis, according to which the land revenue demand was settled in perpetuity with the *zamindar.*
Plassey	site of the battle of that name in 1757, in which the Nawals of Bengal was defeated and which is widely regarded as having

	inaugurated British dominion over India.
pratisthan	institution, league, organization.
Puranas	(from *pur*, to precede); literally, 'connected with what is past'; eighteen poem and prose works concerned with the deeds of the gods, composed in Sanskrit over a wide time span.
purna swaraj	complete independence/self-rule.
Ramarajya	literally, the rule of Ram, legendary ruler of Ayodhya according to the epic *Ramayana*; term used to denote a coming utopia, often invoked by Gandhi.
Ramayana	epic poem.
Rigveda	considered, on linguistic grounds, to be the oldest of the four *Vedas*.
rishi	saint, sage, composer of Vedic hymns.
sabha	meeting, association, assembly, council, convention, committee.
sarpanch	village headman.
Shastras	scriptures, but also books of laws or maxims.
sudra	menial caste, in the four-fold *varna* classification.
swadeshi	literally, 'of one's own country'; home-produced; name given to the movement arising in the aftermath of the first partition of Bengal in 1905.
swadharma	one's own religion/ faith/ virtue (see also *dharma*).
swaraj	self-rule.
talukdar	in British India, a landlord or tenure holder, with regional variations in rank and status, for instance, in the UP a superior *zamindar* who engaged with the state to collect the revenue from his own and other *zamindari* estates, and possessing proprietory rights after 1858 in Awadh over the whole area from which they had previously collected revenue; in Bengal, lower in tenurial or social status than a *zamindar.*

Tavernier, Jean Baptiste	French traveller in Mughal India (1640–1666).
thugs	tribe of allegedly habitual ritual killers of British Indian legend, suppressed by the East India Company's forces.
Upanishads	series of about 150 late Vedic esoteric writings, in which the Self (*atman*) is identified with the Supreme (*paramatman*)
vaisya	trading caste, in the four-fold *varna* classification.
Valmiki	*rishi*, to whom is attributed the authorship of the Ramayana.
varna	(from *varn*, to dye or colour); the four-fold classification of castes.
varnashrama	caste and social order of a person; stages of life which a virtuous individual must pass through (considered together): from *varn* (see above), *shram*, to be peaceful, *ashrama*, resting place, stopping-off point, way-station.
Vedas	(from *vid*, to know); literally, 'knowledge' or 'lore', pragmatically, any or all of the four collections of verbally communicated works in Vedic, a stage of Indo-European related to, but earlier than, Sanskrit: *Rigveda, Samaveda, Yajurveda,* and *Atharvaveda*.
Vyasa	person to whom is attributed authorship of the *Mahabharata*.
yajna	sacrifice, sacred ritual.
zamindar	landholder, often specifically used in British India to refer to landholders under the Permanent Settlement.

Select Bibliography

Manuscript Sources

India Office Library and Records, British Library, London

Committees and Commissions of Enquiry
Economic and Overseas Department Files
Economic and Overseas Department Collections
Finance: Committees and Commissions of Enquiry
Financial Department Files
Financial Department Collections
Indian Political Intelligence Files
Information Department Files
Parliamentary Department Papers
Records Department: Government of India War Department History of the Second World War; Government of India Departmental and Miscellaneous Histories of the Second World War
Secretary of State for India's Private Office Papers: Economic Questions
Secretary of State for India's Private Office Papers: Financial Questions

European Manuscripts

Penderel Moon Collection
S.K. Datta Papers
T.E. Gregory Papers
'Village Uplift Scheme': containing pamphlets published by the anti-revolutionary and officially inspired Agra District League, presented to John Henry Darwin, ICS, UP, 1909–37, and Collector of Agra, 1930–4.

Centre for South Asian Studies, University of Cambridge

Edward Benthall Papers
Malcolm Darling Papers

Churchill College Archives Centre, University of Cambridge

P.J. Grigg Papers

National Archives of India, New Delhi

Government of India, Finance Department, Finance Branch
Government of India, Finance Department, Planning Branch
Government of India, Finance Department, Planning-I Branch
Government of India, Finance Department, Planning-II Branch
Government of India, Finance Department, Planning-III Branch

Jawaharlal Nehru Memorial Museum and Library, New Delhi

All-India Congress Committee Papers
Homy Mody Papers
Jawaharlal Nehru Papers
J.C. Kumarappa Papers
P.C. Mahalanobis Papers
Meghnad Saha Papers
M. Visvesvaraya Papers (microfilm)
Purshotamdas Thakurdas Papers
Walchand Hirachand Archive

P.C. Joshi Archive, Jawaharlal Nehru University, New Delhi

Papers of the Communist Party of India

Indian Statistical Institute, Calcutta

P.C. Mahalanobis Archives

Printed Sources

Newspapers and Periodicals

Amrita Bazar Patrika
Aryan Path
Asiatic Review
Bombay Chronicle
Congress Socialist
Eastern Economist
Economist
Gram Udyog Patrika

Harijan
Hindu
Hindustan Times
Hindusthan Standard
Indian Journal of Economics
Journal of the Royal Society of Arts
Modern Review
National Herald
Prabashi
Science and Culture

Sources Published Before 1950 and Memoirs Relating to that Period

Agarwal, S.N., *The Gandhian Plan of Economic Development for India* (Bombay, 1944).

Ambedkar, B.R., *The Evolution of Public Finance in British India: A Study in the Provincial Decentralisation of Public Finance* (London, 1925).

Amery, L.S., *My Political Life, volume three: The Unforgiving Years 1929–1940* (London, 1955).

——, *The Framework of the Future* (Oxford, 1944).

——, *India and Freedom* (Oxford, 1942).

——, *The Forward View* (London, 1935).

——, *Empire and Prosperity*, (Second edition, London, October 1931).

——, *The Empire in a New Era* (London, 1928).

Anstey, Vera, *The Economic Development of India* (London, 1929).

Baden-Powell, B.H., *The Land Systems of British India*, three volumes (Oxford, 1892).

Banerjee, B.N. *et al*, *People's Plan for Economic Development of India* (Delhi, 1944).

Beveridge, William, *Full Employment in a Free Society* (London, 1944).

——, *The Pillars of Security* (London, 1943).

Birdwood, George, *The Industrial Arts of India* (London, 1880).

Birla, G.D., *In the Shadow of the Mahatma: A Personal Memoir* (Bombay, 1968).

——, *The Path to Prosperity* (Allahabad, 1950).

Bose, P.N., *A History of Hindu Civilisation During British Rule*, three volumes, (Calcutta, 1894–6).

Brayne, Frank Lugard, *Better Villages* (Oxford, 1937).

Carritt, Michael, *A Mole in the Crown* (Calcutta, 1986).

Chettur, S.K., *The Steel Frame and I: Life in the ICS* (Bombay, 1962).

Coupland, Reginald, *India: A Re-Statement* (London, 1945).

Dange, S.A., *Gandhi vs Lenin* (Bombay, 1921).

Darling, Malcolm, *At Freedom's Door* (Oxford, 1949).

——, 'The Indian Village and Democracy', *Journal of the Royal Society of Arts*, Vol. XCI, 6 August, 1943.

——, 'The Indian Peasant in the Modern World', *Asiatic Review*, Vol. XXXVIII, No. 133 (January 1942).

——, *Wisdom and Waste in the Punjab Village* (Oxford, 1934).

——, *Rusticus Loquitur, or the Old Light and the New in the Punjab Village* (Oxford, 1930).

——, *The Punjab Peasant in Prosperity and Debt* (Oxford, 1925).

Dasgupta, Satish Chandra, *The Cow in India*, two volumes (Calcutta, 1945).

Desai, Mahadev, 'Preface' to M.K. Gandhi, *Hind Swaraj*, (revised new edition, Ahmedabad, 1939).

Desai, Valji Govindji, *Cow Protection* (Ahmedabad, 1934).

Digby, William, *'Prosperous' British India* (London, 1901).

Dutt, R. Palme, *India Today* (London, 1940; Second revised Indian edition, Bombay, 1949).

Dutt, Romesh Chunder, *The Economic History of India*, two volumes (London, 1906).

East India Association, Discussion: 'India and Democracy', Tuesday, 14 October 1941, opened by Sir George Schuster, *Asiatic Review*, Vol. XXXVIII, No. 133 (January 1942).

Gandhi, M.K., 'Hind Swaraj,' in Anthony Parel (ed.) *Gandhi: Hind Swaraj and Other Writings* (Cambridge, 1997).

——, *The Story of My Experiments with Truth* (Harmondsworth edition, 1982; first published in two volumes, 1927 and 1929, Ahmedabad, translated by Mahadev Desai).

Grigg, P.J., *Prejudice and Judgement* (London, 1948).

Gyan Chand, *Local Finance in India* (Allahabad, 1947).

——, *Essentials of Federal Finance: a Contribution to the Problem of Financial Re-adjustment in India* (London, 1930).

Hatch, D. Spencer, *Further Upward in Rural India* (Madras, 1938).

——, *Up from Poverty in Rural India* (Oxford University Press, 1932).

Hutton, Thomas, 'The Planning of Post-War Development in India', *Asiatic Review*, Vol. *XLIII* (April 1947).

Jack, J.C., *The Economic Life of a Bengal District* (Oxford, 1916).

Keynes, John Maynard, *A Treatise on Probability* (London, 1921; edn London, 1973).

——, *Indian Currency and Finance* (London, 1913).

——, review of Theodore Morison, *The Economic Transition in India* (London, 1911), in *The Economic Journal*, Vol XXI (September 1911).

Kumarappa, JC, 'The Economy of the Cross', a summary of three addresses to the Mid-India Conference of Christian Students at Nagpur, 5th-7th November 1942, reprinted in *Christianity: its Economy and Way of Life* (Ahmedabad, 1945).

Kumarappa, J.C., *Blood Money* (Wardha, 1948).

——, *The Economy of Permanence* (Wardha, 1948).

——, *Clive to Keynes (A Survey of the History of our Public Debts and Credits)* (Ahmedabad, 1947).

——, *Christianity: its Economy and Way of Life* (Ahmedabad, 1945).

——, *The Practice and Precepts of Jesus* (Ahmedabad, 1945).

——, *Currency Inflation- its Cause and Cure* (Wardha, 1943).

——, *Why the Village Movement? (A plea for a village-centred economic order in India)* (fifth edition, Wardha, 1949; first edition, 1936).

——, *A Survey of Matar Taluka (Kaira District)* (Ahmedabad, 1931).

——, *Public Finance and our Poverty: The Contribution of Public Finance to the Present Economic State of India* (Ahmedabad, 1930).

Law, Satya Churn (ed.), *Acharyya Ray Commemoration Volume* (Calcutta, 1932).

Lohia, Ram Manohar, 'Economics After Marx', written in 1943, reprinted in Rammanohar Lohia, *Marx, Gandhi and Socialism* (Second edition, Hyderabad, 1978; first published 1963).

Lokanathan, P.S., *Industrial Organisation in India* (London, 1935).

——, *Industrial Welfare in India* (Madras, 1929).

Mahalanobis, P.C., 'Analysis of Racial Likeness in Bengal Castes' (Abstract), *Proceedings of the Indian Science Congress (Calcutta), Anthropology Section* 22, (1935).

——, 'Application of Statistical Methods in Industry', *Science and Culture* 1 (1935).

——, 'Revision of Risley's Anthropometric Data relating to the Chittagong Hill Tribes' (Abstract), *Proceedings of the Indian Science Congress (Bangalore), Anthropology Section* 19, (1932); and *Sankhya* 1 (1934).

———, 'Revision of Risley's Anthropometric Data relating to the Tribes and Castes of Bengal', (Abstract), *Proceedings of the Indian Science Congress (Nagpur)* 18, (1931).

——, 'Analysis of Race Mixture in Bengal', *Journal of the Asiatic Society of Bengal*, Vol. XXIII (1927).

——, 'Anthropological Observations on the Anglo-Indians of Calcutta, Part I: Analysis of Male Stature', *Records of the Indian Museum*, Vol. XXIII (April 1922).

Maine, Henry, *Village Communities of the East and West* (London, 1871).

——, *Ancient Law* (London, 1861).

Marx, Karl, 'The British Rule in India', *New York Daily Tribune,* 25 June 1853, reprinted in Karl Marx and Friedrich Engels, *On Colonialism* (Moscow, 1959).

Masani, M.R., *Against the Tide* (New Delhi, 1981).

——, *Bliss was it in that dawn...* (New Delhi, 1977).

——, *The Communist Party of India: A Short History* (London, 1954).

——, *Picture of a Plan*, (Bombay, 1944).

——, *Socialism Reconsidered* (Bombay, 1944).

Mason, Philip, *A Shaft of Sunlight* (London, 1978).

Matthai, John, *Village Government in British India* (London, 1913).

Mitter, S.C., *A Recovery Plan for Bengal* (Calcutta, 1934).

Mookerji, Radhakumud, *Nationalism in Hindu Culture* (London, 1921).

——, *Local Government in Ancient India* (London, 1919).

——, *A History of Indian Shipping and Maritime Activity from the Earliest Times* (London, 1912).

Moon, Penderel, *Strangers in India* (London, 1944).

Morison, Theodore, review of Jadunath Sarkar, *The Economics of British India* (Calcutta, 1911), in the *Economic Journal*, Vol XXI (September 1911), pp. 424–5.

——, *The Economic Transition in India* (London, 1911).

Mukerjee, Radhakamal, *The Foundations of Indian Economics* (London, 1916).

Naoroji, Dadabhai, *Poverty and Un-British Rule in India* (London, 1901).

Narayan, Jayaprakash, 'Letter to PSP Associates', Patna, 25 October 1957, reprinted in Jayaprakash Narayan, *Towards a New Society* (New Delhi, 1958).

——, *Why Socialism?* (Benares, 1936).

National Council, Y.M.C.A. India, Burma, and Ceylon, *The Y.M.C.A. at Work in India, Burma and Ceylon*, pamphlet, (Calcutta, n.d., but after 23 September 1940).

Nehru, Jawaharlal, *The Discovery of India* (Calcutta, 1946).

——, *An Autobiography* (edition New Delhi, 1982; first edition London, 1936).

——, *Whither India?* (Allahabad, 1933).

Ranadive, B.T., *The Tata–Birla Plan: Will it Work?* (Bombay, n.d.).

Ray, P.C., *Life and Experiences of a Bengali Chemist* (two volumes, Calcutta and London, 1932 and 1935).

——, *The History of Hindu Chemistry* (two volumes, London, 1902 and 1908).

Risley, H.H., *The Tribes and Castes of Bengal: Anthropometric Data* (two volumes, Calcutta, 1891).

——, *The Tribes and Castes of Bengal: Ethnographic Glossary* (two volumes, Calcutta, 1891).

Roseboom, Henry E. and Cedric Dover, 'The Eurasian Community as a Eugenic Problem', in *A Decade of Progress in Eugenics* (Baltimore, 1934; reprint, New York, 1984).

Saha, M.N., and S.N. Bose, (transl), *The Principle of Relativity; Original Papers by A. Einstein and H. Minkovski. With a Historical Introduction by P.C. Mahalanobis* (Calcutta, 1920).

Salter, Arthur, *Memoirs of a Public Servant* (London, 1961).

Sarkar, Benoy Kumar, *Hindu Achievements in Exact Science* (New York, 1918).

Sarkar, Jadunath, *The Economics of British India* (Calcutta, 1911).

Schuster, George, *Private Work and Public Causes: A Personal Memoir* (Cowbridge, 1979).

——, 'Indian Economic Life: Past Trends and Future Prospects', *Journal of the Royal Society of Arts*, Vol. LXXXIII, 31 May 1935, address delivered 8 March 1935.

——, 'Empire Trade Before and After Ottawa: A Preliminary Reconnaissance', *The Economist:* Special Supplement, 3 November 1934.

Seal, Brajendranath, *The Positive Sciences of the Ancient Hindus* (London, 1915).

Shah, KT (ed), *Report: National Planning Committee* (Bombay, 1949).

—— (ed.), *National Planning, Principles and Administration* (Bombay, 1948).

—— (ed.), *National Planning Committee: Power and Fuel* (Bombay, 1947).

—— (ed.), *National Planning Committee: River Training and Irrigation* (Bombay, 1947).

—— (ed.), *National Planning Committee; Report of the Sub-Committee on Labour* (Bombay, 1947).

—— (ed.), *National Planning Committee, No. 2: Being an Abstract of Proceedings and other particulars relating to the National Planning Committee* (Bombay, May 1940).

—— (ed.), *Sixty Years of Indian Finance* (Bombay, 1921).

Shaha, A.K., *India on Planning: Planning for Liquidation of Unemployment and Illiteracy* (Calcutta, 1948).

Shaha-Sedina, Tatiana, 'The Problem of Nationalities', in A.K. Shaha, *India on Planning: Planning for Liquidation of Unemployment and Illiteracy* (Calcutta, 1948).

Strickland, C.F., *Indian Village Welfare Association; Review of Rural Welfare Activities in India, 1932* (London, 1932).

Subba Rao, N.S., *Some Aspects of Economic Planning: Sir William Meyer Lectures, University of Madras, March 1933* (Bangalore, 1935).

Sundara Ram, L.L., *Cow Protection in India* (Madras, 1927).

Tawney, R.H., *Religion and the Rise of Capitalism* (London, 1927; this edition Harmondsworth, 1977).

Thakurdas, Purshotamdas, J.R.D. Tata, G.D. Birla, Sir Shriram, Kasturbhai Lalbhai, A.D. Shroff, and John Matthai, *A Plan of Economic Development for India* (Parts I and II, Bombay, 1944).

Third International Conference on Eugenics, 1932, *A Decade of Progress in Eugenics* (Baltimore, 1934; reprint, New York, 1984).

Thomas, P.J., *The Growth of Federal Finance in India: being a survey of India's public finances from 1833 to 1939* (Oxford 1939).

Visvesvaraya, M., *Memoirs of my Working Life* (Bombay, 1951).

——, *Reconstruction in Post-War India: A Plan of Development All Round* (Bombay, 1944).

——, *Indian Automobile Factory Scheme: Government of India's Obstructive Attitude* (Bombay, 1942).

——, District Development Scheme: Economic Progress by Forced Marches (Bangalore City, 1939).

——, *Nation Building: A Five-Year Plan for the Provinces* (Bangalore City, 1937).

——, *Unemployment in India: its Causes and Cure* (Bangalore City, 1932; Second edition 1935).

——, *Planned Economy for India* (Bangalore City, 1934).

——, *Rural Reconstruction in India: an Outline of a Scheme* (Bangalore City, 1931).

——, *Reconstructing India* (London, 1920).

Webb, Sidney and Beatrice Webb, *Soviet Communism: A New Civilisation?*, two volumes, (London, 1935).
Wint, Guy and George Schuster, *India and Democracy* (London, 1941).
Woodruff, Philip (Philip Mason), *The Men Who Ruled India, Part II: The Guardians* (London, 1965).

Official Publications

Bowley, A.L., and H.D. Robertson, *A Scheme for an Economic Census for India, with special reference to a Census of Production and Reorganisation of Statistics* (Delhi, 1934).
Clow, A.G., *The State and Industry: A Narrative of Indian Government Policy and Action in relation to Industry under the Reformed Constitution* (Calcutta, 1928).
Commonwealth Consultative Committee on Economic Development in South and South-East Asia: Report by the Committee (London, 1950).
Government of Bengal, *Report of the Land Revenue Commission, Bengal, Vol. I (with Minutes of Dissent)* (Calcutta, 1940) (Floud Commission).
Government of India, Bureau of Public Information, *Guide to Prominent Newspapers and Periodicals in English and Indian Languages Published in British India and Indian States* (New Delhi, May 1944).
——, Planning and Development Department, *Second Report on Reconstruction Planning* (New Delhi, 1944).
——, Bureau of Public Information, *Guide to Prominent English and Vernacular Newspapers and Periodicals Published in British India and the Indian States, Corrected up to December 1937* (New Delhi, 1938).
——, Home Department, Intelligence Bureau, *India and Communism: Confidential (Revised up to the 1 January 1935:* (Simla, 1935).
——, Home Department, Intelligence Bureau, *India and Communism: Confidential* (Calcutta, 1933).
Gregory, T.E., and W.R. Natu, *Studies in Indian Economics issued by the Office of the Economic Adviser, First Series: Aspects of the Indian Tariff, No. 1: The Burden of the Indian Tariff* (Delhi: Government of India Press, 1939).
Indian Central Banking Enquiry Committee, 1931 Volume I, Part I; Majority Report (Calcutta, 1931).
——, *Volume I Part II: Minority Report* (Calcutta, 1931).
——, *Volume II: Evidence (Written)* (Calcutta, 1931).
Indian Munitions Board, *Industrial Handbook 1919* (Calcutta, 1919).
Petrie, David, *Communism in India, 1924-1927* (Calcutta, 1927).
Report of the Advisory Planning Board (New Delhi, December 1946).
Report of the Central Banking Enquiry Committee, 1931 (Calcutta, 1931).
Report of the Indian Road Development Committee, 1927–28 (Calcutta, 1928) (Jayakar Committee).
Report of the Royal Commission on Agriculture in India (London, 1928) (Linlithgow Commission).

Report of the Royal Commission on Indian Currency and Finance, 1926 (London, 1926) (Hilton Young Commission).

Report of the External Capital Committee, 1925 (Calcutta, 1925) (Blackett Committee).

Report of the Indian Economic Enquiry Committee (Calcutta, 1925) (Visvesvaraya Committee).

Report of the Royal Commission on the Superior Civil Services in India (London, 1924) (Lee Commission).

Report of the Indian Fiscal Commission, 1921–22 (Simla, 1922) (Rahimtoola Commission).

Report of the Indian Industrial Commission (Calcutta, 1918) (Holland Commission).

Report of the Committee on the Subject of Imperial Preference (Calcutta, 1920) (Wacha Committee).

Report on Indian Constitutional Reforms (Calcutta, 1918).

Salter, Arthur, *A Scheme for an Economic Advisory Organisation in India* (Geneva, 1931).

Statement Exhibiting the Moral and Material Progress and Condition of India (London: HMSO, annual).

Published Documents, Correspondence, etc.

Bose, Sisir Kumar, and Bose, Sugata (eds), *Netaji Collected Works, Volume 9: Congress President: Speeches, Articles and Letters, January 1938–May 1939* (Delhi, 1995).

Bose, Sisir Kumar, and Bose, Sugata (eds), *The Essential Writings of Netaji Subhas Chandra Bose* (Delhi, 1997).

Gopal, S (ed), *Selected Works of Jawaharlal Nehru* (15 vols, New Delhi, 1972–1982).

Mansergh, N (ed), *India: The Transfer of Power* (12 vols, London, HMSO, 1970–83).

Moggridge, DE (ed), *The Collected Writings of John Maynard Keynes* vol XI (London, 1983).

Moon, Penderel (ed), *Wavell: The Viceroy's Journal* (London, 1973).

Nehru, Jawaharlal, *India's Foreign Policy: Selected Speeches, September 1946–April 1961* (Delhi, 1961).

The Collected Works of Mahatma Gandhi (100 volumes, New Delhi, 1958–2000).

Published Secondary Works

Ahmad, Aijaz, '*Orientalism* and after: Ambivalence and Metropolitan Location in the Work of Edward Said', in Aijaz Ahmad, *In Theory: Classes, Nations, Literatures* (London, 1992).

Alvares, Claude, *Science, Development and Violence: The Revolt Against Modernity* (Delhi, 1992).

Ambirajan, S, *Classical Political Economy and British Administration in India* (Cambridge, 1978).

Amin, Shahid, 'Gandhi as Mahatma', in Ranajit Guha (ed.), *Subaltern Studies II* (Delhi, 1983).

Andersen, W.K., and S.D. Damle, *The Brotherhood in Saffron: the Rashtriya Swayamsevak Sangh and Hindu Revivalism* (Boulder, Colorado, 1987).

Anderson, Robert S., *Building Scientific Institutions in India: Saha and Bhabha* (Montreal, 1975).

Arndt, H.W., *Economic Development: The History of an Idea* (Chicago, 1987).

Bagchi, Amiya Kumar, *The Presidency Banks and the Indian Economy, 1876–1914* (Calcutta, 1989).

——, *Private Investment in India 1900–1939* (Cambridge, 1972).

Baker, Christopher, Gordon Johnson, and Anil Seal, (eds), *Power, Profit and Politics*, special issue, *Modern Asian Studies*, Vol. 15, No. 3 (1981).

Balachandran, G., *John Bullion's Empire: Britain's Gold Problem and India between the Wars* (Richmond, 1996).

——, 'Towards a "Hindoo Marriage": Anglo-Indian Monetary Relations in Interwar India, 1917–35', *Modern Asian Studies*, Vol. 28, No. 3 (1994).

Bardhan, Pranab, *The Political Economy of Development in India* (Oxford, 1984).

Barrier, N.G. *The Punjab Alienation of Land Bill of 1900* (Durham, NC, 1966).

Basu, Subho, 'Strikes and "Communal" Riots in Calcutta in the 1890s', *Modern Asian Studies*, Vol. 32, No. 4 (1998).

Bates, Crispin, 'Race, Caste and Tribe in Central India: The Early Origins of Indian Anthropometry', in Peter Robb (ed.), *The Concept of Race in South Asia* (Delhi, 1995).

Bawa, Vasant Kumar, 'Gandhi in the Twentieth Century: Search for an Alternative Development Model', *Economic and Political Weekly*, Vol. XXXI, No. 47, 23 November 1996.

Bayly, C.A., *Empire and Information* (Cambridge, 1996).

——, 'Returning the British to South Asian History: The Limits of Colonial Hegemony', *South Asia*, Vol. XVII, No. 2, (1994).

Bayly, Susan, 'Caste and "Race" in the Colonial Ethnography of India', in Peter Robb (ed.), *The Concept of Race in South Asia* (Delhi, 1995).

Berman, Marshall, *All that is Solid Melts Into Air: The Experience of Modernity* (London, 1983).

Bhagwati, Jagdish, *India in Transition: Freeing the Economy* (Oxford, 1993).

Bhattacharya, Sabyasachi, 'Laissez-faire in India', *Indian Economic and Social History Review*, Vol. II, No. 1 (January 1965).

Bhattacharya, Sanjoy, *Propaganda and Information in Eastern India 1939–45* (Richmond, 2000)

——, 'An Extremely Troubled Relationship: The British Colonial State and the Communist Party of India, 1942–44', in Biswamoy Pati (ed.), *Turbulent Times: India, 1940–44* (Bombay, 1998).

Bhattacharya, Sanjoy and Benjamin Zachariah, '"A Great Destiny": The British

Colonial State and the Advertisement of Post-War Reconstruction in India, 1942–45', *South Asia Research*, 19, 1 (1999).

Bose, Sugata, 'Instruments and Idioms of Colonial and National Development: India's Historical Experience in Comparitive Perspective', in Fredrick Cooper and Randall Packard (eds) *International Development and the Social Science* (Berkeley, 1997).

Bose, Sugata and Ayesha Jalal, 'Nationalism, Democracy and Development', in Sugata Bose and Ayesha Jalal (eds), *Nationalism, Democracy and Development: State and Politics in India* (Delhi, 1997).

Brecher, Michael, *Nehru: A Political Biography* (London, 1959).

Bridge, Carl, *Holding India to the Empire* (Delhi, 1986).

Burrow, J.W., *Evolution and Society* (Cambridge, 1966).

Butler, J.R.M., *Lord Lothian (Philip Kerr) 1882–1940* (London, 1960).

Byres, Terence J. (ed.), *The Indian Economy: Major Debates Since Independence* (Delhi, 1997).

——, 'State, Class and Development Planning in India', in Terence J. Byres (ed.), *The State and Development Planning in India* (Delhi, 1994).

—— (ed.), *The State and Development Planning in India* (Delhi, 1994).

Cain, P.J., and A.G. Hopkins, *British Imperialism: Crisis and Deconstruction 1914–1990* (London, 1993).

——, *British Imperialism: Innovation and Expansion 1688–1914* (London, 1993).

Chakrabarty, Bidyut, 'Jawaharlal Nehru and Planning, 1938–41: India at the Crossroads', *Modern Asian Studies*, Vol. 26, No. 2 (1992).

Chakrabarty, Dipesh, *Habitations of Modernity: Essays in the Wake of Subaltern Studies* (Chicago, 2002).

——, *Provincialising Europe* (Princeton, 2000).

Chakravarty, Sukhamoy, *Development Planning: The Indian Experience* (Oxford, 1987).

Chandavarkar, Anand, *Keynes and India: A Study in Economics and Biography* (Basingstoke, 1989).

Chandavarkar, R.S., *The Origins of Industrial Capitalism in India* (Cambridge, 1994).

Chandra, Bipan, 'Jawaharlal Nehru and the Capitalist Class, 1936', *Economic and Political Weekly*, Vol. X, Nos. 33–35 (August 1975).

——, 'British and Indian Ideas on Indian Economic Development, 1858–1905', in B.R. Nanda and V.C. Joshi (eds), *Studies in Modern Indian History* (New Delhi, 1972).

——, *The Rise and Growth of Economic Nationalism in India: Economic Policies of Indian National Leadership, 1880–1905* (New Delhi, 1966).

Charlesworth, Neil, *Peasants and Imperial Rule: Agriculture and Agrarian Society in the Bombay Presidency, 1850–1935* (Cambridge, 1985).

Chatterjee, Partha, 'Development Planning and the Indian State' in Terence J. Byres (ed.), *The State and Development Planning in India* (Delhi, 1994).

——, *The Nation and its Fragments: Colonial and Post-Colonial Histories* (Princeton, 1993).

———, *Nationalist Thought and the Colonial World: A Derivative Discourse?* (London, 1986).

———, 'Gandhi and the Critique of Civil Society', in Ranajit Guha (ed.), *Subaltern Studies III* (Delhi, 1984).

Chatterji, Basudev, *Trade, Tariffs and Empire: Lancashire and British Politics in India 1919–1939* (Delhi, 1992).

———, 'Business and Politics in the 1930s: Lancashire and the Making of the Indo-British Trade Agreement, 1939', *Modern Asian Studies*, Vol. 15, No. 3 (1985).

Chattopadhyay, Gautam, *Subhas Chandra Bose and the Indian Communist Movement* (Calcutta, 1975).

Chattopadhyay, Raghabendra, 'An Early British Initiative in the Genesis of Indian Planning', *Economic and Political Weekly*, Vol. XXII, No. 5: *Review of Political Economy* (31 January1987).

———, 'Indian National Congress and the Indian Bourgeoisie: Liaquat Ali Khan's Budget of 1947–48', Occasional Paper No. 85, Centre for Studies in Social Sciences (Calcutta, August 1986).

Clarke, Peter, *Hope and Glory: Britain, 1900–1990* (Harmondsworth, 1996).

———, *The Keynesian Revolution in the Making, 1924–1936* (New York, 1988).

Clarkson, S., *The Soviet Theory of Development: India and the Third World in Marxist–Leninist Scholarship* (Toronto, 1978).

Cohn, Bernard, *Colonialism and its Forms of Knowledge: The British in India* (Delhi, 1997).

———, *An Anthropologist Among the Historians and other Essays* (Delhi, 1986).

———, 'Representing Authority in Victorian India', in Eric Hobsbawm and Terence Ranger (eds), *The Invention of Tradition* (Cambridge, 1983).

Cohn, Norman, *Warrant for Genocide* (London, 1967).

Constantine, S, '"Bringing the Empire Alive": The Empire Marketing Board and Imperial Propaganda, 1926–33', in J.M. MacKenzie (ed), *Imperialism and Popular Culture* (Manchester, 1986).

———, *The Making of British Colonial Development Policy 1914-1940* (London, 1984).

Darwin, John, *Britain and Decolonisation: The Retreat from Empire in the Post-War World* (Basingstoke, 1988).

Das Gupta, Uma, 'Rabindranath Tagore on Rural Reconstruction: The Sriniketan Programme, 1921–41', *Indian Historical Review*, Vol. IV, No. 2 (January 1978).

Dasgupta, Ajit K., *Gandhi's Economic Thought* (London, 1996).

———, *A History of Indian Economic Thought* (London, 1993).

Dasgupta, Sugata, *A Poet and a Plan (Tagore's Experiments in Rural Reconstruction)* (Calcutta, 1962).

Datta, Bhabatosh, *Indian Economic Thought: Twentieth Century Perspectives* (New Delhi, 1978).

Deutscher, Isaac, *The Prophet Armed* (London, 1959).

Dewey, Clive, *Anglo-Indian Attitudes: The Mind of the Indian Civil Service* (London, 1993).

——, 'The End of the Imperialism of Free Trade: The Eclipse of the Lancashire Lobby and the Concession of Fiscal Autonomy to India' in Clive Dewey and A.G. Hopkins (eds) *The Imperial Impact: Studies in the Economic History of Africa and India* (London, 1978).

——, 'Editor's Introduction' to Malcolm Darling, *The Punjab Peasant in Prosperity and Debt*, fifth edition, (Delhi, 1977).

—— 'Images of the Village Community: a Study in Anglo-Indian Ideology', *Modern Asian Studies*, Vol. 6, No. 2 (1972).

Drummond, Ian, *Imperial Economic Policy 1917–39: Studies in Expansion and Protection* (London, 1974).

——, *British Economic Policy and the Empire, 1919–1939* (London, 1972).

Dumont, Louis, 'The "Village Community" from Munro to Maine', *Contributions to Indian Sociology*, Volume ix (1966).

Duncan, Ian, 'The Politics of Liberalisation in Early Post-Independence India: Food Deregulation in 1947', *Journal of Commonwealth and Comparative Politics*, Vol. XXXIII, No. 1 (March 1995).

Erdman, H.L., *The Swatantra Party and Indian Conservatism* (Cambridge, 1967).

Fanon, Frantz, *Black Skin, White Masks* (London, 1980).

——, *The Wretched of the Earth* (Harmondsworth, 1967).

Frankel, Francine R., *India's Political Economy 1947–1977: The Gradual Revolution* (Princeton, 1978).

Gadgil, Madhav and Ramachandra Guha, *Ecology and Equity: The Use and Abuse of Nature in Contemporary India* (London, 1995).

Gadgil, Madhav, 'On the Gandhian Economic Trail', *Gandhians in Action* (April–June 1994).

Gallagher, J.A., and Anil Seal, 'Britain and India Between the Wars', *Modern Asian Studies*, Vol. 15, No. 3 (1981).

Ganguli, B.N., *Indian Economic Thought: Nineteenth Century Perspectives* (New Delhi, 1977).

Ghosh, Tapan, *The Gandhi Murder Trial* (New York, 1973).

Gilman, Sander L., *Freud, Race and Gender* (Princeton, 1993).

Gopal, S., *Jawaharlal Nehru: A Biography*, volume 1 (London, 1975).

Gordon, A.D.D., *Businessmen and Politics: Rising Nationalism and a Modernising Economy in Bombay, 1918–33* (Delhi, 1978).

Gramsci, Antonio, *Selections from the Prison Notebooks,* edited and translated by Quintin Hoare and Geoffrey Nowell Smith (London, 1971).

Guha Thakurta, Tapati, *The Making of a New 'Indian' Art: Artists, Aesthetics and Nationalism in Bengal, c. 1850–1920* (Cambridge, 1992).

Guha, Ranajit, *History at the Limits of World History* (New York, 2002).

——, *An Indian Historiography of India: a Nineteenth-Century Agenda and its Implications* (Calcutta, 1988).

——, 'On Some Aspects of the Historiography of Colonial India', in Ranajit Guha (ed.), *Subaltern Studies I* (Oxford, 1983).

——, *A Rule of Property for Bengal* (Paris, 1963).

Gupta, Dhruba, 'Indian Perceptions of Africa', *South Asia Research*, Vol. 11, No. 2 (November 1991).

Gupta, Partha Sarathi, *Imperialism and the British Labour Movement 1914–1964* (London, 1975).

Hanson, A.H., *The Process of Planning: A Study of India's Five-Year Plans, 1950–64* (Oxford, 1966).

Hasian, Marouf Arif, Jr, *The Rhetoric of Eugenics in Anglo-American Thought* (Athens, Georgia, 1996)

Hobsbawm, E.J., *Industry and Empire* (Harmondsworth, 1969).

——, 'Where are British Historians Going?', *The Marxist Quarterly*, Vol. II, No. 1 (January 1955).

Hodges, Sarah, 'Indian Eugenics in an Age of Reform', in Sarah Hodges (ed.), *Reproductive Health in India: History, Politics, Controversies* (Delhi, 2003).

Howe, Stephen, *Anticolonialism in British Politics: The Left and the End of Empire 1918–1964* (Oxford, 1993).

Hunt, Roland and John Harrison, *The District Officer in India 1930–1947* (London, 1980).

Hurd, John M., 'Railways', in Dharma Kumar (ed.), *Cambridge Economic History of India*, volume II, (Cambridge, 1983).

Hutchins, Francis, *The Illusion of Permanence: British Imperialism in India* (Princeton, 1967).

Hyam, R., 'Bureaucracy and "Trusteeship" in the Colonial Empire', in W.R. Louis (ed.), *Oxford History of the British Empire*, volume IV (Oxford, 1999).

Indian Statistical Institute, *History and Activities, 1931–1963* (Calcutta, n.d.).

Israel, Milton, *Communications and Power: Propaganda and the Press in the Indian Nationalist Struggle, 1920–1947* (Cambridge, 1994).

Iyer, Raghavan, *The Moral and Political Thought of Mahatma Gandhi* (New York, 1973).

Jaffrelot, Christophe, 'The Idea of the Hindu Race in the Writings of Hindu Nationalist Ideologues in the 1920s and 1930s: A Concept Between Two Cultures', in Peter Robb (ed.), *The Concept of Race in South Asia* (Delhi, 1995).

Jalal, Ayesha, *The Sole Spokesman: Jinnah, the Muslim League and the Demand for Pakistan* (Cambridge, 1985).

Kaushik, Karuna, *Russian Revolution and Indian Nationalism: Studies of Lajpat Rai, Subhas Chandra Bose and Ram Manohar Lohia* (Delhi, 1984).

Kaviraj, Sudipta, 'Democracy and Development in India', in Amiya Kumar Bagchi (ed.), *Democracy and Development* (London, 1995).

——, 'On the Structure of Nationalist Discourse' in T.V. Sathyamurthi (ed.), *Social Change and Political Discourse in India, volume 1: State and Nation in the Context of Social Change* (Delhi, 1994).

Keer, Dhanajay, *Dr Ambedkar: Life and Mission* (Bombay, 1954; this edition Bombay, 1987).

Kevles, Daniel J., *In the Name of Eugenics: Genetics and the Uses of Human Heredity* (New York, 1985).

Kiernan, Victor, 'Farewells to Empire: Some Recent Studies of Imperialism', in *Marxism and Imperialism* (London, 1974).

Kindleberger, Charles, *The World in Depression 1929–1939* (Munich, 1973; new edition Harmondsworth 1987).

Kirk, R.L., 'P.C. Mahalanobis and Population Genetics in India', *Samvadhvam: House Journal of the Indian Statistical Institute*, Vol. 10, Nos. 1–4 (P.C. Mahalanobis Memorial Volume) (December 1974).

Krishnamurthy, Shakuntala, *Dr Mokshagundam Visvesvaraya* (Bangalore, 1980).

Krishnamurti, Y.G., *Sir M. Visvesvaraya: A Study* (Bombay, 1941).

Kuber, W.N., *B.R. Ambedkar* (New Delhi, 1978).

Kudaisya, Medha Malik, *The Life and Times of G.D. Birla* (Delhi, 2003).

Kumar, Deepak, *Science and the Raj 1857–1905* (Delhi, 1995).

—— (ed), *Science and Empire: Essays in the Indian Context (1700–1947)* (Delhi, 1991).

Kumar, Devendra, 'Kumarappa and the Contemporary Development Perspective', *Gandhi Marg*, Vol. 14, No. 2 (July–September 1992).

Lala, R.M., *The Creation of Wealth: The Tata Story* (Bombay, 1981).

Land, Andrew, Rodney Lowe, and Noel Whiteside, *The Development of the Welfare State 1939–1951: A Guide to Documents in the Public Records Office* (London, 1992).

Laushey, David M., *Bengal Terrorism and the Marxist Left: Aspects of Regional Nationalism in India, 1905–1942* (Calcutta, 1975).

Lavin, Deborah, 'Lionel Curtis and the Idea of the Commonwealth', in Frederick Madden and D.K. Fieldhouse (eds), *Oxford and the Idea of the Commonwealth* (London, 1982).

Lee, J.M., *Colonial Development and Good Government: a Study of the Ideas Expressed by the British Official Classes in Planning Decolonisation 1939–1964* (Oxford, 1967).

Leys, Colin, *The Rise and Fall of Development Theory* (London, 1996).

Little, Ian, *Economic Development: Theory, Policy, and International Relations* (New York, 1982).

Louis, William Roger, *In the Name of God, Go! Leo Amery and the British Empire in the Age of Churchill* (New York, 1992).

——, *Imperialism at Bay, 1941–1945: the United States and the Decolonization of the British Empire* (Oxford, 1977).

Ludden, David, 'India's Development Regime' in Nicholas Dirks (ed.), *Colonialism and Culture* (Ann Arbor, 1992).

MacKenzie, J.M., *Orientalism: History, Theory and the Arts* (Manchester, 1995).

—— (ed), *Imperialism and Popular Culture* (Manchester, 1986).

——, *Propaganda and Empire: the Manipulation of British Public Opinion, 1880–1960* (Manchester, 1984).

Madden, Frederick, 'The Commonwealth, Commonwealth History, and Oxford, 1905–1971', in Frederick Madden and D.K. Fieldhouse (eds), *Oxford and the Idea of the Commonwealth* (London, 1982).

Madden, Frederick and D.K. Fieldhouse, (eds), *Oxford and the Idea of the Commonwealth* (London, 1982).

Majeed, Javed, *Ungoverned Imaginings. James Mill's The History of British India and Orientalism* (Oxford, 1992).

Mangan, J.A., *Making Imperial Mentalities: Socialisation and British Imperialism* (Manchester, 1990).

———, *The Games Ethic and Imperialism: Aspects of the Diffusion of an Ideal* (Harmondsworth, 1985).

Marglin, F.A. and S. Marglin (eds), *Dominating Knowledge: Development, Culture and Resistance* (Oxford, 1990).

Markovits, Claude, *Indian Business and Nationalist Politics 1931–1939: The Indigenous Capitalist Class and the Rise of the Congress Party* (Cambridge, 1985).

McGuire, John, *The Making of a Colonial Mind: a Quantitative Study of the Bhadralok in Calcutta, 1857–1885* (Canberra, 1983).

Metcalf, Thomas, *Ideologies of the Raj* (Cambridge, 1994).

———, *The Aftermath of the Revolt* (Princeton, 1965).

Milward, Alan S., *War, Economy and Society, 1939–1945* (Harmondsworth, 1987).

Moggridge, D.E., *Maynard Keynes: An Economist's Biography* (London, 1992).

Moore, R.J., 'The Making of India's Paper Federation', in R.J. Moore, *Endgames of Empire* (Delhi, 1988).

———, 'The Mystery of the Cripps Mission', in R.J. Moore, *Endgames of Empire: Studies of Britain's India Problem* (Delhi, 1988).

———, *Making the New Commonwealth* (Oxford, 1987).

Mukerjee, Hiren, *The Gentle Colossus* (Calcutta, 1964; new edition Delhi, 1986).

Mukherjee, Aditya, *Imperialism, Nationalism and the Making of the Indian Capitalist Class 1920–1947* (Delhi, 2002).

———, 'The Indian Capitalist Class: Development 1927–1947', in S. Bhattacharya and Romila Thapar (eds), *Situating Indian History: for Sarvepalli Gopal* (Delhi, 1981.)

———, 'Indian Capitalist Class and Congress on National Planning and Public Sector, 1930–47', in K.N. Panikkar (ed.), *National and Left Movements in India* (New Delhi, 1980).

Mukhopadhyay, A.C., 'A Brief Account of PCM's Work on Meteorology and Flood Control and Irrigation', in Ashok Rudra, *Prasanta Chandra Mahalanobis: A Biography* (Delhi, 1996).

Muniandi, K., 'Kumarappa the Man', *Gandhi Marg*, Vol. 14, No. 2 (July–September 1992).

Myrdal, Gunnar, *Asian Drama; an Inquiry into the Poverty of Nations*, three volumes (London, 1968).

Nandy, Ashis, *Alternative Sciences: Creativity and Authenticity in Two Indian Scientists* (Delhi, 1980; second edition, Delhi, 1995).

———, 'The Political Culture of the Indian State', *Daedalus*, Vol. 118, No. 4, (Fall 1989).

—— (ed.), *Science, Hegemony and Violence; A Requiem for Modernity* (Delhi, 1988).

——, *Tradition, Tyranny and Utopias: Essays in the Politics of Awareness* (Delhi, 1987).

——, *The Intimate Enemy: Loss and Recovery of Self Under Colonialism* (Delhi, 1983).

——, 'Sati: A Nineteenth Century Tale of Women, Violence and Protest', in Ashis Nandy, *At the Edge of Psychology: Essays in Politics and Culture* (Delhi, 1980).

Nath, Pandri, *Mokshagundam Visvesvaraya: Life and Work* (Bombay, 1987).

Overstreet, G.D., and M. Windmiller, *Communism in India* (Berkeley, 1959).

Pandey, Gyanendra, 'Rallying Round the Cow', in Ranajit Guha (ed.), *Subaltern Studies II* (Delhi, 1983).

Parekh, Bhikhu, *Colonialism, Tradition and Reform: An Analysis of Gandhi's Political Discourse* (New Delhi, 1989).

Pickens, Donald K., *Eugenics and the Progressives* (Nashville, Tennessee, 1968).

Potter, D.C., *India's Political Administrators 1919–1983* (Oxford, 1986).

Pressnell, L.J., *External Economic Policy Since the War, volume 1: The Post-War Financial Settlement* (London, 1986).

Raina Dhruv, 'Visvesvaraya as Engineer-Sociologist and the Evolution of his Techno-Economic Vision', National Institute of Advanced Studies, Bangalore, published lecture, 2001.

Raina, Dhruv and S. Irfan Habib, 'Bhadralok Perceptions of Science, Technology and Cultural Nationalism', *Indian Economic and Social History Review*, Vol. 32, No. 1 (1995).

——, 'The Unfolding of an Engagement: The Dawn on Science, Technical Education and Industrialisation', *Studies in History*, Vol. 9, No. 1 (January–June 1993).

Ray, Rajat Kanta, *Industrialisation in India: Growth and Conflict in the Private Corporate Sector 1914–47* (Delhi, 1979).

Ray, Ravindra Chandra, *Colonial Economy: Nationalists' Response* (Varanasi, 1996).

Reeves, Peter D., 'The Politics of Order: "Anti-Non-Cooperation" in the United Provinces, 1921', *Journal of Asian Studies*, Vol. 25, No. 2 (1966).

Ross, Alan, *The Emissary: G.D. Birla, Gandhi and Independence* (London, 1986).

Rostow, W.W., *How it All Began: Origins of the Modern Economy* (London, 1975).

——, *Politics and the Stages of Growth* (Cambridge, 1971).

Rothermund, Dietmar, *India in the Great Depression 1929–1939* (Delhi, 1992).

——, *An Economic History of India* (London, 1988).

——, 'Die Anfaenge der indischen Wirtschaftsplanung im Zweiten Weltkrieg', in Peter Habluetzel, Hans Werner Tobler, and Albert Wirz (eds): *Dritte Welt: Historische Praegung und politische Herausforderung: Festschrift zum 60. Geburtstag von Rudolf von Albertini* (Wiesbaden, 1983).

——, 'The Great Depression and British Financial Policy in India, 1929–1934',

Indian Economic and Social History Review, Vol. 17, No. 4 (1981) and *Indian Economic and Social History Review*, Vol. 18, No. 1 (1981), reprinted in Dietmar Rothermund, *The Indian Economy under British Rule*.

Roy, Tirthankar, *The Economic History of India 1857–1947* (Delhi, 2000).

Rudra, Ashok, *Prasanta Chandra Mahalanobis: A Biography* (Delhi, 1996).

Sachs, Wolfgeeng (ed.) *The Development Dictionary: A Guide to Knowledge as Power* (London, 1992).

Said, Edward W., *Orientalism* (London, 1978).

Sarkar, Sumit, 'The Communists and 1942', in Biswamoy Pati (ed.), *Turbulent Times: India, 1940–44* (Bombay, 1998).

——, 'The Decline of the Subaltern in Subaltern Studies', in Sumit Sarkar, *Writing Social History* (Delhi, 1997).

——, *A Critique of Colonial India* (Calcutta, 1985).

——, *'Popular' Movements and 'Middle Class' Leadership in Late Colonial India: Perspectives and Problems of a 'History from Below'* (Calcutta, 1983).

——, *Modern India 1885–1947* (Madras, 1983).

——, 'The Logic of Gandhian Nationalism: Civil Disobedience and the Gandhi–Irwin Pact (1930–31)', *Indian Historical Review*, Vol. III, No. 1 (1976).

——, *The Swadeshi Movement in Bengal 1903–1908* (New Delhi, 1973).

Saul, S.B., *Studies in British Overseas Trade, 1870–1914* (Liverpool, 1960).

Schumacher, E.F., *Small is Beautiful* (London, 1973).

Searle, G.R., *Eugenics and Politics in Britain 1900–1914* (Leyden, 1976).

Sen, Amartya, 'On Interpreting India's Past', in Sugata Bose and Ayesha Jalal (eds), *Nationalism, Democracy, Development: State and Politics in India* (Delhi, 1997).

Sen, Asok, 'The Frontiers of the Prison Notebooks', *Economic and Political Weekly*, Vol. 23, No. 5 (1988).

Sen, Shila, *Muslim Politics in Bengal 1937–1947* (New Delhi, 1976).

Shriman Narayan, *Vinoba: His Life and Work* (Bombay, 1970).

Sieberg, Herward, *Colonial Development: die Grundlegung moderner Entwicklungspolitik durch Grossbritannien, 1919–1949* (Stuttgart, 1985).

Simmons, Colin, 'Economic Development and Economic History', in Barbara Ingham and Colin Simmons (eds), *Development Studies and Colonial Policy* (London, 1987).

Singh, Anita Inder, *The Limits of British Influence: South Asia and the Anglo-American Relationship 1947–1956* (London, 1993).

Sitaramiah, V., *M. Visvesvaraya* (New Delhi, 1971).

Skidelsky, Robert, *Politicians and the Slump: The Labour Government of 1929–1931* (London, 1967).

Skinner, Quentin, 'Language and Social Change', in James Tully (ed.), *Meaning and Context: Quentin Skinner and his Critics* (Cambridge, 1988).

——, 'Meaning and Understanding in the History of Ideas', in James Tully (ed.), *Meaning and Context: Quentin Skinner and his Critics* (Cambridge, 1988).

——, 'Some Problems in the Analysis of Political Thought and Action', in James

Tully (ed.), *Meaning and Context: Quentin Skinner and his Critics* (Cambridge, 1988).

———, *The Foundations of Modern Political Thought* (Cambridge, 1978).

Smith, Cyril, *Marx at the Millenium* (London, 1996).

Solodovnikov, V., and V. Bogalovsky, *Non-Capitalist Development: An Historical Outline* (Moscow, 1975).

Som, Reba, *Differences Within Consensus: The Left and Right in the Congress, 1929–1939* (London, 1995).

Spodek, Howard, 'Pluralist Politics in British India: The Cambridge Cluster of Historians', *American Historical Review*, Vol. 84.

Srinivasamurthy, A.P., *Sir M. Visvesvaraya (A Brief Review of His Services)* (Bangalore, 1984).

Stepan, Nancy Leys, *"The Hour of Eugenics": Race, Gender and Nation in Latin America* (Ithaca, 1991).

Stokes, Eric, *The English Utilitarians and India* (Oxford, 1959).

Studdert-Kennedy, Gerald, *British Christians, Indian Nationalists and the Raj* (Delhi, 1991).

Swan, Maureen, *Gandhi: The South African Experience* (Johannesburg, 1985).

Tomlinson, B.R., *The Economy of Modern India, 1860–1970* (Cambridge, 1993).

———, 'Indo-British Relations in the Post-Colonial Era: The Sterling Balances Negotiations, 1947–49', *Journal of Imperial And Commonwealth History*, 13 (1985).

———, *The Political Economy of the Raj, 1914–1947: the Economics of Decolonization in India* (London, 1979).

Tully, James (ed.), *Meaning and Context: Quentin Skinner and his Critics* (Cambridge, 1988).

———, 'The Pen is a Mighty Sword: Quentin Skinner's Analysis of Politics', in James Tully (ed.), *Meaning and Context: Quentin Skinner and his Critics* (Cambridge, 1988).

van den Dungen, P.M.H., *The Punjab Tradition* (London, 1972).

van der Veer, Peter, *Religious Nationalism: Hindus and Muslims in India* (1994).

Voigt, Johannes H., *India in the Second World War* (New Delhi, 1987).

Washbrook, David, 'The Rhetoric of Democracy and Development in Late Colonial India', in Sugata Bose and Ayesha Jalal (eds), *Nationalism, Democracy and Development: State and Politics in India* (Delhi, 1997).

———, 'Progress and Problems: South Asian Economic and Social History, c. 1720–1860, *Modern Asian Studies* Vol. 22, No. 1 (1988).

Watt, Carey A., 'Education for National Efficiency: Constructive Nationalism in North India, 1909–1916', *Modern Asian Studies*, Vol. 31, No. 2 (1997).

Weindling, Paul, *Health, Race and German Politics between National Unification and Nazism* (Cambridge, 1989).

Williams, Raymond, *Keywords: A Vocabulary of Culture and Society* (revised edition, third impression, Glasgow, 1989).

Zachariah, Benjamin, 'Interpreting Gandhi; J.C. Kumarappa, Modernity and the

East', in Tapati Guha Thakurta (ed.), *"Culture" and "Democracy": Papers from the Cultural Studies Workshops* (Calcutta, 1999).

——, 'The Development of Professor Mahalanobis', *Economy and Society*, Vol. 26, No. 3 (August 1997).

Zachariah, Benjamin, Subhas Ranjan Chakraborti, and Rajat Kanta Ray, 'Presidency College, Calcutta: an Unfinished History', in Mushirul Hasan (ed.), *Knowledge, Power and Politics: Educational Institutions in India* (New Delhi, 1998).

Unpublished Dissertations

Bagchi, Amiya Kumar, 'Private Investment and Partial Planning in India', PhD dissertation, University of Cambridge (1963).

Bhattacharya, Sanjoy, '"A Necessary Weapon of War": State Policies towards Propaganda and Information Control in Eastern India, 1939–45', PhD dissertation, School of Oriental and African Studies, University of London (1996).

Charrier, Philip Joseph, 'Britain, India and the Genesis of the Colombo Plan, 1945–1951', PhD dissertation, University of Cambridge (1995).

Chatterjee, Rimi B. 'A History of the Trade to South Asia by Macmillan & Co. and Oxford University Press, 1875–1900', DPhil thesis, University of Oxford (1997).

Chattopadhyay, Raghabendra, 'The Idea of Planning in India, 1930–1951', PhD dissertation, Australian National University, Canberra (1985).

Kudaisya, Medha Malik, 'The Public Career of G.D. Birla, 1911–1947', PhD dissertation, University of Cambridge (1992).

Roy, Sulagna, 'Communal Conflict in Bengal 1930–1947', PhD dissertation, University of Cambridge (1999).

Watkins, Kevin, 'India: Colonialism, Nationalism and Perceptions of Development', DPhil thesis, University of Oxford (1986).

Zachariah, Benjamin, 'Controlling the Economy, Planning the Nation: the Origins of Economic Planning in India, c. 1930–1947', MPhil dissertation, University of Cambridge (1995).

Index

Agriculture, 89
AICC pamphlets, 50, 51, 52
Aman Sabha, 116, objectives of, 117
Ambedkar, B.R., 55
Amery Leo, 32, 100
    forward views on importance of
    imperial market, 34
    not in favour of social clauses,
    106
    white supremacist views of, 33
Arnold, Sir Edwin, 171
Arthashashtra, 41
Ashoka, 41

backwardness, 5
Baden-Powell, B.H. 110
balanced budgets, 28, 29, 31
    collapse in India of, 34
Bata, Thomas, 247
Bentham, Jeremy, 10
Beveridge Report (1942), 99
Bevin, Ernest, 103
Bhave, Acharya Vinoba, 158
Bhore, Sir Joseph, 96
Birdwood, Sir George, 47
Birla, G.D., 163, 247
    deal with Nuffield invited
    criticism, 259
    on British and Gandhi's interests,
    215
    on planned action for rise in
    living standards, 214
Bolshevism, 6

Bombay Plan (1944), 216
    basic industries and self-
    sufficiency, 221
    limits of socialism in, 260
    objectives and references to NPC,
    220–2, 256
    role of the state, 222
    state and private enterprises, 221
    terms emanating from NPC, 257
Bose, J.C., 242
Bose, Nirmal, 167
Bose, S.C., 223, 251
    on Gandhi and socialism, 168,
    169
    presidential election of Congress
    (1939), 234
Bose, Satyendranath, 237
Brayne, F.L., 110
    associations with village
    reconstruction, 112, 113
    Gurgaon experiment of, 118
Brelvi, S.A., 50
British Empire, 27, 124, 292
    differing arguments to local and
    home audiences, 54
    dissenting voices in the
    government, 84
    formula of trusteeship and, 80
    free trade in official economic
    thinking, 30
    shift in official thinking about
    governance in 1930s, 82, 83
    government intervention under, 27

imperial personnel as audience, 55
Indians' role in administration, 87
intervention through protectionist
    model of Friedrich list, 34
laissez-faire as proclaimed
    government doctrine, 27
Lord Curzon's desire to turn
    India into a second military
    centre of, 28
narrow range of ideas in the
    government, 84
protection of peasants under, 27
retrospective view of
    achievements and significance
    of, 124
settling Indian Defence expenses,
    100
several layers of governance
    under, 85, 86
shift in arguments of, 292
social and intellectual environment
    of, 58
British expertise, 5
Brockway, Fenner, 229

Caldwell, Erskine, 231
capitalism, 6
    socialism and relative merits of, 6
    capitalist vision of India, 163
Central Banking Enquiry Committee
    1931, 35
    split into three stages, 41–2
Chamberlain, Joseph, 32
Chamberlain, Neville, 94
Chand, Gyan, 243
Chandragupta Maurya, 41
Chatterjee, Sir Atul, 102
Chattopadhyay, Bankimchandra, 170
Churchill, Winston, 33, 100
circulation of ideas and information,
    48–59
Cole, G.D.H, 32, 229
Colonial Development Act (1927), 3

Colonial Development and Welfare
    Acts (1940s), 3
colonial impact, 1, 81
    intellectual formations under, 1
    structures of exploitation, 81
Committee and Commissions,
    collaboration of Indian on inferior
        terms, 40
    nature of working of, 38, 39
    possibilities of protest in, 40
    selective representation of Indians
        in economic committees
        (1914–47), 37
Congress Socialist Party (1934), 226,
    299
    Congress's transition to, 261–2
    differences with orthodox
        communists, 228
    followers of, 227
    goals and tasks of, 227
    pamphlets by, 51
Congress, 7
    decline in quality membership
        (1946–7), 260
Conservative Party, 32
cow-protection, 175
    economic viability of, 175
    Satish Chandra Dasgupta on,
        175–6
Cripps, Stafford, 103
    for enlisting popular class
        support, 104
    his approach, 105
    responses to Cripps-Bevin
        reforms, 105, 107, 108
Croft, W.D., 102
    views on agricultural development,
        105
Cromwell, Oliver, 247
crossover linkages and social
    mobility, 55

Dalal, Sir Ardeshir, 258

Darling, Sir Malcolm, 101–2, 110
  critical of Penderel Moon's
    writing, 128–9
  ideas of rural development and
    peasantry, 119–23
  influence of Malthus' writings,
    123
  on importance of education and
    Russian model, 106
  on peasantry and norms of sound
    finance, 130
  positive image of British rule, 129
  suggestions of, 101–2
Darwin, 170
democracy, 10
Dev, Narendra, 50, 227
development debates, 1, 211
  coming to the forefront, 80
  conventions of debates, 2
  discursive context in, 25
  Indo-British economic relations as
    background to, 27
  interest of academic institutions
    in, 53
  middle-classness and, 211–13
  possibilities evoked in 1930s and
    1940s, 1
  practical context, 25
  within official and government
    circles, 81
development planning, 256
  businessmen's role during Second
    World War, 256
  under CSP, 227–8
development, 1, 2, 8, 13, 48, 83,
  211, 291
  absences of intellectual history of,
    8
  and planning, 8
  approaches to the study of, 8–13
  arguments addressed to a created
    audience, 48
  concerns as adjuncts to the
    economic part, 292
  connected with ideas of
    regeneration and progress
    (1930s and 1940s), 291
  connection with science, 236–7
  constrained benevolence of, 82
  context of conception, 1
  first extensive discussion on plans
    (1940s), 83
  fora for discussions of, 7–8
  framework for Indian nation, 6
  Grigg's ideas of, 94
  importance of expertise in, 253
  Indian conception of, 5
  Indian path to, 293
  Indo-British partnership in, 293–4
  interpretation of the term, 80, 81
  materialist approach to study of,
    11
  mixing of liberal, illiberal and
    socialist ideas in, 299
  moral question regarding, 247
  national form of, 211
  positions of imperialists,
    nationalists and capitalists in
    1940s, 296–7, 298
  progress, self-government and
    nation-building, 1
  protagonists' history of, 9
  setting in 1930s and 1940s for
    the discussion of, 25
  themes incorporated in 1930s, 44
  three elements of discourse, 211
  various colonial and post-colonial
    uses of, 3–4
Dobb, Maurice, 92
Dover, Cedric, 230

economics, 2, 5
  conception of, 5
  continuity from 1920s to 1930s
    of administrative mechanisms
    of, 29
  early origins and significance of
    concern beyond, 2–3

language of 2,5, 291
management (1930s), 31
nationalist consensus on ascribed
    causes of backwardness, 215
economic depressions (1880s) and
    protectionism, 28
External Capital Committee (1925),
    42

Fa-Hien, 41
Famine Commission (1880), 28
Fanon, Frantz, 47
Fascism, 6, 181
    dangers of, 228
    economy under, 43
    Nehru's opposition to, 233
    success of Fascist Italy, 7
federal finance, 243
Franklin, Benjamin, 247

Gandhi, Gandhian, 2, 114, 247, 294
    addressing the intelligentsia, 176–9
    and mechanization, 157
    against Gandhi, 165–8
    criteria of modernity, 158, 293
    criticism on indigenous solutions
        of, 166
    different audiences of, 161
    distinction between East and
        West, 160
    earlier intervention (pre-1930s),
        168–73
    economic thought, 157
    granting legitimacy to capitalists,
        165
    ideas on science, 239–40
    on cow protection, 174–6
    on material and moral progress,
        46
    overdrawn claims to indigenism,
        172
    planning (1940s), 44
    political manifesto, 169

position, 6, 192–3
    publishing network, 50
    relationship with socialism, 262–3
    retrospective view of ideas of,
        161
    scientific and technologists'
        critique of ideas, 166
    strategic placement of arguments,
        158
    tendency to order retreats, 163
    trusteeship role of the wealthy,
        157
    ventures financed by G.D. Birla,
        57
    western trends in thought, 170
    writings moral in character, 160
Gandhi, Indira, 300
    temporary dictatorship in the
        1970s, 300
Government of India Act (1858), 45
Government of India Act 1919, 46
    nation-building departments in,
        47
Government of India Act 1935,
    moral and material progress in, 45
    Provincial Autonomy in, 85,86
Gramsci, Antonio 212
    concept of 'passive revolution',
        212
Great Depression, 83
    and nationalist discourse of
        development, 6–7
    Soviet Union's prevention of
        impact of, 227
    viability of Soviet Five-Year
        plans, 291
Gregory, Theodore, 97–9
    challenge to tariffs, 98
Grigg, Sir James, 32, 98
    as an imperialist, 94
    plebian origins of, 96
    reaction to economic nationalism,
        93–6

Haldane, J.B.S., 242
Harrappa, 41
Harrison, Agatha, 235
Havell, E.B., 47
Hirachand, Walchand, 255, 259
History writing, 10
  'self-interest' approach to, 10
Hitler, Adolf 233
Hiuen-Tsang, 41
Hobson, J.A., 229

Ibn Batuta, 41
ICS, 87, 95, 112
  Clive Dewey' study of Darling
    and Brayne, 111
  engaged with village
    reconstruction, 112
  Grigg on, 95 Indian members of,
    87–8
  self-image of, 110, 112
ideas, 9, 16
  accommodation in Nationalist
    mainstream, 15
  establishing the place of, 13
  linkages with policy, 9
  linkages with political behaviour,
    10
  regional or local imperatives, 15
  relationship between metropolitan
    and Indian, 15–16
Imperial Council of Agricultural
  Research, 36
Imperial Economic Conference,
  Ottawa (1932), 32
Indian Village Welfare Association
  (1931), 113
India, Indian, 5, 26, 99
  British ideas of backwardness, 4–
    5
  changing assumptions, character
    and future of, 99
  concerns and anxieties of

intellectual bourgeoisie, 9
  exceptional nature of, 26, 30
  first systematic academic
    administration studies of, 110
  indigenous view of backwardness,
    5
Industrial Commission (1916–18), 28
Industrialization, 5
  India unsuitable to in British
    thinking, 35
Iyer, Raghavan, 169
Iyer, T.V. Narayanaswami, 193
  Indian confused with Hindu
    ethos, 194–5

Jack, Major J.C., 110
Japan,7 economic success of, 7, 43
Jatakas, 41

Keynes, John Maynard, 30–1, 93,
  249
  Amery on, 33
  in favour of tariffs, 32
  support to Beveridge Plan, 34
Kisan Sabha, 116
Kripalani, J.B., 260
Kulkarni, Dharmaraj, 260
Kumarappa, J.C., 45, 156, 176, 219–
  20
  adopting Hindu moral bases of
    Gandhian thought, 174
  challenge to yardsticks of
    modernity, 185
  classification of 'pack type' and
    'herd type' by, 179, 180, 181,
    182, 186
  critique of economics, 191–2
  defence of caste, 187–8
  distinction between East and
    West, 188
  Gandhi's dissatisfaction with
    article on industrialization by,
    162

less mystical than Gandhi, 189
on Gandhi's vows, 178–9
on Khadi, 192
on RSS volunteers, 196
opposition to communism, 187
partnership with Gandhi, 178
practical arguments of, 185–7
problems in drawing conclusions,
    187
professional brief, 177
role in formulating Gandhian
    economic thought, 159
speaking for Gandhi, 173
success or failure, 191

Labour Party, 4, 32
Laissez Faire (1920s), 28
Lancashire, 33, 86
    concerns, 33
    economic domination of, 157
language, 211, 255
    inter-war, 211
    uses of legitimacy, 255–63
Laski, Harold, 229
Leggett, Sir Frederick, 106
levels of governance, 81–8
Linlithgow, 36, 100
Lipton, Thomas, 247
Lohia, Ram Manohar, 260
    Gandhism and, 262
Lokanathan, P.S., 57
Lothian, 96, 215
Lotvala, R.B. 192–3

Macaulay, Thomas Babington 241
Macdonald, Ramsay, 242
Mahalanobis, P.C., 237
    on race efficiency, 250
Mahmud, Dr Syed, 50, 223, 232,
    233
Maine, Henry, 170
Marx, Karl, 84, 294
Masani, Minoo, 229, 238, 257

Mason, Philip, 124
Matthai, John, 130, 257, 294
Max Mueller, 171
Maxton, James, 229
Mehta, Ashoka, 165
Metcalfe, Sir Charles, 294
metropolitan ideas, 294–5
    linkages, 55
middle class, 10
    composition of, 212
    opinion (during Second World
        War), 54
Mill, John Stuart, 10
Minority Reports, 38
    Manu Subedar on Central Banking
        Enquiry Committee, 42
Minutes of Dissent, 38
modernity, 11, 12, 190
    compatibility with caste
        principles, 189–90
    connotation of, 12 critique of, 11
modernization, 5
Mohenjo-Daro, 41
Mookerji, Radhakamal, 171
Mookerji, Radhakumud, 46, 171, 244
Moon, Penderel, 124
    retrospective survey of colonial
        exploitation, 124–9
Morality, Modernity, National
    Discipline, 242–55
Morison, Sir Theodore, 28
Mudaliar, Sir Ramaswamy, 102
Mussolini, 92, 233, 242, 247
    Fascists of, 251
Mysore Princely State, 15

Narayan, Jayaprakash, 50, 56, 158,
    237
    advocacy of left unity, 164
    Gandhism and, 262
national, nationalism, nationalist, 11,
    25, 243, 292
    and morality, 243

discipline, workers urged for, 252
discourses, 25
internal differences within, 298
legitimacy of, 12
legitimacy linked to state's ability, 11
physical entity of state, 248
press, 49
technological, social and discipline concerns, 292
National Publication Society (1930), 50, 51
Nazi, Nazism, 6, 181
economy, 43 success of, 7
Nehru, Jawaharlal, 6, 50, 239
circulation of ideas and, 56
relationship with socialist circles, 230–5
Scientific Socialism and, 237
socialism of, 226, 229, 297
New Deal, 30–1, 43
successes of US in, 7
Norman, Montague, 86, 93
NPC, 224, 248, 254, 260
and the question of nationalization, 218–19
comparison Bombay Plan to, 223, 225–6
controversy between modernization and cottage industries, 219
formulations, composition and relationship with socialism, 217
guidelines regarding labour, 219
role in debates of, 249, 250
self-sufficiency urged by sub-committees of, 218
tensions within, 225

Pant, Govind Ballabh, 50
Partition of Bengal, (1905), 157
Pasha, Mustafa Kemal, 247

Patel, Jhaverbhai, 261
physical training and mass mobilization, 251
planned economy, 213, 248
demand as an appeal, 214
demand in 1930s, 213
urged by FICCI members, 214
woman's role in, 248
Planning and Development Department (1944), 99
planning, 44, 216
Gandhian opposition to, 44
Nehru on, 216
political economy, 26
precedents and ideas 26–36
political publications, 50
post-war reconstruction, 44, 83, 109
Gregory on, 105, 106
Linlithgow sent notes of Jenkins and Hutton, 107
Linlithgow's multiple objections, 109
Reconstruction Committee (1943), 99
Second Report on Reconstruction Planning, 258
Post-War Reconstruction and Development, 99–110
proselytizers, 6, 48, 242
protagonists, 9, 14
arguing within conventions, 17
fora of, 9
role in developmental policies of 1950s, 14–15
protective tariff (1931), 31
Punjab, 27
Civilians, 45
images ascribed to tradition and peasants of, 27–8

Quit India Movement, 102

race, 249

Radhakrishnan, Sarvapalli, 244
Rahim, Abdul, 230
Raman, C.V., 242
Ray, Acharya Prafulla Chandra, 175–
   6, 241, 247
Realpolitik, 13, 82, 85, 111
Rigveda, 41
Risley, H.H., 250
Robeson, Paul, 231
Round Table Conference (1931), 163
Royal Commission on Labour
   (1931), 36
Royal Commission on Agriculture
   (1927), 36
Rural Development, 114, 115
Russell, Bertrand, 229
Russian Revolution, 162
   Narodnik-Marxist debates before,
      168

Saha, Meghnad, 53, 55, 57, 195,
   237, 242
   author of several schemes, 236–7
   patronage from Tatas and Birlas
      to, 57
   science and its compatibility with
      socialism, 255
Sarkar, N.R., 247
Sarkar, Sir Jadunath, 47
Sarvodaya Movement, 158
Schuster, Sir George, 32, 100–1
   approach to Indian economic
      planning, 88–93
   Birla's association with, 215
   failure of his conception of an
      accommodating imperialism, 93
   selective appropriation of
      Gandhian ideas, 90, 91
   significance of his Indian years,
      91
science, 235–42
   and modernity, 240
   economics as, 237
   scientists cast as influential group
      in a new India, 236
   teaching for practical application,
      236
scientific journals, 236
Seal, Brajendranath, 53, 244
   influence of P.C. Ray on, 241
Second Civil Disobedience
   Movement, 164
Shah, K.T., 50, 218, 244, 254
Shared Spaces of Domination and
   Resistance, 36–43
Shaw, George Bernard, 229, 246–7
Sinclair, Upton, 230
Sinha, Bisheswar P., 229
Skinner, Quentin, 13–14
Snowden, Philip, 32, 93
social and economic reforms, 100,
   103
   Bevin and Cripps for, 103
socialism, 226–35
   Gandhi's non-acceptance of, 164,
      165
   in 1930s, 162
   ambivalence of business and, 254–
      5
Soviet Union (1930s), 7
specialist periodicals, 49
spinning and weaving Khadi, 164
Stakhanovism, 254
Sterling Balances, 100, 103
Strickland, C.F., 114
Subba Rao, N.S., 213
   on planning and socialism, 213–14
   on role of backward countries,
      215–16
Swadeshi, 169

Tagore, Rabindranath, 45
   review of his conception of a
      rural university, 113
tariff protection, 32
   1920s in India, 28

effects of, 29
Tavernier, 41
Tawney, R.H., 120
terminology, 16, 43–8
  shift in meanings of, 16
  strong extra-economic
    connotations of, 26
The 1930s: Aberrations and Default
  Settings, 88–99
Theosophists, 249
Trivedi, Ramendra Sunder, 170
Tolstoy, 170
  on Gandhi, 171
Tory 'die-hards', 33
Townend, H.P.V., 114
Travancore Princely State, 15
'trusteeship of wealthy', 163, 165
  not an 'indigenous' idea, 167

Unity of Thought, 295

Varnashrama, 183–4
Village Panchayats, 117

village uplift initiatives, 45
Visvesvaraya, Sir M., 5, 195
  belief in science and its
    transformative power, 237
  his approach to development, 45
  industrialization more important
    than social organization, 255
  Mysore Swadeshi Exhibition of,
    (1936), 186
  on modernity and national
    discipline, 243–7
  on planned economy, 214
  professional profile of, 244
von Studnitz, H.G., 233

Wavell, Archibald, 4
Webb, Sidney, 130, 257, 294
Wedgewood, J.C., 234
Wells, H.G., 229

YMCA, 45, 114
  claim of the term 'rural
    reconstruction', 113